ad!

Understanding Whitehead

Alfred North Whitehead

Understanding Whitehead

Victor Lowe

The Johns Hopkins Press
Baltimore · 1962

Library of Congress Catalog Card Number: 62-15312

This book has been brought to publication with the
assistance of a grant from The Ford Foundation.

Preface

A vigorous increase of interest in the philosophy of Alfred North Whitehead began a few years ago. The mathematician who, with Bertrand Russell, wrote *Principia Mathematica*, created in the late 1920s a new world view which, like the world itself, was too big and many-sided to be grasped at once. Now the process is in full swing.

The present volume was originally conceived as a collection of various published papers of mine, to make a series of steppingstones toward the understanding of Whitehead's philosophy. But as the papers were originally written at different levels for different readers, no one reader would have found all of them useful; and there was nothing on Whitehead's philosophy of religion. Furthermore, since the 1940s, when many of them were published, the Whitehead literature has grown profusely; various parts of his philosophy have been newly interpreted, for he offered many things to many minds. The plan was therefore changed, and *Understanding White-head* is offered not as a collection but as a book in which parts of earlier articles are used. All of it is meant to help people understand Whitehead's philosophy, no prior acquaintance with which is assumed. (Readers who have that may want to do some skimming in the first chapter.)

There is nothing in the book which I would not be willing to expand and defend against the criticism of other students of Whitehead's thought. But I am not writing for them alone, or even for them primarily. I know that most of the members of the American Philosophical Association march nowadays to the rhythm of other drums. I believe that Whitehead's philosophy, and any intelligent exposition or discussion of it, is worth their fresh consideration. I believe that the general health of philosophy needs that fresh consideration, perhaps most from them because they publish, teach, and can affect the thought of time to come. However, I write in a hope that extends far beyond my own circle of professionals who hatch and hash philosophies for a living. I write above all for the intelligent human being who has a live curiosity about general ideas which might help him understand life and the world, and who has not really committed himself either to a " nothing but . . ." interpretation of human experience or to a view of philosophy which makes it some kind of linguistic analysis, useful to disputants who " do philosophy " (or the philosophy of science) but to no one else.

Because philosophies which are less ambitious than White-head's naturally appeal to our caution, some attention to some of their rejections of him is included. Because philosophies which are as bold and generous in scope as Whitehead's are easy to misread in vague or alien terms, a good many discussions of likely misunderstandings and of published interpretations which I think miss Whitehead's point, are also included—but only to bring out his point as I see it, not to embark on textual controversies.

The book is not an analysis of the details of Whitehead's work. That would fill a five-foot shelf. And in the nature of the case, a step-by-step analysis of his philosophic writings, in which it can be said at each point, " Clearly, what White-head is saying here is that . . . ," is impossible. You cannot do that with a first-rate philosopher who is saying something new about the broadest questions. My aim is rather to show what Whitehead's philosophy is all about, how it is unique.

I am not a disciple of Whitehead; but this book would never have been written without the conviction that he was a very great man. The expositions in the opening chapters, in the first especially, are wholeheartedly sympathetic. This is necessary if one is to get inside his new way of thinking. Before the last page is reached a good many critical thoughts about the nature and use of some of Whitehead's ideas are suggested.

Part II is the longest stretch in the book. There I trace the path of Whitehead's thought, beginning with his earliest important publication. The titles of his writings suggest that a mathematician turned in his fifties to the philosophy of science and in his sixties to metaphysics and the philosophy of civilization. This was not the familiar case of a scientist setting down philosophical comments in his old age; Whitehead was somehow immediately productive and constructively original in each new field. We are bound to ask how it happened. Without attempting a biography, I describe in order all but his most minor writings in these different fields. The chapters should thus be useful to anyone who wants to know what Whitehead did in this or that published piece. But the main concern is with the distinctive character of each work considered, how it agrees with and differs from its predecessors in its purpose, topics, and mode of treatment. I have tried throughout to find the essential matters and keep them before the reader, so he can see the development of Whitehead's philosophy and come to an over-all comprehension of his way of thinking.

Whitehead's metaphysics having been presented in the earlier chapters, the character of this part of man's philosophizing, and of the Whiteheadian type of metaphysics, provide the subject of Part III, which is less closely tied to exposition of Whitehead. These chapters are included not merely because I had written three papers which dealt with the subject,[1] but because while the heart of a philosophy, for Whitehead, is bound to be its metaphysics, the nature and

---

[1] No use is made of "'Naturalism,' 'Temporalism,' and the Philosophy of Whitehead," which was read to the Eastern Division of the American Philosophical Association in December, 1940. I no longer think well of it.

legitimacy of metaphysics, in relation to human experience, worries almost everyone who is undogmatic. This concern is continued in Part IV.

Chapter 13, "William James and Whitehead's Doctrine of Prehensions," is based on what twenty years ago was one of half a dozen chapters of a comparative study, never completed, of Whitehead and James. It is a good idea to use James as a vestibule—*one* vestibule—to Whitehead. Chapter 12 contains the part of that comparative study which best serves this purpose. In its discussion of alternatives to the empiricism which these two philosophers share, the epistemological positions known as neorealism and critical realism provide the context. They are no longer anything like as familiar as they then were to students of philosophy. In revising this discussion I have not changed the context, because I do not think the linguistic and linguistic-psychological ways in which philosophers are now talking about experience are solid enough. Talk of "direct realism" is already creeping back into the journals. Philosophy cannot indefinitely stay away from the question whether experience is most adequately to be conceived as what Whitehead called *prehension* of its data. I grant that the older positions deserved to be superseded—because Whitehead's was better.

Among the philosophical topics with which Whitehead concerned himself, one is not discussed: education. That is because his essays on education speak for themselves, and are best understood without the use of any external aid.

Whitehead was no iconoclast. His philosophy is more aptly described as a culmination of the Western tradition. Since it is obviously true that we are entering a quite new world for which we are not prepared, some of us may wonder whether Whitehead has anything to say that will help the rising generation solve its terrifying problems, social, political and cultural. The answer is that he has much to say, but not about means. He wrote a philosophy, not a strategy. What we do should be determined by how we see human existence and what we value, our attitudes and emphases. But we must understand a philosophy before we try to use it. That is what is concentrated upon in this book. Implications for the conduct of life and the health of the society are present in Whitehead's thought; they are indicated in the last section of Chapter 1, and briefly touched upon elsewhere.

From references in the text and notes the reader will see various respects in which I have found—and think that he will find—the writings of other interpreters of Whitehead enlightening. In this matter and in others I owe thanks to many more persons than can be named here. The oldest obligation is to my friend Paul Arthur Schilpp for the interleaved copy of my "Development of Whitehead's Philosophy"² which silently encouraged the first enlargement of that essay. In conversations about mathematical topics Professors Francis Murnaghan and Robert Palter, and Mr. Dean Haggard, gave generously of their superior knowledge. I am grateful also to Lord Russell, Professor Garrett Birkhoff, and other correspondents too numerous to mention.

For help in bringing the book to press I am indebted to several persons—especially to Mrs. Thomas Grover who prepared the typescript, and to Mr. Paul Johnson who helped me with the index. I thank my colleagues at Johns Hopkins for the occasions upon which they lightened my academic duties, and the University for grants which defrayed secretarial expenses. By far my greatest debt is to my wife.

Victor Lowe

The Johns Hopkins University
March, 1962

---

² Pp. 15-124 in LLP-W.

Acknowledgments

Portions of Chapter 1 appeared in "The Philosophy of Whitehead," *Antioch Review*, 8 (Summer, 1948); of Part II, in *The Philosophy of Alfred North Whitehead* (Vol. III of *The Library of Living Philosophers*), edited by Paul Arthur Schilpp (Evanston and Chicago, 1941); of Chapter 9, in "The Influence of Bergson, James, and Alexander on Whitehead," *Journal of the History of Ideas*, 10 (April, 1949); of Chapter 12, in "Empirical Method in Metaphysics," *Journal of Philosophy*, 44 (April 24, 1947); of Chapter 13, in "William James and Whitehead's Doctrine of Prehensions," *Journal of Philosophy*, 38 (February 27, 1941); of Chapter 14, in "What Philosophers May Learn from Whitehead," *Revue Internationale de Philosophie*, 15 (1961). Grateful acknowledgment is made to the editors of these publications for permission to use these materials in the present volume.

Thanks are due also to three publishers for permission to incorporate copyrighted material in other chapters: parts of Chapter 2 appeared in my Introduction to the Selections from Whitehead in *Classic American Philosophers*, edited by Max H. Fisch and published by Appleton-Century-Crofts, Inc. (New York, 1951); parts of Chapter 3, in my third of *Whitehead and the Modern World* (by Charles Hartshorne, A. H. Johnson, and myself), published by the Beacon Press (Boston, 1950) ; parts of Chapter 11 and of Chapter 4, Section III, in " The Approach to Metaphysics," a contribution to *The Relevance of Whitehead*, edited by Ivor Leclerc and published by George Allen & Unwin Ltd. (London, 1961) .

I am thankful to Lord Russell for his kindness in granting permission to quote from several letters to me.

Mr. Lucien Price's perfect copy of the Harvard Tercentenary photograph is used as frontispiece, thank to his kindness and the courtesy of Harvard University.

V. L.

Contents

PART III.
EXPERIENCE AND METAPHYSICS

PART IV. CONCLUSION

Abbreviations

chiefly of titles of the principal works of Alfred North Whitehead

Parentheses following an entry show the name of the publisher of the current American paperback issue.

ADG   *The Axioms of Descriptive Geometry.* Cambridge University Press, 1907. Cambridge Tracts in Mathematics and Mathematical Physics, No. 5; reprinted by Hafner Publishing Co.

AE   *The Aims of Education and Other Essays.* The Macmillan Co., New York; Williams & Norgate, London, 1929 (NAL).

AESP   *Whitehead's American Essays in Social Philosophy.* Edited with an Introduction by A. H. Johnson. Harper & Bros., New York, 1959.

AI   *Adventures of Ideas.* The Macmillan Co., New York; Cambridge University Press, 1933. (NAL). In references to xvi the numbering of Sections in the English edition is followed, so as to avoid an error in their numbering in the American edition.

APG   *The Axioms of Projective Geometry.* Cambridge University Press, 1906. Cambridge Tracts in Mathematics and Mathematical Physics, No. 4; reprinted by Hafner Publishing Co.

CN   *The Concept of Nature.* Cambridge University Press, 1920. (Ann Arbor).

ESP   *Essays in Science and Philosophy.* Philosophical Library, New York, 1947. (Wisdom Library; under title, *Science and Philosophy*).

FR   *The Function of Reason.* Princeton University Press, 1929. (Beacon Press).

IM   *An Introduction to Mathematics.* Home University Library
        of Modern Knowledge, No. 15. Williams & Norgate, Lon-
        don; Henry Holt & Co., New York, 1911. (Oxford).

IS   *The Interpretation of Science: Selected Essays.* Edited with
        an Introduction by A. H. Johnson. Library of Liberal Arts,
        Bobbs-Merrill Co., Indianapolis and New York, 1961.

LLP-W   *The Philosophy of Alfred North Whitehead.* The Library
        of Living Philosophers, Vol. 3. Edited by P. A. Schilpp.
        Northwestern University, Evanston and Chicago, 1941;
        second edition, Tudor Publishing Co., New York, 1951.

MC   " On Mathematical Concepts of the Material World." *Philo-
        sophical Transactions, Royal Society of London.* Series A,
        Vol. 205. 1906.

MT   *Modes of Thought.* The Macmillan Co., New York; Cam-
        bridge University Press, 1938. (Putnam).

N&G   *Alfred North Whitehead: An Anthology.* Selected by
        F. S. C. Northrop and Mason W. Gross. The Macmillan
        Co., New York, 1953. (Macmillan).

OT   *The Organisation of Thought, Educational and Scientific.*
        Williams & Norgate, London, 1917.

PM   *Principia Mathematica* (with Bertrand Russell). 3 vols.
        Cambridge University Press, 1910-1913; second edition, 1925-
        1927.

PNK   *An Enquiry Concerning the Principles of Natural Knowl-
        edge.* Cambridge University Press, 1919; second edition,
        1925.

PR   *Process and Reality.* The Macmillan Co., New York; Cam-
        bridge University Press, 1929. (Harper). In references
        to I I the numbering of the Sections in the English edition
        is followed, so as to avoid an error in the American edition.

R   *The Principle of Relativity, with Applications to Physical
        Science.* Cambridge University Press, 1922.

RM   *Religion in the Making.* The Macmillan Co., New York;
        Cambridge University Press, 1926. (Meridian).

S   *Symbolism, Its Meaning and Effect.* The Macmillan Co., New
        York, 1927; Cambridge University Press, 1928. (Putnam).

SMW   *Science and the Modern World.* The Macmillan Co., New
        York, 1925; Cambridge University Press, 1926. (NAL).

UA   *A Treatise on Universal Algebra, with Applications.* Cam-
        bridge University Press, 1898. Reprinted by Hafner Pub-
        lishing Co.

To make references usable by all readers, citations are made, wherever possible, by chapter and section rather than by page (and when a page number is referred to, it is always preceded by a " p." or " pp."). In general, full-sized Roman capital numerals indicate the number of a Part; small Roman capital numerals indicate a Chapter or Lecture; lower case Roman numerals a Section or Article; thus, Section IV, Chapter III, Part II of Process and Reality is cited as PR II III iv. *Arabic numerals are introduced into this system wherever Whitehead himself departed from his wont and employed them to number a section; in addition in some few instances they are used to indicate a further subdivision (i. e., paragraph) when it is judged that such an indication would be helpful to the reader. A few of Whitehead's works are composed of continuously numbered articles or sections; references to these works are made by Article only (e. g., UA 14; PNK 13.2) or Section only (e. g., " Immortality " vi).*

PART I

WHITEHEAD'S WAY

Philosophy is the product of wonder. The effort after the general characterization of the world around us is the romance of human thought. The correct statement seems so easy, so obvious, and yet it is always eluding us. We inherit the traditional doctrine: we can detect the oversights, the superstitions, the rash generalizations of the past ages. We know so well what we mean and yet we remain so curiously uncertain about the formulation of any detail of our knowledge. . . . We have to analyse and to abstract, and to understand the natural status of our abstractions.

A civilization which cannot burst through its current abstractions is doomed to sterility after a very limited period of progress.

—Alfred North Whitehead

Chapter 1

Alfred North Whitehead
and His Philosophy

I

In 1898 the editors of *Mind* (*the* English philosophical quarterly) asked Hugh MacColl to review *A Treatise on Universal Algebra*. It was Whitehead's first book. (Bertrand Russell, eleven years his junior, had already produced two.) No articles had prepared a way for it: *here,* suddenly, was a book of five hundred and eighty-six pages, quarto. As for MacColl, he was an esteemed logician. For twenty years he had been putting out papers on symbolic logic; independently of Peirce and even of Boole, he had invented a calculus of propositions similar to Peirce's; and he was shortly to produce another algebra of logic distinguished by the general features of C. I. Lewis' system of "strict implication." [1] Surely, he was the man to review a treatise on universal algebra.

MacColl wrote the review.[2] It opens with a statement which

---

[1] See the references to MacColl in Lewis' *Survey of Symbolic Logic* (Berkeley, 1918).
[2] *Mind*, n. s., 8 (1899), 108-113.

is often a routine one:

> In consenting to review this important volume for the
> readers of *Mind* I fear that I have undertaken a task for which
> I am but indifferently qualified.

After some explanations, he considers the progress of Whitehead's book.

> His opening chapter, " On the Nature of a Calculus," is very
> interesting, and may be understood by anyone of ordinary
> education and intelligence.

To be sure,

> If the reader knows something of common algebra he will
> grasp the author's meaning more easily; but, for much of this
> chapter, even this modicum of preliminary knowledge is not
> absolutely indispensable.

> When, however, we enter upon the second chapter, which
> treats of *Manifolds*, we find ourselves on very different terri-
> tory. A reader previously unacquainted with the subject can-
> not read this straight through, as he would a novel or a
> paragraph in a newspaper; he will have to make frequent
> halts, and sometimes very long halts, in order to reflect.

The next sentence falls inevitably in place.

> This is not altogether the author's fault.

He was grappling with a subject at once formidable and
elusive:

> The truth is that the subject of manifolds is extremely difficult
> to understand, and still more difficult to explain. The meaning
> of the word *manifold*, as defined by its inventor, Riemann,
> is so very general, not to say vague and attenuated, that it may
> be called the *ether* of mathematical conceptions.

But could we not have been let off a little easier?

> Mr. Whitehead might, I think, with advantage have restricted
> his discussion to the general characteristics of the manifolds

which enter into his compared algebras, and he should have illustrated these more copiously with simple and concrete examples.

Nevertheless, the task which the author set himself,

I consider him to have accomplished with rare ability.

To this conclusion a qualification is attached, namely: "judging of the whole from my knowledge of a part." For, of course, MacColl had been able to read but one fifth of the *Universal Algebra*. He had not anticipated a large mathematical treatise, but a manageable book on the general principles of symbolic reasoning, "with occasional appeals to mathematics and geometrical diagrams by way of illustrations."

How many later voices do we hear in this first of Whitehead reviews! Voices of other logicians, of professional philosophers, professional mathematicians, professional physicists, professional historians; of teachers of philosophy, literary critics, gentlemen and scholars: their surprise, their bewilderment, their irritation, their admission of partial incompetence, and their admiration—all are here.

Alfred North Whitehead was a mathematician during most of his professional life; it was not until he was in his sixties that he undertook to write "philosophy," and became known almost overnight as the leading original thinker in metaphysics. He was then teaching at Harvard, and I remember how he used to walk through the Yard: a little apple-cheeked man, his shoulders much bent, an umbrella often held across his back; his head down, but his clear blue eyes up. I cannot describe his face or recall any printed photograph or sketch that does justice to it. I can only confirm what Edmund Wilson wrote when he introduced Whitehead (as "Professor Grosbeake") into his early novel, *I Thought of Daisy*: that when you looked at him you felt that you were seeing a real face, in comparison with which others looked like mere masks. The general impression given by Whitehead's presence, I should say, was one of kindness, wisdom, and a perfectly disciplined vigor. Both his conversation and his writings showed a wonderful combination of urbanity and zest, rather like the tone of Plato's dialogues. (Whitehead wrote nothing in dialogue form. The insuperable task of showing his conversation to readers who never met him was attempted, and done about as well as is humanly possible, by Lucien Price in *Dialogues of Alfred North Whitehead*.) He loved to follow the minds of young people, and when you came to him to talk about his philosophy, the meeting always began with the eager question, " Tell me what you've been doing."

He was born February 15, 1861, at Ramsgate, a village in the Isle of Thanet on the east coast of Kent. The Whiteheads were schoolmasters and Anglican clergymen; as a boy Alfred often accompanied his father (Vicar of St. Peter's Parish) on visits to the parochial schools which the father headed. At fourteen he went to Sherborne in Dorsetshire, one of England's oldest schools, and received a perfect " classical " education. Then came Trinity College, Cambridge—Isaac Newton's college. There Whitehead took courses in mathematics only. He stayed on to become a Fellow of Trinity and to teach mathematics for a quarter of a century. This was followed by thirteen years in the same field at the University of London. Finally came thirteen years at Harvard. After his retirement in 1937 he continued to serve his adopted university as a Senior Fellow. He died in his small apartment near the Harvard Yard on December 30, 1947. It sounds a most unexciting life, so unexciting as to rouse a suspicion that the emphasis on *adventure* in his philosophy must have been a professor's compensatory gesture.

The adventure was real. In 1910 Whitehead's reputation was considerable; he had been for seven years a Fellow of the Royal Society, and the first two volumes of *Principia Mathematica* by Whitehead and Russell were in the press. A great intellectual adventure was drawing to a close. Yet Whitehead, feeling a need for a new environment with fresh perspectives, moved from Cambridge to London—without securing a position there, or getting an academic appointment until a year later. London was a different world, where he was in the thick of "the problem of higher education in a modern industrial civilization."[3] His interest in this problem drew him into administrative connections with several technical schools as well as into positions of high responsibility at the University of London, where he became Dean of the Faculty of Science. (Some day, I hope, a historian of education will try to estimate Whitehead's effect on the development of that institution after its remodeling by Lord Haldane.) When the time for his retirement approached, he moved across the Atlantic to enter a third world.

If the bare facts about the formal education he received and the subjects he taught in England suggest extreme narrowness and removal from real life, that appearance is wholly illusory. The classical training at Sherborne was in truth highly relevant to the future lives of English boys of the Victorian period. At Cambridge the students covered everything in their reading and conversation—religion, history, poetry, philosophy, politics—and they did this well. (This doubtless reflects in part the fact that they came from the upper middle class which at that time was practically the sole governing class in England; but it also exhibits the absurdity of the assumption, habitually made by twentieth-century Americans, that to discuss anything you must first take a course in it.) Alfred North Whitehead belonged to a famous discussion club at Cambridge, "The Apostles." F. D. Maurice and others had founded it in the 1820s; Tennyson was an early member. When Whitehead was an undergraduate he seems to have been the only mathematician in the group, perhaps because he was the only mathematician interested in general ideas.[4] Throughout his life he kept up the habit of this kind of conversation, receiving and giving facts and ideas with all kinds of people: a Lord Chancellor of England, and

---

[3] LLP-W p. 12; in ESP p. 12. The phrase is from Whitehead's brief "Autobiographical Notes." My account of Whitehead's life is based upon those Notes, unless other sources are mentioned.
[4] Lucien Price, reporting Whitehead's reminiscences, in *Dialogues of Alfred North Whitehead* (Boston, 1954), Dialogue XL.

the Boston reporter who wrote *Ward Eight*; a geneticist, and a translator of Cicero's letters; a physiologist, and a great French historian of early nineteenth-century England; Felix Frankfurter, and the medievalist Henry Osborn Taylor; and nonprofessional people. If anyone supposes that during White-head's long collaboration with Bertrand Russell logic and mathematics monopolized the conversation, Russell will correct him. They "talked about everything under the sun." [5]

I do not mean to give the impression that Whitehead habitually learned from conversation *rather* than from reading. Russell's biographer, Alan Wood, wrote, "Russell probably read more widely than any other contemporary philosopher, with the possible exception of Whitehead." [6] Russell himself has told how Whitehead's knowledge of history used to amaze him. "Whatever historical subjects came up he could always supply some illuminating fact, such, for example, as . . . the relation of the Hussite heresy to the Bohemian silver mines. No one ever mentioned this to me again until a few years ago, when I was sent a learned monograph on the subject." [7]

It seems to me highly probable, though I do not know it for a fact, that Whitehead very early developed a lifelong habit of responding to everything he read with some specific reflection on its general—which is to say, its philosophic—significance. [8] However, one more thing is needed as prepara-tion for the writing of a philosophy: firsthand experience of life—what some would call an "existential" participation in it, of the sort that George Santayana lacked. Whitehead was always alive, not aloof. He never stood for parliament, and he loathed publicity. But he did a good deal of political

---

[5] Letter from Lord Russell to the present author, September 26, 1959. In granting permission to quote, Russell added that this statement " is unduly limited, since we also talked about extra-galactic nebulae " (letter of July 12, 1960) .

[6] Wood in: Bertrand Russell, *My Philosophical Development* (London, 1959) , p. 273.

[7] Bertrand Russell, *Portraits from Memory* (London, 1956) , p. 94.

[8] Lucien Price reports Whitehead as saying (August 30, 1941) , " As a matter of fact, I have not read a great quantity of books; but I think about what I read, and it sticks " (*op. cit.*, Dialogue XXII) .

speaking in his Cambridge years. "Rotten eggs and oranges were effective party weapons, and I have often been covered with them." [9]

Stability, which is as important as adventure for new achievements of thought, showed itself in Whitehead's long-term academic positions, in his constant devotion to his students, and in his family life. (He insisted that his wife had a fundamental effect upon his outlook on the world, especially on that part of it which had to do with the importance of beauty, moral and aesthetic.[10]) And there was tragedy. A whole generation of his English pupils was nearly wiped out in the First World War; his younger son Eric, an aviator, was killed at nineteen.

At present, published knowledge of Whitehead's life is slight. I cannot conceive, however, that any account will ever convey so much so briefly and vividly as do his own descriptions of his English environment and education. These are to be found in the "Autobiographical Notes" and in the articles, "The Education of an Englishman," "England and the Narrow Seas," and "Memories." [11] To supplement the "Autobiographical Notes," there is the admirable Prologue in Lucien Price's book. And do not miss the chapter on Whitehead in Bertrand Russell's *Portraits from Memory* (1956).

II

As a mathematician, Whitehead had not been trying to make direct additions to the superstructure of this science so much as to construct new foundations for its advance, by finding ideas broad enough to include as special cases the concepts of arithmetic, geometry, and mechanics which had

[9] LLP-W p. 13; in ESP p. 13.
[10] LLP-W p. 8; in ESP p. 8.
[11] See n. 3, above. The articles were published in the *Atlantic Monthly*, August, 1926, June, 1927, June, 1936, and reprinted in ESP and AESP.

been considered irreducibly basic. When he brought out the *Universal Algebra* he wrote in the Preface that his object was not completeness in details, but unity of idea. Soon thereafter he joined forces with his most brilliant pupil, Russell, to produce, after a decade of work, the tremendous three-volume *Principia Mathematica*. This, published in 1910-1913, is always called " epoch-making," because the authors enlarged the very meaning of mathematics, and did so not by one more discussion of it but by chains of demonstrations, expressed in precise symbols. The whole familiar apparatus of special indefinable mathematical concepts and premises concerning numbers and quantities was done away with; these were instead deduced from a general theory of logical classes and relations, itself ultimately derived from a few axioms concerning logical relations between propositions. An exact formulation was given to deductive logic, and pure mathematics exhibited as an extension of it. This grand unification of two sciences was incomplete; Whitehead never finished the fourth volume, on geometry, which he alone was to write. Also, the treatment of the logical foundations of arithmetic was complicated by the need to introduce certain dubitable hypotheses. Experts have since devoted much ingenuity to their improvement or elimination, with but partial success; and in 1931 Kurt Gödel proved that no set of axioms can embrace the whole of arithmetic. Still, *Principia Mathematica* is universally, and rightly, admired. Concerning the science of logic, it is not too much to say that Whitehead and Russell made the greatest single contribution to it in the more than two thousand years since Aristotle.

Shortly before this work was done, the principles of physics had become disorganized. Two centuries of repeated success in predicting natural phenomena justified the assurance of educated men that the Newtonian framework was—in Whitehead's words, as reported in Lucien Price's Prologue—" fixed as the Everlasting Seat." The few recently discovered phenomena which, late in the nineteenth century, had still to be fitted in, never were fitted into the framework. It broke down completely. This is something that Whitehead, who as a young man shared that assurance, never forgot. Men of lesser wisdom assumed that certainty lay elsewhere, or just around the corner. Whitehead reflected that all of our best generalizations are subject to qualifications of which we are ignorant, and that a continuing approximation to truth is the most that can be expected of our finite intellects.

In a memoir published in 1906 he had used the symbolism of *Principia* to restate the Newtonian theory of the basic relations between space, time, and matter, and to propose alternative theories; but his point of view then was purely mathematical or logical. With the collapse of the Newtonian scheme it became evident that the pressing question for physics was: Precisely what new conceptual frame can best explain the experimental facts? Whitehead studied Einstein's great contribution, and concluded that it was a brilliant mathematical theory erected upon basic empirical meanings that were too narrowly restricted to laboratory operations plus conventional stipulations. His own adventure, in the latter half of his stay in London, was the ambitious one of replacing the Newtonian concepts with new ones which would both express the general character (basic for all natural sciences alike) of our experience of space, time, and matter, and accommodate results of the most delicate astronomical and physical observations. In three books, published in 1919, 1920, and 1922, he expounded these concepts and offered his reinterpretation of physical relativity, with new formulas for the laws of motion, gravitation, and electromagnetism. Although the great majority of mathematical physicists by-passed Whitehead's work at the time, there was some renewal of interest in it in the 1950s.[12] I do not know whether it has a future.

These three books were thus philosophical as well as mathe-

[12] See Robert M. Palter, *Whitehead's Philosophy of Science* (Chicago, 1960), Chap. IX and Appendix IV. It might be added that J. L. Synge, after working with Whitehead's theories, returned to Einstein's; this appears from the fact that he subsequently devoted a book to Einstein's special theory and another to his general theory.

matical, though the philosophy was limited to what natural
science required by way of general empirical foundation. Still,
the known facts of the extraordinary breadth of their author's
intellectual interests, and of his familiarity with Plato and
Hume and Kant, made it appropriate that he, who had never
heard a lecture in philosophy, should be invited to come to
Harvard as a professor in that department. Throughout his
forty years as a mathematician, in his conversations and reflections he had been touching on the various conditions involved
in human existence. The exchange of a mathematical for a
philosophical professorship was Whitehead's opportunity to
formulate the results and devise a new world view: to transfer
his habitual pursuit of maximum generality to the widest
field there is.

In the Lowell Lectures which he gave within a few months
of his arrival—they were expanded and published in 1925 as
Science and the Modern World—Whitehead showed why it
was important for all of us that the criticism and replacement
of the Newtonian concepts should be carried beyond the
immediate concerns of physical science. Newton's success had
established the reign of what Whitehead called "scientific
materialism"—the mechanistic view of nature which resulted
from the work of the great seventeenth-century scientists.
Dualism was its immediate result: the material world fitted
this scheme of ideas, values were outside it. But as the application of the scheme increased, scientific materialism became
a dominant force affecting morals, politics, poetry, the entire
civilization of the occident. Whitehead sketched its career
as the exciting story of an idea that mankind had got hold
of and "could neither live with nor live without." Idealistic
philosophers did not dethrone it; like the orthodox theologians, they assumed that this was the final scientific truth
about nature, and then strove to mitigate it by arguing that
nature presupposed something beyond nature. That did not
hinder materialism, backed by the power and prestige of science, from controlling human affairs; while philosophy, like
religion, became merely consoling. In the twentieth century,

however, scientific materialism broke up from the inside: " What is the sense of talking about a mechanical explanation when you do not know what you mean by mechanics? " wrote Whitehead. " The only way of mitigating mechanism is by the discovery that it is not mechanism " (SMW pp. 23, 107). The discovery appeared imminent. Could not the dualism be overcome at last by some new conception of the nature of things, which would express the aesthetic and purposive character of immediate experience at the same time that it provided a more adequate frame of reference, basically neither mechanistic nor materialistic, for natural science?

In the mid-twenties there was a fair expectation among educated, thoughtful Americans that this could be accomplished by a philosophical scientist of sufficient genius. So when Whitehead in *Science and the Modern World* combined a stunning historical criticism of scientific materialism with a sketch of such a new conception, the book was immediately hailed (by John Dewey among others), despite the fact that the sketch, like all of Whitehead's first expositions of new ideas, was often perplexing. But the full statement which appeared four years later in *Process and Reality: An Essay in Cosmology*, was too intricate and many-faceted to be popular. Furthermore, the doctrine was becoming increasingly prevalent that the gap between matter and value can be bridged without cosmology by fearlessly applying the scientist's experimental *method* of thinking to questions about values. While he was alive, Whitehead's influence among Americans was by no means as great as Dewey's. (This is now changing, but it would be foolish to expect a reversal in the foreseeable future.) In England, habits of philosophical discussion were such that almost no one was at home to receive Whitehead's metaphysics. (New hosts have lately appeared, but they are still few.) In continental Europe and Latin America phenomenology, dialectical materialism and positivism all easily outdrew Whitehead—less because of their actual merits than by their dogmatic claims to be strictly scientific. Then came existentialism, with an opposite sort of appeal. But the translations of many of Whitehead's philosophical books into Spanish, Italian, French, German, Korean, and Dutch are evidence of his growing influence abroad.[13]

Although *Science and the Modern World* was Whitehead's most influential exposition of his philosophy, *Process and Reality*, for technical reasons, is the indispensable one. He completed a kind of trilogy with the publication early in 1933 of another stout volume, *Adventures of Ideas*. There he discussed so many sides of human experience that, as with Plato's *Republic*, it is not easy to specify the subject of the book as a whole. I should say that the chief of its many topics is the sort of history which general ideas about the human race and about the universe have had and can have in Western civilization. A restatement of the main thought of *Process and Reality* provides a basis for the unforgettable conclusion of *Adventures* in a brief but profound analysis of the qualities which are essential to civilized life: truth, beauty, art, adventure, and peace—the peace of the soul.

Whitehead's next book, his last, was *Modes of Thought* (1938).[14] Here he set aside his technical definitions, and wrote " the first chapter in philosophic approach "—" a free examination of some ultimate notions, as they occur naturally in daily life " (MT I, 1). This is what he usually did in his regular lectures at Harvard. Much of the book has an extraordinary valedictory beauty. Whitehead sometimes said that it was his own favorite, though at other times he preferred *Adventures of Ideas* or *Science and the Modern World*. Undoubtedly, the layman's best choice is either *Adventures* or *Modes of Thought*. One may, if he chooses, make a beginning with Whitehead by observing the character of his philosophic

[13] George L. Kline has compiled a list of translations and a bibliography of writings about Whitehead in languages other than English, through 1961. It will be found in a collection of essays in honor of Charles Hartshorne being edited by William L. Reese and Eugene Freeman, and scheduled for publication at La Salle, Ill., in 1963.

[14] *Essays in Science and Philosophy*, published just before his death, is a collection of papers that first appeared in print between 1910 and 1941.

thought within a limited field, as this appeared in the wonder-ful, *Aims of Education*, or in any of his three short books, *Religion in the Making, Symbolism: Its Meaning and Effect*, and *The Function of Reason*.

III

"Philosophy" is a word that we use a good deal; but the philosophies we talk about are fragmentary creations limited by the word *of*. We have our favorite philosophies of educa-tion, of government, of this, of that; but the wide integrating system which shall embrace the whole show is not in the habit of our thinkers. Whitehead stands out because he was up to doing the big job. The method and temper for which it calls are perfectly indicated in a fine passage from the Preface to *Process and Reality*.

> In putting out these results, four strong impressions dominate my mind: First, that the movement of historical, and philo-sophical, criticism of detached questions, which on the whole has dominated the last two centuries, has done its work, and requires to be supplemented by a more sustained effort of con-structive thought. Secondly, that the true method of philo-sophical construction is to frame a scheme of ideas, the best that one can, and unflinchingly to explore the interpretation of experience in terms of that scheme. Thirdly, that all con-structive thought, on the various special topics of scientific interest, is dominated by some such scheme, unacknowledged, but no less influential in guiding the imagination. The im-portance of philosophy lies in its sustained effort to make such schemes explicit, and thereby capable of criticism and improve-ment.
>
> There remains the final reflection, how shallow, puny, and imperfect are efforts to sound the depths in the nature of things. In philosophical discussion, the merest hint of dogmatic certainty as to finality of statement is an exhibition of folly.

The main reason why it is hard to understand Whitehead is that we naturally suppose we already have in our conscious possession all the fundamental ideas which are applicable to human experience, and the right words to express them. That is what he called The Fallacy of the Perfect Dictionary.[15] The usages of language enshrine our old patterns of thought, so that language has to be given a novel twist if a new idea is to be accurately expressed. A genuinely new philosophy is the hardest thing in the world to read. Complaints against Whitehead on this score have been legion. He has become one of the most quoted and least accepted of twentieth-century thinkers.

His work is exciting because of the way in which he depicts reality; and because he depicts reality, not man alone. In this philosophy, the basic fact is everywhere some process of self-realization, which grows out of previous processes and itself adds a new pulse of individuality and a new value to the world. Nothing that exists is completely passive and inert. But Whitehead does not suppose that this is because everything is its own antithesis as well as itself. Nor is he playing the older, less dramatic game of pushing "matter" out of the way in order to give the prime place to eternal spirit. Like Dewey, George Boas, and all who are rightly called temporalists, he rejects the traditional doctrine which contemplates a being at once infinite and changeless as the sole repository of reality and value. Reality and value lie only in emergent pulsations of individuality.

But can you construct a system of the world on this basis? The amazing thing is that in *Process and Reality* Whitehead did just that.

---

[15] MT Epilogue. The name and the idea will recur in later chapters of the present volume.

IV

In Chapter 2 the structure of the system will be shown. At this point an introductory view of Whitehead's metaphysics is in order.

Our first step, which was also his, is to give up completely the habit of picturing the material world as composed of enduring elements moving about in an otherwise empty space. Long before they split the atom, physicists had substituted vibratory entities for Newtonian corpuscles, and fields (electromagnetic and gravitational) for apparently empty space. Let us then think of the material world as basically not a shifting configuration of substantial things, but a nexus of events, or processes. We are to think of the existence of a mountain as a long process, and the existence of an individual atom in the mountain as a connected series of vibratory processes. And whether we notice much or little change, the present event is displaced by others. As Whitehead wrote in the first chapter of his book of 1919, the fundamental characteristic of nature is this " passage," or " creative advance." These words underscore the force of that rather colorless one, " process."

We used to picture a bit of matter as a certain mass which at any given instant was just where it was and nowhere else; now we realize that we cannot ascribe the existence of an atom to any shorter event than the period of its vibration, and that this vibration, though it has a central region, agitates all of space-time. And of course " mass " no longer means " permanent quantity of matter." As Whitehead says, it is " the name for a quantity of energy considered in relation to some of its dynamical effects "; and energy " is merely the name for the quantitative aspect of a structure of happenings." When a particular structure persists throughout a connected series of events, we speak of an enduring material " thing "; when the pattern of activity changes drastically we say, there's an end of that thing. The property of permanence, relative permanence that is, evidently belongs to the *form* of process;

and it is by this form, within the larger patterns of its environment, that we distinguish one atom from another, and both
from a mountain or a frog. Through the ages new types of
pattern evolve, and in Whitehead's broad view there is none
that may not be replaced by some other in the endless history
of the universe.[16]

As long as we thought in terms of things, it was natural to
look upon the things that were substantial as those that were
themselves under all circumstances. In the Newtonian physics
a massy particle had its location altered by the other particles
in the universe, but not its essential nature. In the popular
mind, Daddy Warbucks was [17] a real man because he was
self-sufficient and unchanging. Many philosophers have produced definitions of Reality which glorify such independent
existence. Language, with its separate words for separate
things, strengthens this habit of thought. But the attitude
becames difficult once we shift our basic concept from things
to process. Historical context is now emphasized; the primary
constituents of every event are the threads which come to it
from earlier events, and live anew in it.

As everyone knows, the process of nature, carefully examined, is not sheer continuity. It is individualized into
natural units of process, each arising from established conditions as a determinate synthesis of available energies. As
the world-process moves on to its next creation, that pulsation
lapses, becomes mere material for the building of the future.
Its sources and effects spread out to infinity; in its moment
of life the event is a strictly limited individual fact.

If, with Whitehead, you turn from the physical world to
consider the way in which your own immediate experiences
occur, you will notice a similar rhythm of wide public origin,
concentrated individuality, and spreading public effect. Your
experience now, though you may not consciously separate it
from those that immediately precede and follow, still has a
unity of its own. In its short life—what psychologists call

[16] Further, see Chap. 2, below, p. 12 and pp. 42–55, *passim*.
[17] Hopefully, I use the past tense here also.

" the specious present "—it arises as an integration of nerve impulses, and of conscious and subconscious emotions and attitudes. All these factors have a vector character; that is, intensity and forward direction. They derived their substance from innumerable earlier processes inside and outside of your body—both " physical " ones and " mental " ones (e. g., intentions) . Your present experience, as a whole, is another *process* —a synthesizing process of feeling this wide environment, that is, of bringing its factors to a new head, self-enclosed and privately enjoyed. Its formation completed, this " drop of experience "—William James's phrase, adopted by Whitehead —becomes a fact of history, part of the unalterable context of your future existence and your neighbor's; in short, a cause with observable effects. The end of its life is the beginning of its career. That is how we experience the irreversibility of time.

If these appear obvious generalities, so much the better. Philosophers have no private information here. Their business, if they would think concretely, is to describe the common texture of these drops of experience, which are the immediate realities of our life. This texture we all enjoy, but do not think about because it is always right under our noses. So its true description, once achieved, is bound to appear obvious. The *general* account is what is so hard to draw up. There is a constant temptation to take a part for the whole: your sharp consciousness of sensations and images, if you are introspective or literary; a succession of causal reactions, if you run to behavior-science.

If you think of the drop of water at the faucet as wholly formed by external forces, then " pulse of experience " is a better metaphor for you. Experiencing is an active process. Whitehead is very insistent on this point. It is not only men of genius who entertain new possibilities in their consciousness and do new deeds. A capacity for the spontaneous introduction of something not present in the environment is part of the structure of every experience. Otherwise the present would be only the sum of what was given it by the past, and any

item, taken by itself, a mere re-enaction. Even when you are
consciously entertaining no new idea and the environment
seems to be supplying all the material for your experience,
the question of exactly how this material, donated by the past,
shall be absorbed and felt, what shall be neglected and what
emphasized, is finally decided only by that nascent moment
of existence. *That* unity of feeling never existed before. A
pulse of existence does, in miniature, what a human being
normally accomplishes in the course of his life: the world
gives him his material, his many alternative potentialities,
and of these he fashions *his* personality, which embodies the
perspective and the feeling with which he now takes in the
world. So does each pulse of experience create its own final
unity, complete its own perspective of the world. It brings
into being a slightly, sometimes substantially, novel pattern
of integrated feeling.

This is an aesthetic achievement. " The mutual adaptation
of the several factors in an occasion of experience " is beauty,
in a primary sense of the word. In that sense, beauty is the
unconscious aim of each moment of our existence—beauty of
some sort, that is, for there are many modes of beauty, not
mutually consistent. The intrinsic value of each pulse of
experience is a function of its inclusions; of the exclusions
which are equally essential to achievement; of the internal
qualitative contrasts, complexity, intensity, and breadth of
the pattern of feeling. This is Whitehead's account of the
essential value of sheer existence. Our discussions of human
life are often based on the premise that " existence is good ";
but we are so concerned with the fluctuations of fortune that
we forget the perpetual aesthetic creation of each moment.

Finally, since, within limits imposed by the environment,
every experience is self-creative, it is indirectly creative of the
future. Directly, too, for every moment includes some anticipatory forward thrust, or purpose.

V

At this point our story is in danger of being permanently divided into a story of purposive, creative activity applicable to human experience but not to nature, and a story of external compulsions applicable to the things of nature but not completely to human experience. This separation has been the headache of philosophers for more than three centuries. If purposive activity does not occur in nonhuman nature, then a pragmatist does not solve the problem by defining the science of nature as an instrument for effecting human purposes. He produces another man-glorifying dualism.

The older dualism, following the lead of Immanuel Kant, held that to the scientist every event, inanimate or human, is bound to appear mechanically caused in its entirety; yet the moralist is bound to think of right and wrong as freely done; and the two beliefs do not really conflict, they are merely asserted from different points of view. We have all heard the problem of science versus religion solved in a similar way. Whitehead believed that this is a bogus solution. Our life is one life; you cannot parcel it out to thinkers sworn not to interfere with each other. Causality and freedom, like all fundamental contrasts, are in existence itself. You cannot reconcile them by distinguishing points of view, but only by finding a way to think them together.

This particular contrast is but one feature of the gap between inanimate nature and human experience. That is the gap the philosopher must bridge, and Whitehead faced up to the fact that this requires general concepts which apply to both extremes. The physicist's concepts of physical existence won't do the job, because they omit altogther the existence of experiences. On the other hand it would be fantastic to generalize, as metaphysicians so often have, from what is peculiar to man or only fitfully exhibited by him—from such traits as his consciousness, sense-perception, or thought. But every quantic event in the universe may at least be thought of as in itself a pulse of experience of a primitive sort, an individual feeling of and reaction to its environment; and this is Whitehead's bold hypothesis: here is his " pluralistic universe." [18]

Each of these pulses of experience occurs as an atom of process, integrative or convergent in shape. Causation, then, is the principle of transition from atoms of process achieved to an atom of process beginning, on which they impose their individual characters, just as your experiences of a second ago automatically become part of your present existence. And the internal principle, consciously or (in the great majority of cases) unconsciously operating in each atom of process, is its individual measure—slight or considerable—of self-creation, by which the process concludes in one way rather than another, and feels itself a new member of the universe. Causation means conditions, conditions imposed by the environment; but conditions do not unify themselves into a novel individual. Without the internal principle of self-creation, there would be no individual pulses of existence and no individual responsibility in our lives, but only a continuous flow of energy. There is no creation without creators, and every new actuality is here and now in some degree creative.

Whitehead did not put out a bare hypothesis, but a developed theory, the first of its kind. Into it he fitted the general ideas of physics: space-time, motion, causality, quantization, vibration, matter, energy flow, and energy transformation. His familiarity with natural science enabled him to follow the contours of nature, and to suggest how, within the framework of his hypothesis, we may distinguish molecules, stones, single living cells, trees, animals, and persons as different organizations—" societies," he calls them—of primitive or complex drops of experience. A considerable application of Whitehead's principles to biological theory may be found in *A*

---

[18] William James wrote a book with this phrase for its title, but he never said what the universe was a plurality *of*. The published and unpublished writings of his last five years, however, contain indications that he would have accepted Whitehead's hypothesis; see Chap. 9, n. 61, and Chap. 12, n. 11, below.

Contribution to the Theory of the Living Organism, by the
Australian zoologist W. E. Agar.[19] Among inanimate things
the autonomous energy which, on Whitehead's view, belongs
in principle to every natural pulsation, generally conforms
to established patterns (as many autonomies in human affairs
do). For the science which is tracing a transmission of energy
up to an observer in a laboratory, such autonomous energy
is negligible, and an atom's experience is nothing. However,
once we recognize that the entities which are the subjects of
physical theory are abstractions—and this cannot credibly be
denied—then if we wish a general theory of existence we must
consider what the more complete things are, from which our
observations and our special sciences make their abstractions.
Whitehead has offered an answer. It does not, I believe, contradict any confirmed result of science. There is an addition
to what science says.

Without this addition, we slip back to a dualistic universe,
and man himself becomes divided. With it, a unity of interpretation comes in at the ground floor. In other words, man's
union with organic nature is not just a scientific fact the
reality of which no one could have felt before Darwin wrote;
it is the basic fact of our existence, and it is perpetually
evidenced by the feeling—" vague but insistent," as Whitehead
liked to say—that our experience derives from a natural world
of " throbbing actualities " whose reality is of the same sort
as our own. (We do not usually extend this feeling to such
things as stones, but then a stone is not a true individual. The
passive uniformity of its behavior, which is all that our eyes
can perceive, is the result of an averaging-out process which
masks the incessant activities of the individual atoms.)

Our reluctance to admit that any beings lower in nature's
scale than our animal pets may have experiences is not entirely
due to unimaginativeness. Our elemental feeling of the living
universe " begetting us " becomes submerged as the autonomous part of each pulse of our experience rises to dominance:
that pulse feels the creativeness of nature here and now as its

[19] See Chap. 3, n. 48, below.

own possession, and the wide universe comes to appear as a collection of things laid out in its immediate neighborhood for it to act upon. In the language of the existentialists, it calls itself " spirit," everything else " thing " or " object." This division is a real phenomenon of human consciousness, and it may take on a myriad fascinating forms. Fasten upon them, dismiss the universe, and you are ready to embrace some kind of existentialism.

Whitehead's philosophy has never enjoyed the popularity which rewards narrowness. A new philosophy which is broad enough to reflect many facets of existence will have many enemies. How many people will go into a rage when they read of elemental feelings, " vague but insistent "! They cannot believe that what is clear in consciousness might be superficial in our existence, that what they are reading is anything but another mystical irrationalism designed to justify brutalities in action. And the scientist may jump to the conclusion that Whitehead's cosmology is an attempt to dictate principles to him. But that is today the special privilege of dialectical materialism; Whitehead did not desire it. Natural science remains, in his view, the systematic study of the causal connections between events. But Whitehead *has* made it possible for thinking man once more to enjoy his organic relationship with nature: to be a Wordsworthian—Wordsworth probably influenced Whitehead as much as any philosopher did, Plato excepted—or to respond to D. H. Lawrence's feeling for nature, without having to swallow Lawrence's antiscientific extravagances. Whitehead's offering is a frame of reference in which there is ample room for science, for poetry, and—as we must next observe—for religion.

VI

Our beliefs that individuality, interdependence, and growth are fundamental ideas find a reconciliation in Whitehead's metaphysics. The members of his pluralistic universe are

organically connected by the fact that each is a growing
together, a " concrescence," of components of earlier members
into a new unity of existence. In *Process and Reality* Whitehead proposed general principles governing concrescence and
a theory of the stages into which each one is analyzable. It
is easy to put a halo on " growth," but this philosophy is a
universal *theory* of growth-quanta as the cells in the process
of the universe. We find this amazing because we are used
to the timid assumption that only mechanical movement and
causal connections can be anlyzed.

Whitehead makes his principles of growth and of dependent
individuality perfectly universal. His system includes a concept of God; but even God is dependent on the individual
processes of the world for the perpetual completion of his
being. He is not self-sufficient, and they are as real as he. Nor
is God omnipotent. Whitehead was convinced that the finer
religious insight sees the divine agency in the universe as
persuasive, not coercive; persuading by the attraction of the
ideals, the new possibilities of value, which it offers to the
finite individuals of the world as each of them, rising into
being, makes the final determination of its character, and so
of what it offers to the future. In this way God, and the
environment consisting of the totality of already completed
finite processes, together make up the infinite background
from which a new event emerges.

Upon its completion, this event becomes part of God's
experience, thus acquiring a further unity with all the others
that have ever been. They are now all included in an infinitely
wide harmony of feeling which grows without fading. This
doctrine reflects Whitehead's acceptance of a purified religious
intuition of a kingdom of heaven. Those who embrace atheism
or agnosticism may still agree with the estimate that this philosophical system incorporates the conviction that God is love
better than any other has.[20] Personal experience of tragedy—

[20] See Charles Hartshorne, " Is Whitehead's God the God of Religion? "
Ethics, 53 (1942/1943), 219-227. Hartshorne and William L. Reese,
Philosophers Speak of God (Chicago, 1953), present a large anthology
and a technical comparative study.

something which threatens all loving souls—lies in the background of Whitehead's metaphysics. He speaks profoundly
to religious men in this destructive century. In particular:
he speaks from a fine imaginative understanding of human
existence, not from anxiety about it.

For Whitehead, the temporal world itself involves more than
process. While " the flux of things is one ultimate generalization around which we must weave our philosophical system,"
he also believes that " the alternative metaphysical doctrine,
of reality devoid of process, would never have held the belief
of great men, unless it expressed some fundamental aspect
of our experience." (PR II x i; MT v 8). Whitehead fashions
his adjustment of this antithesis by interpreting the creative
ness of individual processes as a desire to embody ideal patterns which are ordered in God's experience, and which as
patterns do not change. Thus " the things which are temporal
arise by their participation in the things which are eternal "
(PR II 1 i). Without the latter, Whitehead thinks, definiteness and novelty in the temporal world would be inconceivable.

The contrasts with existentialism, and with nonmetaphysical
philosophies of process (like John Dewey's) are obvious. The
most gifted systematic philosopher of our century was by
second nature a Platonist—not of the unimaginative kind who
by God tells you what the eternal truths are, but of the kind
whose outlook is widened by the thought of countless ideal
patterns in the background of actual existence. If their
Platonism is a mistake, it is a mistake for which their own
humility is half responsible. They cannot give themselves
the whole credit for their creativeness; they say that they have
merely drawn on a boundless realm of ideality, merely *realized*
a value.

Whitehead's Platonism did not lessen, it enhanced, his keen
appreciation of change, of novelty, of the myriad qualities of
transient experience. His writings are full of such phrases as
" the final good of immediate joy." And in his philosophy of
education—a topic of lifelong concern, on which he wrote a
fair number of articles after 1911—it was natural for him to

emphasize experimental activity and living in the present, which is "holy ground." Yet to Whitehead, "we learn by doing" was only half the truth. "Education," he said, "consists in the habitual vision of greatness." *Vision*—there you have the authentic Platonic note.

Plato was far and away Whitehead's favorite philosopher; rightly or wrongly, he believed that his own metaphysics was a systematic modern development of Plato's general point of view. But although he was convinced that the timeless Forms of Platonic philosophy are real, not invented, Whitehead refused to give them the kind of reality which Plato usually gave them—independent of and superior to changing things.[21] Though the forms are undated, and eternally present to God's experience, they are there only as so many possibilities for realization in the flux of things—possible patterns of existence and possible ways of feeling the changing world. As we might expect, Whitehead was especially concerned that the realm of mathematical relationships should not be construed as an exception. "The modern concept of an infinite series," he noted, "is the concept of a form of transition"; he argued that the simple sentence, "twice-three is six," "considers a process and its issue." He called this, his final discussion of the subject (MT v 4, 5), "a belated reminder to Plato that his eternal mathematical forms are essentially referent to process." He concluded: "The discovery of mathematics, like all discoveries, both advanced human understanding, and also produced novel modes of error. Its error was the introduction of the doctrine of form, devoid of 'life and motion.'"[22]

In Whitehead's philosophy, then, the temporal and the eternal are both there; neither is "illusion," but neither is sufficient unto itself. Each, to achieve full reality, needs the other. Never did a philosopher so interweave these opposites. In truth, this metaphysics generalizes perfectly, in the terms

[21] Accordingly, I shall not continue to capitalize "form."
[22] Whitehead also had in mind the current expression of this error in the doctrine that mathematical propositions are tautologies, saying nothing. The phrase, "life and motion," which he cites with approval, is from Plato—Plato in another mood.

of the European philosophical tradition, the attitude of that
rarest of men—he whose feet are on the ground while his eyes
are turned upward.

VII

Whitehead's philosophizing was no mere intellectual game.
In his view, every throb of existence has some value for itself,
for others, and for the universe. Hence a morality founded on
this metaphysics will enjoin respect for others—not (as in the
Kantian and other idealistic philosophies) only for other men
because they are men and man is unique in being more than
a natural animal, but for all beings, and precisely because they
are all individuals in a reconceived natural world. Whitehead's philosophy generates a moral attitude toward nature,
by teaching that there is nothing in the universe that is really
and completely dead, mere material, with which we may do
as our whims dictate. Vegetarianism and kindness to bacteria
do not follow; what follows is that all destruction requires
justification. Whitehead hated violence. Yet he was not a
pacifist, for he believed that no absolute rule is adequate to
the conduct of life.

Whitehead also gives us basic reasons for looking upon the
problem of achievement, both individual and social, as a problem in the co-ordination of living values. The human soul,
like every being, is a synthesizer.

> Its good resides in the realization of a strength of many feelings
> fortifying each other as they meet in the novel unity. Its evil
> lies in the clash of vivid feelings, denying to each other their
> proper expansion. Its triviality lies in the anesthesia by which
> evil is avoided. . . . Evil is the half-way house between perfec-
> tion and triviality. It is the violence of strength against
> strength.—AI xix ii.

The problem of social life is to make possible a harmony of
strong individuals. This " is the problem of the co-ordination

of [various grades of] activities, including the limits of such co-ordination " (AI III i) . Hegel and Marx were wrong; the conflict of unco-ordinated opposites is a disaster. The conditions of synthesis, in every form of existence, are aesthetic contrast rather than strife. High achievement requires a "zest" (one of Whitehead's favorite words) for those contrasting novelties which can enrich human life. It equally requires preservation of those wider social co-ordinations on which the survival of society depends. Whitehead's doctrine is that structures (like everything else in his world view) are interdependent; none can exist save as a part of a wider structure which sustains it. This is a general principle, on which bionomics in all its branches, as well as sociology, and all rational consideration of an individual's possibilities, depend.

Complete preservation of established ways is never possible. Since everything, as it comes into existence, aims at a synthesis of what has been with what may be, the present alters the trend of the past—upward, or downward. The approach to sheer continuation is characteristic of sticks and stones: "The art of persistence is to be dead." Besides, every process, individual or social, in taking on its character rejects a multitude of other characters; in realizing its ideal, it is changing within a limited range of possibilities, and when these are exhausted either staleness or transition to a new type of order, hitherto excluded, must set in. "The pure conservative is fighting against the essence of the Universe " (AI XIX ii) . This is not an apology for revolution. Development, not revolution, is the thing. And development has its optimum pace, which it takes statesmanship to discover.

Every new idea, in particular, is a danger to the existing order. In contrast to the compulsion which is exercised by what exists, the power of an idea is, in the first instance, persuasive. This is a special case, involving consciousness, of the functioning, in each pulse of existence, of "what may be." Behind it is the creative purposiveness which each pulse possesses in some degree. But, says Whitehead, any impartial survey of life on earth shows us that individual purposes tend to be anarchic. The *general* idea, capable of successive partial embodiments, introduces order into the persuasive element, and is the distinctively human agency in man's checkered progress. Here is a typical paragraph from *Adventures of Ideas* showing Whitehead's over-all judgment of this agency:

> The history of ideas is a history of mistakes. But through all mistakes it is also the history of the gradual purification of conduct. When there is progress in the development of favourable order, we find conduct protected from relapse into brutalization by the increasing agency of ideas consciously entertained. In this way Plato is justified in his saying, The creation of the world—that is to say, the world of civilized order—is the victory of persuasion over force.—II vili.

Human experiences, however, are natural events, and their basis is emotional, not intellectual. Conscious thought, according to this philosophy, is a rare thing—the occasional flowering of experience, not its essence. Societies, too, are dominated by habitual modes of feeling, which are the basic facts for wise historians and statesmen. Whitehead had learned, as many thinkers have not, that man is only to a very slight degree a rational animal. But the possibility of rational guidance is there, and progress requires that it be exercised. Reason is no formal thing, but the occasional discipline, ardently to be desired, of life's ubiquitous purposiveness.

Usually this discipline is confined to a pragmatic interest in the control and reconstruction of some limited aspect of the environment so as to improve life in the immediate future. So do we study forestry, electronics, bacteriology, the theory of games. This kind of intelligence begins as shrewdness in observation and manipulation, and blossoms out into a highly organized experimental method appropriate to particular interests. Yet the history of human thought and a glance at the morning paper both confirm Whitehead's judgment:

> The man with a method good for purposes of his dominant interests, is a pathological case in respect to his wider judgment on the co-ordination of this method with a more complete

experience. Priests and scientists, statesmen and men of business, philosophers and mathematicians, are all alike in this
respect. . . . Some of the major disasters of mankind have
been produced by the narrowness of men with a good method-
ology. Ulysses has no use for Plato, and the bones of his
companions are strewn on many a reef and many an isle.—
FR p. 8.

This is the justification of a wider type of reason, unlimited
in its aim at generality—of the sort of thing that Whitehead
did.

Chapter 2

The Metaphysical System

I

The purpose of this chapter is to set forth the main ideas of Whitehead's general theory of existence under their technical names, and to show how they fit together. But something must first be said about the general character of the book, *Process and Reality*, in which Whitehead elaborated his theory.

The work is a very good illustration of one of the frequent characteristics of intellectual landmarks—that of being hard to read just because it is original. In 1948 I wrote that Whitehead's book was about as long as Immanuel Kant's *Critique of Pure Reason*, and quite as backbreaking. This statement has not, to my knowledge, been challenged. But now that a whole generation has passed since *Process and Reality* was published, the book has come to appear less frightening than it did at first. People still complain of its vocabulary, and some always will—those who make the false assumption that really new ideas in any nonmathematical discipline can always be adequately expressed in a good tight system by language that would be acceptable to the editors of the *Reader's Digest*, and that when this doesn't happen the author is at fault: he is obscure either on purpose or because he hasn't taken pains. As a matter of fact, if you come to Whitehead with an open mind and some acquaintance with modern philosophy, you will probably soon agree with him that the introduction of the new terms was a practical necessity, and will find the words themselves peculiarly apt.

Readers who have spent some time on *Process and Reality* now complain rather of the many misprints. One commentator recently observed that we have a better text of Plato's *Republic*. And indeed *Process and Reality* was badly put together, badly proofread, and poorly indexed. Discrepancies and minor inconsistencies abound. These things are characteristic of Whitehead's books. He was absorbed in his ideas, not in ordering them nicely for the public; and long before the publisher sent out galleys his mind had always moved on to some new investigation. All his works are the expressions of an active intellect, not of a writer who sends forth at long last one technically perfect product. In consequence, accurate understanding of many details in Whitehead's thought—and probably of some matters that are more than details—simply cannot be assured until there is a critical edition of his works. The need is greatest in the case of *Process and Reality*, since in it the defects are most pronounced. But this need is primarily a scholar's. The ordinary reader—if he is willing to devote himself to an original thinker—will easily find in this book ideas which make a forcible impact, and which he can use. That is of course what Whitehead most wanted.

Process and Reality is an expansion of a series of lectures— the Gifford Lectures which Whitehead delivered at the University of Edinburgh during the session 1927-28. The book accordingly begins:

> This course of lectures is designed as an essay in Speculative Philosophy. Its first task must be to define ' speculative philosophy ', and to defend it as a method productive of important knowledge.

> Speculative Philosophy is the endeavour to frame a coherent,
> logical, necessary system of general ideas in terms of which
> every element of our experience can be interpreted. By this
> notion of 'interpretation' I mean that everything of which
> we are conscious, as enjoyed, perceived, willed, or thought,
> shall have the character of a particular instance of the general
> scheme.

Here there is no beating around the bush, no attempt to build
up a solemn metaphysical mood in the reader. The style is
the same style of straightforward statement which you would
expect to find on the first page of a mathematical or other
scientific treatise which investigates a new field, or applies a
new method to an old one.

It is the element of novelty which prompts Whitehead to
begin his enterprise by defending it. The opening pages of
his *Treatise on Universal Algebra* likewise contained a defense
of the claims of that subject to be considered an important
branch of mathematics. Whitehead the philosopher had none
of the apologetic nervousness which the writings of philosophers
so often betray in this age of science.

Section I of the first chapter continues in the same plain
way, by stating how the key terms in the definition of " Speculative Philosophy " are to be understood. At once succinct and
comprehensive, these statements do their work well. An attempt to set down their essence here would be at best an
unnecessary duplication. One warning may not be amiss. In
using the word, " necessary," Whitehead is not saying that the
system he is about to offer is necessarily true. He did not
write, " Speculative Philosophy is a coherent, logical, necessary
system . . ." He wrote that it is " the *endeavour to frame* a
coherent, logical, necessary system . . ."

Whitehead's defense of speculative philosophy has become
the classic exposition of that mode of thought, and must be
read. Let us now begin our approach to the content of his
speculative philosophy.

As we pointed out in the first chapter, Whitehead's amazing
philosophical achievement is the construction of a system of

the world according to which the basic fact of existence is everywhere some process of self-realization, growing out of previous processes and itself adding a new pulse of individuality and a new value to the world. So far as familiar classifications of metaphysical systems are concerned, then, I should first of all classify Whitehead's as pluralistic; it denies that ultimately only one individual (God, or the Absolute) exists. But no one-sentence characterization, not even of the roughest kind, is possible for this system. Whitehead the pluralist saw the great monistic metaphysicians as endeavoring to exhibit the unity and solidarity which the universe undoubtedly has, while failing to do justice to the equally evident plurality of individual existents. He saw Spinoza the monist, equally with Leibniz the pluralist, as having made valuable depositions. It is not that their systems, however, should be reconciled (at some cost to each). It is that their insights, along with those of Plato and others, should be reconciled—or better, used—in a new system. It will have its own elements and its own structure. For reasons which will appear, Whitehead named it " the philosophy of organism."

Taken as a whole, this deposition of Whitehead's can neither be subsumed under any movement of the twentieth century nor accurately represented as the joint influence of recent thinkers on its author. It must be understood in its own terms. But it is so complex and elaborate that all but the main concepts will be omitted in the one-chapter summary which follows. These concepts will be presented sympathetically, with some fullness and a little comment, as a bald statement of them would be unintelligible.

II

By way of initial orientation, let us say that Whitehead's universe is a *connected* pluralistic universe. No monist ever insisted more strongly than he that nothing in the world exists in independence of other things. In fact, he repeatedly criticizes traditional monisms for not carrying this principle far enough; they exempted eternal being from dependence on temporal beings. Independent existence is a myth, whether you ascribe it to God or to a particle of matter in Newtonian physics, to persons, to nations, to things, or to meanings. To understand is to see things together, and to see them as, in Whitehead's favorite phrase, " requiring each other." A system which enables us to do this is " coherent."

Each pulse of existence—Whitehead calls them " actual entities "—requires the antecedent others as its constituents, yet achieves individuality as a unique, finite synthesis; and when its growth is completed, stays in the universe as one of the infinite number of settled facts from which the individuals of the future will arise. " The many become one, and are increased by one." The ultimate character pervading the universe is a drive toward the endless production of new syntheses. Whitehead calls this drive " creativity." It is " the eternal activity," " the underlying energy of realisation." Nothing escapes it; the universe consists entirely of its creatures, its individualized embodiments. Accordingly, Whitehead's Categoreal Scheme begins with the three notions, " creativity," " many," and " one," which comprise the " Category of the Ultimate." This category is presupposed by all his other metaphysical categories.

Creativity is not to be thought of as a thing or an agency external to its actual embodiments, but as " that ultimate notion of the highest generality " which actuality *exhibits*. Apart from that exhibition it does not exist. Like Aristotle's " matter," creativity has no character of its own, but is perfectly protean: " It cannot be characterized, because all characters are more special than itself." Nor can its universal presence be explained in terms of anything else; it must be seen by direct, intuitive experience.

The doctrine that all actualities alike are in the grip of creativity suggests a general principle which Whitehead thinks every metaphysical scheme, so far as it is coherent, must follow.

The principle is that there is ultimately but one kind of actuality.

> ' Actual entities '—also termed ' actual occasions '—are the final real things of which the world is made up. There is no going behind actual entities to find anything more real. They differ among themselves: God is an actual entity, and so is the most trivial puff of existence in far-off empty space. But, though there are gradations of importance, and diversities of function, yet in the principles which actuality exemplifies all are on the same level.—PR I II i.

This statement represents an ideal which Whitehead, so far as the concept of God is concerned, does not entirely achieve. But he is distinguished by his conscious adoption and pursuit of it, in place of the more traditional, dualistic doctrine of inferior and superior realities.

Our experience of the universe does not, at first glance, present any obvious prototype of actual entities. Selves, monads, material atoms, and Aristotelian substances have been tried out in the history of philosophy. Whitehead develops a theory of a different entity—an *experience*. The doctrine that experience comes in drops or pulses, each of which has a unique character and an indivisible unity, is to be found in the writings of William James; but James never outlined a metaphysics on this basis. In any case, Whitehead had motives of his own for adopting the working hypothesis that " all final individual actualities have the metaphysical character of occasions of experience."

There was the antidualistic motive: belief that some such actualities are without any experience of their own, when joined to the fact that the human existence with which philosophic thought must begin is just a series of experiences, makes it impossible to think of these extremes as contrasting but connected instances of one basic kind of actuality. But on Whitehead's hypothesis, " the direct evidence as to the connectedness of one's immediate present occasion of experience with one's immediately past occasions, can be validly used to suggest categories applying to the connectedness of all occasions in nature " (AI xv i).

Secondly, we instinctively feel that we live in a world of "throbbing actualities"; and such "direct persuasions" are the ultimate touchstones of philosophic theory.

Thirdly, Whitehead does not wish to think that intrinsic value is an exclusive property of superior beings; rather it belongs to even "the most trivial puff of existence." In human life, he finds value not far off, but at hand as the living essence of present experience. If every puff of existence is a pulse of some kind of immediate experience, there can be no final dualism of value and fact in the universe.

A fourth reason why Whitehead chose occasions of experience for his "actual entities" emerges as a reader becomes familiar with his thought. It is his love of concrete immediacy. An immediate experience, in its living occurrence at this moment—that, to this rationalist's way of thinking, is a full fact, in comparison with which all other things are pale abstractions. It is a mistake for philosophers to begin with substances which appear solid or obvious to them, like the material body or the soul, and then, almost as if it were an afterthought, bring in transient experiences to provide these with an adventitious historical filling. The transient experiences *are* the ultimate realities.

But experience is not restricted to consciousness. "We experience the universe, and we analyze in our consciousness a minute selection of its details." Like most psychologists today, Whitehead thinks of consciousness as a variable factor which heightens an organism's discrimination of some part of its world. Consciousness is no basic category for him, because it is so far from being essential to every drop of experience in the cosmos, that it is not even present in every human experience. The same remark applies—the tradition of modern philosophy to the contrary notwithstanding—to thought and sense-perception.

The chief meaning intended by calling every actual entity a pulse of *experience* is that the entity is conceived as having an immediate existence in and for itself. "Experience" is "the self-enjoyment of being one among many, and of being one arising out of the composition of many." Each appropriation of an item of the many into the arising unity of enjoyment is a "feeling" or "prehension" (literally, a grasping) of that item, and the process of composition is a "concrescence" (growing together) of prehensions. The appropriated "many" are "objects," existing before the process begins; the "one" is the privately experiencing "subject." Thus "the subject-object relation is the fundamental structural pattern of experience."

A good way to continue our exposition now is to connect it with the challenge which William James, who had championed "psychology without a soul," issued to philosophers in his famous essay of 1904, "Does 'Consciousness' Exist?." He there attacked the notion, then current in various forms, that the existence of a conscious subject, if not of a soul, must be assumed in the discussion of experience. Is Whitehead trying to resuscitate the notion which James led many twentieth-century philosophers to reject? No. He does think it obvious that experience is a relation between private centers of experience and public objects experienced. But there are three big differences between his theory of this relation and the views which James attacked.

1) In the earlier views this was a cognitive relation of a conscious mind to objects known. Whitehead's fundamental relation of prehension is something broader and more elemental, the generally unconscious emotional feeling by which one bit of life responds to other realities. An essential factor in every prehension is its "subjective form"—the affective tone with which that subject now experiences that object. An example is the unconscious annoyance with which you experienced this page when you turned to it and saw another solid mass of print. Everything in your environment contributes something both to the tone of your experience and to its content.

2) A prehension is not so much a relation as a relating, or transition, which carries the object into the make-up of the subject.[1] Whitehead's "feelings" are not states, but "'vectors'; for they feel what is *there* and transform it into what is *here*" (PR II iii i 15).[2] He was writing a theoretical transcript of the fact that you feel this moment of experience to be your very own, yet derived from a world without. By taking that elemental assurance at its face value, he was able to accept a primary rule of modern philosophy—that the evidence for an external world can be found only within occasions of experience—without being drawn into solipsism.

Prehensions, like vectors, should be symbolized by arrows. The arrows run from the past [3] to the present—for the "there" is antecedent, however slightly, in time as well as external in space to the "here"—and *from* objects *to* a subject. The method is realistic, not idealistic: Whitehead remarks that instead of describing, in Kantian fashion, how subjective data pass into the appearance of an objective world, he describes how subjective experience emerges from an objective world.

3) For Whitehead the subject which enjoys an experience does not exist beforehand, neither is it created from the outside; it creates itself in that very process of experiencing. The process starts with the multitude of environmental objects awaiting unification in a fresh perspective, moves through stages of partial integration, and concludes as a fully determinate synthesis, effected by a concrescence of feelings. "The point to be noticed is that the actual entity, in a state of process during which it is not fully definite, determines its own ultimate definiteness. This is the whole point of moral

---

[1] Thus there is some analogy between "prehension" and the "felt transition" of which James wrote. This is elaborated in Chap. 13, below.

[2] Vectors, in physical theory, are quantities which have direction as well as magnitude: e. g., forces or velocities. Although it is evident from Whitehead's language, here and in the several other passages where he refers to prehensions as "vectors," that this is the analogy he intends, the meaning of "vector" in biology (the carrier of a microorganism) also provides an appropriate analogy. I owe this observation to Prof. Nathaniel Lawrence.

[3] Except in the case of "conceptual prehension," which will be explained shortly.

responsibility " (PR III iii v). It is also the point of the
descriptive term, "organism," which Whitehead applies to
actual entities, and which supplies the very name of his philosophy. He means that an organism determines the eventual
character and integration of its own parts. Its growth is motivated by a living—if generally unconscious—aim at that outcome. So the brief course of each pulse of experience is guided
by an internal teleology.

Many philosophers consider Whitehead's doctrine of a self-
creating experiencer unintelligible. It certainly contradicts
the mode of thought to which we are accustomed—*first* a
permanent subject, *then* an experience for it. But how did the
subject originally come into being? Whitehead looks upon
process as not only the appearance of new patterns among
things, but the becoming of new subjects, which are completely
individual, self-contained units of feeling. "The ancient doctrine that 'no one crosses the same river twice' is extended.
No thinker thinks twice; and, to put the matter more generally,
no subject experiences twice." "The universe is thus a creative
advance into novelty. The alternative to this doctrine is a
static morphological universe" (PR I ii iv; III i iii).

Whitehead pictures reality as cumulative. When, upon the
completion of an actual occasion, the creativity of the universe
moves on to the next birth, it carries that occasion with it
as an "object" which all future occasions are obliged to
prehend. They will feel it as an efficient cause—as the immanence of the past in their immediacies of becoming. The
end of an occasion's private life—its "perishing"—is the
beginning of its public career. As Whitehead once explained:

> If you get a general notion of what is meant by perishing,
> you will have accomplished an apprehension of what you mean
> by memory and causality, what you mean when you feel that
> what we are is of infinite importance, because as we perish we
> are immortal—ESP p. 117.

Part of the appeal of Whitehead's metaphysics lies in this,
that through his conception of pulses of experience as the

ultimate facts, he invests the passage of time with life and motion, with pathos, and with a majesty rivaled in no other philosophy of change, and in few eternalistic ones.

Our experience does not usually discriminate a single actual entity as its object, but rather a whole nexus of them united by their prehensions. That is how you experience your body or your past personal history. " The ultimate facts of immediate actual experience," then, " are actual entities, prehensions, and nexūs.[4] All else is, for our experience, derivative abstraction." In Whitehead's cosmology, however, some types of derivative abstractions are constituents in every actual entity. Propositions are such; in every experience, conscious or unconscious, they function as " lures proposed for feeling." (Whitehead cites " There is beef for dinner today " as an example of a " quite ordinary proposition.") Because human beings think it important to consciously judge some propositions true or false, all propositions have traditionally been treated as units of thought or discourse, and supposed to be the concern of logicians alone. But we have no space for Whitehead's highly original theory of propositions as factors in natural processes.

We shall confine attention in this chapter to the simplest type of abstract entity. The entertainment of propositions is but one of the ways in which " eternal objects " are ingredients in experience. These entities, uncreated and undated, are his version of Plato's timeless ideal Forms. They are patterns and qualities like roundness or squareness, greenness or redness, courage or cowardice. The fact that every actual occasion in its process of becoming acquires a definite character to the exclusion of other possible characters is explained as its selection of *these* eternal objects for feeling and its rejection ("negative prehension") of *those*. (This is not as fantastic as it sounds; actualities inherit habits of selection, and these habits are so strong that scientists call them laws of nature.)

For Whitehead as for Aristotle, process is the realizing of selected antecedent potentialities, or it is unexplainable. " Pure potentials for the specific determination of fact "—that is what

---

[4] Plural of " nexus." The quotation is from PR I II i.

eternal objects are. And that is all they are. The ideal is
nothing more than a *possibility* (good *or* bad) *for* the actual.
Whitehead so emphatically repudiates the Platonic tendency
to think of the realm of forms as constituting a superior, self-
sufficient type of existence, that he interprets even the propositions of mathematics as statements about certain possible
forms *of process.*

As an antidualist, Whitehead rejects the doctrine that mind
and body are distinct, disparate entities. He generalizes the
mind-body problem, and suggests that a certain contrast between two modes of activity exists within every actual occasion. An occasion is a throb of experience, so of course its
" physical pole " cannot consist of matter, in the sense of a
permanent unfeeling substance; and consciousness is too slight
and occasional to define the " mental pole." [5] The physical
activity of each occasion is rather its absorption of the actual
occasions of the past, its direct *rapport* with the environment
from which it sprang; and its mental side is its own creativeness, its desire for and realization of ideal forms (including its
own terminal pattern) by means of which it makes a novel,
unified reaction to its inheritance. (So there are two species
of prehensions in Whitehead's system: " physical prehensions "
of actual occasions or nexūs, and " conceptual prehensions "
of eternal objects.) Each occasion is a fusion of the already
actual and the ideal.

The subjective forms of conceptual prehensions are " valuations," up or down; this or that possibility is felt to be important or trivial or irrelevant, or not wanted. We see again
how, in trying to make theory correspond to the character of
immediate experience, Whitehead insists that emotional feeling, not pure cognition of a neutral datum, is basic. Except
for mathematical patterns, the data are not neutral either:
red is a possibility of warmth, blue of coolness.

An eternal object, as a form of definiteness, may be realized

---

[5] These terms are prominent in *Process and Reality.* Whitehead privately regretted that he had used them; too many readers thought they
referred to substantially separate parts of each actual occasion.

in one actual occasion after another, through each prehending that form in its predecessor. A nexus composed of one, or simultaneously of many, such strands, Whitehead aptly calls a "society of occasions," which has that eternal object for its "defining characteristic." Such a process of inheritance seems to be the essence of every human "society," in the usual meaning of the word. But the general principle has a much wider application; through it, a metaphysics of drops of experience can define personal identity, and a philosophy of process can account for *things*—for frogs and mountains, electrons and planets—which are certainly neither becomings nor forms. They are societies of becomings—of "atoms of process," as they were called in Chapter 1. Thus personal minds (each with its history of experiences) and enduring bodies finally appear in the philosophy of organism, but as variable complexes rather than metaphysical absolutes.

Though Whitehead's philosophy is very much a philosophy of change, we must notice that according to it the ultimate members of the universe do not, strictly speaking, change— i. e., alter some of their properties while retaining their identities. Because it is a process of self-realization, an actual occasion can only become itself, and then "perish." Whatever changes is a serial "society" of such occasions, and its persistence during the change is not due to any underlying *substance*—Whitehead eliminates that notion—but to retention of one *form* (the defining characteristic) while others vary.

The differences between the kinds of things in nature then go back to the different contrasts, repetitions, divisions, or modes of integration involved in the chains of prehensions by which actual occasions make up societies with different defining characteristics. Whitehead sketched the main principles involved.[6] His universe exhibits societies arising and decaying, societies within other societies which sustain them (consider the animal body), societies on all scales of magnitude. The

[6] It is not only readers interested in natural science who should find the chapters in *Process and Reality* on "The Order of Nature" and "Organisms and Environment" fascinating.

structure of Nature comes out well—in fact beautifully—in this philosophy of the flux.

The bare statement of Whitehead's theory of actual entities, apart from its elaboration, takes the form in *Process and Reality* (I II) of thirty-six principles—twenty-seven "Categories of Explanation" and nine "Categoreal Obligations." Many of his Categories of Explanation have appeared, unnamed, in our exposition. Before we go farther, we must draw attention to three others. The nature of the Categoreal Obligations will be explained in the next section.

The principle that "no two actual entities originate from an identical universe" is one that we should expect in a philosophy of process. An actual occasion's "universe"—also called its "actual world"—is the nexus of all those occasions which have already become and are available for feeling.[7] This nexus is *its* past, and is not quite the same as the past of any other occasion. The part that is the same for both, each will absorb into its unique perspective from its unique standpoint in the cosmos.

The "principle of relativity" applies the doctrine of the relativity of all things to the very definition of "being." The being of any kind of entity is its potentiality for being an element in a becoming. That means: for being felt in an occasion of experience. So, according to Whitehead's cosmology, "There is nothing in the real world which is merely an inert fact. Every reality is there for feeling: it promotes feeling; and it is felt" (PR IV IV i). In this consists the reality even of spatio-temporal relations (see p. 54, below). But there is danger of reading too much into the term, "feeling." Its technical definition is "positive prehension"; thus to be "felt" means to be included as a prehended datum in an integrative, partly self-creative atom of process.

It should now be evident that Whitehead's metaphysical concepts are intended to show the interpenetration of "being," "becoming," and "perishing." Becoming draws on being (or

[7] Contemporary occasions are precisely those, neither of which can feel the other as a cause.

"process" on "reality"); and what becomes, perishes. Becoming is the central notion; for the universe, at every moment, consists solely of becomings. Only actual entities *act*. Hence the "ontological principle":

> Every condition to which the process of becoming conforms in any particular instance, has its reason *either* in the character of some actual entity in the actual world of that concrescence, *or* in the character of the subject which is in process of concrescence. . . . This ontological principle means that actual entities are the only *reasons*; so that to search for a *reason* is to search for one or more actual entities.—PR I II ii Category xviii.

The effect of this fundamental doctrine is to put all thought into an ontological context. In the last analysis, there is no such thing as a disembodied reason; no principles of order—in logic, science, epistemology, even in ethics or aesthetics—have any reality except what they derive from one or more actualities whose active characters they express.

Then what of the realm of eternal objects in Whitehead's system? By the ontological principle, there must be an eternal actual entity whose active character that realm expresses. Whitehead naturally calls this entity "God"; more exactly, this consideration defines the "primordial" side of God's nature, which is "the unconditioned actuality of conceptual feeling at the base of things." Thus "the universe has a side which is mental and permanent." Whitehead's God is not a creator God, and is "not *before* all creation, but *with* all creation"—i. e., immanent in every concrescence at its very beginning. His envisagement of the infinite multiplicity of eternal objects—he does not create them either—bestows a certain character upon the creativity of the universe. Here is how Whitehead asks us to conceive this character:

> Enlarge your view of the final fact which is permanent amid change. . . . This ultimate fact includes in its appetitive vision all possibilities of order, possibilities at once incompatible and unlimited with a fecundity beyond imagination. Finite tran-

sience stages this welter of incompatibles in their ordered relevance to the flux of epochs. . . . The notion of the one perfection of order, which is (I believe) Plato's doctrine, must go
the way of the one possible geometry. The universe is more
various, more Hegelian.—ESP p. 118; IS p. 219.[8]

Whitehead seems never to have considered atheism as a
serious alternative in metaphysics. An atheist would naturally
suggest that all the potentialities for any occasion are derived
from its historic environment. A "society," in Whitehead's
cosmology, is built on this sort of derivation. Why then need
the occasion also draw upon a God? The answer is that if
the past provided everything for the present, nothing new
could appear. Novelty and adventure were too real to Whitehead to permit him to say, like the materialists, that the apparently new is a reconfiguration of the old. Yet his thoroughgoing rationalism did not permit him to say that novelty
just happens. His religious humility told him whence it came.
   Throughout his philosophy, Whitehead contrasts the compulsion of what is with the persuasive lure of what might be.
God's action on the world is primarily persuasive: he offers to
each occasion its possibilities of value. The theory that each
occasion creates itself by realizing an aim internal to it, however, requires that the germ of this aim be initially established
at that spot in the temporal world by God; otherwise the
occasion's self-creation could never commence, since nothing
can come from nowhere. Whitehead's position is that the
initial aim partially defines the goal which is best in the given
situation, and that the temporal occasion itself does the rest.
God thus functions as the "Principle of Concretion," in that
he initiates the move toward a definite outcome from an
indeterminate situation.

---

[8] On the meaning of "flux of epochs," see the end of Sect. III, below.

III

Whitehead calls actual occasions the "cells" of the universe. As in biology, the "cells" are organic wholes which can be analyzed both genetically and morphologically. These two analyses make up the detailed theory of actual occasions in *Process and Reality*.

The genetic analysis is the analysis of the self-creation of an experiencing "subject." In the first phase of its self-genesis an actual occasion merely receives the antecedent universe of occasions as data for integration. None of these can be absorbed in its entirety, but only so far as is consistent with present prehension of the others. In a continuing chain of occasions the past progressively fades, but, like energy radiated from afar, never disappears. Thus the datum for physical feeling by a new occasion consists of some of the constituent feelings of every occasion in its "actual world." The first phase of the new occasion's life is an unconscious "sympathy" [9] with its ancestors. The occasion then begins to put the stamp of its developing individuality on this material: the intermediate phase is "a ferment of qualitative valuation" effected by conceptual feelings, some of them automatically derived from the physical feelings of the first phase, others introduced because of their contribution toward a novel unification. All these are integrated and reintegrated with each other until at the end of the concrescence we have but one complex, integral feeling—"the 'satisfaction' of the creative

[9] As we would say "in the language appropriate to the higher stages of experience" (PR II vii iii). But the word fits Whitehead's technical meaning, namely, feeling another's feeling with a similar "subjective form." This is prominently illustrated in the relation between your present drop of experience and that which you enjoyed a second earlier.

The concept of sympathy is emphasized in Prof. Charles Hartshorne's reading of Whitehead, and in his own metaphysical work. It is more severely treated in Prof. William A. Christian's interpretation of Whitehead (see Chap. 4, n. 14, below).

Among books in print, attention should also be called to Prof. Ivor Leclerc's and Prof. A. H. Johnson's accurate expositions of Whitehead's philosophy.

urge." This final phase includes the occasion's anticipatory feeling of the future as necessarily embodying this present existence.

The difference between the universe as felt in the first phase and as felt in the last is the difference, for that occasion, between the plural public "reality" which it found and the integral, privately experienced "appearance" into which it transformed that reality. Since the difference is the work of the "mental pole," we may say that Whitehead has generalized the modern doctrine that mentality is a unifying, transforming agency. He also makes it a simplifying agency. By an actual entity with a strong intensity of conceptual feeling, the qualities common to many individual occasions in its immediate environment can be "fused into one dominating impression" which masks the differences between those occasions. That is why a world which is really a multitude of atoms of process appears to us as composed of grosser qualitative objects.

In the language of physics, the simplest "physical feelings" are units of energy transference; or, rather, the physicist's idea that energy is transmitted according to quantum conditions is an abstraction from the concrete facts of the universe, which are individual occasions of experience connected by their "physical feelings." Whitehead's principles governing the integration of physical and conceptual feelings, and the way in which an actual occasion's conceptual feelings are physically felt by that occasion's successors in a "society" (so that appearance merges into reality), constitute an original treatment of the interaction of the physical and the mental, which has been such a problem for modern philosophy.

Taken as a whole, this theory of the internal course of process is remarkable in three respects. Efficient causation and teleology are nicely linked in Whitehead's cosmology: the former expresses the transition from completed to nascent becomings, while the latter is the urge toward self-completion, and toward a future career, within each becoming. Nevertheless the system is first and foremost a new teleology, for it makes every activity, in its immediate occurrence, purposive.

The main postulates of the genetic theory—the "Categoreal Obligations"—are the conditions to which every concrescence must conform to achieve a fully determinate end as a unity of feeling. These conditions are very general [10] and do not specify the content of this unity. Each occasion has its own aim, and that is what renders it an individual in a pluralistic universe.

In this concept of existences as teleological processes, Whitehead thought, we find the proper way for the philosopher to perform his task, now that the basic idea of physics has become the flux of energy rather than the particle of Newtonian matter. It is obvious that " physical science is an abstraction "; but to say this and nothing more would be " a confession of philosophic failure." Whitehead conceives physical energy as " an abstraction from the complex energy, emotional and purposeful, inherent in the subjective form of the final synthesis in which each occasion completes itself " (AI xi 17).

Second, this teleology is evidently a universal quantum-theory of *growth*. Whitehead, though sympathetic with Bergson's reaction against materialism, was teaching by example that it *is* possible for theoretical concepts to express the inner growth of things. His conception of growth has points of similarity with Hegel's, but differs in having no use for " contradiction," and in presenting a hierarchy of categories of feeling rather than a hierarchy of categories of thought.

Third, the principles of this teleology are, broadly speaking, aesthetic principles. The culmination of each concrescence, being an integrated pattern of feeling, is an aesthetic achievement. " The ultimate creative purpose " is " that each unifica-

---

[10] E. g., that the feelings which arise in various phases of a concrescence be compatible for integration; that no element in a concrescence can finally (in the " satisfaction ") have two disjoined roles; that no two elements can finally have the same role; that every physical feeling gives rise to a corresponding conceptual feeling; that there is secondary origination of variant conceptual feeling; and that the subjective forms (valuations) of the conceptual feelings are mutually determined by their aptness for being joint elements in the satisfaction aimed at. For the sake of brevity, no attempt at accuracy is made in this list, and three principles are omitted because their gist has been already given.

tion shall achieve some maximum depth of intensity of feeling, subject to the conditions of its concrescence " (PR III iii iii) . God's immanence in the world provides novel possibilities of contrast to this end. The conditions of synthesis are not the dialectical antagonism of opposites, but aesthetic contrast among ideal forms, and between these forms and the occasion's inheritance. The latter contrast is exhibited at its simplest in the wave-vibration which is so prominent in nature. The superiority of a living over an inanimate nexus of occasions is that it does not refuse so much of the novelty in its environment, but adapts it to itself by a massive imposition of new conceptual feeling, thus transforming threatened incompatibilities into contrasts. The very notion of " order " in an occasion's environment is relative to the syntheses which that environment permits; adaptability to an end is what makes the difference between order and disorder. (*Regularity* is a secondary meaning of order, definable by reference to " societies.")

The distinctive character of occasions of *human* experience, to which we now turn, is the great difference between " appearance " and " reality." The genetic process is based on feelings of the causal efficacy of the antecedent environment, and more especially of the body; it generates the appearance called " sense-perception." Of sense-data Whitehead says:

> Unfortunately the learned tradition of philosophy has missed their main characteristic, which is their enormous emotional significance. The vicious notion has been introduced of mere receptive entertainment, which for no obvious reason by reflection acquires an affective tone. The very opposite is the true explanation. The true doctrine of sense-perception is that the qualitative characters of affective tones inherent in the bodily functionings are transmuted into the characters of [external] regions.—AI xiv vii.

> Our developed consciousness fastens on the sensum as datum: our basic animal experience entertains it as a type of subjective feeling. The experience starts as that smelly feeling, and is developed by mentality into the feeling of that smell.—AI xvi v.

According to this fresh treatment of an ancient philosophic problem, the data of sense are indeed received from the external world, but only in the form of innumerable faint pulses of emotion. The actual occasions in the various organs of the animal body, acting as selective amplifiers, gather these pulses together and get from them sizeable feelings; and these— e. g., the eye's enjoyment of a reddish feeling—are intensified and transmuted by the complex occasions of the brain into definite colors, smells, and other instances of qualitative eternal objects, definitely arranged in a space defined by prolongation of the spatial relations experienced inside the brain. In this process the original physical feelings of causal efficacy are submerged (not eliminated) by an inrush of conceptual feelings, so that the throbbing causal world of the immediate past now appears as a passive display of qualities " presented " to our senses. Whitehead calls this new kind of experience " perception in the mode of presentational immediacy."

The higher animals have learned to interpret these sense-qualities, thus perceived, as symbols of the actualities in the external world—actualities which are themselves perceived only by vague feelings of their causal agency. The epistemology of sense-perception is the theory of this " symbolic reference." The recognition of these two levels of perception distinguishes Whitehead's epistemology from other realistic ones.

The practical advantage of sense-perception over causal feeling lies in its superior clarity and definiteness. And of course natural science would be impossible without it. For Whitehead scientific theory refers to causal processes, not, as the positivists think, to correlations of sense-data; but science is accurate for the same reason that it is no substitute for metaphysics—its observations are limited to experience in the mode of presentational immediacy; and science is important because it systematically interprets sense-data as indicators of causal processes.

Presentational immediacy, in addition to its practical value, has the aesthetic value of a vivid qualitative display. Although unconscious feeling is the stuff of nature for Whitehead, his theory of "appearance" is one of the things which brings home the splendor of his philosophy—and that even as this theory emphasizes the fusion of conceptual feeling with physical nature. We cannot go into his discussion of the aesthetics of appearance. This passage will suggest what is meant:

> The lesson of the transmutation of causal efficacy into presentational immediacy is that great ends are reached by life in the present; life novel and immediate, but deriving its richness by its full inheritance from the rightly organized animal body. It is by reason of the body, with its miracle of order, that the treasures of the past environment are poured into the living occasion. The final percipient route of occasions is perhaps some thread of happenings wandering in "empty" space amid the interstices of the brain. It toils not, neither does it spin. It receives from the past; it lives in the present. It is shaken by its intensities of private feeling, adversion or aversion. In its turn, this culmination of bodily life transmits itself as an element of novelty throughout the avenues of the body. Its sole use to the body is its vivid originality: it is the organ of novelty.—PR V I iii.

In his theory of appearance Whitehead also shows how truth-relations, types of judgment, and beauty are definable within the matrix provided by his general conception of prehensions and their integrations. And he advances a striking thesis about consciousness: it is that indefinable quality which emerges when a positive but unconscious feeling of a nexus as given fact is integrated with a propositional feeling about the nexus, originated by the mental pole. Consciousness is how we feel this contrast between "in fact" and "might be." It is well-developed so far as the contrast is well-defined and prominent; this is bound to be the case in negative perception, e. g., in perceiving a stone as not gray, whereas perception of a stone as gray can occur with very little conscious notice. The difference between these two cases supports Whitehead's conjecture about consciousness, and leads him to say: "Thus the negative perception is the triumph of consciousness. It finally rises to the peak of free imagination, in which the conceptual novelties search through a universe in which they are not datively exemplified " (PR III vii ii) .

The morphological analysis of an actual occasion is the analysis of the occasion as completed, no longer having any process of its own; it is only an " object "—a complex, permanent potentiality for being an ingredient in future becomings. Each concrescence is an indivisible creative act; and so the temporal advance of the universe is not continuous, but discrete. But in retrospect and as a potentiality for the future, the physical side (though not the mental) of each atom of process is infinitely divisible. The theory of this divisibility is the theory of space-time—a subject on which Whitehead was expert, original, and involved.

Space-time, he holds, is not a fact prior to process, but a feature of process, an abstract system of perspectives (feeling is always perspectival) . It is no actuality, but a continuum of potentialities—of potential routes for the transmission of physical feeling. (The transmission of purely mental feeling is not bound by it.) " Actuality is incurably atomic "; but potentialities can form a continuum.

Each actual occasion prehends the space-time continuum in its infinite entirety; that, says Whitehead, is nothing but an example of the general principle (also illustrated by prehension of qualitative eternal objects) that " actual fact includes in its own constitution real potentiality which is referent beyond itself." There is a similarity to and a difference from Kant's doctrine of space and time as forms of intuition; each occasion inherits this network of potential relatedness from its past, actualizes a portion of it as its own " region," and (if it has any substantial experience in the mode of presentational immediacy) redefines the network and projects it upon the contemporary world.

We often say that space and time are composed of points and instants; these should be defined as systematic abstractions from empirical facts instead of being accepted as volumeless or durationless entities. Well before he turned to metaphysics,

Whitehead had devised a "method of extensive abstraction"
for doing this.[11] *Process and Reality* includes his final application of the method (IV ii and iii), in which he begins with
a general relation of "extensive connection" among regions.
There is one "extensive continuum" of potential regions;
it is differentiable into space and time according to relativistic
principles. When we consider the vastness of the universe,
it would be rash to ascribe to the entire continuum anything
more than very general properties of extensiveness and divisibility. The dimensional and metric relationships to which
we are accustomed (laymen and physicists alike) are only
local, characteristic of the particular "cosmic epoch" in
which we live—i. e., of "that widest society of actual entities
whose immediate relevance to ourselves is traceable" (PR
II iii ii). Whitehead also suggests that the "laws of nature"
in this epoch are not precisely and universally obeyed; he
adopts a broad statistical view of natural law. The "running
down" of the physical universe is interpreted as a general
decay of the patterns of prehensions now dominant; new
societies defined by new types of order, now perhaps sporadic-
ally foreshadowed, will arise in another cosmic epoch. —And so
on, forever.[12] "This is the only possible doctrine of a universe
always driving on to novelty" (ESP p. 119; IS p. 220).

Whitehead does not say what the time-span of an actual
occasion is, even in the cosmic epoch in which we live. The
theory of actual occasions is a *general way* of thinking about

---

[11] It is the topic of Sect. II-IV of the next chapter.

[12] If we are tempted to call this view impossible in the light of scientific
cosmology, we should notice that "the expanding universe" gets older
in every fresh estimate of its age, and that enigmas seem to be multiplied
by recent galactic studies. Dr. Jon H. Oort, president of the International
Astronomical Union, has been quoted as saying at its 1961 meeting that
some galaxies apparently were created "in past and quite different
phases of the universe." My point is not that this suggests the possibility
of positive support for Whitehead's notion of a variety of cosmic epochs
(on his own theory of perception, it must be impossible for us to make
observations of another epoch) ; my point is the negative one that generalizations from available astronomical data to uniformity throughout the
universe may be precarious.

the pluralistic process of the universe; it suggests basic concepts, but does not automatically apply them. The "specious present" of human experience and the quantum events of physics are perhaps the best samples of actual occasions now discernible.

IV

The philosophy of organism culminates in a new metaphysical theology.[13] In Whitehead's view, "The most general formulation of the religious problem is the question whether the process of the temporal world passes into the formation of other actualities, bound together in an order in which novelty does not mean loss" (PR vi iv) —as it does in the temporal world. Whitehead thought anything like proof was impossible here; with great diffidence he sketched the sort of other "order" which his metaphysics suggests.

Evidently the question is one of permanence; but it is not merely that, for permanence without freshness is deadening. And to oppose a permanent Reality to transient realities is to brand the latter as inexplicable illusions. The problem is the double one of conceiving "actuality with permanence, requiring fluency as its completion; and actuality with fluency, requiring permanence as its completion." Whitehead's solution is his doctrine of "the consequent nature of God." God's primordial nature is but one half of his being—the permanent side, which embraces the infinity of eternal forms and seeks fluency. The temporal world is a pluralistic world of activities, creatively arising, then fading away. But "by reason of the relativity of all things," every new actual occasion in that world reacts on God—is felt by him. The content of a temporal occasion is its antecedent world synthesized and somewhat

---

[13] PR V. This short Part, though often technical, is a fine expression of wisdom and of religious feeling. (The quotation which follows is from I iv.) The interaction of God and the World was also the subject of the last philosophical paper Whitehead wrote, "Immortality."

transformed by a new mode of feeling; the consequent nature of God consists of the temporal occasions transformed by an inclusive mode of feeling derived from his all-embracing primordial nature, so as to be united in a conscious, infinitely wide harmony of feeling which grows without any fading of its members. It is a creative advance devoid of " perishing."

> The theme of Cosmology, which is the basis of all religions, is the story of the dynamic effort of the World passing into everlasting unity, and of the static majesty of God's vision, accomplishing its purpose of completion by absorption of the World's multiplicity of effort.—PR V ii v.[14]

It is essential to note the interdependence of God and the world, and the final emphasis on creativity:

> Neither God, nor the World, reaches static completion. Both are in the grip of the ultimate metaphysical ground, the creative advance into novelty. Either of them, God and the World, is the instrument of novelty for the other.

The story requires a final chapter:

> . . . the principle of universal relativity [or interdependence] is not to be stopped at the consequent nature of God. . . . For the perfected actuality passes back into the temporal world [" according to its gradation of relevance to the various concrescent occasions "], and qualifies this world so that each temporal actuality includes it as an immediate fact of relevant experience.—PR V ii vii.

Whitehead has evidently been concerned to embody the finer intuitions of religion in his cosmology. From these he emphatically excludes the notion of omnipotence. God in his

---

[14] Whitehead thought his conception of the consequent nature of God was close to F. H. Bradley's conception of Reality (PR Preface). Referring to God's primordial nature as " the lure for feeling, the eternal urge of desire " (PR V ii ii), Whitehead noticed a similarity there to Aristotle's conception of the Prime Mover.

primordial nature is rather " the divine persuasion, by reason of which ideals are effective in the world and forms of order evolve " (AI x iv). His consequent nature perfects and saves the world. And its passing into the world is God's love, whereby " the kingdom of heaven is with us today."

Any doctrine of an omnipotent God, Whitehead held, would also undermine the assertion of freedom and novelty in the temporal world. And it would be contrary to his basic metaphysical orientation, which is directed toward showing how God and the World, and the poles of every other perennial antithesis, can be reconceived so as to require each other.

Chapter 3

Whitehead's Philosophy of Science

I

The purpose of this chapter is to be of help in the understanding of Whitehead's philosophy of science—more precisely, his philosophy of natural science. That is the area to which he devoted himself from about 1914 to 1924, and in which he published three books, beginning with *An Enquiry Concerning the Principles of Natural Knowledge* (1919). Nothing will be said here about his work on the foundations of mathematics or his philosophy of history and society.[1]

At the heart of a philosophy of natural science there should be a well-developed conception of the foundations of physics— that is, of principles concerning space, time, motion, and measurement which constitute an adequate framework for physical theory and research. As the title of Whitehead's first book in this field suggests, these principles should also be fundamental for all other " natural knowledge," whether this

---

[1] Some discussion of the first topic will be found in Chap. 6; of the second, on pp. 28-31, 245-246, 269-275, 380-382.

knowledge be developed in some other natural science or be a matter of everyday observation. The task thus demands both a philosopher's discernment of what is universal in our apprehension of external nature, and a mathematician's ability to construct a theoretical framework (including a theory of relativity). Whitehead had both.

A complete grasp of his contribution to this field accordingly requires mathematical preparation as well as philosophic understanding. It is only with regard to the second that I shall try to be helpful. Consideration of technical matters will be kept to the bare minimum needed to give substantive illustration to what is said about Whitehead's distinctive philosophical position. Fortunately the recent labors of Robert M. Palter enable mathematical physicists to go as far as they like in pursuing Whitehead's reasonings step by step. In *Whitehead's Philosophy of Science* [2] Professor Palter united the best versions of constructions and arguments which Whitehead offered in various places, provided technical completeness, and drew a lucid comparison between the principles, procedures, and equations of Whitehead and Einstein.

Whitehead had a keen sense of the imperfection of his results, their need of criticism and revision. Although his emphatic way of expressing himself, together with his habit of looking at a problem in a large perspective, led to an occasional labeling of one of his constructions as " a complete solution," this was not his prevailing attitude. It was rather, " Take it from here." Yet he could say, speaking of his divergence from the operationist way of setting up geometry as a physical science: " I'm sure I'm right "—and Einstein wrong. He could, in short, be quite sure of the soundness of his general approach to a topic. There is a strong tendency for us, his readers in this era of piecemeal philosophic discussion, to survey Whitehead's results, see which one (or possibly two) can be fitted into our approaches to the problems of philosophy, and dismiss the rest. Our attention to *his* approach is

---

[2] Chicago, 1960. See also Palter's article, " Philosophic Principles and Scientific Theory," *Philosophy of Science*, 23 (April, 1956), 111-135.

all too likely to begin and end with the remark that Whitehead was a man of high genius—and, presumably, low utility. This makes an end of his work by treating it as an end in itself, not as means withal. Yet to call a man an intellectual genius is to admit that his way of thinking possesses some unusual virtue. We might do well to consider it possible that our ways are not entirely adequate and to give his a trial, hard though that may be. Otherwise we had better stop paying tribute to his genius.

When we concentrate on Whitehead's approach to philosophical problems rather than on his results, we find two main characteristics which make thinking with him something of a challenge. One, obvious to all, is his bold, untiring rationalism —the rationalism which he defined as the hope " that we fail to find in experience any elements intrinsically incapable of exhibition as examples of general theory " (PR II i ii) . The other is an unusual kind and degree of concreteness. This second characteristic of Whitehead's thought has also been widely felt—for example, by Jacques Barzun:

> Even when his prose is full of snarls and knots, which is usually the result of trying to tame original ideas, one always has the sense of his direct contact with experience, of his concreteness.
>
> This last quality is what is so conspicuously lacking in what is offered us today as thought. We like to believe that it is the Whiteheads of this world who are " abstract thinkers " and need to be brought down to earth. The fact is, only a great mind has the secret of being in touch with things; the abstract ones are the run-of-the-mill philosophers.[3]

The memorial notice of Whitehead in *Philosophy and Phenomenological Research* contains the remark, " In the philosophy of science, Whitehead's major contribution consists of ' The Principle of Extensive Abstraction.' " One might wish to qualify this statement; but I think that if we consider the

[3] *Harper's Magazine,* 148 (March, 1948) , 289.

method of this "extensive abstraction" we shall see how
Whitehead's approach to the philosophy of science, quite as
well as his metaphysics, shows a unique combination of theory
and concreteness. Most expositions of the method treat it
simply as an epistemological device (for replacing inferences
to unknown entities by constructions out of known ones),
and do not fully catch its broader significance.

II

"Extensive abstraction" is the name of the technical instrument which Whitehead invented for defining, in terms of
relationships evident in the perceptual flux, those apparently
simple concepts of space and time, such as "point," "line,"
and "instant," in terms of which all exact natural science is
expressed. Whitehead's work on this problem, or parts of it,
runs from 1905 to 1929, and some of the research was once
intended for the fourth volume, on geometry, which he was
to contribute to *Principia Mathematica*.[4] In the peculiar place
it holds in the general history of its problem, the work with
extensive abstraction resembles that great book. Inquiry into
the relation of geometry to our experience of nature has if
anything a longer history than inquiry into the logical foundations of mathematics. Protagoras, as we know from Aristotle's
approving report, cited the fact that a hoop does not touch
a rod merely at one point, to show that the geometer's straight
lines and circles do not exist in nature; and Heath thinks that
one of Democritus' lost works was probably directed against
this sort of criticism.[5] Now, just as the authors of *Principia*

[4] Cf. Bertrand Russell, *Our Knowledge of the External World*, Preface
to 1st ed. (London and Chicago, 1914).

[5] Aristotle, *Metaphysics*, B 2 998a2; Sir Thomas Heath, *History of
Greek Mathematics* (Oxford, 1921), I, 179. Those who study Whitehead's
theory of extensive abstraction with care will find that the problem of
tangent boundaries was the very one which gave him most trouble!

Mathematica undertook actually to derive mathematical concepts—actually deduce them, no matter how great the labor—so Whitehead with his method of extensive abstraction undertook to execute some actual derivations [6] instead of merely continuing a discussion begun in Socratic times. His was a rationalism that *went to work*.

The general acceptance of relational conceptions of space and time should have brought such work into being before a Whitehead appeared. According to the relational point of view, anyone who makes a statement about a point P in physical space is really talking about a certain set of relations between extended things. What are these relata and relations? By this formulation of the problem (to be found in AE pp. 235 f. [pp. 92 f. in IS]; PNK 2.1; CN p. 136), the interest in "bridging the gap" between spatial experience and scientific concepts is centered upon a demand for a definition of the point of physical space, i. e., the space in which natural phenomena occur, and which the mathematical physicist has in mind when he writes ordinary differential equations. Similar definitions are needed for all other "ideal" spatial entities, and for the instant of time and the point-instant (and more complex ideal entities) of space-time, but so far as this crucial ideality is concerned, the point may serve as the representative of them all. The application of Whitehead's method to the subject of the first definition in Euclid's *Elements* ("A point is that of which there is no part") is the natural one to choose for brief discussion. It is the one on which Whitehead lectured to his classes at Harvard; the one through which many students first became—and still become—acquainted with the method; [7] the one usually chosen for discussion by Whitehead's critics.

[6] This word requires some qualification; see p. 78, below.

[7] Namely, in Chap. I of C. D. Broad's influential book, *Scientific Thought* (London and New York, 1923), or in some exposition based on it. On p. 79, below, we point out a respect in which Broad's exposition of Whitehead's method is seriously misleading; apart from that, it is still useful to laymen—for example, in showing why some such method is necessary, and how it is like the modern way of defining an irrational number as a class of rational numbers.

Before proceeding with this illustrative case, we should realize how very much we leave out of consideration by limiting ourselves to it. For Whitehead the subject matter on which extensive abstraction operates also has a temporal aspect—as it must have if the method is to connect scientific concepts with our experience of nature. Furthermore, we are ignoring the fact that there are two ways of abstracting from the passage of time: one results in a concept of instantaneous space, the other in a concept of permanent space. Mathematical physics uses both, and Whitehead brings both into his construction; but we shall ignore their distinction.

Whitehead not only made several applications, but wrote several expositions, of his method of extensive abstraction. These show differences, but in each exposition there is something of value for a student who wants to make sure that he is rightly interpreting the method. I shall draw on more than one source, but confine the summary which immediately follows to the familiar version contained in his *Principles of Natural Knowledge*. A full account of all Whitehead's procedures and what he did with them is available in Chapters V and VI of Professor Palter's book.

Whitehead's systematic development of extensive abstraction in the *Principles* begins with a set of axioms which state the fundamental properties of the whole-and-part relation of " extension " among events. We continually observe that one event extends over (or " encloses ") another, either spatially or temporally or in both ways. Since we are now ignoring the temporal dimension, we may substitute the word " volume " for " event," provided we remember that the word does not stand for the volumes of pure geometry, but for portions of the expanse of nature displayed to perception, like the volume of the room in which we sit. Whitehead assumes that the relation of extending over is transitive (i. e., if A extends over B and B over C, then A extends over C) and asymmetrical; that its field is compact (or, as some say, dense, i. e., between any two volumes, one of which encloses another, there is a third which encloses the second and is enclosed by the first; that every volume encloses other volumes and is itself enclosed by other volumes; and that for any two volumes there exists a third enclosing both of them.[8] The spatial continuity of nature is further expressed by the assumption that every volume joins others. This relation of junction is defined in terms of extension,[9] and will make it possible to speak of two volumes as having an exact common boundary— if we have made the general assumption that volumes have exact demarcations, instead of the vague ones which they exhibit in perception. Whitehead's making of that general assumption is a topic to which we shall return in Section IV.

The next step in the method is the definition of what Whitehead called an " abstractive set " of volumes. An example is the set of all spheres concentric to a certain point. But neither this notion of a point, nor that of any regular geometrical figure, enters into the definition. An abstractive set is defined [10] by only two conditions. First, of any two of its volumes, one encloses the other. Second, there is no volume which is a common part of every volume of the set; thus the set has no minimum volume, but is an infinite series whose members diminish without end. By ingenious technical devices, Whitehead gathered abstractive sets into classes and types of classes, so that sets which diminish in all three dimensions are distinguished from those which diminish in one or two dimensions only; thus the sets which are needed to define points are separated from those which are needed to define lines and planes. The class of all equivalent abstractive sets (if we imagine the superposition of a set of spheres on a set of cubes, with every sphere in one set enclosing a cube in the other and *vice versa*, the two sets are equivalent) is an " abstractive element "; this concept secures impartiality between all shapes of volumes in abstractive sets of the same type. We are then ready to translate any statement about points into a statement about abstractive elements. Whitehead once used

---

[8] See PNK Art. 27, for Whitehead's exact formulation.
[9] PNK Art. 29; cf. CN p. 76.
[10] PNK 30.1; the set is there called an " abstractive class."

as an example " the points A and B are two feet apart " (AE p. 216) . That is to say that the abstractive elements A and B are such that by going down their tail-ends we can always find a volume x in A and a volume y in B such that the distance between x and y approximates two feet within any limit, however small, that we may wish to assign. The abstractive element replaces the notion of a point as an entity radically different from anything known in our experience of the physical world, but believed to be an ideal limit of diminution of extensions.

In an essay of 1917, " The Anatomy of Some Scientific Ideas," Whitehead remarked (AE pp. 207 f.) that his method for defining points might, if desired, be considered an elucidation of the phrase, " ideal limit." It is important to see the need for elucidation. Without it, we find ourselves thinking of points as tiny volumes when we say that any volume is composed of points, and thinking of points as *really* unextended when we talk about the distance between two points. The notion of an ideal limit relieves our feeling of contradiction. But what does it mean? " Limit " has a precise meaning in the mathematical theory of series, and in the theory of functions.[11] But our diminishing volumes are not mathematical functions of anything, and the notion of a limit as a term to which the summation of a series of terms approximates does not apply. The transition from ever-diminishing volumes to an unextended entity is a transition from something to nothing. There is no objection to saying that a physical *property*, like electric charge or a component of field intensity, becomes zero; this is to say that it drops out of the picture. But when volume becomes zero, the picture itself disappears. An unextended entity cannot harbor any kind of physical existence.

Defective though it is, Euclid's definition of a point has been so successful in the development of natural science that we are bound to conclude that it is associated with some universal,

----

[11] AE p. 207. Whitehead's own statements of the precise mathematical meanings may be found in IM pp. 200 f., 227 ff.

sound practice. This practice is the key to understanding Whitehead's method of extensive abstraction. He represented the method as "merely the systematization of the instinctive procedure of habitual experience" (PNK 18.3). He continued:

> The approximate procedure of ordinary life is to seek simplicity of relations among events by the consideration of events sufficiently restricted in extension both as to space and as to time; the events are then "small enough." The procedure of the method of extensive abstraction is to formulate the law by which the approximation is achieved and can be indefinitely continued. The complete series is then defined and we have a "route of approximation."

This approach of Whitehead's to the theory of physical space is like his approach to metaphysics, in that he conceived metaphysics as "nothing but the description of the generalities which apply to all the details of practice" (PR I i v). His general comment on Hume was that instead of supplementing conclusions with an appeal to practice, a philosopher should put our invariable practice into his premises. The devilishly hard thing to do, of course, is to state the systematization of this practice with some completeness. To Whitehead that meant looking for the types of relata and relations with which it universally deals and rendering these into a coherent set of concepts. Such was his aim in both his philosophy of science and his metaphysics. John Dewey's *Experience and Nature* contains much description of habitual human practice, but no such *theory*; Whitehead once said to me that he didn't see why in heaven's name Dewey didn't go ahead and construct one.

The proper Deweyan answer to this challenge is fortunately not our business at the moment; it seems fairly clear that the ideal of science is to systematize our heterogeneous practice in determining spatial positions into a universal rule stated in terms of a universally applicable definition. So I am shocked whenever a critic suggests that the method of extensive abstraction is quite unnecessary because all that physics ever needs or uses is the notion of an entity which differs from perfect punctuality by an extent which is negligible for the purposes of the occasion. When C. J. Ducasse offered this criticism,[12] he seems to have recognized the desirability of uniting these many definitions for many occasions into one, for he went on to offer this general definition: a point is " an entity the size of which would be undetectable through any test whatever, and therefore negligible for every purpose." It is very hard to see how such an entity could be of the slightest use, or what meaning it gives to such statements as " The intensity of the electric field at the point P is I." We do not have to make points entities, but to give a universal definition of this at-a-point-ness, or punctuality, which stands for an ideal exactness in the determination of spatial position. The introduction of an eternally undetectable entity is nothing but an interesting example of reification. I have taken a moment to notice it because it shows the Nemesis which awaits one kind of anti-Whiteheadian empiricism—the kind which, lacking Whitehead's full appreciation of the systematic pursuit of exactness by science, thinks that no ideally exact concepts are required in the foundations of physics. Ideal exactness cannot be shrugged off like that.

But neither can it be assumed. Approximation is the only way in which we can handle space and time. Many persons (we may call them, philosophically, intuitionists) think that Whitehead assumed exact points—otherwise he would not have been able to construct his abstractive sets. Certainly no one

[12] As one which had occurred to both R. M. Blake and himself: *Symposium in Honor of the Seventieth Birthday of Alfred North Whitehead* (Cambridge, Mass., 1932; printed for private circulation), p. 10. In this symposium Whitehead did not reply to Prof. Ducasse's criticisms of the method of extensive abstraction. However, in the paper of 1914 which is described in Chap. 8, Sect. I, below, he had noticed the idea of taking a point of physical space as an area or volume so small that its division is " pointless " in the existing state of science, and had set this idea aside as one of those approximations which get replaced by exact concepts in the progress of deductive science (" La Théorie Relationniste de l'Espace," p. 432) .

approximates in a vacuum. The assumed idea is the idea of
" being precisely *there*." That is what we intend to talk about
when we talk about a point; we imagine the possibility of
perfect precision. But—how possible? This is the idea of an
undefined superlative not exemplified in experience. All that
we experience is the comparative, " being in this smaller
region." The definition and realization of the ideal, the superlative, can be achieved only by an unending series of compara-
tives. That is the lesson of extensive abstraction; and I know
of no one who taught this lesson, both in the philosophy of
physical science and in that of other human activities—such as
government—better than Whitehead. The advantage enjoyed
by physical science is the double one, that our emotions are
not involved, and that the subject matter permits us to " convert [the] process of approximation into an instrument of
exact thought." [13]

It must not be supposed that there is a simple, perfect idea
of punctuality which sits in judgment on these approximations. No such idea is necessary or statable. In Whitehead's
view, our most exact knowledge of basic concepts is a systematic
formulation, as exact as may be, of relations universally " had "
in direct experience.

I think most scientists would say, offhand, that Whitehead's
definition of a point was unnecessary. They would distinguish
instead two meanings for " point," one purely abstract, the
other concrete. The former is provided by such a set of postulates for geometry as Oswald Veblen's, published in *Mono-
graphs on Topics of Modern Mathematics*.[14] " Point " there
is the sole undefined relatum; what it means is *any* thing,
spatial or nonspatial, which conforms to the postulates. The
concrete meaning is obtained by turning to actual space and

[13] From PNK 18.3, where this object of the method of extensive abstraction is compared to that of the differential calculus. The comparison with
politics was a favorite one in Whitehead's lectures at Harvard. The
answer to the intuitionist is drawn from my notes of Whitehead's lectures
in the spring of 1937.
[14] Edited by J. W. A. Young (New York, 1911; reprinted, New York,
1955) .

pointing at such visible extended things as chalk-dots on a
blackboard; and the two meanings are united by the observation that experiments with the chalk-dots reveal an approximate exemplification of the point-properties laid down in the
formal postulates. Unfortunately the mathematical physicist,
for whose sake the two meanings were united, will observe
that in the sense in which he uses the word "point" in his
equations, the chalk-dot is itself a volume composed of points.
What has been left out of the account is that "unconscious
act of speculative thought"[15] by which the physicist has conceived the observed dot in this way. It *can* be included and
made explicit—by taking the dot as the large end of one of
Whitehead's abstractive elements. Obviously the same sort
of omission is made in talking about the straight line between
two points if, with the operationists, we take our concrete
meaning from a pair of fine marks on a special rod kept under
glass in a laboratory or a government bureau. We are not
given a meaning for that punctuality and that straightness
which are potentially present in every bit of space, rod or
no rod.

Thus Whitehead's concreteness is, that the spaciness of
space is in his geometry from the start. Furthermore, his
abstractive sets have the logical properties which will enable
us to say that points form a continuum and to deduce all the
familiar properties of points and of other geometrical elements
—properties which in Veblen's theory are enunciated in purely
abstract terms. There is a union of the formal with an infinitude of specific meanings for the operationist to draw upon.

When John Dewey wrote his *Quest for Certainty*, he thought
that "extensive abstraction as a mode of defining things" was
"similar in import" to the operationist identification of scientific concepts with sets of operations.[16] He failed to observe
that the possibility of the operations of approximation, by
which Whitehead defines a point, depends entirely on the
properties of the relation of "extending over," which is a

---

[15] Whitehead's phrase: see AE. pp. 157 f., 245 f. (in IS pp. 22, 101).
[16] P. 111 and note (New York, 1929).

directly observed relation. There are also other divergences; an interesting paper can still be written on the similarities and contrasts between Whitehead's epistemologically realistic approach and Dewey's instrumentalist approach to the scientific concepts of space and time. Dewey sticks close to what the scientist consciously does; Whitehead reminds him of what he unconsciously assumes. When Dewey regards " space " in physics as a name given to operations possible with respect to things having the quality of spaciousness, the physicist says, " Yes "; and, thinking of nothing useful to say about this quality of spaciousness, turns at once to a yardstick. Whitehead is the one man in a million who found that something could be said about the spaciousness that was in front of the physicist's nose before he ever thought of that yardstick.

III

Dewey's comment on Whitehead's method, published in 1929, was one of the last of the misconceived appreciations which it got. From the mid-twenties on, misconceived rejections have been frequent. Most frequently, specialists in the philosophy of science have said that instead of showing how connections are made between geometrical concepts and sensible experience, Whitehead merely produced another ideal construction. It may be helpful to bring out the differences between Whitehead's procedure and certain habits of thought from which this criticism arises.

The first divergence concerns the way in which a set of postulates is to be read and applied. Sixty years ago, when Hilbert, Veblen, Whitehead, Russell, and others were constructing or discussing sets of postulates for geometries, it was important for them to remind readers that the meanings of the undefined terms were limited only by the postulates. Accordingly, Russell [17] and Whitehead [18] said that the postulates, being without determinate subjects, were not propositions but propositional functions; in the phraseology now current, they are not statements but only statement-forms, collectively presenting a logical skeleton which may then be exhibited in a variety of specific examples—say, by persons and the clubs to which they belong, as well as by points and the lines to which they belong.[19] Such reminders have long since become unnecessary; it is assumed that anything which appears to be a set of postulates specifies a logical skeleton and nothing more. This suggests to the unwary a negative verdict on extensive abstraction. Professor V. F. Lenzen's statement of it is representative: " As a matter of fact the method of extensive abstraction is purely formal and never comes in contact with physical reality. *Inasmuch as the abstractive sets are defined by postulates,* they are just as abstract as the points of an abstract geometry as expounded, for example, by Hilbert." [20] (Veblen's set of postulates, which we noticed in the preceding section, would be an equally good illustration.)

The purely formal, abstract character of a set of postulates was originally insisted upon because the area of investigation was a branch of pure mathematics; indeed, this character is summarized in Russell's famous remark that pure mathematics is the subject in which we do not know what we are talking about, nor whether what we are saying is true. If Whitehead had offered his work with extensive abstraction as a piece of

[17] *Principles of Mathematics,* Sects. 13, 108, 353, and Chap. I.

[18] APG 2; " Axioms of Geometry " (Div. III of " Geometry," *Encyclopaedia Britannica* [11th ed.]; reprinted in ESP p. 245) .

[19] Cf. Raymond L. Wilder, *Introduction to the Foundations of Mathematics* (New York and London, 1952) , Chap. I, " The Axiomatic Method." The chapter is reprinted, along with expositions of this feature of the method by Hempel, and by Nagel and Newman, in Pt. XI (Vol. 3) of James R. Newman, ed., *The World of Mathematics* (New York, 1956) .

[20] *The Nature of Physical Theory* (New York, 1931) , Chap. II, Sect. 8 (italics added) . Prof. Lenzen informed me in September, 1961, that he still adheres to this criticism.

The reference which concludes the quotation is to David Hilbert's celebrated axiomatization; it was first published in 1899 and soon translated into English as a small book, *The Foundations of Geometry.*

pure mathematics, no one should expect it, unaided, to make contact with physical reality. In fact, Whitehead explicitly turned from "geometry as an abstract science deduced from hypothetical premisses," to investigate " geometry as a physical science "—to " show how the geometric relations between points issue from the ultimate relations between the ultimate things which are the immediate objects of knowledge " (PNK Preface and 2.1). There would be some excuse for ignoring this and similar explanations by Whitehead if he had begun his statement of " Principles of the Method of Extensive Abstraction " by writing something like, " Let K represent any dyadic relation and $a, b, c, \ldots$ any elements in its field, which are such that (1) If aKb, then $a \neq b$; (2) If aKb and bKc, then aKc; " etc. Actually, he began: " The fact that event a extends over event b will be expressed by the abbreviation aKb " (PNK 27.1). Here " event " names a natural entity, one of " the ultimate things which are the immediate objects of knowledge," and " extends over " names one of " the ultimate relations " which we observe in every perception of nature; from the start, the symbols in Whitehead's " postulates " have just these meanings; the " postulates " are propositions about events. So far is Whitehead's procedure from being purely formal! To be sure, anyone who pleases may ignore these concrete meanings and extract a roughly organized formal calculus from Whitehead's text—he will find it deliberately rough, because Whitehead was " not thinking of logical definition so much as the formulation of the results of direct observation " (CN p. 76; and see PNK 18.2)—if for _his_ purposes it is advantageous to do this. But judgment of Whitehead's work is another matter.

In investigations of empirical phenomena, efforts are often made to find a logical structure and to state it in terms which are as general and abstract—as pure-mathematical—as possible. Such generalization is highly desirable, as Whitehead often said. But philosophers of science frequently associate with it the assumption that every formal expression of general relationships must be counted as simply a pattern of symbols (as pure cogitation, according to an older philosophy) until a laboratory use for it is specified by declaring that a particular physical body (fortunately there available) gives the symbols their meaning for physical reality.[21] This concentration of the empirical reference, and reading of theory as devoid of empirical meaning, constitute a dualistic position which White-head opposed. He held that all natural science and all philosophy is an endeavor to gain a self-consistent understanding of what we observe, and his own objective was a theory *of* the concrete, that is, of some or all of its most general aspects.

The conflict between these two views comes to a head over the definition of congruence. Whitehead offers axioms for the congruence-relation,[22] axioms which apply to geometrical elements defined by further applications of extensive abstraction. The opponent, who may call his own position either operationism or a species of conventionalism, offers a rationale of measurement in which the length of the chosen body is declared to be unaltered by any change of its position; but having observed that the lengths of bodies vary with heat and under the application of force, he stipulates that only a solid body which is kept at a certain temperature and so far as possible undisturbed by external differentiating forces is to count as a rigid rod. Congruent lengths are then defined by the coincidence of pairs of marks with a pair on such a standard rod. Whitehead, by contrast, went back to the most general facts about our practice. We measure as accurately

---

[21] "Thus the postulates of Euclidean geometry define the formal properties of rigid bodies. This, however, is not enough for physics—we must also have contact with bodies given in experience, and so we point to a concrete body which serves as a standard. . . . We point to a concrete thing and declare that it is a rigid body of length *l*."—Lenzen, *op. cit.*, Chap. II, Sect. 9.

Ernest Nagel authoritatively explains a similar doctrine in *The Structure of Science* (New York, 1961). In *The Philosophy of Bertrand Russell*, edited by P. A. Schilpp (Evanston, Ill., 1944), p. 345, he referred to the outcome of the method of extensive abstraction as "in effect another set of abstract formulae, quite out of touch with the accessible materials of the world."

[22] See CN vi, or (better) Sects. 10, 12 of Chap. V in Palter, *op. cit.*

as we need to and can; " the ideal of accuracy shows that the meaning [of spatial congruence] is not derived from the measurement " (PNK 12.5) . And every measuring operation presupposes perceptions. For example, the use of coincidence as a test for congruence depends on direct perceptions that the yard measure remains congruent to its previous self as it is transferred from one place to another. Whitehead did not question the practical need for official standards, nor the process of successive definition by which more reliable ones are chosen; he *was* concerned to argue (AE p. 129; PNK Art. 12; CN VI; R pp. 58 f.; PR IV v iv) that a standard is but a device for making more evident the exemplification of ante-cedently meaningful relationships, and that the use of any instrument—say, the use of an interferometer to apply the wave length of the unperturbed .606μ spectral line of krypton 86 to the calibration of a meter bar [23]—rests on perceptual judgments of constancy throughout the operation.

The basis of measurement is a question on which positions are taken and tenaciously held. However, one philosopher who might have been expected to favor operationism, C. I. Lewis, has written [24] a sympathetic exposition of Whitehead's alternative. By and large, operationists are quick to assume that Whitehead's position must be archaic. My explanation is, that although he was thoroughly competent in mathematics and all relevant parts of mathematical physics, his philosophy was the opposite of a technician's. The technician is always tempted to elevate his techniques for making tests into sole criteria for basic meaning. He knows that for his purposes he can make sufficient determinations of rigidity, straightness, and congruence by experimental procedures and conventional stipulations.[25] The question to ask is, What general assump-

[23] In October, 1960, the Eleventh General Conference of Weights and Measures redefined the International Meter in terms of this wave length.
[24] In his contribution to the second edition of LLP-W (New York, 1951) .
[25] Sir Harold Jeffreys on rigidity, in Art. 6.1 of his *Scientific Inference* (2nd ed.; Cambridge, 1957) , is a simple example: " We can make per-manent marks on bodies, which we can recognize afterwards. By means of compasses or calipers we can compare pairs of marks with one another. All pairs of marks that can be fitted by the compasses in the same adjust-

tions has he made? But he is seldom challenged, for this is the day of the technician. It is also the day of the businessman, of the board of managers; and the speech of the operationist is very businesslike. Managers are necessary, but one may doubt that all matters are matters for practical decision, and also regret that S. J. Perelman has not written a parody upon the directors of the Physical Corporation, deciding the foundations of natural science.

Whitehead's view, that the scientific concepts of space and time are based upon relationships which are disclosed to everyone in every perception of nature, is in marked contrast not only to pure operationism but also to Einstein's view. In the latter, a degree of operationism is combined with belief that scientific concepts are free creations of the mind, creations whose successful application to nature is a mystery which "we shall never understand." [26] Whitehead, more than any philosopher of science, demanded understanding. In seeking its basis he developed (as will be explained shortly) a different empiricism from the traditional British sensationism which Einstein rejected.

Before passing on to other things, I would like to say that in bringing up the question of the basis of measurement I have not been trying to demonstrate that Whitehead had the answer. It is a complicated question, involving types of geometry and their relation to physics. I merely suggest that Whitehead had something distinctive and important to say about this problem.

---

ment can be classified together. We abstract the common property of *distance* and say that all such pairs are equidistant. Now when a fit of pairs of marks on the same body has been obtained, it may be found that a fit is always obtained again in subsequent trials. If this holds for numerous pairs of marks on the same body, we can generalize it as a law for that body. Such a body is called *rigid*. Compasses are rigid bodies provided their adjustment is not altered. If there is a doubt as to whether their adjustment has altered, they can be tested by application to several pairs of marks that they previously fitted, and if they fail we can tighten up the hinge or get a new pair. In the first place distance is simply a property of pairs of marks on rigid bodies."

[26] A. Einstein, "Physics and Reality," *Journal of the Franklin Institute*, 221 (1936), 351; Sects. I and II, *passim*.

IV

If we now think back to Whitehead's definition of an abstractive set and the properties he ascribed to the observable relation of " extending over," we shall see another important respect in which his philosophy of science diverges sharply from what most philosophically educated readers expect. Surely a dense, unending series of volumes, an infinite number of them below the limits of sense perception, is never observed! Empirically, the objection runs, there will always be a smallest volume in an observed series of diminishing volumes.[27] Since only pseudo-empiricisms deal in "actual infinites," Whitehead's definition of a point can be only an ideal construction, not a solid bridge between experience and geometry.[28]

The simplest answer is that in defining *point* Whitehead was defining an exact theoretical *concept*, and that in defining

[27] Cf. Lenzen, " Scientific Ideas and Experience," *University of California Publications in Philosophy*, 8 (1926) , 173-189.

[28] Ernest Nagel writes: " The principle of extensive abstraction succeeds in doing none of the things that may reasonably be expected from an instrument devised for the criticism of abstraction. It is a mathematical calculus whose application to the matters at hand raises the very problems it was intended to solve. Thus, for mathematical purposes, a point may be defined as an infinite set of overlapping volumes. But no empirical subject-matter involves *infinite* sets of volumes, and no experiment could decide whether something alleged to be a point is indeed a point if the relations between an infinite set of objects would first have to be determined " (*Sovereign Reason* [Glencoe, Ill., 1954], pp. 41 f.; italics in text) .

The passage provokes two questions. First, if Whitehead meant to offer " an instrument devised for the criticism of abstraction," it is odd that he should have christened it " the method of extensive abstraction." His purpose was, rather, to replace the unclear idea of an extensionless point by a systematically stated abstraction from spatial experience. Second, what sort of something is it which should be subjected to experiment to determine whether it is a genuine point or an impostor? It is precisely because chalk-dots *can* be seen, magnified, erased, etc., that we know they are not points.

That " no empirical subject-matter involves *infinite* sets of volumes " is undeniable, if " involves " refers to the possibility of actually discriminating volumes by observation or experiment. But the spatiality that is empirically given seems to involve something more—as we shall soon observe.

any concept of that sort it is not necessary, nor indeed possible, to restrict oneself entirely to entities which individually are physically observable. The solid-bridge notion, as usually understood, is nonsense; what we want is an analysis of the bridgework on which we have been walking since men first thought of nature in terms of points. For this purpose we must start with observed entities and relations, then interpolate and extrapolate. Thereby, as Jean Nicod wrote, "instead of postulating entities which nature does not exemplify [extensionless points], we confine ourselves to positing new members of a known class, not different from the known individuals except as the latter differ among themselves." [29] "This," he continued, "is an intelligible and modest hypothesis."

So far as the properties which Whitehead ascribed to extension are hypothetical, the commentators who have found a conceptual element, contributed by the mind rather than by sense perception, in Whitehead's method of extensive abstraction are quite correct.[30] When the original task of the method is described—whether by Whitehead, by Ernest Nagel and other critics, or by us in Section II, above—as that of *deriving* geometrical concepts from our perceptions, we must not understand the word with absolute literalness. Our comparison with what the authors of *Principia Mathematica* undertook still has point: their derivation of mathematical from logical concepts also required hypotheses, such as the Axiom of Infinity. But since Whitehead did not try to exhibit any deductive system in his applications of extensive abstraction, it is better to call those applications empirically well-based constructions of ideal concepts than to call them deductions.

A second answer to the empiricist criticism goes deeper. We must be sure that the empirical base of Whitehead's construc-

[29] *Foundations of Geometry and Induction*, trans. P. P. Wiener (London, 1930), p. 47.

[30] Nathaniel Lawrence comes first to mind, in virtue of his article, "Whitehead's Method of Extensive Abstraction," *Philosophy of Science*, 17 (1950), 142-163, and Chap. 6 of his book, *Whitehead's Philosophical Development* (Berkeley, 1956). See Chap. 8, n. 33, below.

tion is correctly identified. C. D. Broad's familiar exposition (in Chapter I of *Scientific Thought*) suggests that Whitehead began with the colored patches we see and the lumps we touch—things which are quite crude in comparison with the exact concepts of geometry, but *are* undeniably given to sense-awareness—and by gathering them into classes and filling these out, arrived eventually at complex entities which have the logical properties of points. Whitehead's most vigorous recent critic, Adolf Grünbaum, in 1953 attacked conceptions of extensive abstraction which "require with Broad that the Method rest on *sensationist* foundations, as in Whitehead's earlier books," [31] i. e., books prior to *Process and Reality*. (One should add: as in Broad's own constructions, Jean Nicod's, and some of Russell's.) Grünbaum easily showed that the existence of a threshold of spatial perception for objects of sense-awareness makes it quite impossible to construct from them that continuum of punctual elements which physics requires. Thus he wrote finis to what is probably the most frequent reading of extensive abstraction, namely, as a "positivistic construction" (Grünbaum's phrase) of points out of discrete sensa. But this is a misreading of Whitehead.

It is true that his first sketches of the method convey this conception of it.[32] And many phrases in his books on the philosophy of science—e. g., "the immediate data of perception" and "what sense-awareness delivers over for knowledge" —will not be construed otherwise by anyone for whom "empiricism" first of all means Hume or Russell. (Grünbaum wrote, "Whitehead has given no reason why we should not regard Hume's characterisation of *the structure of appearance* as undeniably correct." [33]) Whitehead's theory of sensa,[34] however, is only part of his characterization of "what sense-aware-

---

[31] "Whitehead's Method of Extensive Abstraction," *British Journal for the Philosophy of Science*, 4 (1953/1954), 220; italics in text.

[32] They are described in Chap. 8, Sect. II, below.

[33] *Op. cit.*, pp. 223 f.; italics in text.

[34] Whitehead called them "sense-objects," but I use the now more familiar name, there being no difference in meaning which is crucial for this discussion.

ness delivers over for knowledge." The other part, the part that is distinctive of Whitehead—even ten years before *Process and Reality* was published—is his doctrine of the primary fact for sense-awareness. This doctrine will claim more of our attention in Chapter 8. It is sufficient here to note that according to Whitehead, ". . . awareness of nature begins in awareness of a whole which is present," [35] and that the parts of this whole are apprehended as extensively related events. These events (reduced to volumes in our discussion), not the sensa which we perceive as qualifying some of them, are the terms with which extensive abstraction operates. The unseen but unquestioned interior of a tennis ball is thus taken—and according to the dictates of my own experience, rightly taken— for as good a part of perceptual space as is the seen white surface. I do not wish to say that Whitehead's unusual empiricism is safe from all empiricist criticism. My point is that if the only terms we will accept are sensa on the one hand, and entities which are conceptually postulated on the other, than *we* are safe from making sense of Whitehead.

Once we realize that the topic of Whitehead's geometry is the extensive field *within* which discriminations are made, we can see that the meaning he provided for punctuality is not canceled by discovering that, below some minimal volume, operational answers to "Where?" questions cannot be determined. On the contrary: approximation to punctuality must be meaningfully thought in asserting that physically we can get only so close to it. A similar rejoinder can be made to the claim that modern quantum theory requires us to accept a minimum for meaningful length (the so-called "hodon," computed at approximately 10^{-13} cm.): the mathematical formulations of the theory presuppose a continuous spatio-temporal framework.

In Section II we noted that in his *Principles of Natural Knowledge* Whitehead assumed that events (volumes, in our limited context) have exact demarcations, even though our

[35] IS p. 58 (reprinted from a 1919 symposium).

perceptual determinations of *actual* events show vague boundaries and a continuity of transition. This assumption complicated his task and was explicitly adopted only after hesi-
tation.[36] Critics were quick to claim that it made Whitehead's
whole procedure for defining points and lines circular. I
think that the necessity of the assumption was merely, as
Whitehead said (PNK 17.4), that of "the claim which is
implicit in every advance towards exact observation, namely
that there is something definite to be known ": "what has
been apprehended as a continuum is a potentially definite
complex of entities for knowledge." This claim is *consistent
with* the perception itself, and seems supported by Whitehead's
final view (to be noted in our next paragraph) of spatial
experience. As for the logical circularity, it is avoided by the
procedure Whitehead adopted in *Process and Reality* (IV II).
There he introduced the idea of regions in exact contact only
as a case to be *excluded* from his definition of an abstractive
set, which was then made in terms of non-tangential enclosure.
Thus Whitehead used the fact that perfect accuracy in the
determination of relative position, though definable only by
a process of approximation, nonetheless has at every stage a
perfectly definite negative; thereby he avoided assuming that
any region actually has just one unextended point or breadth-
less line in common with another.

   Supposing the empiricist's conception of Whitehead's perceptual base corrected by substituting events for sensa, the
objection to an actual infinite, composed of endlessly diminishing volumes, remains. This infinity does not appear to be
observed. What, then, other than the convenience of what
appears to be a product of our creative imagination, justifies
the conception of infinite spatial divisibility? I believe there
is an empirical justification. I do not think it can be extracted
from the *Principles of Natural Knowledge* without a reinterpretation, but it appears clearly in *Process and Reality*. There
Whitehead holds that we experience space-time as a con-

[36] See AE pp. 213 f.

tinuum of potentialities.[37] We perceive an actual spaciousness
not as an infinity of individual existents, but as a potentiality
of *heres* and *theres* unlimited in number. This seems to me
part of the perceptual meaning of spaciousness, something to
be admitted by an empiricism that is not artificial. We might
put it this way for vision: the immediate datum is an expanse
which *looks* infinitely divisible. There is no contradiction
between granting this and admitting that when we make trial
to see how finely our eyes can discriminate portions of this
expanse (by color differences, necessarily) we come up against
minimum visible sensa.

Whitehead's combination of techniques of mathematical
logic with an empiricism which refers us *au fond* to "the
general character of our direct experience" (R p. 4) has
aroused some fear among logicians that he opened the door
to the dogmatic assertion of nonsense as a mere transcript of
basic experience, and the only possible transcript. Such politic
considerations have no rightful claim on science. And while
it *would* be dogmatic to say that our basic experience of space
and time can be formulated in only one set of terms, Whitehead always insisted that there were a variety of possible
formulations. His own definitions of points and instants in
terms of the relation of enclosure among events were shown
by Theodore de Laguna to contradict our direct experience
by entailing an excessive dependence of spatial meanings on
temporal meanings.[38] (This defect could not appear in the
present exposition, because—unlike Whitehead—we artificially
eliminated the temporal dimension from the start.) Whitehead avoided that result in *Process and Reality* by beginning
with a different relation, called "extensive connection" among
"regions," and postponing the distinction between space and
time.[39] Later he expressed a private opinion that a relation

[37] Cf. the second half of Sect. III in the preceding chapter; and Ivor
Leclerc, "Whitehead and the Problem of Extension," *Journal of Philosophy*, 58 (September 14, 1961), 559-565.
[38] *Philosophical Review*, 30 (1921), 217.
[39] The significance of this alteration is a complex question, on which
the student who has read Whitehead will want to consult pp. 101-103,

of " betweenness " among regions would be a still better choice for the undefined initial relation.

Before we leave the method of extensive abstraction, something more must be said about the use of it in *Process and Reality*. The theory of extension developed there has the new merit of defining points, lines, volumes, and surfaces by extensive abstraction without presupposing any particular theory of parallelism.[40] The theory culminates in a definition of a straight line, made without reference to measurement. Whitehead attached great importance to this. It is a pity that it appeared, badly stated, on page 465 of a book on metaphysics.[41] It appears that he defined the *projective* straight line, which, it may be argued, has the intuitive properties of the straight line of naïve experience. For sense perception, he held, " the fundamental notion of 'straightness'" is " straight-away in such-and-such a direction "; " the shortest distance " (measured or estimated) is a further notion; in the theory of extension, projective geometry supplies the antecedent system into which the concept of distance is introduced (AI xiv viii).

116-118 of Palter's book. Palter minimizes the significance, which Whitehead (PR IV i iii) undoubtedly exaggerated.

Whitehead gave credit to De Laguna for the idea of extensive connection and the definition of inclusion adopted in *Process and Reality* (IV i iii, IV ii ii). The former was suggested to him by the use of " can connect " as the undefined relation in De Laguna's construction, published in " Point, Line, and Surface, as Sets of Solids " (*Journal of Philosophy*, 19 [1922], 449-461). But De Laguna had limited himself to spatial concepts; and, as the choice of " solid " for his undefined relatum suggests, dissented from Whitehead's view of the ultimate perceptual data, to find his own point of departure " in the behavior of things toward one another, as we manipulate them " (De Laguna, " The Nature of Space, Part I," *Journal of Philosophy*, 19 [1922], 394).

[40] Cf. Art. 3.9 of William W. Hammerschmidt, *Whitehead's Philosophy of Time* (New York, 1947). This monograph, though it attempts much less than Palter does, is still a helpful one.

[41] In the British edition, p. 432. A clear exposition, and some indication of unresolved issues, may be found in Palter, especially Sects. 3 and 4 of Chap. VI. Other studies are beginning to appear. I hope that Mr. Dean Haggard will soon publish his.

V

On p. 67 I referred to the similarity between Whitehead's approach to the philosophy of science and his approach to metaphysics. But there is more than a similarity. As he developed his philosophy of science, he placed it in a metaphysical setting, so much so that in his later years he sometimes said that he didn't really think there was such a subject as the philosophy of science. My choice of the method of extensive abstraction for illustrative purposes may have given a misleading impression of Whitehead's thought; for in the construction of the concept of a point from the general character of our perceptions of space, metaphysical considerations are irrelevant. This would also be true, had we chosen instead to construct the concept of an instant of time. In both cases a measurable aspect of nature has been abstracted from what Whitehead, even in 1919, considered the " fundamental characteristic " of nature: its " passage . . . or, in other words, its creative advance," also called *process* (PNK 3.7; CN p. 54). The enlargement of the concept of process into the ultimate category of Whitehead's metaphysics will be described in Chapters 8 and 9. The points here to be noted are two. First: whatever may be the full story of the occurrence of our perceptions of space, the spatial relatedness which they display is an ultimate datum for science; Whitehead always insisted upon this. Second: the perceptions, after all, do arise and pass, and the static display is implicated in the process of nature. When we try to understand the relation of the display to the process, we are beginning to address " the nature of things." There is no escape, and Whitehead sought none. His general philosophy of science cannot without distortion be separated from his metaphysics, and should never be evaluated on the lazy assumption that it is entirely contained in the books of 1919 to 1922, which he devoted exclusively to the philosophy of science.

To help balance our picture of Whitehead's philosophy of

science in this chapter, let us turn from spatial constructs to a brief consideration of his approach to causality and induction. There can no more be a natural science without causal laws in the form of functional correlations than there can be a mathematical physics without equations whose variables are interpretable as space-coordinates. But to express what we *mean* by space, Whitehead held, we must go behind those variables to the general character of space-perception.[42] Neither can causal laws reveal the nature of causality. Causality is a character of every experience or it is no generic character of nature. Whitehead described it as the compulsion of the past on the present. On men's opinions of this, their attitude toward Whitehead's entire philosophy largely depends. I find Whitehead's rehabilitation of causality persuasive; but the tail-end of the present chapter is not the place to set out its merits.[43] In the spirit of Whitehead himself, let me rather suggest, to those who have not a priori dismissed his doctrine, two respects in which his *theory* of the matter might conceivably be improved.

First, the distinction which he drew between causal experience and sensory (" presentational ") experience may be sharper than the facts allow. In the philosophy of organism this sharpness is an inevitable reflection of the basic ontological distinction between actual occasions and eternal objects. It is also the natural result of Whitehead's charity in attributing entire accuracy to Hume's description of sense impressions.

Second, the methodical connection between causal experience, to which Whitehead remanded us, and the causal laws of natural science needs to be filled out more at its upper end—particularly by philosophers with some special knowledge of a natural science. Among recently published interpretations of the structure of science, the prevalence of those which are of a logical positivist (or " scientific empiricist ") cast is

[42] Cf. (one of many possible references) PNK 10.7.
[43] It is much more radical than A. Michotte's view, presented in his monograph, *La perception de la causalité* (Louvain, 1946; the English translation will soon appear as one of " Methuen's Manuals of Modern Psychology ") .

something which the advocates of such interpretations have earned by their unflagging exertions. Philosophers of other persuasions have not been doing enough in this area.

In Whitehead's view, the inductive logic that is involved in the use of causal laws has a metaphysical ground. This does *not* mean that we cannot make and communicate inductive inferences until we have agreed upon our metaphysics. (The doctrine does however imply that so far as we have not developed a common metaphysics of nature, we have no common awareness of what makes our inductions valid, and are successful only because we act better that we know.) What Whitehead's reference to metaphysical grounds means first of all is, in his own words, that "Either there is something about the immediate occasion which affords knowledge of the past and the future, or we are reduced to utter skepticism as to memory and induction" (SMW p. 62).[44] This strikes me as one of the soundest, most down-to-earth remarks ever made on the problem of induction. If we do not assume that earlier events have powers to affect later events (identified by reference to them), our thought merely dances in some ethereal region. Nothing but suspicion need be accorded any theory of causal induction, however elegant and economical, which, if it were true, would be (like the laws of arithmetic according to one interpretation of them) just as true in Plato's heaven as in this world of past, present, and future.

The dependence of a scientist's inductions on metaphysical principles is a reflection, in his conscious awareness of what he is doing, of his general dependence as a natural scientist on nature. It is merely superficial to take metaphysics out of this relationship and treat it as if it were a theory about the cause of some disease—one more hypothesis awaiting inductive verification, hence itself incapable of supporting inductions.

[44] Whitehead's first argument for looking in this direction if we hope to solve the problem of induction was made in the second half of his presidential address to the Aristotelian Society in 1922 (" Uniformity and Contingency "—reprinted in ESP and IS). The nature of the argument will be indicated in Chap. 8, Sect. VII, below.

Of course every metaphysical system is a complex hypothesis; none is certain and complete. Whitehead insisted on that.[45] But this fact does not prevent the system, as a speculative concept of the universe,[46] from including a conceptualization of the traits of nature on which induction depends. To recognize its hypothetical character is but to recognize that the system, as a human product, is an imperfect verbalization of those traits. Experience is dumb; only by speculative trial can the philosopher formulate concepts which express with some adequacy the generic traits of existence which he enjoys. The philosopher must always face the questions, " Does this speculative concept of the universe accord with the persistent character of our experience and practice? " and " Does it work well as a frame of reference for thought in the special sciences? "

In the last two paragraphs I have been defending Whitehead's position in quite broad terms. I believe that the position can be analyzed and argued in detail, and I hope that someone will undertake to do this more completely than in any hitherto published study.[47] In particular, it should be possible within Whitehead's perspective to do full justice to the further dependence of the inductive process on the ways in which the scientist defines the terms of his questions. This element is most obvious in deductive logic, where it accounts for the apparent autonomous subsistence of logical principles, independent of nature. But, to borrow a word from Santayana, it would be a mere egotism to leave nature out of that story too.

When a human being tries to formulate a general concept of the universe, he is bound to use his favorite preconceptions in his descriptive generalizations of experience. Whitehead's preconceptions were largely Platonic and religious. The part

[45] Cf. PR Pref. and I i; AI ix iii, and, more generally, xv and all of ix.
[46] In this discussion I am using " nature " and " the universe " synonymously (in the broad meaning which Whitehead gives the second term in his metaphysical writings) , but avoiding " concept of nature " because of possible confusion with Whitehead's use of that phrase in PNK and CN.
[47] The topic is not taken up in Palter's book, *Whitehead's Philosophy of Science*.

of his theory of induction that will be least acceptable is his addition, in *Process and Reality*, of an appeal to a theological ground (II ix viii). The experiment of naturalizing Whitehead's metaphysics of nature might well be tried. The idea has long been attractive to a few students of Whitehead, but I know of no attempt to carry it out full-scale. This would be a large and difficult enterprise, from which both theistically inclined and naturalistic philosophers could profit greatly.

VI

It has often been said that the wise scientist is the one who, at the height of his triumph, confesses his abysmal ignorance. The thought were better put positively: a scientist is philosophical if he enjoys a sense of the tremendous variety of unexplored ideas lying beyond those used in current explanations. One of the greatest possible values for science of a system of philosophy is its cultivation of that sense. The scope and the entire temper of Whitehead's philosophy admirably fit it for this service. But also, the general categories of thought which a philosophy conveys may sometimes turn a scientist's imagination in just the direction needed for solving his problems. Though Whitehead's philosophy has been ignored by the vast majority of scientists, there are instances of such applications. I recall Agar's book on the theory of the living organism, and a paper by a student of ethnology, William Morgan, on "The Organization of a Story and a Tale." [48]

[48] *Journal of American Folklore*, 58 (1945), 169-194; W. E. Agar, *A Contribution to the Theory of the Living Organism* (Melbourne, 1943; 2nd ed., 1951). Agar found Whitehead's philosophy valuable for understanding the generation, in the embryology of the higher organisms, of a perceptive central agent; for understanding the subsequent relation between the central agent and its immediate environment of lesser organisms, the cells throughout the mature animal body; for understanding the linkage between mechanism and purposive action; and for conceiving the difference between animate and inanimate as one of degree.

There can of course be no assurance that something which begins as a promising application of Whitehead's ideas will not turn out to be a dud. Whitehead himself claimed no indispensability or " correctness " for his results. He would have been satisfied were scientists more willing to acknowledge the principles—amply confirmed by the history of science— that the fruitfulness of observation depends on having general schemes of thought in mind, and that it is " treason to the future " to lay down limits in advance for such schemes. " A self-satisfied rationalism," he wrote, " is in effect a form of anti-rationalism " (SMW p. 281).

The self-satisfaction is today linked with an uncritical worship of clarity and " reliable information." There is something depressing about the way books on scientific method put a halo around " reliable information." To Whitehead this meant a trivialization of science, the death of intellectual adventure. Contrary to a widespread opinion, he never thought clarity was anything but desirable. What he taught was that scientific and philosophic theory, like the infinite sets by which he defined punctuality, can never achieve perfect precision and must never abandon its pursuit. (If only the universe allowed the philosopher to concentrate on the definition of one character to the exclusion of others, as in our example we concentrated on punctuality!) In this pursuit— in all our discussions—" clarity always means ' clear enough ' " (ESP p. 123 [p. 205 in IS]. —Even as precision in the determination of spatial position always means " precise enough." This relativity of clarity, springing from the fact that we are (as Whitehead liked to say) finite creatures living in an incompletely analyzed environment, should be the first principle of all philosophic thought. It dominated Whitehead's mind. The result of its interfusion with his concreteness and his adventurous rationalism was a quality of wisdom not elsewhere to be found in the philosophy of science.

Chapter 4

Whitehead's Philosophy
of Religion

I

The reader will see from our first and second chapters that the important theistic element in Whitehead's world view can scarcely be understood without keeping the main outlines of the whole in mind. If this is done, it will be useful to know where his chief discussions of religion and the concept of God appear. In chronological order, we have:

Science and the Modern World (1925), Chapters xi (God) and xii (Religion and Science). Whitehead's concept of God in this book is not the complete concept which appears in the later ones. The partial concept is founded on general experience only, not on religious experience. Only the " primordial nature " of God, under the name of " the Principle of Concretion," is explained. The distinction of God's primordial from his " consequent " nature is introduced in *Process and Reality,* but the corresponding ideas can be discerned in *Religion in the Making.* It would be a gross error to dismiss

Whitehead's concept of God on the ground that a Principle of Concretion is not an object of worship.

Religion in the Making (four lectures) (1926) .

Process and Reality (1929) : In Part I, Chapter i, Section vi; in Part II, Chapter iii, Section x, and the last two pages of Section i, also Chapter ix, Section viii; in Part III, Chapter iii, Section i; and Part V.

Adventures of Ideas (1933) : In Part I (Sociological) , especially Chapter ii, Sections iv, v, vii, and viii; Chapter iii, Sections i, iii, and iv; Chapter v, Section vii; Chapter x (The New Reformation) ; and Chapter xx (Peace) .

Modes of Thought (1938) : Lectures v and vi.

" Immortality " (1941) .[1]

These are indispensable; but the indices to *Science and the Modern World, Process and Reality, Adventures of Ideas,* and *Modes of Thought,* though poor, must also be consulted—not forgetting such terms as " Harmony " and " Eros."

This list I set down with some confidence; but the topic of the present chapter is one which I write about with the greatest diffidence. I have mulled it over at intervals for many years, and I think I understand a good deal in it; but my reaction to the whole is not settled. Some explanations of Whitehead's meaning and comments on it, which I hope will be useful to others, are set down here. Reference to other writers will be omitted, in view of my vast ignorance of theologies and of philosophies of religion.

II

Whitehead presented a concept of God, and theses concerning God's relation to the world, which he stated as definitely as he could. He also emphasized religion's need for

---

[1] Printed in LLP-W, ESP, and IS.

this intellectual element. He most emphatically held that religion is something to live by; but he equally opposed the reduction of it to an emotion or an attitude. The following passage is a good example:

> The witness of history and of common sense tells us that systematic formulations are potent engines of emphasis, of purification, and of stability. Christianity would long ago have sunk into a noxious superstition, apart from the Levantine and European intellectual movement, sustained from the very beginning until now. . . .
>
> Thus the attack of the liberal clergy and laymen, during the eighteenth and nineteenth centuries, upon systematic theology was entirely misconceived.—AI x i, ii.

Here Whitehead is applying to a particular instance his usual high—perhaps unduly high—estimate of the beneficial agency of general ideas. He is not simply defending traditional dogmatic theology against the liberals. So far as they objected to the notion of dogmatic finality, they were entirely right. Whitehead considered that notion wicked in every department of human thought. Theology, like metaphysics, is dead when it ceases to be a continuing business. The absence of certainty does not mean, as many people might fear, that the whole subject is unimportant. It means that possession of the exact verbal formulation is not to be claimed. Precision is always hard to achieve when we are dealing with matters of the highest importance: the figures which correctly state the density of iron are far easier to discover than the words which will accurately state the destiny of man.

To people engaged in the continuing effort to refine and restate theological principles, Whitehead's support is the more welcome because it comes from a man who was not at all naïve about the relations between thought, emotion, and language. He made a point of insisting that being true or false was only one of the functions of propositions: ". . . a Christian meditating on the sayings in the Gospels . . . is not judging ' true

or false '; he is eliciting their value as elements in feeling "
(PR II ix i). And, because of our tendency toward unwarranted dogmatism, Whitehead suggested " that the development of systematic theology should be accompanied by a
critical understanding of the relation of linguistic expression
to our deepest and most persistent intuitions " (AI x ii). He
wrote *accompanied by*; any idea of *replacing* the theological
effort to understand the nature of things by a study of theological language must be, for Whitehead, a mistake. Such a
study can be no more than an auxiliary investigation.

Whitehead's concern over theological expression was not a
concern that it might be devoid of what is usually called
"cognitive" meaning; it was a concern over ambiguities of
meaning, and over unwitting reliances upon unformulated
metaphysical preconceptions. These two are connected: ". . .
it is impossible to fix the sense of fundamental terms except
by reference to some definite metaphysical way of conceiving
the most penetrating description of the universe " (RM ii iv).
Of course this does not mean that there can be no theology
without a completed metaphysics. It does mean that terms
which we think are fixed, will not stay fixed; that there never
has been an exact, complete system of metaphysics; that
dogmas are only bits of truth. But dogmas are important: to
illustrate their value, Whitehead compares it to that of the
Greeks' precise formulation of general mathematical truths
which the Egyptians had acted upon for centuries (RM iv i).
He finds the real roots of religion, however, in religious experience and history. "Religions commit suicide when they find
their inspirations in their dogmas. The inspiration of religion
lies in the history of religion " (RM iv iii). —But it is quite
impossible for me to convey, except by massive quotation,
the remarkable union of penetrating criticism and wise appreciation which characterizes Whitehead's concise statements of
the significance of religious experience, truth apprehended but
unformulated, dogmatic expression, the history of religion, and
metaphysics. Each of these is illuminated in more than one
Section of *Religion in the Making*, the most concentrated

discussion of their relationships being in Sections i-iii of Chapter IV.[2]

Whitehead understands religious beliefs in the light of " the two levels of ideas which are required for successful civilization, namely, particularized ideas of low generality, and philosophic ideas of high generality " (AI Pref.). Their interplay is a central theme in *Adventures of Ideas.* He was not alone, of course, in lamenting with horror the bitter quarrels over particularized ideas, the blood cruelly shed because of creedal differences. But he saw that the production of a proper excitement and sense of importance, *without* hatred, was the great difficulty in the checkered history of religion. In an unpublished address to the Augustinian Society in Cambridge, Massachusetts on March 30, 1939, I heard him explain what strikes all his readers, namely, his excessive dislike of St. Paul, on the ground that, although St. Paul was perhaps not himself a hater, he had the way of going at religious things that leads to the development of hatred. (I think he was often unfair to Paul; but this question will inevitably be settled more by temperament than by reason.) Generally speaking, " The Anti-Christ is the fusion of religious feeling with hatred." Because this has been too frequent, he could write, " Religion is the last refuge of human savagery." [3] His reminder that religion, though of the highest importance, is not necessarily good, is

----

[2] I must quote at least this from Sect. ii:

" In particular, the view that there are a few fundamental dogmas is arbitrary. Every true dogma which formulates with some adequacy the facts of a complex religious experience is fundamental for the individual in question and he disregards it at his peril. For formulation increases vividness of apprehension, and the peril is the loss of an aid in the difficult task of spiritual ascent.

" But every individual suffers from invincible ignorance; and a dogma which fails to evoke any response in immediate apprehension stifles the religious life. There is no mechanical rule and no escape from the necessity of complete sincerity either way.

" Thus religion is primarily individual, and the dogmas of religion are clarifying modes of external expression. The intolerant use of religious dogmas has practically destroyed their utility for a great, if not the greater part, of the civilized world."

[3] RM I v; also i.

one which, now and in the foreseeable future, human beings need constantly to bear in mind.

To return to the two levels, general and particular. In the address of 1939 Whitehead likened religious utterances to poetry: they are particular statements with universal connotations. But literal accuracy belongs to prose, not to poetry; it is the mathematician who rightly dotes on the accuracy of his symbols. For all his recommendation that theologians strive for as much accuracy as possible, Whitehead felt that they should prize Love more than accuracy.

III

I have now to notice that Whitehead does not in fact often speak of theology. The one notable exception is the chapter called " The New Reformation," in *Adventures of Ideas*, which reads as if it were written as an address to a group of Protestant theologians. His real topic, in that and all his other discussions in this general area, is religion as a whole and its relation to philosophy. R. Das, in *The Philosophy of Whitehead*,[4] saw Whitehead as emerging with religious feeling on the one hand, and philosophic ideas on the other, no place being left for theology. I note that in *Religion in the Making* theology, under the name, " rational religion," is an important topic to which Whitehead gives positive treatment. But it is a part of metaphysics: " The doctrines of rational religion aim at being that metaphysics which can be derived from the supernormal experience of mankind in its moments of finest insight " (i, v). If this metaphysics is disjoined from general metaphysics the outcome is an extreme example of the incoherence of first principles; if it presumes to dictate the general metaphysics, it attempts the impossible business of determining what are actually its own presuppositions—presuppositions con-

---

[4] London, 1938.

cerning the many and the one, finitude and infinitude, process and form, and so on. Das's interpretation of Whitehead, though put in extreme terms, was essentially correct. It can be supported by many quotations. For example: "Religion should connect the rational generality *of philosophy* with the emotions and purposes springing out of existence in a particular society, in a particular epoch, and conditioned by particular antecedents." [5] That is how "it is directed to the end of stretching individual interest beyond its self-defeating particularity." Among Whitehead's several semidefinitive descriptions of religion,[6] it is important to notice this one:

> Religion is an ultimate craving to infuse into the insistent particularity of emotion that non-temporal generality which primarily belongs to conceptual thought alone.—PR I i vi.

Whitehead continues with an explanation which for the moment lets us down:

> In the higher organisms the differences of tempo between the mere emotions and the conceptual experiences produce a lifetedium, unless this supreme fusion has been effected. The two sides of the organism require a reconciliation in which emotional experiences illustrate a conceptual justification, and conceptual experiences find an emotional illustration.

However,

> This demand for an intellectual justification of brute experience has also been the motive power in the advance of European science.

[5] PR I i vi; italics added.
[6] It may be doubted that Whitehead anywhere offered a general definition of religion. True, the opening section of *Religion in the Making* is entitled, "Religion Defined," but the definition offered is of "a religion, on its doctrinal side." Whitehead wrote many statements of the form, "Religion is . . ."; they supplement each other. The most well-known one, no doubt, is "Religion is what the individual does with his solitariness." A better candidate for a general definition is this: "Religion is the art and the theory of the internal life of man, so far as it depends on the man himself and on what is permanent in the nature of things" (RM i i).

He then points out "a grave divergence between science and religion in respect to the phases of individual experience with which they are concerned." It comes to this: "Religion is centered upon the harmony of rational thought with the sensitive reaction to the percepta from which experience originates," that is, with the value-enjoyment in our reaction to the given world; while science "is concerned with the harmony of rational thought with the percepta themselves." [7] We shall return to the concentration of religion upon value-experience. Let us consider here the idea which may be disturbing—the idea that religion is a kind of craving. Is this a retreat from Whitehead's oft-expressed claim that religion is a kind of apprehension of truth?

His position is best seen by considering the way in which his philosophical theology offers a justification for two cravings which seek to be somehow jointly satisfied. One is, that the future which is bound to follow upon the present shall bring novelty, freshness. The other is the craving for permanence: ". . . the culminating fact of conscious, rational life refuses to conceive itself as a transient enjoyment, transiently useful" (PR V I iv). Whitehead's solution was summarized in the final section of our second chapter. We recall that one aspect of God, his "primordial nature," is an unchanging unity of conceptual feeling which embraces all eternal objects in its vision, and thereby serves the temporal world as its instrument of novelty; that the temporal world of finite occasions is itself the instrument of novelty for God, in that its process "passes into the formation of other actualities, bound together in an order [God's 'consequent nature'] in which novelty does not mean loss"; and that the passage of this—of the satisfaction of the divine process—into the temporal world [8] completes the

---

[7] Cf. Whitehead in 1917, explaining the "scientific validity" of Occam's razor: ". . . every use of hypothetical entities diminishes the claim of scientific reasoning to be the necessary outcome of a harmony between thought and sense-presentation" ("The Anatomy of Some Scientific Ideas," AE p. 218).

[8] God as thus immanent in the world, Whitehead calls his "superjective nature."

process by which the universe perpetually "accomplishes its
actuality." *Process and Reality* concludes with these words:

> Throughout the perishing occasions in the life of each temporal
> Creature, the inward source of distaste or of refreshment, the
> judge arising out of the very nature of things, redeemer or
> goddess of mischief, is the transformation of Itself, everlasting
> in the Being of God. In this way, the insistent craving is
> justified—the insistent craving that zest for existence be re-
> freshed by the ever-present, unfading importance of our im-
> mediate actions, which perish and yet live for evermore.

What Whitehead offers here is no bland assurance in the
face of our mortality; his tone is suggested by the phrases,
"tragic Beauty," and "the sense of Peace," which he uses in
the last paragraph of *Adventures of Ideas*. (In Section iii of
Chapter xx he called Peace "primarily a trust in the efficacy
of Beauty.") Plainly, Whitehead is not injecting any of the
traditional theologies into his world view. He is offering
something which, if true, is of the utmost value. Its truth,
as he so wisely (and more than once) says, is nothing that
can be demonstrated by logical argument.[9] Neither, to be sure,
is the truth of a formulated metaphysical system so demon-
strable. But in all four of his books which deal with this
subject he indicated a distinction between "a metaphysics
which founds itself upon general experience"[10] and further
metaphysical notions whose source is religious experience.
General experience includes—indeed, first of all *is*—an enjoyment of *value* here-now, and acknowledgment of value-exist-
ence elsewhere in the temporal world. The broad contribution
of religious experience to metaphysics, according to White-

---

[9] I regret to note one apparent exception, the passage in which Whitehead offers this argument for the consequent nature of God: "there
can be no determinate truth, correlating impartially the partial experiences of many actual entities, apart from one actual entity to which it
can be referred" (PR I i v). Not even Whitehead could produce a valid
version of the argument from the "existence" of truth to the existence
of God!

[10] RM iv iv. See SMW xi, first paragraph; PR V i iv; AI xx x.

head, is a widespread direct apprehension of a character of rightness and a unity of value in the universe. There is also the possibility of supplementing this with more definite content drawn from exceptional intuitions, provided they are trustworthy.

Whitehead wisely insists that the verbal formulation of any religious intuition is always imperfect and fallible. If it expresses something more than strong emotion, it must be capable of integration with the (also imperfect) formulations of the nature of existence which are suggested by the general texture of general experience. Assuming that this is possible, the philosophic use of an exceptional intuition rests upon this argument (stated by Whitehead in setting forth the culmination of his philosophical theology) : [11]

> It must be remembered that the present level of average waking human experience was at one time exceptional among the ancestors of mankind. We are justified therefore in appealing to those modes of experience which in our direct judgment stand above the average level.

No special intuitive experience, I take it, is justified for all time; any one may be superseded by finer intuitions. The many intuitions of an omnipotent perfection, reported in religious literature, have been superseded in Whitehead's eyes; and they fail to pass the test of being formulatable in a metaphysical system which is self-consistent and consistent with general facts of experience.

Whether widespread or special, religious intuitions vividly arise only because " religion is the longing of the spirit that the facts of existence should find their justification in the nature of existence. ' My soul thirsteth for God,' writes the Psalmist " (RM III i) . One reason for prizing Whitehead's philosophical theology is that his language often reflects perfectly the peculiar character of those religious cognitions which

[11] AI *loc. cit.* The argument applies also to the corresponding exposition in *Process and Reality* (*loc. cit.*)

have metaphysical meaning. For example: " the higher intellectual feelings are *haunted by the vague insistence* of another
order, where there is no unrest, no travel, no shipwreck:
' There shall be no more sea.' " [12] It would be vain to object
that the phrasing is ambiguous, to ask whether it refers to an
intuition or a craving. The language is accurate as it stands.

This mutual involvement of craving and insight inevitably
makes the value of religious evidence for metaphysics prob-
lematic for those who have had no personal experience of
insight. The occurrence of just such experience demands
explanation, but does not determine the soundest mode of
explanation. We know too little about ourselves to eliminate
the possibility that no religious experience, frequent or infre-
quent, reveals anything about the universe.

But the metaphysics which Whitehead drew from general
experience and speculatively formulated as the philosophy of
organism was already theistic. Unless it is willing to hand
over religious experience to the philosophy and sciences of
man, a " properly general metaphysics " must be more than
merely consistent with additions drawn from religion. Whitehead gave the undeniable reason for this: " nothing, within
any limited type of experience, can give intelligence to shape
our ideas of any entity at the base of all actual things, unless
the general character of things requires that there be such an
entity " (SMW p. 243) .

To summarize Whitehead's exposition of this requirement:
The world consists of individual temporal occasions, becoming
and perishing. Each arises from a situation which includes
an antecedent world of occasions, a creativity with infinite
freedom, and a realm of forms with infinite possibilities. These
Whitehead, with his generalizing mind, discerns in the universe.[13] A new concrescence must in its process achieve a perfectly determinate novel issue of the underlying energy of

---

[12] PR V i iv; my italics. Note also " the notion of redemption through
suffering, which haunts the world " (PR V ii vi) .
[13] There is a brief explanation of such speculation as a method of
analyzing the world in Chap. 12, Sect. I, below.

creativity; it must come to stand in perfectly definite positive or negative relations to every entity (of every type) in its universe. Otherwise the finite process would achieve neither a complete individuality, nor a definite shape of value. If there is to be such an outcome, the creativity must bring to the new concrescence not only the deposition of the past, but a gradation of relevance among the countless possibilities of value presented by the realm of realized and unrealized forms. The actual entity that is needed to order the possibilities is called the primordial nature of God. We have here a definite argument from a speculative analysis of the world to the necessary existence of an ordering entity.[14]

We remember another feature of Whitehead's exposition of the general nature of things. His view of the world-process is dominated by a profound and wholly ingenuous temporalism.

> All relatedness has its foundation in the relatedness of actualities; and such relatedness is wholly concerned with the appropriation of the dead by the living—that is to say, with ' objective immortality ' whereby what is divested of its own living immediacy becomes a real component in other living immediacies of becoming.—PR Pref.

[14] Cf. SMW xi; RM iii iv, and last paragraph of vii; PR I iii i. To what we said at the end of Sect. II, Chap. 2, above, we should add Whitehead's argument (in *Process and Reality* it is from his " ontological principle ") that the necessity for all temporal occasions to conform to mathematical and logical relationships can only be understood as the immanence in the world of an aspect of God's primordial nature; his vision includes that eternal logical order as well as an aesthetic ordering of value-possibilities (cf. SMW end of i). I cannot agree with Prof. Christian's argument, in Chap. 14 of his *An Interpretation of Whitehead's Metaphysics* (New Haven, 1959), that after *Science and the Modern World* Whitehead dropped the idea that there is some fixed order among eternal objects (though the *grading* of *value*-possibilities appears to be, as Prof. Christian argues, new for every new occasion). Examination of this matter would require a detailed discussion of texts, for which this is not the place.

Other respects in which Christian's careful study of the structure of Whitehead's metaphysics is challenging, or enlightening, or both enlightening and challenging, are indicated in my review of his book: *Philosophical Review*, 70 (1961), 114-116.

> Philosophers have taken too easily the notion of perishing. . . .
> Almost all of *Process and Reality* can be read as an attempt
> to analyse perishing on the same level as Aristotle's analysis
> of becoming.—ESP p. 117; IS pp. 217 f.

Throughout the elaboration of his general metaphysics, Whitehead makes us feel the sole value and the creativity of immediate life, and the poignancy of the fact that time is a " perpetual
perishing." And that *is* the way things are. But it is hard for
most of us to read this account without experiencing a strong
emotional need for a concluding conception of " another
order."

If a thinker produces a theistic metaphysics which, among
other things, justifies an insistent religious craving, this result
does not discredit the metaphysics. There is after all a type
of experience to be explained in this case, " the zest of self-
forgetful transcendence belonging to Civilization at its height "
(AI xx xi) . Whitehead offered an explanation in his concept
of God, particularly of God's consequent nature and its immanence in the World. More: the general success of the
system as a whole in explaining other things is a strong
argument for the theistic concept, if the theistic concept is
so integral a part of the system that without it we could
not apply the system to anything. And that is the case with
the philosophy of organism. If you start to use its fundamental
categories—creativity, actual entities, and eternal objects—in
the manner prescribed by Whitehead's categoreal scheme, you
cannot avoid introducing an actual entity which from eternity
to eternity holds the entire multiplicity of eternal objects in
its conceptual experience. And once you have this primordial
nature of God, the completeness of the system in its own terms
necessitates some doctrine of God's consequent nature. I
think that the marvelous coherence of Whitehead's completed
metaphysics constitutes the strongest argument for the theistic
element in it—provided this general characterization of the
universe has any considerable success as an interpretation of
mundane experience, which to my mind it does.

There is one more thing that I want to say about White-head's appeal to religious intuitions. He writes of Peace as "the intuition of permanence" amid the passing of beauty, heroism, and daring (AI xx iv). Theologians would doubtless be better pleased if Whitehead had written, "the intuition that so-and-so is the case." Sometimes he does write in that way—but not dogmatically. I think that the frequency with which he uses the vaguer form of expression—"intuition of permanence"—is significant. The phrase presents a continuing challenge to our conceptual powers. The intuition of permanence will not be denied, but it does not formulate itself in propositions. We must do that; and every formulation may be questioned, and should be questioned. When Newton's statement of the laws of motion was found wanting, more than that set of propositions was overthrown for Whitehead. His way of thinking in all fields was affected.

IV

In our efforts to understand what Whitehead means by God, there are three points which we must constantly keep in mind. They by no means exhaust his concept of God, which is quite complex; I single them out because, for thinkers in the Western religious tradition, they are the points from which any slipping away will let us drift from Whitehead's ideas toward more familiar ones. Hence a bit of repetition here does no harm.

The first point is that the only proper concern of religion is with the *value*-aspect of our lives and of the universe. Quotations to show Whitehead's insistence on this could be multiplied indefinitely. Thus: ". . . religion is wholly wrapped up in the contemplation of moral and aesthetic values" (SMW p. 258). "The peculiar character of religious truth is that it deals explicitly with values" (RM iv i). "Deity . . . is that factor in the universe whereby there is importance, value,

and ideal beyond the actual "; and, " There are experiences
of ideals—of ideals entertained, of ideals aimed at, of ideals
achieved, of ideals defaced. This is the experience of the
Deity of the universe " (MT v 9).

The second point is that value is always individual, and
intrinsic to every actual entity. The first positive use of the
term *value* in Whitehead's philosophical writings was in
Science and the Modern World. The way in which it was
introduced is revelatory. " 'Value ' is the word I use for the
intrinsic reality of an event " (SMW p. 131).[15] " An event "
here means the prehensive unity which is called an actual
occasion in *Process and Reality*. In lectures at Harvard,
Whitehead persistently rejected the tendency of monistic idealists to make the one Absolute realize all value, while a temporal
creature is only one item for the Absolute. His comment on
Bradley's view that Wolf-eating-Lamb is a qualification of the
Absolute was, " Hang it all! The wolf was enjoying himself
and the lamb was in torture." Our sense that value-experience
belongs intrinsically to finite individuals is overwhelming.
God's realization of value occurs by his absorption of the finite
value-achievements in the world.

The third point is that Whitehead always conceives of God
according to the philosophic method which he applies to
everything short of all reality—as " an aspect of the Universe."
The phrases vary: In our last paragraph but one, " factor in
the universe " and " the Deity of the universe " appeared. Elsewhere this factor is described as " that ultimate unity of direction in the Universe, upon which all order depends " (MT
III 3). This way of speaking of God is maintained in Whitehead's last utterance on the subject, the Ingersoll Lecture on

[15] In his last discussion of Value, the Ingersoll Lecture on Immortality,
Whitehead introduces the word in what at first appears to be a contrary
way. Attention to just what he says about value-possibilities and value-
realizations shows that there is no doctrinal contradiction. His constant
position is that the finite occasions and the infinitude of God's experience
require each other, if there is to be any value-realization. " Those
theologians do religion a bad service, who emphasize infinitude at the
expense of the finite transitions within history " (MT IV 7).

Immortality. It becomes natural to ask, then, whether Whitehead's thought is an example—a somewhat unusual one—of
the kind of theism called "naturalistic." (It should be obvious, from the way he writes about man in relation to the
universe, that there is no possibility of reading his philosophical theology as "humanistic.") The summary reply to
this question is to point out that Whitehead always conceives
of God as a being, an actual entity; we may not say, "aspect,"
and stop. He transcends the world as much as he is immanent
in the world. However, there is one fact, often mentioned by
Whitehead, which limits our thought about God transcendent.
It is, that the only Kingdom of Heaven which anyone is
acquainted with is the kingdom that is with us today, a kingdom "in the world and yet not of the world" (RM iii ii).
The account of God's consequent nature is an *interpretation*,[16]
an explanation of the source of the quality of immortality
which haunts our own experience of transient actualities. God
may be, as Whitehead says, a being whose consequent nature
is conscious; what we *experience* is what Whitehead calls his
superjective nature. We may recall [17] the feature which distinguishes Whitehead's theory of perception of the external
world from other realistic ones; in his theory there are two
levels of intuitive perception: causal perception (vague, haunt-
ing, insistent) and presentational perception (clear, definite,
limited) which are joined by symbolic reference. Only a
similarly complex account will do justice to our perception
of the creative advance of existence. We have a clear perception of the finality with which a finite occasion is superseded;
and in our religious moments, at least, we are haunted by a
sense of the immortality of the passing fact. No one-level
all-of-a-kind perception, no vestibule-of-eternity idea of the
temporal world can do justice to the religious consciousness,
least of all for any consciousness of a redeeming God.

   I think that Whitehead in his philosophical theology never
gave up, nor wished to give up, that insight into the supreme

---

[16] Cf. the end of Chap. i in PR V.
[17] See Chap. 2, Sect. III, above.

importance of *present* fact, which he expressed before he wrote even his philosophy of natural science. He concluded his fine address, " The Aims of Education," delivered in January, 1916, by saying that our educational ideal must conceive of education as religious, that is, inculcating duty and reverence. " And the foundation of reverence is this perception, that the present holds within itself the complete sum of existence, backwards and forwards, that whole amplitude of time, which is eternity " (AE p. 23). I doubt that Whitehead ever turned longingly away from this world. To him every escapist metaphysics was self-condemned.

It is both amusing and scandalous that he was himself accused of such a view. Thanks to D. H. Lawrence, there is one passage in *Religion in the Making* that has very likely been read more than any other in the book. In Chapter XVI of *Lady Chatterley's Lover* Clifford, who has been " reading one of the latest scientific-religious books " (author not named), reads the final four sentences to his wife, who has just returned from a tryst with Mellors; she responds with contempt. In those final sentences Whitehead was presenting the idea of an indefinite succession of cosmic epochs; of new orders of nature, unimaginable but equally with ours dependent upon the divine wisdom. Lawrence read this as predicting a nonphysical order of nature; in terms of Whitehead's system, this is a complete mistake, since the physical and the mental are universal features of every actual entity, including God. By seeing in Whitehead only another despiser of the body, Lawrence completely mistook Whitehead's attitude toward this world.

V

Some of the hearers of Whitehead's Ingersoll Lecture asked each other, as they left the Harvard Memorial Church, " Does he believe in immortality, or doesn't he? " The old notions die hard. If I may risk putting Whitehead's position in a

nutshell, it is this: we are already immortal. But we must
not suppose that this is merely a fancy way of saying that a
man lives after his death in the books he has written or the
houses he has built. What is meant concerning the *future*
is the difficult notion, beyond our imaginations to conceive,
that a quality, derived from the man's life and purified in
the harmony of God's experience, contributes good to the
world for evermore. More precisely, *every* occasion in the life
of *every* temporal creature has this immortality in God and
thence in the temporal world. Whitehead himself wrote,
" This immortality of the World of Action, derived from its
transformation in God's nature is beyond our imagination to
conceive " (" Immortality " xvii). I should add that any conception which was not at least extremely difficult for us to
imagine, could not be of much value either as metaphysics, or
in its religious character. A little further statement, in the
terms of Whitehead's metaphysics—more, that is, than Whitehead himself wrote—has been attempted by many close students of this part of his work, with conflicting results; whether
God's experience of a temporal occasion abstracts from some
aspects of that occasion, how similar God in his consequent
nature is to a " society " in Whitehead's theory of actual occasions, and other such questions, have been argued. I rather
doubt that definite answers can be derived from the system.
What I find most significant in these discussions is the varia-
tion in distance which the interpreters keep between Whitehead's metaphysics and traditional theologies.

We should also note that some critics of Whitehead find
the primordial nature of God an impossible notion, because
the collection of all the eternal objects, including all value-
possibilities, is an infinitude incapable of being well-ordered.
Whitehead himself spoke of this fecundity of possibilities as
" beyond imagination " (ESP p. 118; IS p. 219). It seems to
me inevitable that *we* should be unable at present to conceive
the unity and order of this totality, in any sense of order that
would be acceptable to our best mathematical minds. I do not
see that this is any more fatal than the difficulty we have in

conceiving any other aspect of God. We may still read Whitehead as offering a *general* idea of God, big enough to accord
with the scale on which he wrote his theory of actual occasions.
In Whitehead's metaphysics, "The limitation of God is his
goodness" (RM IV iv). That which in itself is unlimited,
he termed Creativity. The fact has been misleading, but can
be enlightening. The mistake is thinking that Whitehead
erected creativity into a kind of God beyond God. Creativity
is the ultimate, inexplicable stuff of the universe—not an entity.
Whitehead called it "the universal of universals characterizing
ultimate matter of fact" (PR I II ii). Some readers may find
Charles Hartshorne's suggestion helpful: creativity is the ultimate analogical concept for a philosophy of process, as
"being" is in Aristotelian and Thomistic philosophy.[18] Its
nonentitative character should not tempt us (at the opposite
extreme) to suppose that it is peripheral to Whitehead's
categoreal scheme. It and his two other ultimate terms,
"many" and "one," are, as he says (PR I II ii), presupposed
by all his other categories.[19]

In this handling of creativity in relation to actual entities,
Whitehead noted,

> the philosophy of organism seems to approximate more to
> some strains of Indian, or Chinese, thought, than to western
> Asiatic, or European, thought. One side makes process ulti-
> mate; the other side makes fact ultimate.—PR I I iii.

This is one of the few passages in which Whitehead says something about the partial affinity of his metaphysics of process
to Buddhism.—But I must leave this subject to those who
know Buddhistic thought.[20]

[18] "Whitehead's Metaphysics," in Lowe, Hartshorne, and Johnson,
Whitehead and the Modern World (Boston, 1950), pp. 40 f.
[19] If this is forgotten, Prof. Christian's remark that "creativity" is not
a term in Whitehead's categoreal scheme will have misleading consequences (William A. Christian, "Some Uses of Reason," in *The Relevance
of Whitehead*, ed. Ivor Leclerc [London and New York, 1961], p. 80 n.).
[20] My friend William Ernest Hocking suggests that there are some

Whitehead's own emphasis in theology comes out best in one of his comparative remarks about the great religions of mankind. "I hazard the prophecy that that religion will conquer which can render clear to popular understanding some eternal greatness incarnate in the passage of temporal fact" (AI iii iv).

VI

In 1925 Whitehead said that apart from the religious vision, "human life is a flash of occasional enjoyments lighting up a mass of pain and misery, a bagatelle of transient experience" (SMW xii, last page); and in 1941, that apart from the "immortality of the World of Action, derived from its transformation in God's nature . . . every activity is merely a passing whiff of insignificance" ("Immortality," xvii). These are strong expressions. Whitehead *also* held that it is possible to exaggerate the importance of religion. He had this to say about the fundamental idea of Importance (roughly, another name for Value):

> Importance is a generic notion which has been obscured by the overwhelming prominence of a few of its innumerable species. The terms "morality," "logic," "religion," "art," have each of them been claimed as exhausting the whole meaning of importance. Each of them denotes a subordinate species. But the genus stretches beyond any finite group of species. There are perspectives of the universe to which morality is irrelevant, to which logic is irrelevant, to which religion is irrelevant, to which art is irrelevant. . . . The generic aim of process is the attainment of importance, in that species and to that extent which in that instance is possible.—MT i 6.

---

analogies between Whitehead's metaphysics and the Buddhist rejection of Advaita Vedantism.

An interesting short paper is Charles Hartshorne's "The Buddhist-Whiteheadian View of the Self and the Religious Traditions," *Proceedings of the Ninth International Congress for the History of Religions* (Tokyo, 1960), pp. 298-302.

The passage is from his last book; from our survey of the
development of his philosophy in Part II we shall see, if it is
not already evident, that the passage expresses a kind of wide
outlook that was second nature to him. It is a just view concerning Importance, and it is not at all to be read as watering
down his conception of a religion as, on its doctrinal side,
" a system of general truths which have the effect of transforming character when they are sincerely held and vividly
apprehended " (RM I i).

In the same paragraph of *Modes of Thought* Whitehead
refers to " the final unity of purpose in the world " as including
religious, moral, logical, aesthetic, etc., aspects. Thus the
concept of God in his philosophy is much more than a religious
concept. It does have entirely to do with values; God's function in the world is described, to a first approximation, as
being " to sustain the aim at vivid experience " (MT v 5).
But in Whitehead's system, we remember, there are no value-
less actualities, and a subjective aim is of the essence of the
individual existence of every actual occasion, human or sub-
human. In his cosmology, his concept of God enters systematically into an understanding of the order and processes of
nature. The significance of the concept is not limited to the
religious feelings of mankind. In fact Whitehead, advancing
the idea that the immanence of God's primordial nature in
the world provides a possibility for a supplementary, non-
statistical, ground for judgments of probability, pointed out
that such judgments are in no sense religious, and urged a
" secularization of the concept of God's functions in the world "
(PR III ix viii). The challenge to religious people is to contemplate these secular functions of Whitehead's God without
jumping to the conclusion, as some have, that the concept is
not available for religious purposes. Such thinking is too com-
partmentalized, or too exclusively concerned with man.

Of more concern to us in this chapter is correct identification
of the source of those religious functions which Whitehead
attributes to God. Here the danger is that we might forget
or scornfully repudiate what he plainly said.

Religion insists that the world is a mutually adjusted dispo-
sition of things, issuing in value for its own sake.—RM IV iii.

The metaphysical doctrine, here expounded, finds the foundations of the world in the aesthetic experience, rather than—as
with Kant—in the cognitive and conceptive experience. All
order is therefore aesthetic order, and the moral order is merely
certain aspects of aesthetic order. The actual world is the
outcome of the aesthetic order, and the aesthetic order is
derived from the immanence of God.—RM III v.

Although "morality" and "art" name comparable species of
Importance for human beings, we are here reminded that
Whitehead has a generalized concept of the aesthetic which
really is metaphysical; it applies to every bit of existence and
to ideals in the universe.[21] If any actual religion ever is
"morality tinged with emotion," which I suppose Whitehead
doubted, it falls far short of his notion of the religious ideal.
Unlike most systematic philosophers, he never wrote an essay
or a chapter on ethical theory; in fact he disliked the subject.
He was more concerned with tragedy, the disclosure of ideals,
and the union of these two. One implication of his work is
that instead of separating ethics and aesthetics we should
bring them together in such notions as "harmony," "feeling,"
"adventure," and, of course, "value." But these terms are
first aesthetic terms; they are moral terms in a derivative sense.
In some passages Whitehead touches on right and wrong,
which were important notions to him as to other men. (I
never expect to see a human being whose life exhibits a more
complete and perfect *discipline* than his did. Russell's "Por-
trait" of Whitehead emphasizes this.) He speaks of "the
beauty of right conduct," which is *one kind of beauty*. The
notion that human conduct can be understood, or appreciated,
or guided with any largeness of spirit, by taking the right
as a more fundamental concept than the concept of value,
is indefensibly narrow. The ideas to be got from Whitehead's

---

[21] "The teleology of the Universe is directed to the production of
Beauty" (AI XVIII i).

writings are, rather, such as these: that the touchstone of
good is the intuition of beauty, harmony; that nothing good
is lost; that the difference between good and bad is largely
the difference between diversities which contrast with each
other and diversities in conflict. The notion that a civilized
religion can either support or be supported by a deontological
ethics is fantastic. Only a large-minded teleological ethics,
using concepts which are in effect aesthetic,[22] can suggest
to religion ideas of charity and mercy which are neither
sentimental nor false.

As for sin, I don't think Whitehead discusses it anywhere.
It would be a great mistake to suppose that he held a rosy view
of human nature; he simply had no occasion for a theological
concept of sin, since he did not conceive God as omnipotent
or issuing decrees. Whitehead saw these conceptions as originally modeled upon the kings of the earth, who wielded arbitrary absolute power over their subjects; and the concept of
" a Divine Despot and a slavish Universe " is still with us
(AI III i; MT III 3) . (Psychologies—or phenomenologies—of
religious experience which purport to give a modern foundation for the idea of original sin, he would likewise have
criticized for magnifying our slavish tendencies and devotion
to power.) In recommending the idea of " the divine persuasion " instead,[23] he thought of this as suggested by Plato and
revealed in act by Christ (AI x iv) .

The universal immanence of God's primordial nature is not
a simple doctrine, for the eternal forms include forms of
evil as well as forms of good; but the unity of the realm of

[22] Notice the language Whitehead uses when he indicates his own
concept of morality: " Morality consists in the control of process so as
to maximize importance. It is the aim at greatness of experience in the
various dimensions belonging to it. . . . Morality is always the aim at
that union of harmony, intensity, and vividness which involves the
perfection of importance for that occasion " (MT I 7) .

[23] I have found Maud Bodkin's article, " Physical Agencies and the
Divine Persuasion " (*Philosophy*, 20 [July, 1945], 148-161) , a good statement of the distinctive value of this concept for religious minds in our
time. The article includes brief comparisons of Whitehead with Buber
and Santayana.

forms is the unity of God's vision, and the gradation among forms which he effects suggests for each temporal actuality the best that is possible on that occasion. A theistic metaphysics which frames its explanations in terms of divine will, rather than the logical and aesthetic harmony which God brings to the creativity of the universe, abandons the ideal of rational explanation in metaphysics. It would be more appropriate in an earlier stage of religious evolution. Here is the contrast that Whitehead would have us keep in mind:

> In a communal religion you study the will of God in order that He may preserve you; in a purified religion, rationalized under the influence of the world-concept, you study his goodness in order to be like him.—RM i vi.

In concluding this chapter I am aware that pointing out various emphases, familiar in the philosophy of religion but partial and inadequate in Whitehead's large view, may have had the effect of lessening the chances that his thought will be appreciated. His own addresses on religion evoked some of this reaction; evoked, for example, the exclamation that it is the particular creed on which one sect differs from another that *is* all-important. Rushing to the defense of our loyalties, we do not like to allow that Whitehead may have reached more truth by going farther. But we can try.

Whitehead's philosophy of religion is something that will bear thinking about for a good long time.

PART II

THE DEVELOPMENT OF
WHITEHEAD'S PHILOSOPHY

Chapter 5

Introduction to Part II

I

Our problem in Part II is the unity of Whitehead's thought. A somewhat analogous but simpler problem occurs in the case of William James, whose first and biggest book was a psychological treatise, and who was academically a physiologist and then a psychologist before he became officially a philosopher. His bibliography, however, includes philosophical titles from his thirty-first year onward, and in his forties he was teaching philosophy. In the definitive biography, Ralph Barton Perry showed that there never was a time when James did not entertain philosophic as well as scientific questions, and concluded, "If he was ever a philosopher, he was always a philosopher." [1]

The case of Whitehead is rather different. There came first a period of more than twenty years of mathematical and logical investigations, then a shorter period in which he concerned himself with the technical and philosophical foundations of physics, and a final period explicitly devoted to philosophy.

---

[1] *The Thought and Character of William James* (New York, 1935), I, 228, 449 f.

Not until he is in his mid-fifties does his bibliography show a philosophical title. During far the greater part of his life he not only was regarded as a mathematician and not as a philosopher, but so regarded himself. The two decades before 1918 were a time of lively debate among English-speaking philosophers on epistemological and metaphysical issues. Whitehead's collaborator in mathematical logic, Bertrand Russell, was one of the leading participants in those debates. In all probability Whitehead was little more than an interested spectator. This appears not only from the absence of publications but from Russell's remark that before 1918 Whitehead had no definite opinions in philosophy.[2]

Discussion of questions currently being argued by philosophers, however, is not the only way in which a human mind may show itself to be that of a philosopher. In what ways and how far Whitehead's "nonphilosophical" works may have a philosophic character, and what ways of thinking come later, is a real question. More generally: What, in any one book of Whitehead's, shows that it was aimed at different objectives but written by the same man who wrote his other books? The question is not to be taken to imply that a sufficiently penetrating study of Whitehead's intellectual creations will reveal an "organic development." The more definite metaphor of a spiral (also used by some commentators) is likewise not justified *ab initio*, and as a conclusion is probably too strong. ("Linear" is too simple a word. All these metaphors are dangerous.)

In this Part, I sit down to consider Whitehead's writings *seriatim* and to note the ways in which each in its purpose and his treatment of its topics compares with its predecessors and successors. The origins of the problems he dealt with and

---

[2] Letter of Lord Russell to the present author, July 24, 1960. Exception must of course be made concerning opinions in the philosophy of space and time, and topics closely related thereto, on which Whitehead published papers before 1918 (see Chap. 8, below). I read Russell's remark (see p. 199, below) as referring to the justification of induction and similar problems under debate by philosophers. Possibly 1918 is, even so, too late a date; that question I leave to future biographers.

the probable success of his solutions will naturally enter into the discussion. Since I cannot assume that the reader is acquainted with Whitehead's early writings, they must be described, and a good deal of exposition given to the less familiar ones. This will ensure the performance of a useful service whether or no my conclusions are accepted.

II

The limitations of this study must be carefully noted. The topic is Whitehead's published work, not his life. Some day, I trust, a scholar or (better) group of scholars by writing a biography will cast further light on Whitehead's work. At present the contrast with the case of William James, who left a copious supply of letters and other biographical material, is sharp. And our expectations for the future had better not be great. Whitehead was famous for not writing letters.[3] His unpublished manuscripts were destroyed at his death (as his widow informed me through Professor W. V. Quine) in accordance with his own request. His general answer to questions about how he came to think as he did was that only his published works were of public interest. Though I sympathize with this desire for privacy, it is evident that the sheer greatness of this man—to mention no other consideration—makes his life a worthy subject for a valuable book. That a biography will not some day be attempted (provided civilization continues) is unbelievable. But these pages are no part of such an attempt.

Neither do they add up to a history of Whitehead's intellectual experience. I was not in his study, still less inside his brain, when he developed his ideas or moved from one problem to another. In accepting this limitation which affects anyone

[3] Bertrand Russell, *Portraits from Memory* (London, 1956), p. 96. Although some allowance for exaggeration in Russell's amusing description of this trait may well be made, I do not doubt its truth in substance.

who writes about another's work, I do not suggest that because of it, or for some historiographic reason, it is bad to try to rethink the subject's thoughts. On the contrary, this is an ultimate desideratum. But the foundation must be adequate to what is asserted. My foundation, like that of everyone who has commented on Whitehead, is practically limited to his published writings. I shall try to maintain a corresponding caution in my assertions, though I may not always succeed.

Whitehead's prefaces are particularly valuable for the plainness with which they say just what he is undertaking. At the same time, they occasion an all too familiar way of misconceiving the large transitions in Whitehead's intellectual adventures. His statements of his problems are almost always such as no other man would write. Because most of us were brought up on other men, nothing is more natural for us than to find Whitehead's statement of his problem off center; subsequently we discover that when he takes up a larger problem in a later book he is correcting himself, " driven " by logical necessity to see matters as we always saw them. Thus his later utterances are "explained" as the result of a process of thought which we know he must have gone through, though he understandably failed to say so. This type of distortion, from which no commentator is exempt, I should wish above all others to avoid. Possibly the circumstance that I first came to the field of philosophy from a reading of *Science and the Modern World*, rather than from the field to Whitehead's books, will slightly lessen the ever-present danger of slipping into extraneous conceptual frameworks when trying to interpret Whitehead.

The various kinds of documents which give a scholar some basis for shrewd inferences about what his subject did not plainly say in print, though scarce, are not altogether absent. In the present effort to understand Whitehead's works, bits of published information about the man will be used—sparingly, and only when they are clear, credible, and to the best of my knowledge uncontroverted. Apart from a few brief letters from Lord Russell, the only private materials used are the clearest among my notes of occasional conversations about his published work which I myself had with Whitehead between 1932 and 1946.

III

The grouping of Whitehead's works into the three periods mentioned at the beginning of this chapter has long since become commonplace. And for good reason: it is immediately suggested by the stated objectives of his books. (The dates I assign to these periods are uncertain, since the years meant are not publication dates, but the years in which he probably began a new type of investigation.) I hope in the end to show what the writings of his first and second periods provide for those of the second and third. This is not a simple question, to be answered by the word " premises," or by " presuppositions "—with or without the vague qualification " in principle," used by Rudolf Metz.[4] One strong impression I got as I talked with Whitehead was that he never paid any special attention to being consistent with his former self. Critics, he once said, assume that when a man sits down to write a book he has all his previous books spread out before him; for his part, he had merely tried to handle to the best of his ability the topic before him at the time. All his prefaces bear out this remark. There is no published evidence that he ever envisaged an integrated sequence of investigations, philosophically exhaustive—in the manner of Comte, Spencer, or the young Bertrand Russell. Whitehead wrote no synthesis of his life's work, and I do not wish what I shall set down in the next five chapters to be called a synthesis of it. The word is too strong. Nevertheless, after the reader has made all the reservations suggested in this chapter, I think he will discover in the earlier works philosophic elements which are

[4] *A Hundred Years of British Philosophy* (Eng. trans.; London, 1938), p. 592.

rather more substantial than he would have anticipated before attending to the development of Whitehead's philosophy.

The reception of my earlier study of the present subject [5] has confirmed my belief in the value of surveying Whitehead's work as a whole. In returning to the topic I have seen how unguardedly I wrote about it twenty years ago. I am also increasingly aware of how much we students of Whitehead have still to find out. In saying this I am not thinking only of our paucity of biographical facts. I am thinking primarily of the impossibility of exhausting the significance which any one of his major books has in its own right, except by reading it again and again.

Not being a mathematician, I am not competent to master all of Whitehead's works. The discussion of the mathematical ones is perforce not detailed, and must not be considered authoritative. My purpose is centered upon what they show about Whitehead's interests and ways of thinking, and the philosophical significance of his mathematical creations.

---

[5] " The Development of Whitehead's Philosophy," in LLP-W pp. 15-124.

Chapter 6

The First Period of Whitehead's Work, c. 1891-1913:

Universal Algebra and *Principia Mathematica*

I

In January, 1891, Alfred North Whitehead commenced *A Treatise on Universal Algebra, with Applications.* In the preceding month he had married Evelyn Willoughby Wade; [1] in the following month he would be thirty years old. A Fellow of Trinity College, Cambridge, and Lecturer in Mathematics, his professional publications at the time consisted of two papers in mathematical physics. He now devoted seven years to the *Universal Algebra.* An account of the development of his philosophy must begin with it. The *Treatise* is entirely mathematical—but in an unusual way that is relevant to the rationalistic metaphysics which he produced late in life. To show the significance of this book without technicalities—for I wish the present chapter to be useful to all who are inter-

---

[1] "Autobiographical Notes," LLP-W pp. 8 f., is the authority for this statement and the preceding one.

ested in Whitehead's philosophy—is the object of my first seven sections.

The title phrase calls to mind Leibniz and his vision of a universal calculus of reasoning. C. I. Lewis, in his examination of Leibniz' contribution to symbolic logic, concludes that this calculus, as conceived in Leibniz' later studies,

> was intended to be the science of mathematical and deductive form in general (it is doubtful whether induction was included), and such as to make possible the application of the analytic method of mathematics to all subjects of which scientific knowledge is possible.[2]

Compare this with the statement in Whitehead's Preface:

> The ideal of mathematics should be to erect a calculus to facilitate reasoning in connection with every province of thought, or of external experience, in which the succession of thoughts, or of events can be definitely ascertained and precisely stated. So that all serious thought which is not philosophy, or inductive reasoning, or imaginative literature, shall be mathematics developed by means of a calculus.

The exception made of *philosophy* is to be noted. We do not know its reason, nor what Whitehead's conception of philosophy was. I should doubt that " logic as the essence of philosophy "—a Leibnizian conception—ever came as close to gaining complete possession of Whitehead's pioneering but judicious mind as it did in Russell's case.

This view of the ideal of mathematics Whitehead maintains (roughly speaking) throughout the years. I find in its first working out three points of particular interest with respect to his later thought.

---

[2] *A Survey of Symbolic Logic* (Berkeley, 1918), p. 9.

II

In the first place, there is an emphasis on the provision of means (a "calculus") for the *facilitation* of reasoning. Of course this strain is extremely Leibnizian; though with a difference. The universal calculus which Leibniz conceived was intended, in Lewis' words, "to afford some systematic abridgment of the labor of rational investigation in all fields, much as mathematical formulae abridge the labor of dealing with quantity and number." [3] It should be possible to devise labor-saving symbolic schemes for other fields, Leibniz asserts, because, "All our reasoning is nothing but the relating and substituting of characters, whether these characters be words or marks or images." [4]

This last statement has a positivistic sound; as Professor Quine once said to me, it "has quite a modern ring." But Whitehead does not subscribe to it. His recognition of the tremendous importance of a comprehensive symbolism rests on a conception of the fundamental difference between reasoning and the manipulation of characters. The importance of the latter is that it conserves the precious supply of the former, and places it at new vantage points. "The use of a calculus," Whitehead writes, "is after all nothing but a way of avoiding reasoning." "The signs of a Mathematical Calculus are substitutive signs": they are not, like words, instruments for thinking about the meanings expressed, but rather, as Stout had roughly put it, "means of not thinking" about the meanings symbolized.[5] In the chapter on "Symbolism" in his *Introduction to Mathematics* (1911), Whitehead brings the point home with one of his most beautiful similes:

> It is a profoundly erroneous truism . . . that we should culti-
> vate the habit of thinking of what we are doing. . . . Civiliza-

---

[3] *Op. cit.*, p. 6.

[4] C. J. Gerhardt, *Philosophischen Schriften von Leibniz*, VII (Berlin, 1890), 31; quoted by Lewis, *op. cit.*, p. 9.

[5] UA 47, 1; G. F. Stout, "Thought and Language," *Mind*, 16 (April, 1891), 187.

tion advances by extending the number of important operations which we can perform without thinking about them. Operations of thought are like cavalry charges in a battle—they are strictly limited in number, they require fresh horses, and must only be made at decisive moments.—P. 61.

In the *Universal Algebra*, he equates the difference between the factors that Leibniz (sometimes, at least) tended to identify, explicitly with Bradley's distinction between "inference" and "external demonstration." Inference Whitehead describes as "an ideal combination or construction within the mind of the reasoner which results in the intuitive evidence of a new fact or relation between the data."[6] In external demonstration, the combination is performed with marks on paper in accordance with fixed rules, and this art of manipulation throws up the result for sense-perception and subsequent interpretation.

(Since Leibniz' mind is more akin to Whitehead's than is that of any other philosopher, except possibly Plato, it is worth pointing out that the divergence just noticed is symptomatic of an important general difference between the two men. Whitehead lacks a certain mechanical, metallic quality that Leibniz possessed. I do not mean that Leibniz' thinking in any sense lacked elasticity. He had a very superior, active mind. He could have written *Universal Algebra*, or the categoreal framework of *Process and Reality*, and probably he would have made them shorter and more elegant. I doubt that he could have written *Modes of Thought* or *The Aims of Education*. He had a concern and an unparalleled ability for a meticulous efficiency in thinking out the formal interrelations between the things that make up the world. Whitehead has a much deeper feeling for the inner natures of these things, and a more delicate perception of the inquiring mind's relation to their totality. This difference is in part the difference between the late seventeenth century and the wisdom that was possible two hundred years later. But there is also

[6] UA 6; F. H. Bradley, *Principles of Logic*, Bk. II, Pt. I, Chap. III.

an ultimate difference of the individual minds, which can be brought out in this way: If we imagine Leibniz now alive, and universities at the low level to which they had sunk in his time, we can easily conceive his service of a prince replaced by the service of a large corporation in the capacity of chief accountant. We see him devising some beautiful systems, with much of the work done by machines of his own invention. But Whitehead as an accountant is not conceivable.)

Whitehead's early appreciation and contrasting of two elements essential to the advance of thought, is to be compared on the one hand with the doctrine of self-evidence as the goal of thought, which is set forth in his last book, *Modes of Thought* (1938—especially Lecture III) ; and, on the other hand, with the high place which, in various books of all periods, he gives to the invention and organization of mechanical aids to thinking. John Dewey quoted with emphatic approval the declaration in *Science and the Modern World*, that " the reason why we are on a higher imaginative level is not because we have finer imagination, but because we have better instruments." [7] The instruments referred to are physical instruments, but their relation to discovery in physical science is analogous to the function of symbols in pure mathematics. Instruments and calculi are like railroads, which make walks in distant mountains possible.

All the expressions on this topic that are scattered through Whitehead's writings should, furthermore, be set in the context of his observations on education, observations which penetrate to the general nature of advance in human knowledge. From the " Autobiographical Notes," written when he was eighty,[8] we can see how great a part of Whitehead's activity, all through his life, was expended on education. He wrote essays on it before he began to write as a philosopher, even a philosopher of physics.[9] But just as education is not an

[7] SMW p. 161; Dewey, *Logic* (New York, 1938) , p. 391 n.

[8] For LLP-W; reprinted in ESP.

[9] For their appearance in book form, see OT, AE, and ESP; for further details, consult the Bibliography in **LLP-W**.

isolable subject, irrelevant if one does not happen to possess children or an interest in schools, so Whitehead's reflections on education are not confined within these essays. *Principia Mathematica* is probably the only book bearing his name in which an interest in the workings of the mind does not often show itself. To quote one example from the *Universal Algebra* (Section 7): " No sooner has a substitutive scheme [of manipulable symbols] been devised to assist in the investigation of any originals, than the imagination begins to use the originals to assist in the investigation of the substitutive scheme." A simple remark this, doubtless not original with Whitehead. A logician might describe it as " of merely psychological interest." What is it doing in a mathematical treatise? I take it to be true, and to indicate that this mathematician notices mental processes as well as schematic forms. A mind that will remark the psychological interplay that occurs in the consideration of symbols and things symbolized is perhaps not so likely to take the pains always to distinguish the two in the sharp manner required by modern semantics. Such a mind will instinctively go ahead and develop its subject, allowing the analyses that add precision and fix the theory of the subject to constitute a second stage. By then that type of mind will probably have passed on to other subjects, leaving the original field to specialists.

III

The second point about Whitehead's early conception of mathematics that we have to consider is its relation to the logic of propositions. The Preface to the *Universal Algebra* offers this definition: " Mathematics in its widest signification is the development of all types of formal, necessary, deductive reasoning." Perhaps the most important part of this statement is the implied suggestion that there are a great many unexplored deductive sciences.

The passage continues: " The reasoning is formal in the sense that the meaning of propositions forms no part of the investigation. The sole concern of mathematics is the inference of proposition from proposition." The second sentence expresses what Whitehead has since come to consider an unwarranted limitation. But the general definition of mathematics represents what was then a great advance in the conception of the subject. (It is formally expressed in the opening sentence of Russell's *Principles of Mathematics* (1903) : " Pure mathematics is the class of all propositions of the form ' p implies q,' where p and q are propositions containing one or more variables, the same in the two propositions, and neither p nor q contains any constants except logical constants.") At the time *Universal Algebra* was written, the development of a wide variety of geometries from alternative hypotheses (axioms) , along with the extrusion of appeals to spatial intuition from geometrical proofs, had led many mathematicians to identify geometrical propositions with logical implications. The eventual extension of this view to all mathematics was, I take it, a plausible supposition to those who, like Whitehead, had observed the success of Boole and Schroeder in organizing deductive logic itself as an algebra. But this must be distinguished from the thesis of *Principia Mathematica*. In 1898 neither Whitehead nor anyone else (except Frege, whose work was unknown) had advanced toward the exhibition of mathematics as entirely an extension of formal logic. According to Whitehead,[10] the expression of that idea and its development into a philosophy of mathematics is due to Russell in his *Principles of Mathematics*. Russell's book, published in 1903, was for the most part written in 1900,[11] but in 1898 Russell's ideas were still in confusion.[12]

As for the calculus of propositions itself: the symbolic rela-

[10] " Mathematics, Nature of," *Encyclopaedia Britannica* (14th ed.) , XV, 87 n. (first published in 11th ed., 1911) .

[11] Bertrand Russell, *The Principles of Mathematics*, beginning of Introduction to the Second Edition (1938) .

[12] According to a letter from Lord Russell to the present author, June 18, 1941.

tions worked out in the *Universal Algebra* hold between "terms," and the interpretation of the primitive terms as propositions is but one, and not the first, interpretation of the algebra of logic as Whitehead expounds it; furthermore, that algebra takes up but a small fraction of Whitehead's book.

The point of view of the *Universal Algebra* toward the rules of inference is stated in the Preface:

> The justification of the rules of inference in any branch of mathematics is not properly part of mathematics: it is the business of experience or of philosophy. The business of mathematics is simply to follow the rule.

This is an early point of view; Whitehead's later transcendence of it is probably due in the main to Russell. No one should turn to the *Universal Algebra* to study the whys and wherefores of inference, or—speaking generally—the ultimate problems since raised for logicians by the near unification of mathematics and logic in *Principia*, or by proof theory.

IV

The third feature of the philosophy of mathematics held by Whitehead in 1898 is of the greatest importance for an understanding of the method and many of the special theses of his later philosophy. This feature is an attack on the classical conception of mathematics as the science of number and quantity only (or, as it was sometimes expressed, " of discrete and continuous magnitude ") : a conception then accepted by a great many mathematicians, and still assumed by many teachers today and by the great majority of laymen. The mathematical constructions of the *Universal Algebra* constitute an exhibition of the inadequacy of the traditional conception; which is furthermore, as in Whitehead's writings of all periods, subjected to direct criticism. It is in the highest degree doubtful if the Whiteheadian type of rationalistic method in the field of metaphysics would have been developed at all, had not the traditional conception of the scope of mathematics first been transcended.

The fact is that in Whitehead's work as a whole there are three great assaults on traditional notions, which pave the way for his own contributions. (Of course the phrase, " pave the way," is most inadequate as a description of the intimate connection between his criticism of a narrow concept and his envisagement of a wider one.) The first assault is this, on the quantitative conception of mathematics. One reason for its importance is that the other two do not merely succeed it, but are superimposed while it is maintained, as it were, a pedal point. The second assault is directed against " scientific materialism " as a cosmology of the physical world. The third attacks the sense-percepta conception of experience, especially as expressed by Hume. These three assaults pretty well determine the problems of Whitehead's three periods of activity.

Let us make a rough catalog of the origins of Whitehead's first attack. We have already come upon one. The identification of mathematical meanings with logical implications, while in one sense a restriction, at the same time liberates mathematics from confinement within certain frontiers of fact, and gives it, in theory, free rein in the realm of possibility. The full effect of this line of thought waited upon the composition of *Principia*. Whitehead's attack on the traditional limits of mathematics was stimulated in the first place by certain achievements that may be singled out from the tremendous progress made by that science in the half-century preceding the composition of the *Universal Algebra*. Besides the invention of the algebra of logic by George Boole, four other advances, having nothing directly to do with mathematical logic, had a great effect. They are: (*1*) the discovery of means to eliminate " infinitesimals " and to replace statements involving them by statements about classes of finites; (*2*) the enlargement of algebra effected by the introduction of the complex quantity and similar conceptions; (3) the invention of non-Euclidean geometries; (4) the expansion of that type of geometry, called " projective," which involves no reference to size, distance or measurement, and the subsequent demonstration that the various metrical geometries, Euclidean and non-Euclidean, can be regarded as so many alternative specializations of this geometry.

One or another of these four advances, selected from nineteenth-century mathematics, affects Whitehead's thinking in every one of his books. Taken together, the four are capable of inspiring, in a mathematician inclined toward philosophy, a vision of a new cosmology to be developed by a mathematics no longer held within the bounds of the quantitative. In comparison with what might be developed, mathematics that labors under this restriction appears to Whitehead much as " school-mathematics " appeared to Descartes. Of course the analogy must be qualified: in Whitehead's case I know of no youthful dream, and suppose that the vision opened up gradually; the advance in mathematics that formed its basis was not provided by the philosopher himself, but by the specialists of the preceding generation; the reason Whitehead prizes the *mathematical* investigation of the world is not the absolute certainty which Descartes fancied was thereby gained; non-mathematical factors are equally important in the genesis of Whitehead's philosophy, whereas the mathematical vision is the central factor in Descartes'. But for all that, with respect to the significance of recent mathematical discovery for cosmology,[18] Whitehead is the modern Descartes.

The first of the four developments named above is not particularly relevant to any of Whitehead's work before his invention of the method of extensive abstraction. But inasmuch as a sense of the importance of the other three dominates the *Universal Algebra*, I shall at this point introduce a partial, nontechnical account of their meaning.

To an unprejudiced observer, it is plain that the world in

---

[18] " Cosmology " is here, as elsewhere in the present volume, used in its philosophical rather than its astrophysical meaning.

which we live is by no means exhausted by those properties
which can be measured, added, subtracted, multiplied. Such
properties are, in the strict sense, quantitative. But suppose
we deal with that which cannot be added or multiplied, by
specifying that the definitions of addition and multiplication
shall be enlarged so as to be adequate to this instance and
still include their ordinary meanings as particular cases. If
we then continue to speak of terms so operated upon as quantities, we have enlarged the field of "the quantitative." A very
important step of this kind was taken in algebra when expressions involving the square root of minus one were so handled,
and christened "complex quantities." Bigger steps beyond
numerical quantity were taken in the 1840s, when Hamilton
invented quaternions and Grassmann invented his calculus of
extension. Now how, or indeed why, should any stop be put
to this process, so long as conventional definitions set up in
this way prove useful in exhibiting widespread patterns of
connection among the elements of some subject matter? The
process has in fact gone so far that dictionaries now give as
the first meaning of "quantity" in mathematics, "whatever
may be operated upon according to fixed mutually consistent
laws." In short, the elements of any pattern the conditions of
which can be precisely stated may now be called quantities—
so far have mathematicians gone beyond the original meaning
of the word.

Whitehead observed this process; the idea of "universal
algebra" is an expression of its possibilities, then not nearly so
well recognized as now.

In almost all his books, Whitehead somewhere points the
moral for philosophy of the discoveries of geometries alternative to what had been supposed to be the one system of geometrical knowledge. The *Universal Algebra* weaves Euclidean
and non-Euclidean geometries into its framework. Almost all
the algebraical developments in Whitehead's book are worked
out in terms of a geometrical interpretation, so that the book
might be said to be mainly about geometry. At the time it was
written, the subject of non-Euclidean geometry had passed

through the stage in which it merely presented one alternative
to Euclid (that developed by Lobachevski, Bolyai, and Gauss) ;
and through a second stage in which another alternative (the
Riemannian geometry) was developed, and the investigation
of the possible types of geometry was provided with a wide
field through generalization of the ordinary conception of
three-dimensional space into that of an n-dimensional structured aggregate, or manifold, of points. In the latter decades
of the nineteenth century, a third stage was in full progress:
it was being shown that transformations from any one of these
geometries to another were possible through alteration of the
definitions of " distance " in the manifold; more, it was demonstrated that the very idea of distance, with all its possible
specifications, could be introduced as a late addition to the
axioms and definitions of nonmetrical geometry. Thus the
line of mathematical development which began with the invention of one alternative to the geometry of Euclid was
opening up the vista of a vast and extremely general science
of order in which the metrical systems appear as so many
subsciences.[14]

There were hints that an existing but neglected algebra
contained powerful symbolic machinery for handling this rich
new field as one unit. In 1844, prior to all but the first stage
of non-Euclidean geometry, Hermann Grassmann had published his Calculus of Extension (*Ausdehnungslehre*) . Its
leading idea, for which its author gave the original credit to
Leibniz, was to set up, by means of a calculus, a general science
of form, to which the sciences of geometrical magnitude should
appear as subordinate and posterior. This work was far ahead
of its time, and began to be recognized only a decade before
Grassmann died in 1877.[15] Whitehead's chief debt in the

[14] There are many accounts to which the reader may turn for a fuller
description of the historical development. A good full account, written
by Whitehead and Russell, is Part VI, " Non-Euclidean Geometry," of
the article, " Geometry," in the *Encyclopaedia Britannica* (11th ed.) .
[15] Historians of ideas may wish to consult A. E. Heath's three articles on
Grassmann in the *Monist*, 27 (1917) , 1-21, 22-35, 36-56; or Ernest Nagel,
" The Formation of Modern Conceptions of Formal Logic in the Develop-

Universal Algebra is to Grassmann; after him, to Hamilton and Boole (UA Preface; LLP-W p. 9).

These, then, are the mathematical developments that gave Whitehead his initial push. Algebra and geometry were both advancing to new fronts. In the *Universal Algebra* an attempt is made to integrate many of the new sectors.

V

The aim of this treatise as stated in its Preface is " to present a thorough investigation of the various systems of Symbolic Reasoning allied to ordinary Algebra " (which is assumed). These systems have two characteristics in common. (*1*) All the algebras, regardless of subject matter, deal in some sense with the composition of terms, and employ two general types of composition: addition and multiplication. Accordingly, Whitehead defines " Universal Algebra " as " that calculus which symbolizes general operations, . . . which are called Addition and Multiplication " (Section 12). He then introduces a few laws (the commutative and associative laws for addition, and the distributive law) which he regards as holding generally, and indicates others by reference to which

algebras are to be distinguished (e. g., the commutative law for multiplication, and the law,

$$a + a = a,$$

which is characteristic of the algebra of symbolic logic but not of " numerical " algebras). (*2*) The terms which are thus operated on seem, in all algebras, to be susceptible to interpretation as spatial elements (not necessarily points). To give

---

ment of Geometry," *Osiris*, 7 (1939), 168 ff.; mathematicians, H. G. Forder's book, *The Calculus of Extension* (Cambridge, 1941). My mathematical colleagues tell me that in the twentieth century Grassmann's ideas continued to percolate into present-day mathematics, e. g., via E. Cartan's theory of " exterior multiplication."

a few examples: ordinary algebra was developed with the numerical interpretation of its terms in mind; none other was thought of; but with Descartes an associated geometrical interpretation was discovered. Boole's algebra of logic is capable of a spatial as well as a propositional interpretation. Grassmann's algebra is a "geometrical calculus."

Thus Whitehead envisaged a comparative study of algebras, brought together both formally (through the specification of abstract laws) and concretely (through uniformity of interpretation); the entire project, by its performance, *to provide evidence* for those interested in the general theory of symbolic reasoning.

Whitehead did not complete his program. As he explained in his Preface, "The detailed comparison of their [the algebras'] symbolic structures" was to be made in the second volume, along with studies of quaternions, matrices, and the general theory of linear algebras. That volume never appeared, the work which he had for several years done on it being set aside in order to combine forces with Russell in the writing of *Principia Mathematica*. The published first volume is devoted to separate studies of two unusual algebras which attracted Whitehead's attention precisely because of their "bold extension beyond the traditional domain of pure quantity" (UA p. viii) : these are Boole's algebra of logic, and the algebra of Grassmann referred to above. Four fifths of the bulk of the volume are taken up by the statement of Grassmann's principles in an appropriate form and their extended application in turn to a nonmetrical theory of forces (which may be called line geometry or a contribution to pure dynamics, depending upon one's interest), to non-Euclidean geometry, and to the ordinary Euclidean space of three dimensions.[16] Whitehead shows how this calculus can get behind even projective geometry, the theorems of which can be set out as consequences of the definitions of the calculus.

---

[16] James R. Newman's statement that the "major concern" of the *Universal Algebra* "is the algebra of symbolic logic" (*The World of Mathematics* [New York, 1956], I, 396) is a slip. Nor is that algebra, after its presentation, compared with Grassmann's.

He aims not so much at discovering new propositions, as at proving whole groups of known propositions more simply, from new and more general standpoints, thus showing the power and the use of a branch of mathematics which many members of the profession had looked upon as queer and excessively philosophical.[17]

[17] As to the achievement of the book, only a mathematician would be competent to judge. W. V. Quine has reviewed the section on the algebra of logic on pp. 130-138 of LLP-W. There are very few reviews of the *Universal Algebra* as a whole. The mathematician G. B. Mathews, writing in *Nature*, thought it brilliant: the wealth of applications removed the last excuse for ignoring Grassmann; while it was too early to say whether a great instrument of discovery had been presented, the power of the calculus as a means of expression and organization was amply demonstrated; and the author included substantial contributions of his own to mathematical research. In England, the book led to Whitehead's election to the Royal Society. But its general reception was not helped by the fact that the specific contributions which Whitehead considered most novel had been anticipated in C. Burali-Forti's *Introduction à la géométrie différentielle, suivant la méthode de H. Grassmann*, published in Paris the year before but not seen by Whitehead until the *Universal Algebra* was through the press (see UA, concluding " Note on Grassmann "). In 1941 I wrote, after some conversations with mathematicians (LLP-W p. 30 n.) : " What mathematicians usually say about the UA is that ' there are some good things in it,' but that it ' had no influence.' Symbolic logicians read the short section on the algebra of logic only; algebraists, interested mainly in the theory of equations and the theory of numbers, continued to develop their own discipline; geometers gathered, at second hand, that some of the discoveries of Cayley and Klein on the relations among the non-Euclidean geometries had been restated and discussed from a slightly different point of view. The fact is that Whitehead's work suffered (in a lesser degree) the fate of Grassmann's, and for a like reason." (It had been called " too philosophical.") These are overstatements, but I cannot believe they are wholly wrong. It is impossible to say, without specially investigating the matter, how much they should be toned down. Sir Edmund Whittaker wrote in 1948 that the *Universal Algebra* " was acclaimed on all sides as a splendid piece of learning and research " (*Obituary Notices of Fellows of the Royal Society*, VI [1948], 282 f.) ; Newman (*loc. cit.*) passes this view on to a wider public. Whittaker's statement might be correct, but it would not follow that Whitehead's book had had much influence on mathematicians, even in England. Bertrand Russell, who was " greatly excited " by the *Universal Algebra*, says that " Cambridge paid [it] much less attention than it deserved " (*My Philosophical Development* [London, 1959], pp. 39, 43 n.) . Informal inquiries suggest to me that probably mathematicians today rate Whitehead's first book a bit more highly than they did twenty years ago.

VI

The *Universal Algebra* is philosophical in more than one respect. To begin with, there is an implication of this in Sir Edmund Whittaker's description of its author's mathematical interests. " In my undergraduate days at Trinity [c. 1893] when he was the junior member of the mathematical staff, he had a place apart among our teachers, chiefly because his philosophic urge to grasp the nature of mathematics in its widest aspects led him to study what were at that time considered out-of-the-way branches of the subject: for instance, he offered a course of lectures on ' Non-Euclidean Geometry.' " [18] There is the further fact that scientific research usually proceeds by deducing new possibilities of detail from the deposition of recent work in a specific field and but seldom turns round deliberately to reorganize general ideas, whereas Whitehead's work on universal algebra, like his later work, goes in both directions. And he was always eager to show the *use* of ideas more general than those currently employed. To quote again from his Preface:

> It is the object of the present work to exhibit the new algebras, in their detail, as being useful engines for the deduction of propositions; and in their several subordination to dominant ideas, as being representative symbolisms of fundamental conceptions. In conformity with this latter object I have not hesitated to compress, or even to omit, developments and applications which are not allied to the dominant interpretation of any algebra. Thus unity of idea, rather than completeness, is the ideal of this book.

Uninterpreted calculi, I think, never interested Whitehead. The subtitle, " With Applications," is of the essence of the *Universal Algebra.* (And it is not the only book of his which bears that subtitle.) Even that phrase may mislead if it suggests that the interpretations of an algebraic scheme are

[18] *Obituary Notices of Fellows of the Royal Society,* VI (1948), 281.

tacked on to it; they are worked out concurrently with it (Sections 2, 22, 25).

The view that a spatial interpretation will apply to every algebra that may be discovered is one to which, Whitehead told me in 1941, he would no longer subscribe. His thought, naturally, was narrower at the time he wrote the *Universal Algebra*. And that was much more a work of comparison and deduction than of speculative integration such as we find in *Process and Reality*. It is possible to exaggerate their common nature, and I may have done so at that time (in **LLP-W**). But there are many respects in which the *Universal Algebra* is recognizably Whiteheadian. An important one will be discussed in our next Section.

We conclude the present Section by noting some secondary characteristics of the book. It displays the Whiteheadian ingenuity of thought and the Whiteheadian complexity of presentation so often complained of. There is the Whiteheadian carelessness, too: in Section 22 an appendix is promised " on a mode of arrangement of the axioms of geometry," but the appendix is not in the book. The *Universal Algebra*, in its treatment of Grassmann, also shows Whitehead's characteristic desire to bring out the truth and power of general ideas earlier stated, but short-circuited by history and left out of account in prevalent modes of thought.

VII

Since this first book of Whitehead's deals with abstract ideas in hierarchical patterns, it is natural for a philosopher to raise in connection with it the question as to the genesis of the Platonic strain in Whitehead's metaphysics, manifest in his doctrine of " eternal objects." If one reads his works in chronological order, one comes upon no evidence whatever that this doctrine ever appeared doubtful to Whitehead, or that he adopted his Platonic attitude at a certain juncture for specific reasons. Of course there is no telling what might not be turned up in private sources. What I am saying is, that so long as our texts are limited to Whitehead's published works, the most likely supposition—reinforced for me by my acquaintance with him, beginning in 1929—is that a Platonic attitude was almost second nature; possibly intensified gradually through the years.

It is otherwise with the question whether Whitehead ever had the *pure* Platonic temper of mind. The *Universal Algebra* does not enter upon metaphysics, but there are indications that its author might be expected, were he a metaphysician, to adopt a *modified* Platonism. There are a fair number of philosophical remarks in the opening chapters; none hint that concepts have a status superior to things. The position taken is that the importance of a logical scheme derives from its interpretation as "representing" properties of "the world of existing things" (p. vii; also Sections 5, 8). Before long he comes to ask, "Just what is a 'point,' in Nature?" Such questions are not raised in the *Universal Algebra*; but its author does take care to state that his logically primitive conception, that of a "manifold of elements," is abstracted from the concrete situation, a "scheme of things," which is first explained (5, 8).

If we were to compare Whitehead's handling of pure concepts in this book with Russell's in his Platonic period and with G. E. Moore's early articles, we should first have to observe that as a working mathematician he was not and did not need to be concerned over the issues which were soon to agitate them. Even so, I can sense in Whitehead's case a certain sobriety and absence of single-minded faith, which would naturally lead to a modified rather than an extreme Platonism. If the young Whitehead was ever inclined toward the naïve and dogmatic Platonism of earlier times, I should infer from his writings that the doctrine of evolution and the discovery of alternative geometries—both of which suggest that Nature is patient of many patterns of order—had entirely unbent him.

Consider also Whitehead's discussion of the fundamental idea expressed by " = " in an algebraic calculus. He calls it "equivalence," and explains that two things (of any kind) are equivalent when *for some purpose* they can be used indifferently: "a certain defined purpose in view, a certain limitation of thought or of action," is implied (UA 3). Our mathematician shows the reflective self-consciousness of a philosopher! When he goes on to distinguish equivalence from identity, we are reminded of Bradley's view of equality as an identity in difference; indeed, Whitehead mentions Bradley's and Lotze's logical treatises in his notes. But he expresses his view as a mathematician would: "Equivalence . . . implies non-identity as its general case. Identity may be conceived as a special limiting case of equivalence." The significance of Whitehead's reading of " $=$ " as expressing equivalence rather than identity can be brought out by considering Quine's critical comment on it.

> His [Whitehead's] defense was that laws such as ' $x + y = y + x$ ' would otherwise, like ' $z = z$ ', make no assertion at all. This reasoning . . . loses its force if we attend closely to the distinction between notation and subject matter. Let us tentatively suppose, contrary to Whitehead as of 1898, that ' $x + y = y + x$ ' does hold as a genuine identity; i. e., that the order of summands is wholly immaterial. A notation of addition more suggestive than ' $x + y$ ', then, would consist in simply superimposing ' x ' and ' y ' in the manner of a monogram.—LLP-W, p. 128.

But, Quine observes, the expense of casting monograms, and the difficulty of imagining a notation to carry out a similar procedure in more complex cases, cause us to keep "a linear notation which imposes an arbitrary notational order on summands." We then have, he says, two ways of expressing "one and the same sum"; and the law " $x + y = y + x$," with " $=$ " strictly construed as identity, acquires a real function, that of "neutralizing this excess of notation over subject matter." But—and here we come to the purpose of our discussion— just what is the subject matter? The point of the argument which Quine criticized was to show that "it is essential to the

importance of the commutative law " that we should not state
it in the form, " order is not involved in the synthesis " (UA
15). If the ambiguous word, " synthesis," names the result
of the operation, then order is not involved, and its appearance
in the notation is explained by Quine. But Whitehead's
notion of the subject matter was that it consisted of two processes of synthesis and a comparison of their results. Concerning that subject matter, we may agree with Whitehead
when he flatly says, " $2 + 3$ and $3 + 2$ are not identical; the
order of the symbols is different in the two combinations, and
this difference of order directs different processes of thought "
(3). To this we must add what Whitehead (following Grassmann) says in the full-scale discussion by which he introduces
the concept of addition (14) : the symbols symbolize a " process
of forming a synthesis between two things [" concrete or abstract, material things or merely ideas of relations between
other things "] . . . and then of considering . . . [them], thus
united, as a third resultant thing . . ." Quine and Whitehead,
then, were discussing different topics. Whitehead in 1898 was
not far from the Whitehead who argued in 1938 against the
view that " ' twice-three ' says the same thing as ' six,' " and
contended that " twice-three is six " " considers a process and
its issue " (MT v 4) .[19]

Finally, I think that anyone who reads through Book I,
" Principles of Algebraic Symbolism," of the *Universal Algebra*
cannot but be reminded of the general line of Whitehead's
discussion (in a famous symposium held late in 1936) of the
deceptive simplicity of words like " is," " of," " and," " plus,"
by which we express the simplest interconnections between
things, and his statement of the assumptions we make when
we use the method of algebra, with " real variables," to set
limits to the ambiguities (ESP pp. 126-128; in IS pp. 208-210) .
I quote two sentences from the early discussion which particu-

[19] Also, W. Mays, in Sect. 5 of " Whitehead and the Idea of Equivalence,"
Revue internationale de Philosophie, 15 (1961) , 167-184, has adduced
Whitehead's 1922 treatment of equality (R III) against Quine's remark
(LLP-W p. 130) that treatment of " $=$ " " as equivalence-in-diversity does
not reappear in his later work."

larly struck me; they are from Section 14, where Whitehead is moving from the general notion of synthesis to the concept of addition, and stating the conditions involved.

> Let the result of the synthesis be unambiguous, in the sense that all possible results of a special synthesis in so far as the process is varied by the variation of non-apparent details are to be equivalent. It is to be noted in this connection that the properties of the synthesis which are explicitly mentioned cannot be considered as necessarily defining its nature unambiguously.

The conclusion of our discussion in this Section is that the mathematician who wrote the *Universal Algebra* was neither an out-and-out Platonist, nor a thinker inclined (like Quine) toward nominalism. He was quite sensitive to the existential context of mathematical thought.

VIII

The year in which *Universal Algebra* appeared saw also the publication of a paper by Whitehead on non-Euclidean geometry. In 1899 he submitted to the Royal Society a paper entitled, " Sets of Operations in Relation to Groups of Finite Order." The Abstract, which is all that was published,[20] shows that the topic of this paper was an algebra which has many affinities with the algebra of symbolic logic set forth in his treatise. Whitehead's own studies of Boolean Algebra were continued in a memoir published in 1901, and concluded with a paper published in 1903 (but dated July 4, 1901) .[21] I say,

[20] So far as Prof. Robert C. Baldwin and I could discover when compiling the Bibliography, " Writings of Alfred North Whitehead to November, 1941" (LLP-W [1941]; revised edition in second edition of LLP-W [1951]) . The Abstract is in the *Proceedings of the Royal Society of London*, 64 (1898/99) , 319 f.
[21] These may be found in the *American Journal of Mathematics*, Volumes 23 and 25, respectively. Both are summarized by W. V. Quine in LLP-W pp. 131-133.

"Whitehead's own studies," because his chief published work in mathematical logic was for a decade—perhaps from late in 1900 to late in 1910—done, as everyone knows, in collaboration with Bertrand Russell.[22]

Russell wrote, as we saw, that he was "greatly excited" by the *Universal Algebra*. Since I cannot find any elaboration of this statement in his works, I quote from a letter he wrote to me on June 18, 1941:

> As far as I remember, I was interested: (1) because queer algebras suggested, on the one hand, a purely formalistic treatment of pure mathematics, and, on the other hand, the need for some exact treatment of the conditions for the truth of formal laws (commutative, associative, etc.), which were conventionally taken for granted; (2) because it showed the existence of important branches of mathematics not derived from arithmetic or dependent on number.

[22] The dates I have given are subject to considerable uncertainty. The Preface to *Principia Mathematica* is dated November, 1910, and Russell says (*My Philosophical Development*, p. 74) that the authors delivered the whole manuscript to the Cambridge University Press in 1910. The beginning of the collaboration—if it can be said to have had a precise beginning—is usually given as 1900—the year mentioned in their Preface. It must be placed after Russell's meeting with Peano in late July (*My Philosophical Development*, p. 72; *Mind*, 57 [1948], 138; Quine, LLP-W pp. 132, 138 f.). Russell in a letter to me (September 16, 1941) referred to the collaboration as beginning "late in 1900 or early in 1901"; but what he composed in late 1900 was the first draft of his *Principles of Mathematics*. A considerably later date may be called for if we are thinking of the actual start of work on *Principia*. In 1941 Whitehead remembered this as having occurred in 1903, and added: "between 1898 and 1903, my second volume of Universal Algebra was in preparation. It was never published" (LLP-W p. 10; ESP p. 11). If Whitehead's memory was accurate, Russell's contribution to Whitehead's paper, "On Cardinal Numbers," published in 1902 (*American Journal of Mathematics*, 24; see esp. pp. 367-370) must be accounted an instance of pre-*Principia* collaboration, rather than (as by Quine: LLP-W p. 158) a progress report on the *Principia*.

These matters might be thought unimportant; but this was such a great collaboration, that it would be worthwhile to know its history better than we do. For the present, I should not want the phrase, "Whitehead's own studies," to be applied to the paper of July 4, 1901 in an absolute sense.

The second part of this sentence shows that Whitehead's book of 1898 either implanted or reinforced—the difference is not relevant to our purpose—in Russell's mind what we have noted as a central conviction in Whitehead's: the conviction that mathematics extends far beyond "number and quantity." Whitehead's interest in this extension seems to have been that of a mapper and an explorer of the enlarged world of mathematics. Russell, as always, was passionately interested in the grounds of mathematical *truth*. *Universal Algebra* " suggested . . . the need for some exact treatment " of this; it did not try to show how the need could be met. The ground of arithmetical truth was the central problem which baffled Russell. He had abandoned Kant. In *My Philosophical Development* (pp. 65 f.) he mentions, along with Whitehead's book, the contributions made to mathematical logic by Leibniz, Boole, Peirce, and Schröder, and says that he " had not [in 1900] found that they threw any light on the grammar of arithmetic." Consequently he could not " make even a beginning of solving the problems which arithmetic presents to logic "— until he met Peano at the International Congress of Philosophy in Paris, to which Russell went with Whitehead in July, 1900.

Guiseppe Peano, Professor of Mathematics at Turin, had constructed the theory of the natural numbers from five postulates using " zero," " number," " successor," and some purely logical notions; he had given new life and a new turn to symbolic logic by investigating it as an instrument of mathematical proof; he had given it new precision, not only by insisting (as his predecessors had not) upon careful enunciation of postulates and definitions, but above all by introducing superior ideograms for symbolizing many logical notions (e. g., class membership) .[23] " As soon as I had mastered his notation," Russell recalls, " I saw that it extended the region of mathematical precision backwards toward regions which had been

---

[23] This summary is drawn chiefly from C. I. Lewis' history; see, in particular, pp. 115 f., 281 n. in his *Survey of Symbolic Logic*; also Chapter 1, and other references to Peano, in Russell's *Introduction to Mathematical Philosophy* (London, 1919) ; *My Philosophical Development*, Chap. 2.

By " the natural numbers," above, the finite cardinals are meant.

given over to philosophical vagueness. Basing myself on him,
I invented a notation for relations. Whitehead, fortunately,
agreed as to the importance of the method. . . ." [24] (Whitehead
said in print, " I believe that the invention of the Peano and
Russell symbolism . . . forms an epoch in mathematical reasoning." [25]) Russell has called his visit to the congress at Paris the
most important event of his life; [26] its immediate result was his
writing, in the last three months of 1900, of *The Principles
of Mathematics*, in which he brilliantly argued that arithmetic,
analysis, geometry, and dynamics (considered as a branch of
pure mathematics) found their true places as prolongations
of symbolic logic. His proof " that all pure mathematics deals
exclusively with concepts definable in terms of a very small
number of fundamental logical concepts, and that all its
propositions are deducible from a very small number of fundamental logical principles " was to be formally stated in the
new symbolism in a second volume, to be " addressed exclusively to mathematicians." [27] It was on this that Whitehead
agreed to collaborate. Forty years later, Whitehead wrote,
" We hoped that a short period of one year or so would complete the job. Then our horizon extended and, in the course
of eight or nine years, *Principia Mathematica* was produced "
(LLP-W p. 10) .

IX

That great work has often been described, and I do not
propose to go over its content. The classic exposition is the

[24] *The Philosophy of Bertrand Russell*, ed. P. A. Schilpp (Vol. V in
" The Library of Living Philosophers "; Evanston and Chicago, 1944) ,
p. 12; cited hereafter as " LLP-R."
[25] " On Cardinal Numbers," *American Journal of Mathematics*, 24
(1902) , 367; quoted by W. V. Quine in LLP-W p. 138. It should be
noted that Russell later called his relational notation clumsy, and credited
improvements in *Principia* to Whitehead; see *Mind*, 57 (1948) , 138.
[26] LLP-R p. 12.
[27] Russell, *The Principles of Mathematics* (Cambridge, 1903) , first and
second pages of Preface.

Introduction to Mathematical Philosophy which Russell published in 1919. Two much shorter summaries of *Principia*, written by Whitehead, are not sufficiently known. The account given in the latter half of his 1916 essay on " The Organisation of Thought " [28] is a masterpiece of exposition. Attention should be called to Whitehead's way of expressing the significance of the achievement:

> . . . the whole apparatus of special indefinable mathematical concepts, and special *a priori* mathematical premises, respecting number, quantity, and space, has vanished.—AF. p. 172.

The other account of *Principia* is incidental to Whitehead's article, " Mathematics," written for the eleventh edition of the *Encyclopaedia Britannica.* [29] The article is almost entirely an attack on the traditional definition of mathematics as the science of magnitude. The main attack is the novel one developed by Whitehead and Russell themselves. The central point is that the theory of cardinal numbers is shown in *Principia* to be but a subdivision of the general theory of classes and relations; and the proof of Peano's " axioms of cardinal number " takes us to the premises of logic only. After placing ordinal numbers, infinite numbers, the real number system, and geometry also within the general science of classes and relations, Whitehead in this article explains Russell's contradiction concerning classes and how this is avoided by Russell's theory of types, so as to make possible the deduction of the general properties of classes and relations from the ultimate logical properties of propositions. The conclusion is that mathematics in general is the " science concerned with the logical deduction of consequences from the general premises of all reasoning." [30]

Although Whitehead attached to this definition a footnote which gives Russell the credit for expressing and developing

[28] OT (1917) , pp. 116-128; reprinted in AE pp. 163-175.
[29] XVII (11th ed., 1911) , 878-883; reprinted under the title, " Mathematics, Nature of," in the fourteenth edition, Vol. XV, pp. 85-89.
[30] XV (14th ed.) , 87.

the idea, the words, " the general premises of all reasoning," have rather, to my mind, a Whiteheadian tone. At any rate, this is a way of speaking which he continued to use, but which is not natural to anyone who believes that both logic and mathematics consist entirely of tautologies. That view has been adopted by most of the people who accepted the thesis of *Principia* concerning mathematics (now usually called the " logicist " thesis) . Wittgenstein developed it just before World War I, and afterward urged it upon Russell, who reluctantly agreed. It was a quite natural sequel to accepting *Principia* as a full-scale demonstration that mathematical propositions were not synthetic in Kant's sense and treating the " official " or non-English part of the work as a new formal *language*. A logicist would have had to possess a strong— we might say, a metaphysical—conviction that mathematics is directly about the real world, to reject Wittgenstein's taut- ologist doctrine. I know of no evidence that Whitehead ever sympathized with this doctrine; his published pronouncements, which occur later, strongly repudiate it. (There was an ex- ample—his interpretation of " twice-three is six "—in Section VII, above.)   His metaphysical books construe mathematics ontologically. And I should think that since he probably did not start with Russell's extreme position, he was not so much tempted toward the opposite extreme. (" I set out," Russell has written, " with a more or less religious belief in a Platonic eternal world, in which mathematics shone with a beauty like that of the last Cantos of the Paradiso. I came to the con- clusion that the eternal world is trivial, and that mathematics is only the art of saying the same thing in different words." [31])

Not long after the *Principia* was laid before the world, Hilbert's formalist conception of mathematics and Brouwer's intuitionist conception (championed also by Weyl) became prominent. Though Whitehead was not swayed, he published no explicit answer. Russell's may be found in the Introduction to the second edition of his *Principles of Mathematics*, issued in 1938. Present positions on the foundations of mathematics

[31] *Portraits from Memory* (London, 1956) , p. 56.

are not classifiable into three main groups. That, however, is not our concern. The reviews of *Principia Mathematica*, listed in the Whitehead Bibliography in LLP-W, show the responses to the work; in that same volume Quine's essay, " Whitehead and the Rise of Modern Logic," not only lucidly summarizes it [32] for readers who have some education in mathematical logic, but also explains its chief shortcomings in the eyes of America's leading logician.

Something must be said about the efforts of the authors to relieve defects which they recognized. In a second edition (1925-27) Russell tried to lessen the complications caused by the theory of types, and also recommended some basic changes not related to that theory. These matters were set forth in the Introduction and Appendices to the new edition, the text itself being reprinted without change. The new work was entirely Russell's; Whitehead, then at Harvard, said in a Note to the Editor of *Mind* [33] that he was under the impression that this fact would be indicated in the first volume. A paper he published in 1934 expressed dissent from Russell's recommendations, in the course of sketching a new doctrine of classes, a new treatment of relations, and a new definition of number. [34] Whitehead's idea was to show how these could be constructed in " purely logical terms." Thus (for one thing) the obvious defect of the *Principia* definition of a number as a class of similar classes—that " a new litter of pigs alters the meaning of every number, and of every extension of number, employed in mathematics "—was to be escaped. [35] Whitehead urged that the notion of truth-value be put in the background, and logic conceived as dealing with the " validation-values "— validating, invalidating, or neutral—possessed by complex

[32] Along with Whitehead's other contributions to mathematical logic: see notes 17, 21, and 22, above.

[33] Published in 35 (January, 1926), 130.

[34] " Indication, Classes, Numbers, Validation," *Mind*, 43 (July, 1934), 281-297. The *Corrigenda* (*ibid.* [October, 1934], 543) are essential to anyone who would follow the symbolism; unfortunately they are omitted in the ESP reprint of the paper.

[35] *Ibid.*, p. 288.

propositional forms in virtue of their structure.[36] This advice fell on unsympathetic ears. In addition, a few inquiries I have made suggest that the paper was not widely studied among mathematical logicians. To some extent its author's standing with them had been affected by his publication of metaphysical books, almost as being divorced affects a man's standing in some communities.

X

We must return to the years in which *Principia Mathematica* was written. It is of course an oversimplification to ascribe its existence, as I did in Section VIII, to the confluence of Whitehead's explorer's interest in widening mathematics, Russell's keen interest in reaching firm conclusions about the nature of mathematical truth, and Peano's successes with a new symbolism. Although Russell has written, " The work that ultimately became my contribution to *Principia Mathematica* presented itself to me, at first, as a parenthesis in the refutation of Kant," [37] his constructive genius was evident in many chapters of his *Principles* (e. g., in his providing the first precise definition of series). Also, the work of Cantor (creator of transfinite arithmetic) must be mentioned—as Whitehead and Russell do, early in their Preface to *Principia*. Still, the main causes of the writing of the work seem to be the three mentioned above.

After Whitehead's death Russell described their division of labor. This was published in *Mind*,[38] and began, " There is in some quarters a tendency to suppose that Whitehead's part in our joint work was less than in fact it was." The error was natural. The thesis of *Principia* was Russell's, and so were

---

[36] Whitehead's simple examples are: " p.q. ⊃ .p " is a validating form; " p.∼ p ", invalidating; " p.q ", neutral.
[37] LLP-R p. 13.
[38] Vol. 57 (April, 1948) , 137 f., under the title, " Whitehead and *Principia Mathematica*."

the topics in it which were of greatest and most controversial interest to logicians, e. g., material implication, the theory of descriptions, and the theory of logical types. He had published on all of them. There was also a rough sort of division between mathematical and philosophical questions. This is foreshadowed in Section 357 of *The Principles of Mathematics*, where Russell, referring to the problems of universal algebra, wrote:

> These problems cannot, in my opinion, be dealt with by starting with the genus, and asking ourselves: what are the essential principles of any Calculus? It is necessary to adopt a more inductive method, and examine the various species one by one. The mathematical portion of this task has been [*sic*] admirably performed by Mr. Whitehead: the philosophical portion is attempted in the present work.

Concerning the problems which faced the authors of *Principia*, Russell wrote recently that they " were of two sorts: philosophical and mathematical." He continued:

> Broadly speaking, Whitehead left the philosophical problems to me. As for the mathematical problems, Whitehead invented most of the notation, except in so far as it was taken over from Peano; I did most of the work concerned with series and Whitehead did most of the rest. But this only applies to first drafts. . . . There is hardly a line in all the three volumes which is not a joint product.[39]

However, our main present interest is in the development of Whitehead's philosophy. In this long collaboration each author must have got some general ideas from the other. Whitehead of course attributed the fundamental thesis of the work to his partner. But in the Preface to *The Principles of Mathematics* (dated December, 1902) , Russell had said, " On fundamental questions of philosophy, my position, in all its chief features, is derived from Mr. G. E. Moore," adding that

[39] *My Philosophical Development*, p. 74.

"in the more philosophical parts of the book I owe much to Mr. G. E. Moore besides the general position which underlies the whole." Did young Mr. Moore's philosophy, through Russell, have an important influence on the development of Whitehead's?

I do not think Moore is named anywhere in Whitehead's books. And I have never caught an echo of Moore in anything Whitehead wrote at any time. It is true that our question obviously cannot be settled by what the three men have published. But I think some probabilities can be indicated.

Russell's several accounts of Moore's influence all say that what Moore did was to speed him away from Hegelianism and into common sense, pluralism, Platonism, and the doctrine of external relations. The force of these doctrines for him lay largely in their contrast with the Hegelian ones which they supplanted. He recalls: "With a sense of escaping from prison, we allowed ourselves to think that grass is green, . . ." [40] But Whitehead's passages touching on common sense are distinctively Whiteheadian in character. Although we cannot exclude the possibility of something rather different among Whitehead's earlier beliefs, we do know that he did not—as Russell did—come to his thinking about the foundations of mathematics as a recent escapee from Hegelianism. Exactly the same thing is to be said about Whitehead's pluralism. The matter of Platonism we have already considered, and shall return to. The doctrine that relations and their terms are independent entities is the critical one for us. Its significance for Russell's philosophy of mathematics lay in his belief that both the monadistic theory that a relation between two terms is a property of them, and the monistic theory that a relation implies an inclusive whole made mathematics inexplicable. But the doctrine of external relations which liberated Russell, Whitehead later repudiated. He repudiated it in his metaphysics (including, for good measure [AI xv xi-xiii], an appeal to Bradley's authority!), and, before that, in his philosophy of nature ("The explanation of nature which I urge . . . is

[40] LLP-R p. 12.

that nothing in nature could be what it is except as an ingredient in nature as it is ") (CN pp. 141 f.) . Whitehead
developed these views after his work with Russell was over.
The question, then, is whether during the collaboration he
was committed to the contrary doctrine of the externality of
relations.

I suppose it is *possible*, but doubtful, that he was an adherent of the doctrine; and not likely, I should think, that
he was a strong one. His memory, as expressed to me in 1941,
was that this doctrine, though the foundation of Russell's
thought, had never been the foundation of his; and that at the
time, he neither agreed nor disagreed with his collaborator.
I do not see why their common purpose should have required
it. The symbolism of *Principia*, as Russell says, " assumed
that there are ' things ' which have properties and have, also,
relations to other ' things '." [41] Very good; this is nothing that
Whitehead ever quarreled with. Also, the discussions in
Principia always assume that truth is a matter of relation to
fact; [42] this, too, Whitehead continued to assume, though he
eventually added a metaphysical supplement. The decision of
the authors to avoid " both controversy and general philosophy," and let their massive logical system provide its own
justification, made it quite unnecessary for them to hold
identical opinions about Lotze and Bradley, Kant and Cohen,
who appear so much in the pages of Russell's book. Their
subject now was, as the first sentence of their Preface says,
" the mathematical treatment of the principles of mathematics."

I assume that Whitehead admired Russell's brilliance in
philosophy, and that he sympathized with many of his rejections and with some of his positive ideas. In particular,
Bradley's way of constructing a philosophy was not one that
Whitehead could approve. But probably he was not given to
debating, nor asking for a settlement of, the current philosophical questions.

Russell's influence on the development of Whitehead's phi-

[41] *My Philosophical Development*, p. 158.   [42] *Ibid.*, p. 157.

losophy is a question on which, for want of data, little can be concluded at this time. I have tried to show reasons for not *assuming* that Whitehead must have held the doctrines which his collaborator shared with G. E. Moore. I should rather seek Russell's effect on Whitehead in ideas which Russell himself originated. The idea of the incomplete symbol—key to Russell's theory of descriptions—was one such; many years later, Whitehead was telling his Harvard seminars that although this idea had difficulties it raised the right points. But the most important matter—as important for Whitehead as the logicist thesis itself—does concern relations. In 1900 Russell published *A Critical Exposition of the Philosophy of Leibniz*—the outcome of lectures given at Trinity College, Cambridge the preceding year. From Whitehead's many footnote recommendations—from 1906 to 1925—his admiration for this book is evident. Russell there exhibited the monadology as the inevitable and unacceptable result of assuming that every proposition attributes a predicate to a subject and every fact consists of a substance having a property. He also underscored the difficulties of a subject-predicate logic in understanding mathematical propositions. Whitehead, who knew Peirce's logic of relatives but had not discussed it in his *Universal Algebra* (see p. 115 n.) , was impressed when Russell in *The Principles of Mathematics* showed what could be done with a universe of terms and polyadic relations. As we shall see in our next chapter, Whitehead soon developed a variety of ways of conceiving the material world as the field of one or more relations. In his later work, he moved away from Russell by making relatedness his key idea, rather than relations independent of their terms. But the doctrine of substance and attribute, which Whitehead knew from his youthful reading of Kant and must once have respected if not used, never returned.

To conclude this tentative discussion of Whitehead's relation to Russell, we might ponder a passage from one of the Autobiographical Talks in Russell's *Portraits from Memory*: [43]

[43] Pp. 40 f.

For some years after throwing over Hegel [that occurred in 1898] I had an optimistic riot of opposite beliefs. . . . I, in rebellion, maintained that there are innumerable absolute truths, more particularly in mathematics. Hegel had maintained that all separateness is illusory and that the universe is more like a pot of treacle than a heap of shot. I therefore said, "the universe is exactly like a heap of shot." Each separate shot, according to the creed I then held, had hard and precise boundaries and was as absolute as Hegel's Absolute. Hegel had professed to prove by logic that number, space, time and matter are illusions, but I developed a new logic which enabled me to think that these things were as real as any mathematician [Whitehead was one] could wish. . . . Pythagoras and Plato had let their views of the universe be shaped by mathematics, and I followed them gaily.

It was Whitehead who was the serpent in this paradise of Mediterranean clarity. He said to me once: "You think the world is what it looks like in fine weather at noon day; I think it is what it seems like in the early morning when one first wakes from deep sleep." I thought his remark horrid, but could not see how to prove that my bias was any better than his. At last he showed me how to apply the technique of mathematical logic to his vague and higgledy-piggledy world, and dress it up in Sunday clothes that the mathematician could view without being shocked. This technique which I learnt from him delighted me, and I no longer demanded that the naked truth should be as good as the truth in its mathematical Sunday best.

Possibly this is exaggerated. Still, it speaks volumes; especially the phrase, "At last he showed me . . ." *At last.* There were opposed biases, but Whitehead was not in a hurry to demonstrate the superiority of his. If at the beginning of their collaboration he thought Russell's absolutism excessive, as I suspect he did—well, Russell himself was capable of loosening it, in his own way (by wrestling with the logical paradoxes, and with the logical status of descriptive phrases). In the matter of Sunday clothes, what Whitehead finally showed Russell was merely a technique which delighted him. I imagine Whitehead knew it would delight him.

In the history of men's intellectual products the ten-year collaboration which created *Principia Mathematica* stands out. The nature of the project did a great deal to make joint work possible; in many other fields, it would surely not have been possible for these two men. As I see their collaboration (in the light of what Russell has published about it, and of my later acquaintance with Whitehead; I hope Lord Russell can verify my picture) , the wonderful thing about it is the perfect preservation of the strong individuality of each man, made possible by their mutual affection and respect.

In consequence, each was free thereafter to develop his own philosophic views in his own way, not predetermined by their long work together.

Chapter 7

The First Period of Whitehead's Work (Continued):

" On Mathematical Concepts of the Material World " and Later Writings

---

I

The middle of the *Principia* decade is marked by the appearance of a memoir, " On Mathematical Concepts of the Material World," which Whitehead considered one of his best pieces of work.[1] It was read before the Royal Society of London late in 1905, and published in their *Philosophical Transactions* in 1906. It begins:

> The object of this memoir is to initiate the mathematical investigation of various possible ways of conceiving the nature of the material world. In so far as its results are worked out in precise mathematical detail, the memoir is concerned with the possible relations to space of the ultimate entities which (in ordinary language) constitute the ' stuff ' in space.

[1] Conversation with the present author, December 2, 1936.

157

This paper was submitted to the Royal Society in the same year, 1905, in which Einstein's first paper on relativity appeared. Einstein's paper presented only the Special Theory of Relativity, and did not touch the unification of the theory of space and the theory of matter. But " Mathematical Concepts of the Material World " presents several proposals for their unification into a single theory of the material world. (I am not suggesting that any of Whitehead's proposals are at all similar to the General Theory of Relativity presented by Einstein in 1916.) Such a diving behind the apparent independence of sciences is just what we should expect from the author of the *Universal Algebra*. Yet, very few students of Whitehead's work have paid any attention to the memoir. It *is* formidable; Professor Mays, in his article on it, aptly says, " The closely packed lists of definitions, axioms and derived propositions, make, for example, Carnap's work seem simple by comparison." [2] The symbolism used—it is concisely explained early in the memoir—is that in which *Principia Mathematica* was being written.

In the history of Whitehead's philosophical development, the memoir of 1906 is noteworthy because it presents his first criticism of " scientific materialism." The criticism is logical, not physical or philosophical. Also, what is criticized is not called " scientific materialism " (a term introduced in *Science and the Modern World*, 1) , but " the classical concept of the material world." Evidently it is of the first importance to know clearly what this classical concept, as conceived by Whitehead, is.

The memoir was written during a period of great activity in the investigation of various sets of axioms for geometry. Oswald Veblen, for example,[3] had just constructed the non-

---

[2] P. 236 in *The Relevance of Whitehead*, ed. Ivor Leclerc (London and New York, 1961) . Professors F. S. C. Northrop and Mason W. Gross, happily, print the memoir in its entirety as the opening selection in their *Alfred North Whitehead: An Anthology* (New York, 1953) .

[3] *Transactions of the American Mathematical Society*, 5 (1904) , 343-384. Our reference to Veblen in Sect. II of Chap. 3, above, was to his improved later statement of this axiomatization.

metrical part of Euclidean geometry from axioms referring to
but one class of undefined entities, " points," and one undefined
triadic relation among points, " between." [4] Whitehead, in his
memoir, makes use of Veblen's set of axioms as the most con-
venient organization of geometry; his own great originality
lies in applying this axiomatic method to the expression and,
beyond that, the improvement, of the theoretical basis of
physics:—truly a grand enterprise! The explicit goal is to
try out different ways of embracing in a single deductive
scheme both the relations of points *inter se* and the relations
of points to matter. A " concept of the material world " is
the name he gives to such a complete set of axioms, definitions,
and resulting propositions.

The " classical concept " embodies the prevailing habits of
thought. It employs three mutually exclusive classes of entities:
points of space, instants of time, and particles of matter. The
theory of the motion of matter is superposed on a presupposed
independent theory of space and a presupposed independent
theory of time. (In fact, the classical concept arose in an age
when geometry was the only developed science.) The superposition (according to an analysis first suggested by Russell
in *The Principles of Mathematics* [5]) requires a class of relations of " occupation of a point at an instant," a new relation
being required for each permanent particle. The general laws
of dynamics, and all independent physical laws, are then added
to the deductive scheme as axioms about the properties of this
class of relations.

The criticism which Whitehead, as logician and mathematician, makes of the classical concept, is as follows. Occam's
razor gives a sufficient reason for trying to reduce the number
of relations involved, and to make a construction which does
not require three independent classes of entities, if fewer will

[4] The properties of points and of betweenness are said to be " defined "
solely by the axioms.

[5] (Cambridge, 1903), Chap. LIII. See MC p. 479; N&G p. 29. Russell's
treatment of Rational Dynamics is an important part of the background
of Whitehead's memoir.

suffice. And Whitehead, being Whitehead, looks upon the segregation of geometry from the other physical sciences as a challenge to theoretical thought. His aim in this memoir is to propose alternative concepts of the material world.

After formulating the classical concept ("Concept I") in terms of the precise symbolic logic of relations developed for the *Principia*—something in itself well worth doing—Whitehead states two others in which geometry is brought into closer contact with physics. Concept II, based on a suggestion of Russell's,[6] replaces "material particles" by dyadic relations between points and instants; Concept III, which may in part be traced back to Leibniz, replaces the two classes, points and particles, by what may be called either moving points or particles of ether. Then in Concepts IV and V ultimate physical entities that are *linear* rather than punctual in nature are introduced, resulting in a tremendous difference from the classical concept. These linear or directional ultimates are analogous to lines of force, though endless. The points of space are defined in terms of their properties, and the lines and figures of ordinary geometry are defined as complexes of these *defined* points. In Concept V, the development of which climaxes the memoir, particles of matter are also derivative. The memoir concludes with a sketch of a way in which Concept V might be used to make possible a simple formulation of electromagnetic physics. Classical dynamics and, Whitehead hopes, eventually all of physics, is in this concept expressible in terms of a single polyadic relation between the members of a single class of ultimate physical entities and the instants of time, and one auxiliary relation (required to determine kinetic axes of reference). The single undefined relation, R, is the intersection in order of three linear ultimates by a fourth at an instant of time.

---

[6] *The Principles of Mathematics*, Chap. LIII.

II

Certain specific features of this work now claim our attention. First, Whitehead's treatment of time. There is here no trace of the novel idea which forms the basis of his later physical constructions and is carried over into his metaphysics: the idea that the instant of time, or, in physics, the " configuration at an instant," should not be assumed as primitive and undefined, but, like the point of space, be derived from physical elements which are epistemologically more primitive, though their logical properties are more complex. Whitehead here asserts, on the contrary: " Time must be composed of *Instants. . . . Instants of time* will be found to be included among the ultimate existents of every concept." Again, " In every concept a dyadic serial relation, having for its field the instants of time and these only, is necessary." [7]

Having been educated in the post-Relativity era, most of us may suppose it to be obvious that instants of time should have been treated as points of space were treated in the memoir. Besides committing an anachronism, we should be forgetting that the purposes of the memoir were mathematical, not at all epistemological. And we ought not to expect a man who is very busy working a new field with a new instrument (symbolic logic) to think up a new theory of time as well as new theories of space and matter. It is not humanly possible to make progress if one tries to revise all prevailing concepts at one stroke. Whitehead had been a geometer for years, and the idea of the point as complex was easily suggested to him by the " projective point " of geometry, which is a bundle of straight lines. I know no evidence that in 1905 Whitehead gave any appreciable thought to the analysis of time; he

---

[7] MC pp. 467, 468; N&G pp. 13, 15; italics in text.

In each Concept the relation from whose properties geometry issues is called " the essential relation." In Concept I the essential relation is triadic, and gives rise to geometry *only*; in Concept V it is the pentadic relation just described. Relations other than the essential relation and the time-relation are called " extraneous." Cf. MC pp. 468 f.; N&G pp. 15 f.

appears to have assumed the obvious, accepted analysis, into instants.

Whitehead's treatment of points next requires comment. He writes that " Geometers are already used to the idea of the point as complex," but adds that they nevertheless assume points as ultimate entities, since the definition of the projective point is introduced subsequently to a geometry of points; in fact, the straight lines referred to in the definition are those concurrent at a point. His investigation, he says, grew out of an endeavor to remove this circularity (pp. 482, 483, 466; N&G pp. 12, 32, 33). Two independent geometrical theories, the " Theory of Interpoints " [8] and the " Theory of Dimensions," are offered to that end. The place they merit in the history of twentieth-century mathematics must be left to the judgments of experts. (His Theory of Dimensions, Whitehead says, " is based on a new definition of the dimensions of a space " [p. 466; N&G p. 12]. Here, much has happened since 1905.) The general significance of these theories to us lies in the fact that they make possible in the memoir the mathematical development of the two " concepts of the material world " that differ most widely from the classical concept. The theories themselves are unintelligible if one is not acquainted both with advanced geometry and with the symbolism of *Principia Mathematica*. The facts about them which can here be set down for students of Whitehead are as follows.

First, logicians and mathematicians interested in the full project of *Principia* will find in these theories (along with a paper written in 1914, to be discussed below) the closest existing indication of the manner in which the polyadic relations, essential to geometry, would have been worked out in the unwritten fourth volume of the *Principia*. That volume, on geometry, was to have been entirely Whitehead's work. Russell's recollection, as set down in " Whitehead and *Principia Mathematica* " [9] in 1948, is that Whitehead proposed to

---

[8] I. e., intersection-points (MC p. 484; N&G p. 35).
[9] *Mind*, 57: 138.

treat a space of n dimensions as the field of an $(n + 1)$-adic relation, "a treatment to which, he said, he had been led by reading Veblen." Russell also wrote there, "A good deal of this [the fourth volume] was done, and I hope still exists." Alas! —as we noted in Chapter 5, it appears that the work was already destroyed.

The Theory of Dimensions is first presented in its most general form, in which it is a contribution to the theory of classes, before the application to geometry is made.

Secondly, in the Theory of Interpoints, Whitehead for the first time employs the procedure which he pushed to the limit in his books on the philosophy of physics, namely, the inclusion of temporal entities (the instant in this case, the "duration" later) in the statement of the point-defining relation. Thirdly, one notices in these theories Whitehead's first employment of certain terms, notably "primeness" in the Theory of Dimensions (p. 493; N&G p. 46) and "cogredience" in the Theory of Interpoints (pp. 508 f.; N&G p. 64), which have a basic role in the technical development of the theories of space and time in all his later works. The meanings of these terms are generalized later on, to be sure. Thus, in the later books, cogredience is the common characteristic of those events which are comprised within a temporally thick slab of three-dimensional nature, which is taken to be what is given to sense-perception; whereas cogredience here has no perceptual significance; it is merely an abstract characteristic (suggested by the idea of points at infinity) possessed, under certain conditions, by the linear ultimates at an instant of time. Nevertheless there is a recognizable similarity, which deserves to be investigated by anyone interested in Whitehead's physical theory. Fourthly, these two theories must be looked upon by students of Whitehead's "method of extensive abstraction" as the first beginnings of that method, though the name is only introduced later. This is particularly true of the Theory of Interpoints, which explicitly defines points of space in terms of proposed ultimate material entities. The method of extensive abstraction, as later developed, grows out of two purposes: to define meanings for " point," " line," " instant," etc., thus giving the relational theory of space and time the exact mathematical formulation which its adherents had previously neglected to provide; and to answer the epistemological question (of central importance for an empirical science) : " how is the space of physics based upon experience? " Whitehead's first discussions of extensive abstraction will join the two questions in the way they are customarily joined, or rather fused, by relationists—through the fact that our experience of space is an experience of the order of physical things, not of points. But only the first question is raised in the 1906 memoir, all epistemological questions being excluded from an investigation that is purely logical.

On the relative merits of the relational and absolute theories of space and time, " Mathematical Concepts of the Material World " makes no decisive pronouncement; quite properly, since the memoir is not concerned with philosophical questions, nor with winning acceptance for any theory of the material world. It is quite plain, however, from the memoir and from subsequent papers, that Whitehead was interested in this controversy but had not made up his mind about it; and there is no indication in the memoir that he had yet really tried to do so. The topic is not discussed in its application to time, but the treatment of time is entirely in accord with the absolutist point of view; and when Whitehead asserts that " Time must be composed of *Instants*," he refers the reader to Russell's article, " Is Position in Time and Space Absolute or Relative? " [10]—an article devoted to demolishing the relational theories, and to showing that it is far better to assume points and instants as ultimate simple entities, independent and prior to matter. Yet in his discussion of theories of space Whitehead indicates a preference for the relational type (which he calls " Leibniz's theory of the Relativity of Space "), on the ground that since " entities are not to be multiplied beyond necessity," space elements and material elements should not be accepted as two ultimately independent

[10] *Mind*, n. s., 10 (July, 1901) , 293-317.

classes, if a monistic alternative be possible. Thus the absolute theory of space is part of the classical concept of the
material world, as here conceived,[11] and is a source of weakness
in it. The concept which Whitehead emphasizes, Concept V,
is a "Leibnizian monistic concept" (pp. 467 f., 505; N&G
pp. 14 f., 60).

III

Theoretical thought, when philosophic or nearly philosophic
in its breadth, is likely to be mere star-gazing unless it springs,
in part at least, from specific advances in knowledge. The
reader will have already perceived how very much " On Mathematical Concepts of the Material World " has to do with the
progress of geometry. Two points concerning geometry remain
to be noticed. (*1*) Whitehead, as we might expect of the
author of the *Universal Algebra*, chooses for his concepts of
the material world sets of axioms which contain no reference
to metrical ideas. Such ideas, which must of course appear
in any geometry that is to meet the demands of physics, are
subsequently introduced by definition.[12] (*2*) Non-Euclidean
geometries are not discussed. Whitehead adopts the natural
course of taking the geometry as Euclidean throughout, and
remarks that non-Euclidean structures can be obtained, if
desired, by appropriate alterations in the properties of the
fundamental polyadic relation from which the propositions of
geometry spring in each concept (p. 476; N&G p. 24). However, a novel analysis of Euclidean parallelism is an essential
part of Concept V as elaborated with the aid of the Theory
of Interpoints and the Theory of Dimensions. One wonders
whether this fact has anything to do with Whitehead's choice
of a Euclidean structure for the geometry of space-time in his

---

[11] And as repeated elsewhere, e. g., AE p. 235 (written ten years later).
[12] " According to the well-known method of projective metrics " (MC
p. 477; N&G p. 26).

later work on the Theory of Relativity as developed by extensive abstraction.

In this memoir we meet, for the first time, the plain and decisive contribution made by physical conceptions to Whitehead's speculative thought. In Whitehead's work as a whole, five or six influences from physics may be found. This group and the group of mathematical advances discussed in Section IV of the previous chapter were equally indispensable stimuli— though the physical influences have been more favored by the notice of commentators. At this point I shall touch only on the three that antedate the memoir of 1906. They are: the development of *vector* physics, the development of the theories of molecular and submolecular energetic vibration, and thirdly the rise of *field* as a basic concept. (" Clerk Maxwell's great book on electricity and magnetism," Russell recalls, " had been the subject of Whitehead's Fellowship dissertation." [13]) Later come the statistical conception of physical laws, the theory of relativity, and perhaps the quantum theory.

The first of these six is probably the weightiest of all scientific influences on Whitehead's philosophy. A favorite comparison in *Process and Reality* is that of " prehension " with its physical model, the " vector," or directed magnitude describing transmission. In all his later books Whitehead makes it clear that he thinks the great advance of modern over ancient and medieval cosmology has been the gradual replacement of a " procession of forms " by the various " forms of process "— and this achievement is mainly the gift of physics.[14] The achievement was gradual, and effectively began with the establishment of the transmission theories of light and sound in the seventeenth century: an event of the greatest importance to philosophy,[15] though one usually misunderstood as merely providing the most conspicuous historical occasion for making an epistemological distinction among perceived qualities. The

---

[13] Bertrand Russell, *My Philosophical Development* (London, 1959), p. 43.
    [14] *Nature and Life* (Chicago, 1934), p. 15; reprinted in MT p. 192.
    [15] See CN p. 26.

molecular theories developed in the nineteenth century, such as the kinetic theory of gases, extended the process, and applied the concept of energy, to all bodies. Finally, in the late nineteenth century the mathematical theory of vectors and the physical concept of a field provided the means for tracing and integrating the propagation of vibratory energy through all space.

In the latter chapters of the *Universal Algebra* Whitehead made contributions to vector theory. In " Mathematical Concepts of the Material World " the term, " vector," is not used, for a vector requires an origin and a length. But it is highly significant that, in order to embrace all geometrical concepts and so many physical concepts as possible in a single-based set of axioms, Whitehead chose for his base-class physical lines considered as simple entities. He notes, too (p. 484; N&G p. 34), that on this basis the controversy as to how physical forces can possibly act at a distance (which bears some analogy to the epistemological controversy as to how a subject can possibly have knowledge of a world external to him) is resolved by the fact that two distant particles possess linear ultimates in common.

In the memoir of 1906, the essential thing that is done with each concept of the material world is the demonstration that the theorems of Euclidean geometry follow from its axioms and definitions, and that the motion of matter is expressible. (More exactly, demonstration is made only for Concepts IV and V; it was sufficient to indicate this result for the punctual Concepts. I should add that Whitehead states two variants of Concept III and two forms of Concept IV.[16]) But the existence of relatively permanent " corpuscles," that is, units of matter such as electrons,[17] is also considered. Generally speaking, in the linear concepts a corpuscle is defined as a volume whose permanence is the persistence of some peculiarity of

[16] A summary of this and other details of the memoir may be found in Mays's article (cf. n. 2, above), which concludes with a condensed summary of the whole.

[17] Not, however, quanta of radiation (Planck, 1901).

motion of the linear ultimates "passing through" it. This suggests, to one familiar with Whitehead's metaphysics, his interpretation there of a relatively permanent body, such as an electron, as a succession of occasions, or space-time regions, in each of which a characteristic togetherness of pre-hensions is repeated. There, as here, Whitehead is carrying out the scientific effort to conceive of that which seems to be an ultimate, enduring entity as in reality a particular result of the aggregate operation of vector forces.

It is a curious fact that this magnificent paper had even less influence on the development of physics than did the *Universal Algebra* on the development of mathematics. Though Whitehead offered only a few general suggestions as to how physicists might fit existing theories into the structure of Concept V, the advantages to be hoped for from success in this enterprise were so great that the attempt might well have been worth while.

> What is wanted at this stage is some simple hypothesis con-cerning the motion of [the linear ultimates] . . . and correlating it with the motion of electric points and electrons. From such a hypothesis the whole electromagnetic and gravitational laws might follow with the utmost simplicity. The complete concept involves the assumption of only one class of entities as forming the universe. Properties of 'space' and of the physical phe-nomena 'in space' become simply the properties of this single class of entities.—P. 525; N&G p. 82.

Whitehead's knowledge of the psychology of research warned him that this ideal would not be carried out in the near future.

> . . . in physical research so much depends upon a trained im-aginative intuition, that it seems most unlikely that existing physicists would, in general, gain any advantage from deserting familiar habits of thought.—P. 466; N&G p. 12.

But the chief reason why the attempt was not made seems to me to have been the nonexistence of a sufficient number of theoretical physicists who were both interested in the axiomatic

method and willing to work through the highly complex
Principia symbolism of Whitehead's memoir.

IV

There remains to be considered the relation of "Mathematical Concepts of the Material World" to logic and to philosophy.

What Whitehead calls "philosophic questions" are excluded. To give a striking example: on remarking that possibly
the material world, as described in Concept II, "labours under
the defect that it can never be perceived," he adds, "But
this is a philosophic question with which we have no concern"
(p. 480; N&G pp. 29 f.). The general problem, of formulating
mathematical concepts of the material world, is, then, "discussed purely for the sake of its logical (i. e., mathematical)
interest. It has an indirect bearing on philosophy by dis-
entangling the essentials of the idea of a material world from
the accidents of one particular concept." (p. 465; N&G pp.
11 f.).

The most obvious characteristic of the memoir is that it was
written by one of the authors of *Principia Mathematica*, who
was fired with a vision of the possibilities of mathematical
logic, and was applying it to new regions, geometry and
physics. (The proofs, Whitehead says [p. 471; N&G p. 19],
were mostly elaborated in symbolic form, then translated into
words.) Logic, as a body of principles of inference, is assumed
and employed in the memoir just as in any other mathematical investigation; there are no pregeometrical propositions (except in the Theory of Dimensions). But all the
relations between the variables are expressed in terms of
logical constants, such as negation, disjunction, class membership, etc. The primitive symbols and first definitions are thus
a selection from the first symbols and definitions of the *Principia*; and from propositional functions the memoir passes to

the symbolic definitions of nonpropositional functions and of relations. The first propositions that are asserted are hypotheses as to the formal conditions satisfied by the entities forming the field of the "geometrical" relation, R; these hypotheses are the axioms of a concept of the material world. Thus the fundamental relation in terms of which all geometry and, in the advanced concepts, dynamics as well, is expressible, is itself specified by logical ideas only, though it is immediately given a physical interpretation. Consequently, the paper may be said to broach the idea that physics is "one application of a logical system"; or, alternatively, to exhibit the logical component of physics.

This way of putting the matter—natural for a pure logician—carries some risk of misconceiving "Mathematical Concepts of the Material World." The phrases used at the close of the preceding paragraph are accurate only when applied to the logician's endeavor to state the conceptual structure of physics *as physics stands*, the existing science being called upon to supply the entities and relationships among entities which, substituted for the logical variables, give the conceptual structure its important interpretation. But it is of the essence of Whitehead's work to propose for physics new entities and new relationships among entities. Symbolic logic is only the great instrument, which by its generalizing symbolism makes these novel possibilities visible. Thus the work is more than a logician's analysis of the structure of physics. It is also an excursion into mathematical cosmology.

Attention to that fact will save us from falling into what used to be the standard misconception of Whitehead—that until he began to write philosophy (by responding to the magic of Bergsonism, it was believed)—he was simply a mathematician whose only philosophic interest was in mathematical logic.[18] Is not the logical inelegance of the classical concept

---

[18] It is possible to overcorrect this view. It would be surprising if anyone were able to show what Prof. F. S. C. Northrop says is "likely"—that "one of the mathematical possibles listed in . . . 'On Mathematical Concepts of the Material World' is the metaphysical system which was stated in his [Whitehead's] technically modified English prose in *Process*

of the material world, as exhibited in this memoir of 1906, a good example of that unnecessary disconnection of first principles which is named "incoherence" in the opening chapter of *Process and Reality*? Whitehead's career as a whole shows the kinship between the mathematician's interest in creating a single theory where formerly two were required, and the philosopher's interest in gaining synoptic vision. *Principia Mathematica* itself is a colossal endeavor to replace two sciences, logic and mathematics, by one.

It is important to observe that logic does not provide the reason for the logical inelegance of the classical concept. The situation, as Whitehead describes it after setting forth a modified form of Veblen's axioms for geometry, is this:

> Nothing could be more beautiful than the above issue of the classical concept, if only we limit ourselves to the consideration of an unchanging world of space. Unfortunately, it is a changing world to which the complete concept must apply, and the intrusion at this stage into the classical concept of the necessity of providing for change can only spoil a harmonious and complete whole.—MC p. 479; N&G p. 28.

The integral inclusion of geometry—the perfect static science— within the world of change: that was to be a favorite problem of Whitehead's.

V

Whitehead's next publications are two short companion books, *The Axioms of Projective Geometry* (1906) and *The Axioms of Descriptive Geometry* (1907) —numbers 4 and 5, respectively, in the series of "Cambridge Tracts in Mathematics and Mathematical Physics." Their interest is almost entirely mathematical. They present no original set of axioms. Yet they show their authorship. The axioms of projective geometry are presented only after a chapter is devoted to the

---

and Reality."—Foreword (p. xxii) to Donald W. Sherburne, *A Whiteheadian Aesthetic* (New Haven, 1961).

nature of the axiomatic method and an original definition of geometry in general. On the former subject, this chapter deserves recognition as a marvelously compressed account, still worth reading. The definition of geometry makes it "the science of *cross*-classification," [19] in contrast with the mutually exclusive classification of things into species and genera according to the Aristotelian system. This definition—Whitehead repeats it in 1933 (AI VIII ix) —accords with the view that geometry as pure mathematics has no determinate subject matter in the usual sense of the term, but deals merely with types of relation, and applies to any entities whose interrelations satisfy the formal axioms.[20]

Whitehead's division of geometries into "projective" and "descriptive" is rather unusual, though Russell also employed it in his *Principles of Mathematics*.[21] A geometry is called "projective" if two coplanar lines necessarily intersect (taking points at infinity into account) , "descriptive" if they do not.[22]

---

[19] APG 3. On this conception Whitehead later made the following comment, of capital importance: "Projective Geometry is only one example of a science of cross-classification. Other such sciences have not been developed, partly because no obvious applications have obtruded themselves, and partly because the abstract interest of such sciences have not engaged the interest of any large group of mathematicians. For example, in *Principia Mathematica*, Section 93, 'On the Inductive Analysis of the Field of a Relation,' is a suggestion for another science of that type. Indeed, the whole of Vol. I is devoted to the initiation of non-numerical quasi-geometrical sciences, together with a technique for their elaboration. The subsequent parts of the book specialize on those more special mathematical sciences which involve number and quantity" (AI VIII ix) .

[20] The definition of geometry given by Russell in *The Principles of Mathematics* emphasized this: "Geometry is the study of series of two or more dimensions" (Sect. 352) . On the actual usage of mathematicians, O. Veblen and J. H. C. Whitehead (a nephew) have written that there is probably no definite answer to the question why the name "geometry" is given to some mathematical sciences and not to others: "A branch of mathematics is called a geometry because the name seems good, on emotional and traditional grounds, to a sufficient number of competent people" (*Foundations of Differential Geometry* [Cambridge, 1932], Sect. 1.)

[21] Sect. 362, 374. For a recent discussion of this, consult H. S. M. Coxeter, *Non-Euclidean Geometry* (3rd ed.; Toronto, 1957) , pp. 159-178.

[22] The subject matter of the first tract is easily seen to coincide with "geometry of position," or "projective geometry" in the usual meaning

A special Whiteheadian touch is the endeavor to fit the expositions in these tracts to the preparation of students, already introduced to the subject, for reading the detached treatises on it. Thus the effort is not to exhaust the possibilities of a set of axioms, but to lead the reader to see whether and when a fresh axiom is required if a particular proposition is to be proved. I am not sure that the tracts alone, without a teacher, easily accomplish their educational aim—because of their extreme compression and the absence of external aids such as boldface type.

A condensed account of the two tracts, together with some interesting philosophical discussions, may be found in Whitehead's article on " The Axioms of Geometry," which appears in the eleventh edition of the *Encyclopaedia Britannica*. It is Division VII (in Volume II, pp. 730-736) of the many-authored article, " Geometry." [23] This was published in 1910. Here Whitehead associates the respected name of Kant with the quantitative conception of the subject. We should not say that " space is a quantity," but rather that " systems of quantities can be found [as properties of congruence-groups] in a space " (p. 734; ESP p. 264). Another interesting point occurs in Whitehead's discussion of the controversy between adherents of the relational and the absolute theories of space. The latter is defined as asserting, " it is not intrinsically

---

of the phrase. The set of axioms used is mainly due to Pieri. Axioms of order are introduced subsequently to axioms of classification. The latter part of this tract stresses the fact that numerical coordinates can be introduced without having recourse to distance as a primitive idea. The tract on Descriptive Geometry deals first with what others might call affine geometry; Veblen's axioms, for which the undefined ideas are " point " and " between," are mainly used, though others are discussed. The latter half of this tract is written round the theory of transformation groups, and stresses Sophus Lie's work on the analysis and definition of congruence, as superior to using congruence as an undefined idea. This mathematical definability of congruence later becomes an essential point in Whitehead's battle against the operational approach of orthodox Relativity Theory (thus, Lie's work is again appealed to on p. 49 of *The Principle of Relativity* [1922]).

[23] Not reprinted in the fourteenth edition. Whitehead's article is reprinted in ESP.

unmeaning to say that any definite body occupies *this* part of space, and not *that* part of space, without reference to other bodies occupying space." Whitehead offers the opinion that "No decisive argument for either view has at present been elaborated" (p. 730; ESP p. 244). This remark makes it possible to date his own arrival at a conclusion, in favor of the relational theory, at some time between 1910 and early 1914. (Whitehead read his paper, "La Théorie Relationniste de l'Espace," in April of that year.[24])

The importance of this decision of Whitehead's, as will appear from the sequel, extends far beyond the mere philosophy of space. What caused him to adopt the relational theory can at the present date only be conjectured; but a credible conjecture seems possible. Whitehead was getting the fourth volume of *Principia*, on Geometry, under way. In view of his habit of concentrating on the particular task in hand, it would be most improbable if his rejection of the absolute theory were not closely connected with his plans for that volume. Russell's very brief published recollection of them, reported on p. 162, above, may be supplemented by the following unsurprising reflection.[25] It would have been hardly worth while to treat geometry as arithmetic, by construing points as triples (or, more generally, as *n*-ads) of numbers; it would be more interesting to develop points as classes of entities of some general type not peculiarly "geometrical" in nature—just as in the earlier volumes cardinal numbers were developed as particular classes of entities not essentially numerical in nature—these aggregates to be so chosen that the relations between them would have the precise mathematical properties of points. This would also be in line with Whitehead's bias against the absolute theory with its purely spatial entities, which was manifested in "Mathematical Concepts of the Material World." A second influence, which I should suppose was equally important, is the continued effect of Whitehead's philosophic or reflective way of thinking of in-

---

[24] It is briefly discussed in Sect. I of the following chapter.
[25] Based on Lord Russell's letter of June 18, 1941, to me.

tellectual processes; this factor, which gives the method of extensive abstraction its epistemological aspect, I shall describe in the following chapter.

VI

No account of Whitehead's writings in this period would be complete if it omitted mention of his masterly "shilling shocker," *An Introduction to Mathematics,* written for the Home University Library, and published in 1911. It shows his great ability in sheer exposition, divorced from the working out of new ideas. With reference to the four advances in nineteenth-century mathematics that I singled out as particularly influencing Whitehead, it is to be noted that while the *Introduction to Mathematics* quite properly stops short of projective and non-Euclidean geometry, it does include a superb account of the enlargement of algebra effected by the introduction of complex quantities, and of the elimination of the infinitesimal (Chapters VI-VIII; XI, XV). Students of Whitehead's philosophy could also profit by looking between the covers of this book, since the explanations of the nature and importance of exact science contain short statements of philosophical doctrines, not intended to be such, but therefore all the more revealing of the selective emphases and the natural bent of Whitehead's thoughts in his—so-called—prephilosophical period. Thus, there is the discussion of the value of symbolism, referred to earlier; [26] a discussion of the *periodicity* exhibited in nature (XII); an assertion that the idea of a vector "is the root-idea of physical science" (p. 126); a characteristic insistence that "The really profound changes in human life all have their ultimate origin in knowledge pursued for its own sake" (p. 32); simple expositions of the abstract character of mathematics (Chapters I, II, XVI); and an account, using coordinate geometry as an example (IX), of the importance for the growth of science of that integrating generalization which is characteristic of Whitehead's own writings.

[26] P. 125, above.

Chapter 8

The Second Period of Whitehead's Work, c. 1914-1923

Philosophy of Natural Science

I

Whitehead is set apart from the typical philosophers of our time by having produced a metaphysics instead of confining himself to the philosophic problems of meaning and knowledge. But he is a typical modern in this, that reflections on the nature of meaning and knowledge in science prepared him for eventual metaphysical speculation. The fact is not generally appreciated, and his critics have a habit of supposing that the connection consists in minimizing the importance of clear knowledge and assigning a high value to the vague merely in order to have an excuse for "going off the deep end." Actually, Whitehead's epistemological preparation was an inquiry into the basic framework of the evident model of clear and precise knowledge of the world—mathematical physics. This is an epistemological study, to which logical construction, and physical and common-sense knowledge, are relevant.

My references to " epistemological preparation " and " metaphysics " are not meant to assert or even suggest that the work of Whitehead's second period was undertaken in preparation for the construction of his metaphysical system. He said more than once (though never, I think, in print) that these works were all preliminaries to Volume IV of *Principia Mathematica*, which for a long time (even after he went to America) he hoped to complete in such a way that Minkowski, Einstein, and the growth of logic after 1910 would be taken care of.[1]

The phase now to be described begins somewhere between 1911 and 1914, its initial motive being merely to provide a logical analysis of space for the *Principia*. Reflections on what is meant by space inaugurate an epistemological development which culminates in an *epistemological* criticism of the classical concept of the material world and the elaboration of a new concept from a different empirical base. The books published in 1919, 1920, and 1922 present the culmination of this development.

What Whitehead wrote between 1914 and 1919 suggests tentative groping, and manifests shifts in position and emphasis. Compared with this progress, the expansion of the new concept of the material world into a metaphysics, that is, a concept of the world in all its aspects, is fairly straightforward. But in that development, which takes place in the 1920s, epistemological reflection—on our experience of causality—is again an essential step, though not one marked out as a temporally separate phase.

The published evidence of the first epistemological phase consists of four papers, completed, respectively, in 1914, 1915, 1916, and 1917. (And the educational essays of this period have a general relevance.) Every one of these papers is impor-

---

[1] Conversation with the present author, May 14, 1941. The meaning here is decidedly not that these developments could be taken care of for all time. Whitehead also, about 1941, remarked that he came to see that logic was undergoing a new synthesis which would not reach culmination for some time. I think, however, that the devotion of most of his creative energies after 1924 to metaphysics and the philosophy of civilization was quite enough to keep him from realizing his earlier hopes.

tant, but it would be tedious to analyze each in turn. The last three are written from one and the same point of view, and I shall accordingly treat them as a unit after briefly noticing the first, in which the discussion is on a different level.

The paper of 1914 is called " La Théorie Relationniste de l'Espace." It was read before a congress of mathematical logicians which met in Paris, early in April.[2] The paper seems poorly written and unnecessarily long. But to the student of Whitehead's development it is an interesting document of transition—of the typical Whiteheadian transition, which is not a change of opinion so much as an enlargement of interest.

The relational theory of space is now adopted, and its standpoint expressed in a manner that will evidently take its adherent far afield: it forbids us to consider physical bodies as first in space and then acting on each other—rather, they are in space because they *interact*, and space is only the expression of certain properties of their interaction.[3] (The doctrine of *Process and Reality* is that " geometry is . . . the morphology of nexūs." [4]) The exact point of application of the relational theory, i. e., what the original relata should be, Whitehead has not settled upon. It will be another year before he has his epistemological bases organized and ready for publication. He is now in the process of making the necessary distinctions, e. g., between four possible meanings of " space ": the abstract space of abstract geometry, the physical space of mathematical physics, " immediate apparent space " (a fragment of the world as perceived at a moment by a particular individual), and " complete apparent space " (the public space of common

[2] Publication, in the *Revue de métaphysique et de morale*, was delayed two years. A report of the meeting, given in *L'enseignement mathématique*, 16 (1914), records (pp. 375-376) a delegate's remark that Whitehead's opinions did not agree with Russell's conclusions in *The Principles of Mathematics*; and Whitehead's reply—that his collaboration with Russell did not preclude divergences, and that, besides, Russell's ideas on space had since developed.

[3] *Revue de métaphysique et de morale*, 23 (1916), 429-30.

[4] IV iii i. I am not implying that in 1914 Whitehead had worked out a doctrine of interaction.

sense, constructed from immediate apparent space) . Whitehead is also trying to clear the way of a priori dogmatisms,
such as the dictum that space must be infinitely divisible.
The *must* is better replaced by an expression of infinite divisibility in precise logical symbolism, and a study of the way
the assumption affects the mathematical statement of the
relational theory of space.

Thus the epistemological discussions are accompanied by
contributions in mathematical logic, along the lines of " extensive abstraction "; for the fact that one is not ready to
speak one's mind about the data of perception and the meaning of " space " does not prevent one from working out some
of the formal conditions that must obtain if geometry, as
used in physics, is to be the issue of the investigation. The
chief contribution is a definition of " point " in the manner
explained in Chapter 3, above: the assumption of a point is
the assumption that relations of inclusion-of-a-part-within-a
whole exist among extended objects, such that we can define
the class of all those convergent series of objects which would,
in ordinary language, be said to include the point. The
symbolism of *Principia Mathematica* is employed to state the
axioms required. Whitehead's position is that undoubtedly
there are many possible ways of defining geometrical entities;
he urges that a variety of ways be tried, and an effort made
to find those that best accord with the facts of perception (for
apparent space) or with scientific hypotheses (for physical
space) .[5] Evidently, his conviction that geometry concerns the
same world as physics does has pushed Whitehead's problem
of working out the foundations of geometry for the *Principia*
into an epistemological arena.

II

The papers of 1915, 1916, and 1917 are entitled, respectively, " Space, Time, and Relativity," " The Organisation of

[5] *Revue de métaphysique et de morale*, 23 (1916) , 441-442.

Thought," and "The Anatomy of Some Scientific Ideas."
They were first published in book form in 1917 as the concluding chapters of *The Organisation of Thought*,[6] a book
otherwise devoted to essays on education.

These papers are the first pieces of writing that would
ordinarily be called "philosophical." Whitehead has come
to questions that are immediately—as opposed to ultimately—
of interest to scientists as a group and to philosophers, not
only to mathematicians and logicians. He is now taking an
active part in the discussions of the Aristotelian Society in
London,[7] and in the British Association for the Advancement
of Science. His essays consist of suggestions proposed for the
consideration of such audiences. The symbolism of *Principia*
does not appear in print again for twenty years.

The nerve of the epistemological thought developed in these
essays is contained in the following quotation.

> I insist on the radically untidy, ill-adjusted character of the
> fields of actual experience from which science starts. To grasp
> this fundamental truth is the first step in wisdom, when con-
> structing a philosophy of science. This fact is concealed by
> the influence of language, moulded by science, which foists
> on us exact concepts as though they represented the immediate
> deliverances of experience. The result is, that we imagine that
> we have immediate experience of a world of perfectly defined
> objects implicated in perfectly defined events which, as known
> to us by the direct deliverance of our senses, happen at exact
> instants of time, in a space formed by exact points, without

[6] These were reprinted, with slight omissions, in 1929 as Chapters x,
VIII, and IX, respectively, of *The Aims of Education and Other Essays*.
The first two papers are included in the collection recently edited by
Prof. A. H. Johnson, entitled *The Interpretation of Science: Selected
Essays by Alfred North Whitehead* (New York and Indianapolis, 1961);
he uses earlier texts (from *Proceedings of the Aristotelian Society*) and
omits technical material in "Space, Time, and Relativity."

[7] On reading his first paper to the Aristotelian Society ("Space, Time,
and Relativity," published in their *Proceedings* for 1915/1916), Whitehead referred to himself as "an amateur" in philosophy (IS p. 99).
Russell had been reading papers there for twenty years.

parts and without magnitude: the neat, trim, tidy, exact world which is the goal of scientific thought.

My contention is, that this world is a world of ideas, and that its internal relations are relations between abstract concepts, and that the elucidation of the precise connection between this world and the feelings of actual experience is the fundamental question of scientific philosophy.—AE pp. 157 f.; IS p. 22.[8]

This passage is of the utmost importance. It beautifully states the main problem for all who concern themselves with the relation of experience to scientific concepts; it shows how Whitehead's position in these essays has its origin in his great natural gift of psychological awareness; and it shows how his position is connected, on the one hand, with his examination of geometry as a physical science, and on the other hand with the criticism of abstractions—what his critics call his anti-intellectualism—which dominates *Science and the Modern World*. It is not too much to say that the chief condition for understanding the development of Whitehead's philosophy is: bear jointly in mind his aim at mathematical cosmology and his doctrine of "the rough world and the smooth world" (as I shall for convenience call the doctrine that is expounded in this quotation [9]). Notice that in the passage there is nothing that the author of *Process and Reality* need reject.

[8] The date of the passage is 1916. But the serpent presumably said much the same thing to Russell (quoted on p. 155, above) some years earlier.

[9] Its language is recalled by the invaluable passage in which Whitehead thirteen years later (while *Process and Reality* is in press) discusses the general character of experience and its relation to systematic thought:

"There is a conventional view of experience, never admitted when explicitly challenged, but persistently lurking in the tacit presuppositions. This view conceives conscious experience as a clear-cut knowledge of clear-cut items with clear-cut connections with each other. This is the conception of a trim, tidy, finite experience uniformly illuminated. No notion could be further from the truth. In the first place the equating of experience with clarity of knowledge is against the evidence. In our own lives, and at any one moment, there is a focus of attention, a few items in clarity of awareness, but interconnected vaguely and yet insistently

Whitehead's method of solving " the fundamental question of scientific philosophy," however, is built round four ideas which are all severely modified later on. To state the four ideas: *First*, an acceptance of the characteristic starting point of British empiricism:

> . . . fragmentary individual experiences are all that we know, and . . . all speculation must start from these *disjecta membra* as its sole datum.—AE pp. 245 f.; IS p. 101.

> Consider in your mind some definite chair. The concept of that chair is simply the concept of all the interrelated experiences connected with that chair—namely, of the experience of the folk who made it, of the folk who sold it, of the folk who . . .—AE p. 159; IS p. 23.

> The material pyramids of Egypt are a conception, what is actual are the fragmentary experiences of the races who have gazed on them.—AE p. 243; IS p. 99.

> . . . an extended body is nothing else than the class of perception[s] of it by all its percipients, actual or ideal.—AE p. 176; IS p. 34.

There is no evidence in the Whiteheadian corpus that Whitehead considered any alternative to this empiricism. We might almost say that it was the natural beginning for an English discussion of the data of science. This Englishman is a philosopher of experience in all his later writings. His metaphysics of occasions of experience will need a bigger runway, and the ground now occupied will look a bit different from its point of view; but he is now excluding all metaphysical questions, and asking only about the observational basis of science. The only special comment I would make on this empiricism is to conjecture that his notion of the primacy

---

with other items in dim apprehension, and this dimness shading off imperceptibly into undiscriminated feeling.

" Further, the clarity cannot be segregated from the vagueness. The togetherness of the things that are clear refuses to yield its secret to clear analytic intuition. The whole forms a system, but when we set out to describe the system direct intuition plays us false " (FR pp. 62 f.) .

of immediate experience was strengthened at this time by his concern with the education of London youth, by the contrast between that world and the learned world of Cambridge, and by the rise of relativity in physics.

Whitehead, become conscious of his empiricism, is no longer interested in the absolute theory of space.

> All space measurement is from stuff in space to stuff in space. The geometrical entities of empty space never appear. The only geometrical properties of which we have any direct knowledge are properties of those shifting, changeable appearances which we call things in space. It is the sun which is distant, and the ball which is round, and the lamp-posts which are in linear order.—AE p. 233; IS p. 91.

And obviously the same reasoning applies to time.

> It needs very little reflection to convince us that a point in time is no direct deliverance of experience. We live in durations, and not in points.—AE p. 237; IS p. 93.

Whitehead's empiricism in this stage approaches the narrow "scientific empiricism" of the positivists, but that is mainly because of a *second* idea, that of the independence of science from metaphysics.

> One of the points which I am urging in this address is, that the basis of science does not depend on the assumption of any of the conclusions of metaphysics; but that both science and metaphysics start from the same given groundwork of immediate experience, and in the main proceed in opposite directions on their diverse tasks.

> For example, metaphysics inquires how our perceptions of the chair relate us to some true reality. Science gathers up these perceptions into a determinate class, adds to them ideal perceptions of analogous sort, which under assignable circumstances would be obtained, and this single concept of that set of perceptions is all that science needs; unless indeed you prefer that thought find its origin in some legend of those great

twin brethren, the Cock and Bull.—OT pp. 113 f.; IS pp. 24 f.; cf. AE p. 161.

Its task is the discovery of the relations which exist within that flux of perceptions, sensations, and emotions which forms our experience of life. The panorama yielded by sight, sound, taste, smell, touch, and by more inchoate sensible feelings, is the sole field of activity. It is in this way that science is the thought organisation of experience.—AE p. 157; IS p. 22.

How different from the metaphysical Whitehead that we know! I imagine that reference to the " more inchoate sensible feelings " (which are of no value to science) was less noticed by Whitehead's public than the reference to a cock-and-bull story. The latter is probably a thrust at the current idealistic metaphysics; it was deleted in the 1929 reprint, but originally it was printed not only in *The Organisation of Thought,* but in the *Proceedings of the Aristotelian Society* and in the *Report of the British Association for the Advancement of Science* as well. The wide circulation of the essays of this period among English philosophers and men of science is doubtless one cause of the resentment later entertained in many quarters toward the doctrines of *Science and the Modern World.* In America, where these essays are too little known, the process is sometimes reversed: an antimetaphysical friend of mine, who saw no merit in Whitehead as a philosopher, after reading the essays changed his opinion; he recommended them to his class, which was studying modern developments from Hume's position.

For Whitehead's work in this period is indeed—we are coming to his *third* idea, which may be called the idea of inferential constructions [10]—in many respects a fresh development of Hume's principle that the connected world we take for granted is in reality a product of the habits of the imagination. " In my view," writes Whitehead, " the creation of the world is the first unconscious act of speculative thought; and the first task of a self-conscious philosophy is to explain how

[10] The phrase occurs in AE p. 191.

it has been done " (AE p. 246; IS p. 101) . In the long essay on " The Anatomy of Some Scientific Ideas " (1917) he digs out several " fundamental principles of mental construction according to which our conception of the external physical world is constructed " (AE p. 191) . These principles are not a priori, as in Kant, but matters of fact observed through empirical reflection. Their origination and their present automatic operation are viewed as due to long ages of historical evolution (AE p. 158 f.; IS p. 23) .

Our idea of a thing, such as an orange, is built up out of percepts (" sense-objects," in Whitehead's terminology) by the unconscious application of various principles. For example,

> The essential ground of the association of sense-objects of various types, perceived within one short duration, into a first crude thought-object of perception is the coincidence of their space-relations, that is, in general an approximate coincidence of such relations perhaps only vaguely apprehended.—AE p. 193 f.

There are also various principles of association according to type, quality, and intensity of sense. This is the kind of analysis that is continued by C. D. Broad in the Second Part of *Scientific Thought.*

Such concepts as a " force *at a point,*" and a " configuration *at an instant*" are indispensable to the physical scientist in his effort to attain accuracy and system. What is the origin of these concepts?

> The master-key by which we confine our attention to such parts as possess mutual relations sufficiently simple for our intellects to consider is the principle of convergence to simplicity with diminution of extent.
>
> The origin of points is the effort to take full advantage of the principle of convergence to simplicity.
>
> What are the precise properties [of classes of thought-objects of perception] meant when a point is described as an ideal limit?—AE pp. 191, 206, 207.

The answer to the question is the method of extensive abstraction, which Whitehead now applies to time as well as to space. It is the advance of mathematics that makes it impossible for us any longer to shirk the problem:

> It may be observed that, before the ordinary mathematical meanings of limit had received a precise explanation, the idea of a point as a limit might be considered as one among other examples of an idea only to be apprehended by direct intuition. This view is not now open to us.—AE p. 207.

The *fourth* idea is that with mathematical logic, which can precisely specify the conditions required for membership in a class if the class is to have certain formal properties, we can hope to exhibit *all* the concepts of science as concepts of classes of percepts. The process begins with concepts that are directly exhibited, as, e. g., the whole-part relation is exhibited in space-perception, and proceeds to concepts of classification and order which apply to these primary concepts, and so on, until conceptions are reached

> whose logical relations have a peculiar smoothness. For example, conceptions of mathematical time, of mathematical space, are such smooth conceptions. No one lives in "an infinite given whole," but in a set of fragmentary experiences. The problem is to exhibit the concepts of mathematical space and time as the necessary outcome of these fragments by a process of logical building up.—AE p. 243; IS p. 99.

Whitehead at this time held high hopes for the class theory. It would have been most unnatural to confine the exploration of its possibilities to the concepts of space and time alone.

III

One reason, besides intrinsic importance, for quoting at such length from Whitehead's essays of 1915 to 1917 is that Russell also devoted much effort to answering what Whitehead called

" the fundamental question of scientific philosophy " by the technique Whitehead showed him; and Russell's expositions, which begin with *Our Knowledge of the External World*, are better known; but the language is not quite the same. (The difference between them becomes greater when Whitehead modifies the four ideas just set forth, in ways which are not possible for Russell.) Another source of misunderstanding of Whitehead is familiarity with later positivist statements of and answers to the question, e. g., with Rudolf Carnap's *Der Logische Aufbau der Welt*.

We may discern in Whitehead's exposition of his problem five traits which are distinctively un-Russellian, un-Humian, and un-positivistic.

1) Consider Whitehead's attitude toward metaphysics. Here is a man who has been developing the logic of classes and relations and applying it to space, and who has an eye on what I have called mathematical cosmology. He wants to work his instruments of discovery to the uttermost. But his metaphysical friends tell him that the meaning of scientific concepts requires reference to the nature of ultimate reality, not forgetting mind. Naturally he retorts:

> But, for the purpose of science, what is the actual world? Has science to wait for the termination of the metaphysical debate till it can determine its own subject-matter?—AE p. 157; IS p. 22.

The initial independence from metaphysics that is here claimed for science is, like Whitehead's slightly later (and better known) insistence that the philosophy of natural science should proceed without discussing the mind's union with nature, essentially the natural demand of the creative intellect for freedom from interference in its chosen task. Later still, Whitehead the metaphysician held that the manner in which a scientist approaches his subject matter reflects his implicit metaphysics. But there would be no excuse for a positivist's supposing that the premetaphysical Whitehead was antimeta-

physical. On the contrary, " Science does not diminish the
need of a metaphysic." The relationship of possibility to
actuality, in particular, calls for metaphysical analysis. And,
stronger yet, " Science only renders the metaphysical need more
urgent " (AE pp. 229, 231). The conclusion of " The Anatomy
of Some Scientific Ideas " runs,

> We commenced by excluding judgments of worth and onto-
> logical judgments. We conclude by recalling them. Judgments
> of worth are no part of the texture of physical science, but
> they are part of the motive of its production. . . .
>
> Again, ontological judgments were not excluded by reason
> of any lack of interest. They are in fact presupposed in every
> act of life: in our affections, in our self-restraints, and in our
> constructive efforts.—AE pp. 228 f.

There is here, in short, no closed positivism, but a development of thought within a certain region, namely the analysis
of the perceptual basis (as opposed to the ontological significance) of scientific concepts.

2) Consider the total absence in these essays of the skeptical
motive which is so characteristic of Russell, of Hume, and
of most positivists. Radical skepticism does not interest Whitehead:

> The question which I am inviting you to consider is this:
> How does exact thought apply to the fragmentary, vague
> *continua* of experience? I am not saying that it does not apply:
> quite the contrary. But I want to know how it applies . . . in
> detail how the correspondence is effected.

Whitehead goes further and asserts that

> science is rooted in . . . the whole apparatus of common-sense
> thought [which has been developed in the evolution of man
> and by which he arranges his experience]. That is the *datum*
> from which it starts, and to which it must recur. . . . You may
> polish up common sense, you may contradict in detail, you
> may surprise it. But ultimately your whole task is to satisfy
> it.—AE pp. 158, 159 f.; IS pp. 22, 23.

The refusal of the philosophy of organism to accept Hume's epistemology is based on the doctrine that practice is the ultimate touchstone of theory.[11]

3) By Hume, Russell, and the Carnap of *Der Logische Aufbau der Welt*, the construction of the concepts of common sense and of science is looked upon as the building up of a *public* world from *private* experiences. But Whitehead's emphasis is in another direction, namely, the attainment of accuracy, logical smoothness, and completeness of detail. In a few more years he will denounce the problem of building up publicity from privacy as a false one; now he seems to agree that there is a problem; and he enumerates " universal logical truths, moral and aesthetic truths, and truths embodied in hypothetical propositions," as being " the immediate objects of perception which are other than the mere affections of the perceiving subject " (AE p. 230). This is Russell's position in *Our Knowledge of the External World*. Furthermore, when Whitehead read " Space, Time, and Relativity " before the Aristotelian Society in 1915, he commented that there may be a good deal in the time-lag argument against " an immediate presentation to us of an aspect of the world as it in fact is." [12] Plainly he is not at this time a neorealist, so far as perception of external nature is concerned. But, unlike Russell, he initiates no attack on natural realism. Since his epistemological inquiry does not revolve around the antithesis between the private and the public, his subsequent move into realism will require no revolution in his ideas.

4) Were we to search the doctrines of metaphysics to find that one which is most uncongenial to positivism, we might well choose the doctrine of the immanence of the past in the present, which is emphasized by Bergson's and Whitehead's metaphysics. But Whitehead now, although suggesting that our conception of past events is built up from the before-after relation observed in the present event by means of repeated

---

[11] See Chap. 3, Sect. II, above.
[12] OT p. 225; IS p. 105. The passage is omitted in AE.

applications of a " Principle of Aggregation," also anticipates
the doctrine of immanence:

> If it be admitted, as stated above, that we live in durations
> and not in instants, . . . the distinction between memory and
> immediate presentation cannot be quite fundamental; for
> always we have with us the fading present as it becomes the
> immediate past.—AE pp. 189 f.

The passage reminds us of William James; indeed, Whitehead's view of the field of perception is James's, not Hume's.

5) We come finally to what will turn out to be the most
important deviation from " scientific " empiricism. After
describing the manner in which he proposes to arrive at " that
connected infinite world in which in our thoughts we live,"
Whitehead comments,

> The fact that immediate experience is capable of this deductive
> superstructure must mean that it itself has a certain uniformity
> of texture. So this great fact still remains.—AE p. 246; IS pp.
> 101.

Whitehead's system of natural knowledge in *The Principles
of Natural Knowledge* (1919) rests on this doctrine—here so
briefly alluded to—of the *texture* of immediate experience.
The doctrine seems to me to be the progenitor of the metaphysical doctrine of prehensions.

In fact, Whitehead's fundamental object of explicit criticism
in these essays is no particular doctrine (save that of absolute
space and time, and, in passing, the subject-predicate logic),
but the false neatness of abstract intellectualism, the attitude
of mind which supposes that there is a stock of concepts, at
once general and precise, on hand for use by scientists and
philosophers. The physicist " assumes geometry," and is satisfied. He has another job to do. The intellectualist philosopher, without the physicist's justification, thoughtlessly
assumes a similarly precise set of concepts. Evidently, while

Whitehead's intentions at this time are limited, he is attacking the great "fallacy of misplaced concreteness."

IV

The three books—the *Enquiry Concerning the Principles of Natural Knowledge* (1919), *The Concept of Nature* (1920), and *The Principle of Relativity* (1922) —may for our purpose be considered as forming a unit.[13] I shall call them, for short, the 1920 books. They have, all of them, but one subject—a new philosophy of natural science, with special applications to physics. Inconsistencies between the three are minor. The first is the indispensable volume, *The Concept of Nature* being mainly a more polished and less technical explanation of its predecessor, whereas the chief new element in the last of the three is the deduction of a General Theory of Relativity.

The main specific changes that lie open to inspection in Whitehead's philosophical writings are the considerable modification of his empiricism and the almost entire rejection of the three other ideas which were presented above (Section II) as involved in his first epistemology. The changes were well

---

[13] As C. I. Lewis puts it, they "have a common subject-matter and intent, with respect to which they are mutually supplementary statements"; on p. 704 of "The Categories of Natural Knowledge" (LLP-W 2nd ed., pp. 703-741). This is the best article-length account of the philosophy of the 1920 books that I know of, written by someone other than Whitehead.

In treating these books as a unit I am not denying that Whitehead's thought shows some significant advances between 1919 and 1922. We shall in fact notice two extensions of his concept of "significance" in this period; a more detailed study would reveal other advances. Several such studies, published or unpublished, have been made; thus Nathaniel Lawrence, in Part Two of *Whitehead's Philosophical Development* (Berkeley and Los Angeles, 1956), has paid special attention to the new points contained in *The Principle of Relativity* and in the 1922 paper, "Uniformity and Contingency." (The paper is briefly discussed at the end of Sect. VII, below.) See also n. 28 in our next chapter.

under way by the time *The Concept of Nature* appeared; in fact, practically all that their completion then required was the expansion of certain doctrines of that book beyond the field of the philosophy of science. The chief reason why this change was not much noticed, until *Science and the Modern World* startled the public, is that *The Concept of Nature*, by reason of its analyses, its realism, and its scientific background, enlarged the number of sympathizers with Whitehead among philosophers who inclined toward Hume and analysis or positivism. Whitehead was conquering new worlds, and had so far given little encouragement to metaphysicians. One outcome of the discussion of the 1920 books will be to show how very much the antimetaphysicians should have been on their guard. For Whitehead's empiricism, in appearance retained, is now in fact greatly altered through the replacement of the base-class, viz., sense-objects (percepts), by two types of primitive entities, " objects " and " events." The class theory is gradually seen to involve a false simplification when extended beyond purely spatio-temporal concepts like points and instants. Principles of inferential construction play a correspondingly lesser role than formerly. Only Whitehead's working attitude toward metaphysics remains what it was.

He is, as before, discussing the rationale of natural science. But his discussion is now inspired by the conviction that the classical scientific materialism, taken as a whole, does not stand up under empirical examination any better than did the absolute theory of space; and furthermore in certain respects (beyond those noticed in the memoir of 1906) it lacks coherence. Scientific materialism was already under attack from all sides, but the usual mode of its correction consisted in restricting meanings to laboratory operations together with conventions. The problem of the philosophy of natural science, for Whitehead, is to offer the scientist, in place of the ancient trinity of time, space, and matter, a coherent set of meanings based on relations exhibited in all sensory observation. Such a set of general meanings will constitute a philosophy for the reorganization of theoretical physics.

V

The relation of Whitehead's thought to physical science is easily misconceived. Theodore de Laguna wrote in his review of *The Principles of Natural Knowledge*:

> Mr. Whitehead seems to have felt very keenly the force of Bergson's criticism of natural science as incapable of expressing the continuity of things. . . . the ulterior aim of his whole work is to reform science so that it shall no longer be open to any such criticism.[14]

On putting this opinion before Whitehead in 1937, I received the reply that he had read Bergson but was not much worried by him; what did worry him at that time was "the muddle geometry had got into" (in relation to the physical world). The Preface to the book bears this out. However, as we proceed in the next Section with our discussion of Whitehead's purpose we shall see that adequate conceptual expression of the continuity of events was an essential part of it, as much so as the definition of geometric (and kinematic) elements by extensive abstraction. The mistake to be avoided is that of taking an essential part for the whole of Whitehead's purpose.

Several persons who knew Whitehead when he was writing the *Principles* or shortly afterward attribute an important influence to Bergson,[15] and none that I know of deny this. Hence I am no longer as skeptical about it as I was in "The Influence of Bergson, James and Alexander on Whitehead," published in 1949.[16] But very little documentation of the causal relationship has yet been published;[17] there is a biographical job to

[14] *Philosophical Review*, 29 (1920), 269.
[15] Sir Edmund Whittaker, in *Obituary Notices of Fellows of the Royal Society*, VI (1948), 286; Bertrand Russell, *Portraits from Memory* (London, 1956), p. 93, and letter of July 24, 1960, to the present author; earlier, F. S. C. Northrop, LLP-W pp. 168 f.
[16] *Journal of the History of Ideas*, 10 (1949), 267-296.
[17] Northrop (*loc. cit.*) says that the influence came during the war

be done. It needs to be shown that certain problems and/or doctrines of Whitehead's 1920 books are more likely to have come to him from Bergson than from any other source— including his own originative power—which research can suggest. The chief doctrine in question is that of "the primacy of process," as F. S. C. Northrop calls it; another which he has stressed is "Bergson's emphasis upon the all-sufficiency of immediate intuition" (LLP-W pp. 169, 194 f., 205). My paper of 1949 examined the apparent evidence in Whitehead's writings of Bergson's influence in these respects; such matters as the priority of temporal over spatial concepts in Whitehead's construction are taken up there.[18] My conclusion was, and is, against Northrop's thesis that the Bergsonian influence "can hardly be exaggerated." What future biographical research will show, is another matter. We should most like to get documented knowledge about when and how Whitehead's conviction of the primacy of process grew upon him.[19] Bergson undoubtedly had something to do with it, possibly a good deal. (For all I know, Whitehead may have long had a latent inclination toward temporalism.)

Another view of Whitehead's movement from logic and mathematics into the philosophy of physics and beyond is that Einstein's theory of relativity acted on him as an impulse from the outside that released latent philosophical powers. Thus Dr. Rudolf Metz:

> His awakening from dogmatic slumber resulted, as he himself confessed, from the great changes in the field of mathematical

---

years, through Whitehead's friend H. Wildon Carr. Stahl (see next note) has found evidence of Whitehead discussing Bergson in minutes of the meetings of the Aristotelian Society.

[18] See especially pp. 273-278; also R. M. Palter's comment in *Whitehead's Philosophy of Science* (Chicago, 1960), Chap. V, Sect. 6. Northrop indicated but did not detail the possible evidence in Whitehead's 1920 books. Dr. Ronald Stahl undertook this in his unpublished dissertation at Boston University in 1950, which is summarized in his article, "Bergson's Influence on Whitehead," *The Personalist*, 36 (1955), 250-257.

[19] The relation of Bergson to Whitehead's later metaphysics of process is discussed on pp. 278-289 of "The Influence of Bergson, James and Alexander on Whitehead," and more briefly in Chap. 9, Sect. X, below.

physics that came especially from Einstein's theory of relativity
and its criticism of the traditional doctrine of space and time.[20]

The confession referred to appears in the opening paragraph
of the preface to *The Principle of Relativity*, as follows:

> The present work is an exposition of an alternative rendering
> of the theory of relativity. It takes its rise from that ' awakening
> from dogmatic slumber '—to use Kant's phrase—which we owe
> to Einstein and Minkowski.

Now as to the inferences drawn from the above. In the first
place, the plural " we " is converted into the singular " I."
Whitehead's allusion to Kant's " dogmatic slumber " is im-
personal, and refers to a general awakening to possibilities,
formerly undreamt of, concerning the relativity of space, time,
and matter. Metz's reading may have been a simple slip, or
it may have been the result of unconsciously assuming that
the subject whose philosophy he was reviewing was at that
time thinking of himself as the author of a philosophy. In
the second place, even if Whitehead had said " I " instead
of " we," such a statement, coming from a notoriously modest
man, would have proved little about what the man might
have done in the absence of Einstein's work. Thirdly, although
it is doubtless quite improbable that the theory of relativity
contained in the book would have been written had Einstein's
theory not preceded it, that still leaves us a long way from
philosophy. Fourthly, there is the implication that Whitehead
had been quietly acquiescing in " the traditional doctrine of
space and time." As a matter of fact, he had for years been
criticizing the traditional doctrine, both from a logical and
from an epistemological point of view—as we have seen. He
was now spurred on by the great advance toward unification
initiated by physicists.

We naturally make the assumption of a slumber and a need
to be wakened if we interpret Whitehead's pre-*Principia* work

[20] *A Hundred Years of British Philosophy* (English trans.; London and
New York, 1938) , p. 591.

as that of a member of the mathematical profession who has no philosophy even in the back of his mind, and then have his collaborator impose some philosophical ideas upon him. This was Metz's view. So, "There was needed a further impulse from without to bring him finally into the paths of philosophy and to release him from the fetters of Russell's way of thinking."[20a] But Whitehead had developed his own epistemology of space and time (the technique of which, Russell had accepted). I think Metz's interpretation is thoroughly German and no more than one-third true of Whitehead, whose make-up and education (and sympathies) were very un-German.

Exactly what role is to be ascribed to the theory of relativity in Whitehead's development, I find it impossible to say. His own intellectual history never interested Whitehead, and nothing would have appalled him more than the idea of putting out in speech or writing a "General Confession" in the manner of Santayana. The observer can construct no *neat* picture of the whole. He *can*, by studying the so-called non-philosophical writings, avoid the deeper pitfalls; and he can, on the basis of the published evidence, draw probable conclusions. In the case of the theory of relativity, it is practically certain that Minkowski's work influenced Whitehead considerably, and that Einstein's spurred him on. The whole physical development agitated him very much, as it did every live mind that had an interest in the philosophy of science. It incited Whitehead to devise a theory of space-time, from which both the Lorentz Transformation and the observable consequences of Einstein's general theory could be deduced, but which should have an altogether different foundation.

In the fourth volume of *Principia Mathematica* he would have to take cognizance of the interrelations of space, time, and matter—both because the author of "Mathematical Concepts of the Material World" was inclined to do so, and

---

[20a] Metz, *op. cit.*, p. 590. John Passmore's brief account of Whitehead's second period (*A Hundred Years of Philosophy* [London, 1957], pp. 340-342) avoids this mistake, but wrongly calls Whitehead's problem and strategy concerning the rough world and the smooth world "still . . . Russellian."

because experimental physics demanded it. Meantime, physicists would be getting fixed in their minds a conception of these interrelations which was, according to Whitehead, far too narrow. In these matters, time is of the essence. So, I take it, nothing was more natural than to postpone the completion of the *Principia* in order to " lay the basis of a natural philosophy which is the necessary presupposition of a reorganised speculative [i. e., theoretical] physics " (CN p. vii) , and to deduce the accepted experimental results from that basis.

In fact, Whitehead failed to deflect the path of physics. In 1933 Eddington, who had done much to get Einstein's interpretations accepted, remarked that he could now see that the philosopher's insight had been superior, but that it had come out of season for the physicist.[21] There is a bare possibility that Whitehead's theory of relativity may yet affect the history of science, for he deduced several consequences which differ from those of Einstein's theory by minute quantities still beyond our powers of observation.[22]

The main effect of relativity theory on Whitehead was probably to accelerate the application of his logical and epistemological studies on a grand scale. A comparison of *The Principles of Natural Knowledge* with his earlier writings suggests that, among specific ideas, thinking about the idea of *time* was what the physical theory most sharply stimulated in him. But he had long been peculiarly interested in relating geometry to motion, and, but for the time consumed by the *Principia* and by the educational activities he plunged into after that was done, he might much earlier have worked out a theory of space-time. Einstein's special theory, and Minkowski's work, had been before the public for years. Whitehead in 1915 had pointed out (AE p. 232 f.; IS p. 90) the desirability of conducting dicussions of relativity on a broad basis, in which the points of view of psychology and of the

---

[21] However, this refers to only one important aspect of the general divergence between the two. Eddington's remark was made in a lecture on " Physics and Philosophy," *Philosophy*, 8 (1933) , 31.

[22] See Robert M. Palter, *Whitehead's Philosophy of Science*, Appendix IV, and Sect. 5, 6 of Chap. IX.

axiomatic foundations of mathematics should be joined to the physical point of view. Now the general theory of relativity had brought matters to a head. A new theory of natural science was required of him.

VI

The pith of Whitehead's theory is to be found by consulting Chapter I of *The Principles of Natural Knowledge* and then the fine untechnical summary of that book written by him for a meeting of the Aristotelian Society.[23] The first chapter of the *Principles* is magnificent and much more important than Whitehead's celebrated polemic against the bifurcation of nature. The indispensable rule for reading Whitehead's books is to study and never forget his prefaces and opening chapters; there he usually states very clearly what he is about.

The argument starts from a fresh criticism of that traditional "Concept of the material world" which Whitehead had examined in his memoir of 1906. But now his interest is not purely logical; it is concentrated on *observable* nature. He conceives the classical concept to be based upon the idea that spatial and temporal extension express disconnection, and he proposes to remedy this: ". . . in the place of emphasising space and time in their capacity of disconnecting, we shall build up an account of their complex essences as derivative from the ultimate ways in which those things, ultimate in science [i. e., events], are interconnected" (Article 1). He does not deny the separative function of space and time, but plainly he is rejecting the kind of account of space, time, and motion which Russell had so clearly elaborated in *The*

---

[23] "Symposium: Time, Space, and Material," *Problems of Science and Philosophy* ("Aristotelian Society Supplementary Volume, 2"; 1919), pp. 44-57; now reprinted in IS. C. D. Broad's well-known summary (*Mind*, 29 [1920], 216-231), though very useful, fails to reflect the essential character of the book, as presenting a unitary *theory of nature*, and converts it into a series of chapters in what Broad calls Critical Philosophy.

Principles of Mathematics. (Whitehead does not mention Russell, who for his part seems to have thought that his former collaborator was letting himself be unduly influenced by Bergson.[24])

In his criticism of the traditional scheme Whitehead fastens first upon its employment of "nature at an instant" (an instantaneous configuration of material) as a fundamental conception.[25] It will be recalled that in the memoir of 1906 he had assumed this to be ultimate in all concepts of the material world, and had found no fault with it. But in fact the idea of "nature at an instant" embodies the classical prejudice that "the essential relationship between bits of matter is purely spatial." [26]

> The [classical] theory demands that there should be an instantaneous space corresponding to each instant, and provides for no correlation between these spaces; while nature has provided us with no apparatus for observing them.—PNK 2.2.

Thus "no physical relation between nature at one instant and nature at another instant" [27] is provided for. Conceptions like velocity and kinetic energy, which express such relations and are essential to physics, are tacked on, instead of being integrally included in the foundations. The remedy is to include among the undefined elements of science the notion of a state of change (PNK 1.2) .[28] Furthermore, if a relational theory of space be adopted (and the absolute theory is of no use to an observational science) , it will be seen that the

[24] See Chap. 9, first paragraph of Sect. X, below. In a letter to the present author, July 24, 1960, Russell describes Whitehead's recommendation to him of "some such philosophy as Bergson's" as part of a new attitude which he discovered in Whitehead after 1918.

[25] PNK 1.2, 2.5; "Symposium: Time, Space, and Material," pp. 44-46 (IS pp. 56-58) .

[26] This phrasing, so reminiscent of Whitehead's 1906 memoir, is from *Nature and Life* (1934) , p. 5 (as reprinted in MT, p. 179) .

[27] "Symposium: Time, Space, and Material," p. 45 (IS p. 57) .

[28] Contrast Sect. 327 and Chap. LIV of Russell's *Principles of Mathematics*!

persistence of matter (e. g., of a measuring rod or other instrument during the time required to make an observation) is not expressible in the traditional scheme, since we cannot then appeal to "occupation of the same *spatial* entities at two different instants" as the basis of the observed persistence. We must set instants aside, and admit that "the ultimate fact for observational knowledge is perception through a duration" (PNK 2.4).

An analogous difficulty prevents the classical materialism from expressing a physical relation between two *places* even (e. g., a stress). For the physical entities of the scheme are point-particles, and no two points are in contact, nor are there any "infinitely small volumes"—the notion of such being in fact a muddled notion that was plausible only so long as it seemed necessary to the infinitesimal calculus: but Weierstrass and his school had knocked the bottom out of that necessity.[29] Of course, this difficulty of defining physical relationships that extend across space had been discussed for generations, but without much effect on either physics or metaphysics. Whitehead himself had discussed it on previous occasions without arriving at a conclusion;[30] and in 1906 he had pointed to its avoidance as a merit in his proposed linear concepts of the material world. But he had not dealt with the full application of the difficulty to physical action through time.

That the ultimates of natural science are states of change, conceived as single unities and extended in both space and time—this is a fundamental result which Whitehead carries over bodily into his metaphysics. That the specious present is an example of such a unity is for him at once the ground of the harmony of his theory of nature with observation, and the ground of the possibility of applying his result to a meta-

---

[29] PNK 1.3. The effect of this mathematical advance was to immensely clarify and sharpen the problem of relating geometrical to natural entities.

[30] In Sect. II, concerned with Physical Objects and Physical Space, of his 1914 paper, "La Théorie Relationniste de l'Espace"; and in "The Anatomy of Some Scientific Ideas" (1917; see AE pp. 222-225).

physics of experience. Thus Whitehead's unification of experiences and nature in one concept has its first origin here.

In *The Principles of Natural Knowledge* these unities are termed "events." Whitehead proceeds to state the facts about them that are exhibited in every observation of external nature. He calls these facts the "constants of externality"; they are the assumptions common to all the sciences of nature. They concern chiefly the relations called "cogredience" (definition of a presented expanse by a percipient event) and "extension" (the mutual overlapping and inclusion of events).[31] The development of Whitehead's scheme is dominated by the embracing of spatial and temporal extendedness as two species of a general relation of extension. That is the sort of thing we should expect from the Whitehead we became acquainted with in the earlier portions of this Part. Besides, Minkowski's unification encouraged it.

Of course Whitehead does not ask physics to confine the span of an event to that of the specious present; his point is that the idea of spatio-temporal spans, of whatever magnitude, must replace instants and points, if what is observed (not in its specificity, to be sure) is to fall within the concept of the material world. The unusual character of Whitehead's theory of nature, which distinguishes it both from contemporary theories and from his mathematical theory of 1906, is precisely this statement of the general character of observation and the inclusion of the general character as the basis of a unified speculative construction. The whole thing is the product of a most unusual English philosopher-scientist, who *fuses* (and does not merely happen to hold simultaneously in his mind) the Berkeleian criticism of scientific concepts and an unlimited interest in mathematical cosmology.

The relation which holds between the basis adopted in the *Principles of Natural Knowledge* and the bricks and mortar of Whitehead's metaphysical system can be expressed in another way, the full import of which will appear in our next

[31] Cf. "Symposium: Time, Space, and Material," pp. 47-50 (IS pp. 59-62).

section. The physicists had discovered the relativity of space and time to the circumstances of the observer, but they had not been bold enough to build entirely on the general character of a-perception-from-a-standpoint-here-and-now. It is because Whitehead's physical inquiry does build on this basis, that the conclusion of the inquiry leads naturally to the further question:—what is the full character of the relation which holds between a percipient event and other events?—in other words, what base-relations for a pluralistic and temporalistic cosmology are discernible in the percipient event? [32]

VII

One of the most striking features of Whitehead's philosophy of nature is its sharp distinction between two fundamentally different sorts of entities in nature: "events" and "objects," or "recognita," [33] which are recurring characters of events. This distinction is the clear beginning of the great duality in his metaphysics between "actual occasions or entities," and "eternal objects." And, of course, the analysis of the celebrated relation of "ingression" by which Whitehead connects these two classes of elements begins here, so far as the relationships evident in sense-perception are concerned. The original duality, however, was not intended to be an assertion about the ultimate character of reality, but only to correspond to a difference evident in perception and indispensable for a clear philosophy of natural science. [34] My own

---

[32] When he presented his metaphysics of Time to the Sixth International Congress of Philosophy in 1926 (one year after *Science and the Modern World*), Whitehead said that his "whole paper" was directed toward explaining "the relativistic conclusion that individual perceptivity is the ultimate physical fact" (Sect. V of "Time," in *Proceedings of the Sixth International Congress of Philosophy* [New York, 1927]; in IS p. 245).

[33] "Symposium: Time, Space, and Material," p. 51 (IS p. 62).

[34] C. I. Lewis in his exposition (see n. 13, above) brings out very well the advantage which Whitehead gains—especially for the ultimate basis of measurement—by distinguishing the structure of events from the theory of objects.

belief is that nothing better than a pragmatic reason can be given for making "recognita" as ultimate as "events" in the theory of nature. Only a platonically minded writer would assert, without attempting to justify himself, that "Objects are of course essential for process, as appears clearly enough in the course of any analysis of process" (PNK 2nd ed., Note II). To some English philosophers the fundamental distinction between recognita and events was the source of the greatest merit in Whitehead's work: he had produced a philosophy of nature in which universals and particulars could not be confused.[35]

The purpose of the dual apparatus is, with the help of the method of extensive abstraction, "to express the essential scientific concepts of time, space and material as issuing from fundamental relations between events [extension and cogredience] and from recognitions of the characters of events" (PNK 2.5). The choice of the object and the event for this purpose is natural enough; and the new basis is what makes possible Whitehead's advance from the mere suggestions of his epistemological period to the grand construction of a theory of nature. But in the process, Whitehead's previous sense-empiricism is left far behind. His main classification of recognita—into sense-objects, perceptual objects (called "physical" if non-delusive) and scientific objects—reflects his distinctions of 1915-1917; but he mentions percipient objects, discusses figures and rhythms, and admits an indefinite number of types of objects. He is emphasizing both the inexhaustible diversity of the subject matter of perceptual experience (PNK 13, 16, 22.1). His manner of describing our awareness of events in "nature as a present-whole" is particularly crucial.

[35] See, e. g., L. S. Stebbing, "Concerning Substance," *Proceedings of the Aristotelian Society*, n. s., 30 (1929/1930), 300:

Because clearing away confusion was a necessity, much of the *Principles of Natural Knowledge* is given over to drawing distinctions of one kind or another; and this was a source of delight to many intellectualist philosophers with whom Whitehead had little in common (see the close of Sect. III, above).

The fundamental datum is a "duration"; other events and various objects are discriminated only as given in a duration. This givenness is of two kinds. There is full awareness, and there is awareness of "significance." Thus we look at the closed door of a cupboard, and are aware that an event (bounded by the edges of the cupboard and by the beginning and end of our act of seeing) has a certain character (color and form). But we are also aware that inside the cupboard there are events whose space-relations complete the space-relations of the things that are fully seen (the exterior of the cupboard, other objects seen in the room) to myself as a point of origin. Similarly for contemporary events so distant that we can learn of their characters only indirectly, say by reading newspapers. And this awareness of the relations of which undiscriminated events are known to be relata is for White-head as immediate, as given, as plainly posited in an act of observation, as awareness of sense-data, strictly so called.

The difference between these two types of perception is described in *The Concept of Nature* as the difference between " the discerned" and " the discernible," in *The Principle of Relativity* as the difference between " cognizance by adjective " and " cognizance by relatedness only." The doctrine is called the doctrine of " significance," namely, events whose characters are not discerned are known through being signified, in a uniform manner, by other events (PNK 3.3-3.8, 16.1, 16.2, 19.4, 20, 21; CN pp. 49-53, 186-188, 184, 197 f.; R II, IV). You may discern in the doctrine a touch of Kant's transcendental aesthetic; or you may see in it other historical affiliations. Whitehead observes that to start with an experience of per-cepts, and then to add a theory of significance, is to subject yourself to Hume's criticism of Berkeley; Kant's method, " the essential point " of which was " the assumption that 'signifi-cance' is an essential element in concrete experience " (PNK 3.4), was superior. Whitehead argues also that the modern method (practiced by Russell) of constructing a visual space out of colored patches, an auditory space out of sounds, and so on for the other senses, and then fitting all these spaces

together, sets an impossible task for " inferential construction "
(PNK 62-63).

Two facts stand out. *First, the doctrine of significance
underlies Whitehead's whole theory of nature.* Every application of the method of extensive abstraction is based on it.
This doctrine also (together with his appeal to a uniform
nonmetrical geometry as presupposed in every application of
metrics) makes possible the distinction he draws between
geometry, which studies this uniformity, and physics, which
investigates the contingent properties of events.[36] This distinction is the root of the essential difference between his
theory of relativity and Einstein's. *Second, the doctrine of
significance is not a doctrine of ordinary empiricism.* Every
orthodox empiricist (and also every Critical Realist and positivist) will insist that the network of relationships affirmed
by Whitehead is not a direct datum of knowledge, but *either*
(as for Russell prior to *The Analysis of Matter*) a shorthand
way of referring to classes of hypothetical percepts *or* (and
this is more usual) a result of inference. Thus, in *The Revolt
Against Dualism*, part of Lovejoy's argument that Whitehead
merely re-enunciates epistemological dualism in novel terminology is a warning to the reader to bear in mind " a rather
constant peculiarity of Professor Whitehead's way of putting
things—his custom of speaking of that which is cognized
indirectly or inferentially in terms which would ordinarily be
regarded as appropriate only to the ' objects of immediate
appearance.' " [37] On the contrary, Whitehead means what he
says when he includes in immediate experience what is excluded from it by orthodox epistemology.[38]

[36] To insist upon the stock alternatives, that geometry is either pure
mathematics or empirical in the same manner as, say, the study of
strengths of materials, is to rule out Whitehead's position in advance.
[37] *The Revolt Against Dualism* (La Salle, Ill., 1930), p. 180.
[38] Whitehead's divergence from Kantian positions should also be noted.
(Nathaniel Lawrence's extended criticism in *Whitehead's Philosophical
Development* is largely an attempt to show that Whitehead was unable
to maintain this divergence.) The following passage (CN p. 143) throws
a flood of light on what Whitehead was trying to do, and shows that

As for the antecedents of " significance " in his own writings, one has already been mentioned: the ascription of a " uniform texture " to "immediate experience" in the essay of 1915. At that time Whitehead spoke of this uniformity as " a most curious and arresting fact," and remarked that he was " quite ready to believe that it is a mere illusion " (AE p. 245; IS p. 100) . Perhaps he was; and perhaps he was not so ready as he thought. The expansion of this ascription of "texture " into a central doctrine was probably due to his search—evident in the essays of 1915 to 1917 [39]—for the best way to formulate the ideal or hypothetical perceptions which seemed to be necessary additions to sense-data if a geometry, smooth and complete enough to be a scientific concept, was to be constructed.

In a note which Whitehead appended to *The Concept of Nature* while reading proof (this is in 1920) , he removes the limitation of significance to space-relations within a duration, and asserts that there is a significance of a percipient event "involving its extension through a whole time-system [of durations] backwards and forwards.[40] In other words the essential 'beyond' in nature is a definite beyond in time as well as in space " (CN p. 198) . The expansion pleases him, because it furthers the assimilation of time and space in one theory of extension.

Any reader of *Science and the Modern World* will see how readily this doctrine suggests the description given in that book, of the perceiver as cognizant of " aspects " of an entire universe of other events.

But Whitehead, while still engaged on the philosophy of

------

his position was not an incredible one: " I am quite willing to believe that recognition, in my sense of the term [i. e., as 'sense-recognition '], is merely an ideal limit, and that there is in fact no recognition without intellectual accompaniments of comparison and judgment. *But recognition is that relation of the mind to nature which provides the material for the intellectual activity.*" (Italics added.)

[39] Cf. AE pp. 160, 177 (IS pp. 24, 35) , 218-220.

[40] As he later puts it, " my life in the morning " and " my life in the afternoon of the same day " fit on to each other in a continuum apprehended as dominating my experience (" Uniformity and Contingency " [cited below, n. 42], p. 7; ESP p. 137; IS p. 113) .

natural science, carries the doctrine of significance well beyond the scope assigned to it in *The Concept of Nature*. In a lecture delivered in June, 1922,[41] he expounds it as central to the general question of the relation of finite to infinite: each finite fact is embedded in the whole of factuality, but a uniform significance, pervading experience in certain respects, makes it possible to know something without knowing everything. Whitehead's presidential address to the Aristotelian Society in November, 1922, is entirely concerned with the doctrine of significance.[42] It is there described as the doctrine of spatio-temporal relations covertly assumed by Hume, and the first conception that we have to make explicit if we are to solve the problem of induction bequeathed by him. Whitehead agrees with Hume's principle, that " there is nothing in a number of instances, different from every single instance, which is supposed to be exactly similar "; [43] he infers that " the key to the mystery is not to be found in the accumulation of instances, but in the intrinsic character of each instance "— " its significance of something other than itself." [44] Whitehead incidentally distinguishes his conception from those by which idealists have usually tried to secure the conformation of experience not yet examined to present experience. The main argument continues: the passage of the mind from sense-data to an ordinary perceptual object (e. g., of a dog's mind from " smell and a pat " to " master ") is in that address said to be no inference from a class of sense-data, but a further instance of significance: this is Whitehead's first adumbration of his conception of " symbolic reference," which gets fully developed in the little book on *Symbolism*, published in 1927. We must finally notice in this address an identification [45] of

[41] Before the Royal Society of Edinburgh. The lecture is printed as Chapter II in *The Principle of Relativity* (1922).
[42] " Uniformity and Contingency," *Proceedings of the Aristotelian Society*, n. s., 23 (1922/1923), 1-18; reprinted in ESP and IS.
[43] Essay VII, " The Idea of Necessary Connection," in Hume's *Philosophical Essays Concerning the Human Understanding*.
[44] *Op. cit.*, p. 14; ESP p. 144; IS p. 120. Compare SMW pp. 62 f.
[45] *Op. cit.*, p. 17; ESP p. 147; IS p. 123.

the converse of significance with the transmission of causal force from a focus throughout a field: apparently Whitehead, thinking often both of induction and of field physics, is slowly transmuting his idea of significance from a mere description of the spatial relatedness disclosed in a single perception, into a description of the causal bonds—prehensions—through which one occasion affects the rise of another in the creative advance of nature. In a few years that train of thought will be completed, and (in *Symbolism*) the concept of a secondary significance that is again purely spatial will be introduced as a product of the temporal action of prehensions.

Whitehead's investigation of significance cannot safely be assimilated to any other development in modern philosophy. With a non-Newtonian physics of vector fields in his mind, Whitehead seems to be giving us a progressive elaboration of the premise that " perception is a natural event."

Also in his mind is an inclination to think in terms of polyadic relations instead of being content with dyadic ones or, worse, with the substance-attribute relation. From the *Principles of Natural Knowledge* onwards, his treatment of sense-objects is intrinsically connected with his doctrine of the mutual significance of events by the concept called (in *The Concept of Nature*) "multiple ingression." "The sense-awareness of the blue as situated in a certain event which I call the situation, is . . . the sense-awareness of a relation between the blue, the percipient event of the observer, the situation, and intervening events " (CN p. 152). This doctrine is equally indispensable for Whitehead's discussion of Nature in *Science and the Modern World*.

VIII

There has thus far in this chapter been no occasion to allude to the school of modern realism. I think that no decisive influence from it is discernible in any of Whitehead's

writings prior to *The Principles of Natural Knowledge*; and
the main object of that book was easily describable without
reference to realistic doctrines. Whitehead does not write
his books out of a desire to decide the battles of epistemologists.
However, his familiarity with realistic doctrines is attested by
his reference, in the Preface, to discussions with Dawes Hicks
and T. P. Nunn, and, of course, Russell; and also by references
in later books. That his sympathies were with the realists as
against the idealists, there can be no doubt. But there is no
evidence in his books that he was a member of the Moore-
Russell school, as is commonly supposed. In fact, anyone who
accepts the doctrine of the rough world and the smooth world,
which is the central doctrine of his epistemological period
(1914 to 1917), will have Moore's and Russell's early epistemological essays thoroughly spoiled for him.

It is an important characteristic of Whitehead's *metaphysics*
that it is realistic, in a fundamental sense; this depends on
his pluralism, and his final doctrine of prehensions as causal
links. The natural philosophy of his 1920 books adumbrates
this metaphysical realism through its doctrine of the mutual
significance of events. But in these books the obvious realism,
which readers noticed and either hailed or rejected, is of a
more special kind. Its thesis is that immediate appearance is
a datum which, for the philosophy of natural science, can
and must be considered without reference to the mind to which
it appears. Whitehead makes the essential and simple claim
that when we make an observation we perceive something that
is not mind or thought. G. E. Moore's celebrated article, " The
Refutation of Idealism," had been one of the principal agents
—perhaps *the* agent—in getting this claim before the philosophic public. *The Aims and Achievements of Scientific
Method*, published in 1907 by Whitehead's friend Nunn, pro-
pounds a general doctrine of " the Objective " that was probably closer to his own mode of thought. " The Objective "
is a closed system, separate from and " prior " to perception
and thought; the chief basis of this assertion is " the direct
and simple perception of the presence of Objectivity as

such "; [46] also, the assumption of this objectivity is tacitly made in every scientific investigation. Both these arguments are congenial to Whitehead. But sufficient reasons for the realistic character of his philosophy of nature may be found by considering in order his statements: *1*) " Nature is the terminus of sense-perception "; *2*) " Nature is closed to mind " (CN p. 4).

1) The first statement itself includes two propositions, both of which are emphasized by Whitehead in this period, and which are too seldom distinguished by him. As defining the status of sensa for natural science, the statement is indispensable, and is never repudiated in Whitehead's writings. As a sweeping definition of nature, that is, of the subject matter of the natural sciences, the statement is thought indispensable, but is dropped in a few years. The point of the narrower proposition is that what is perceived is a part of nature and not merely content of mind; in fact, for natural science the datum is not mental at all. Whitehead subjects the opposite opinion to a variety of devastating criticisms, but it will be sufficient to state his reason for including this polemic in his exposition of the concept of nature—a reason noticed, he said, by hardly any of those who had commented on the polemic.[47] If what is perceived be considered a fact of individual psychology only, no assertions about nature can be verified (IS p. 155). This is the indispensable core of Whitehead's protest against bifurcation.

Just what the definition of nature as solely " the terminus of sense-perception " comes to, is very hard to say, in view of the broad manner in which—owing to his doctrine of significance—Whitehead understands sense-perception. Clearly his theory is no simple phenomenalism. But his often repeated references to " sense-awareness " have naturally led people to think of these books as phenomenalistic. An example is his declaration, in *The Principle of Relativity*, that " the keynote

[46] Nunn, p. 6.
[47] IS pp. 155 f.; originally in *Aristotelian Society Supplementary Volume*, 3 (1923), 41.

of everything " in that book is adherence to Poynting's aphorism, " I have no doubt whatever that our ultimate aim must be to describe the sensible in terms of the sensible " (R p. 5). Now " the sensible," in the philosophy of science, is a pinning-down word. I do not think Whitehead realized how very far he was from pinning himself down to its usual meaning. Of course, these contexts are complicated by his desire to pin Einstein down, and to make individual perceptivity the basis of relativity.

We can imagine several possible causes for Whitehead's adoption of this definition of nature, though we are in the dark as to their relative weights. He appreciated the new realism, and Bergson's emphasis on immediate intuition. But perhaps Whitehead's definition is also to be understood as the remaining effect of the narrow empiricism and the class-theory he was gradually shedding; perhaps he was much influenced by the importance of defining nature as one homogeneous subject; or by the fact that his defense of simultaneity would get no hearing on any other than an empiricist basis. Probably his choice of the definition was " instinctive " rather than the result of specific deliberation.

2) If we follow the course of the argument in the opening chapter of *The Concept of Nature,* the reason for adopting the closure of nature to mind is the adoption of the definition of nature described above, as " that which we observe in perception through the senses," followed by adoption of the realistic premise that the object of sense-observation is not thought but something which is " self-contained for thought " (CN pp. 3, 4). In his next chapter Whitehead gives other reasons—weightier, it seems to me—for closing nature to mind. These reasons would be sufficient even if nature were not defined in neorealistic fashion. The point is that the aim of the whole inquiry is not to state everything that is true about nature, but to express the unity of the initial subject matter of the natural sciences in a single concept, with interrelated factors. It is a fact, acknowledged by everyone, that the natural sciences form a group with a certain unity; and essential factors

in this unity are the assumption (made in every observation of nature) of the externality of nature to mind, and the concentration on that which is external. The study of mind forms another department of science, and the synthesis of nature and the observant mind is a task for metaphysics. Trying to embrace either of these other studies in the chosen inquiry is a fatal distraction: " It blows up the whole arena " (CN p. 29). What minds do in the natural sciences is not left out of the account, but on the contrary investigated; thus the mind—Whitehead usually writes " we "—achieves accuracy by confining its attention to places and times of small extent. But in all this the assumption of the externality of the object of the mind's attention is maintained. What has to be made explicit is the unity which nature has *for the natural scientist*.

It would be a great mistake to identify this point of view with that of positivism. Surely we must distinguish between a limited inquiry and the philosophic doctrine of positivism. Here are no declarations that metaphysics is merely emotive. Instead, Whitehead writes of the " need of a metaphysics whose scope transcends the limitation to nature " (CN p. 32). He postpones the attempt to satisfy that need, because there is another job which he must first do cleanly. Yet philosophers have been known to quote, " Nature is closed to mind," and disregard the sentence that follows it: " This closure of nature does not carry with it any metaphysical doctrine of the disjunction of nature and mind " (CN p. 4).

Whitehead's whole procedure here is really an example of one of his primary metaphysical tenets—that all achievement requires exclusion.

IX

The condemnation of the bifurcation of nature has probably been more debated than anything else in Whitehead's work. The core of his criticism has already been pointed out. We may add the observation that nothing was more natural for Whitehead than to criticize this bifurcation. For years he had been fastening on incoherence, or absence of rational connection, between two theories, each accepted; and particularly on incoherence in the theory of the relation of geometry to physics—" the muddle geometry had got into." Now he notes the general acceptance of a bifurcation of nature into data which appear to a mind, and are really subjective, mental, and private; and physical objects that cause perceptions to occur, but do not themselves appear at all. Yet the relational theory of space is also accepted, and rightly so. Take this relational theory seriously, and we must say that

> the space in which apparent nature is set is the expression of certain relations between the apparent objects. It is a set of apparent relations between apparent relata. . . . Similarly the space in which causal nature is set is the expression of certain relations between the causal objects. . . . of certain facts about the causal activity which is going on behind the scenes. Accordingly causal space belongs to a different order of reality to apparent space. Hence there is no pointwise connexion between the two. . . . The case is even worse if we admit the relativity of time.—CN pp. 41 f.

It was probably through some such line of thought as this, that Whitehead first became an enemy of bifurcation. In his logical-epistemological essay on the relational theory of space, written in 1914, he had, we remember, joined the analysis of the relational theory with the drawing of distinctions between the diverse meanings of " space," apparent or physical.

It should be noticed that the argument given above would not occur to anyone who had not passed beyond a purely logical point of view. The natural comment of a logician on the argument would be that it is the relations, not the relata, that are essential to geometry, which deals with any relata whatever, so long as they satisfy the specified relations. Whitehead would recommend the logician's point of view so far as research in geometry is concerned; but he is now asking how geometry applies to nature. The import of the relational theory is that the relata do make a difference; if they don't, we had better keep on with the clean and simple points of the absolute theory of space.

An important fact, which may be inferred from the preceding chapters of this Part but deserves to be stated explicitly, is that much of Whitehead's work in his second, or physical, period was instigated through the success of mathematicians in their investigations into the axioms of geometry. He observes that if the absolute theory of space be true, the mathematicians have said all that needs to be said about space (PNK Pref. and 2.1). But if points are not natural entities, a whole new region for inquiry appears: what *are* the entities of the spatial world we live in?

To recur to Whitehead's argument against bifurcation. Some philosophers think that it is essentially an attack on the causal relation as the instrument of physical explanation. They then infer that his metaphysics repudiates his philosophy of nature. In fact, the polemic contains no objection to causal explanation—*within nature*. (Whitehead draws the distinction: CN p. 31.) What he does require of the causal relation is exactly what he requires of every other relation employed in natural science: that it should operate in a single field, and not mysteriously leap a chasm between two alien types of entity, namely, material molecules and affections of the mind. Also, it is a mistake to suppose that causality enters into Whitehead's philosophy only with the lectures on *Symbolism*, delivered in 1927. What is true is that the role of causality is then greatly expanded. But his position now is (to quote from an explanation of the point of his chapter on bifurcation) :

> It is the problem of science to conjecture the characters in the three-way spreads [durations] of the past which shall express the dependence of the three-way spread of my present experience upon the past history of Nature. These characters are collections of molecules, . . . and light waves [in the case of vision] . . . , and finally disturbances in my body.—IS pp. 155 f.

Again, no objectionable bifurcation is introduced by recognizing that perceived change in what is regarded as the same object is a function of a number of variables. The causes of change may be as many and as complex as you please—provided only that they are not wholly alien in nature from the perceived datum that changes.

What must be acknowledged about Whitehead's protest against bifurcation is that in his zeal he overstates his case. Harping so much on "apparent nature," he must describe causes as "characters of apparent characters" (PNK 61), which does violence to what the scientist means by a cause. When he says, "Our experiences of the apparent world are nature itself" (R p. 62), the conception that these experiences, which display an apparent world, are processes of reception and appropriation of not-alien antecedent causal events, is needed to distinguish his resolution of bifurcation from that of ordinary scientific phenomenalism. For you cannot get away from a division into past world and present experience: you must unite the two through the idea of an immediate experience of causal process. This is what is supplied in 1927. A beginning for it was already made by the application of the doctrine of our awareness of significance to temporal extension, and by the doctrine of the "passage" of events. In Note II (written in 1924) to the second edition of *The Principles of Natural Knowledge*, Whitehead said of the first edition (1919) that ". . . the true doctrine, that 'process' is the fundamental idea, was not in my mind with sufficient emphasis."

X

The final comment to be made on the 1920 books is that there is both much more and much less in them than is commonly supposed. For example: Whitehead did not simply decide that the world consists of many actualities when he came to write a metaphysics. The 1920 books, which showed the preoccupation with the continuity of change that is natural for a man reforming the theory of space and time, also search for unities of rhythm which require blocks of time for their realization. In the magnificent attack on the classical conceptions of time, space, and matter with which *The Principles of Natural Knowledge* opens, not the least of Whitehead's criticisms is that the classical scheme makes such unities illusory or at the most derivative facts. The book closes with a chapter on rhythms, which adumbrates his later conception of " living occasions." In fact, the kinship of that final chapter with the whole theory of grades of organic and inorganic occasions that appears in *Process and Reality* will be evident to anyone who reads it.

There is also less in the 1920 books than is commonly found there. In order to " prevent the reader from bolting up side tracks in pursuit of misunderstandings," Whitehead began *The Concept of Nature* with two chapters of a philosophic character, which inevitably trod on the toes of some philosophers and elated others. As a result there has arisen a bad habit of discussing these philosophical chapters in separation from the inquiry to which they are but auxiliaries; and this habit (which in itself would not have such evil effects, if the chapters were but carefully read) has engendered the worse habit of forgetting the specific and philosophically limited context of all of Whitehead's assertions in each of these three books. This in spite of very plain warnings in the texts. These books are admittedly philosophical, but in a limited sense only:

> . . . ' philosophy' in this connection . . . is solely engaged in determining the most general conceptions which apply to things observed by the senses. Accordingly it is not even metaphysics: it should be called pan-physics.—R p. 4.

Moreover, there are specific warnings to philosophers not to look to " pan-physics " for solutions of metaphysical problems. The entire project is relative to the reorganization of physics.

Concerning " the values of nature," the introduction of which, in *Science and the Modern World*, surprised so many of the tough-minded, Whitehead wrote, " The values of nature are perhaps the key to the metaphysical synthesis of existence. But such a synthesis is exactly what I am not attempting" (CN p. 5). Of course,

> It is difficult for a philosopher to realise that anyone really is confining his discussion within the limits that I have set before you. The boundary is set up just where he is beginning to get excited.—CN p. 48.

Some philosophers are excited about teleology, perhaps rightly; but certainly they go wrong if they assert that "According to these . . . works the external world had little if any teleology within it," and argue that the subsequent expansion of the "events" of this Whiteheadian period into the "prehending subjects" of the philosophy of organism shows that Whitehead was driven to acknowledge his philosophy of natural science to be "weak," "inadequate," or "wrong."[48] The cause of the expansion is not so simple as this. Teleology in nature, or the efficacy of mental functionings in nature, is perfectly compatible with the answers the books of this period give to their own questions. They make no attempt to assess the degree or state the kind of teleology that exists; for their purpose no attempt is necessary, unless one believes that a man in love, for example, "necessarily measures space and time differently from a man given over to avarice."[49]

Whitehead's philosophy of nature, then, "speaks to the condition" of physics only. It cares not a whit for the intrinsic significance of any event.[50] The understanding of the physical

[48] David L. Miller, "Purpose, Design and Physical Relativity," *Philosophy of Science*, 3 (July, 1936), 267-285, esp. p. 268.

[49] Whitehead, replying to H. Wildon Carr in a symposium on the idealistic interpretation of the theory of relativity: *Proceedings of the Aristotelian Society*, n. s., 22 (1921/1922), 133 f.; in IS p. 147.

[50] The subject of this sentence is "It"—Whitehead's philosophy of nature—, not Whitehead. I assume that Whitehead cared. F. S. C. Northrop wrote recently, ". . . in the early 1920's when he took me page by page and chapter by chapter through *The Principles of Natural Knowledge* and *The Concept of Nature*, he often stopped to point out the aesthetic character of the concrete facts from which all science, philosophy and reflection take their inception."—Foreword to Donald W. Sherburne, *A Whiteheadian Aesthetic* (New Haven, 1961), p. xxviii.

level from the perspective of a metaphysical level is postponed. It is promised in the Preface to the second edition of *The Principles of Natural Knowledge,* written in August, 1924. Since " nature " is then used with a wider meaning," Whitehead's philosophy of natural science " is a better name for what we have been examining than " Whitehead's philosophy of nature."

We must not be so naïve as to suppose that any expanding and philosophic mind succeeds in confining itself absolutely to a specified level of thought. Whitehead's way of talking about the " creative advance " of nature, for example, is sometimes a metaphysical note in these books. There is in the production of ideas a ferment which interferes with their bottling. This remark applies in some degree to every part of Whitehead's work.

But the only course open to a philosophic critic who has doubts about Whitehead's philosophy of natural science is to show that in some respect—for example, in stating what we mean by measurement or by extension—Whitehead falsifies the *essential* character of all scientific investigation that is directed toward nature. Conversely, if a philosopher disbelieves, let us say, Whitehead's Platonism, he must criticize the doctrines of *Process and Reality*; he must not rest content with demolishing the special form in which that Platonism appears earlier—the theory of the " recognition of natural objects "— and then referring to *Process and Reality* merely in passing.[51] Nothing is proved by showing that a theory, offered as adequate for physics, is inadequate for metaphysics. And if it be shown that " recognition of objects " is not an irreducible *in physics,* that is a blow to the general (metaphysical) theory of objects, but no disproof of it; since the theories, and the physical-metaphysical relationship, and the possibilities of demonstration, are never so precisely drawn that this situation is an instance of the situation in formal logic where a universal proposition may be disproved by a single negative instance.

----

[51] Most of A. A. Bowman's extensive criticism of Whitehead, in Chap. 3 of his *A Sacramental Universe* (Princeton, 1939), rests on this mistake.

Chapter 9

The Third Period of Whitehead's Work, c. 1924-1947:

The Philosophy of Organism

I

For three reasons I count 1924 the first year of Whitehead's third period. (*1*) In that year he left England and his professorship in Applied Mathematics to take up an appointment (originally for five years) as Professor of Philosophy at Harvard; he held the position for thirteen years, and the American Cambridge was his home for the remainder of his life. (*2*) In the preliminary correspondence his letter of January 13, 1924, to an intermediary, Mark Barr, included these statements: " The post might give me a welcome opportunity of developing in systematic form my ideas on Logic, the Philosophy of Science, Metaphysics, and some more general questions, half philosophical and half practical, such as Education . . . I should greatly value the opportunity of expressing in lectures and in less formal manner the philosophical ideas which have accumulated in my mind." [1] This list of subjects includes areas of his previously published work and adds metaphysics, as a field in which he has ideas that he would like to develop. Thus both continuity and expansion are indicated. (3) Whitehead's bibliography includes nothing for 1924, but the one published item which he dated in that year, the Preface to the second edition of *The Principles of Natural Knowledge* ("August, 1924"), is accompanied by Notes which, as we shall see, show a very important movement beyond the point of view of the first edition (1919).

Whitehead's turning toward an all-inclusive speculative construction after his books on the philosophy of natural science ought not to surprise us. He had written several times of the need for a metaphysics which should synthesize mind with nature, and value with fact. In his Tarner Lectures of 1919 he had described the aim of philosophy as "attainment of some unifying concept which will set in assigned relationships within itself all that there is for knowledge, for feeling, and for emotion " (CN p. 2) —which is both an accurate prescription for the philosophy of organism, and the sort of conception of philosophy we should expect from the unusual mathematician who wrote the *Universal Algebra* and " Mathematical Concepts of the Material World."

But he was also led toward metaphysics by external events. (I do not mean that we can safely assign great weight to these external events.) His appointment to a philosophical professorship and his migration to America [2] probably stimulated him enormously. Also, tragedy has a liberating effect on minds that are capable of expansion. Probably the national tragedy and the personal tragedy of the war of 1914 to 1918 played a part in extending the horizon of his thoughts. However, in Whitehead's published work there is nothing which I can construe as conclusive evidence that but for these tragic events

---

[1] Quoted by W. E. Hocking in " Whitehead as I Knew Him," *Journal of Philosophy*, 58 (September 14, 1961), 508.

[2] Hocking's invaluable article (*op. cit.*) includes the only account so far published of how Harvard came to offer the appointment, and a persuasive explanation of part of its attractiveness to Whitehead.

he would never have written a metaphysics, and nothing I can construe as good evidence that his metaphysical views in the nineteen-twenties would have been markedly different. But in 1956 Bertrand Russell wrote about the 1918 death of Whitehead's younger son Eric in the war: " The pain of this loss had a great deal to do with turning his thoughts to philosophy and with causing him to seek ways of escaping from belief in a merely mechanistic universe." [3] Some day, I hope, biographers will find out what can be known, and will evaluate Russell's implication that Whitehead at one time privately favored a mechanistic world-view. Since Whitehead expresses substantial dissent from recent antimechanical systems of metaphysics, in his few published references to them, the tragedy of 1918 *may* have been a cause of his eventually working out his own system.

It seems likely that the production of a grand metaphysical scheme by Samuel Alexander somewhat encouraged him to try his hand. But although Whitehead thinks highly of Alexander's work, and has been sensitive to the lively originality of James and Bergson also, it is not easy to find in his metaphysical writings *clear demonstrations* of their influence either in his choice of problems or in the essentials of his solutions.[4]

As regards Bergson, it should be noted here that Whitehead's advance from physics to metaphysics is of an entirely different type from the French philosopher's. In an Aristotelian Society symposium on the question, " Time, Space and Material: are they, and if so in what sense, the ultimate data of science?," Mrs. Adrian Stephen (Karin Costelloe), a skillful interpreter of Bergson, said, " If our question were put to him, Bergson would, I think, reply: Material is the ultimate datum of science, space is the form which science imposes upon its objects, science cannot deal with time." [5]

[3] *Portraits from Memory* (London, 1956), p. 93.
[4] See Sect. X, below.
[5] *Problems of Science and Philosophy*, (" Aristotelian Society Supplementary Volume, 2 "; 1919), p. 87. The summary of his *Principles of Natural Knowledge*, mentioned and drawn upon in Sect. VI of the preceding chapter, was Whitehead's contribution to this symposium.

Whitehead's answer, however, is not, like this, *restrictive*. His advance is toward a single unifying concept, not toward a contrasting pair of concepts, the inferior member of which is to be supplied by physical science. When Whitehead first (in print) looks toward metaphysics, he writes that he hopes to *embody* his philosophy of nature " in a more complete metaphysical study " (PNK Preface to 2nd ed.) .

In all of Whitehead's later writings one can see that a strong motive for metaphysical exposition is his belief that the educated man's implicit conception of the universe has not responded to the advance from the seventeenth-century physics of inert matter to the late nineteenth-century physics of energetic vibrations described in terms of vectors. He sees that, whereas a number of philosophic systems have been produced in the modern period, it is not any system of philosophy, but the success of the materialistic ideas of science, which has shaped the philosophy unconsciously held by mankind. No epistemology and no philosophy of religion, but only a new and equally scientific set of ideas about nature and nature's relation to human experience, can hope to get this philosophy displaced.

There is no evidence in Whitehead's writings that any twentieth-century developments in the field of science lured him into metaphysics at this time. The four mathematical developments and the three physical developments earlier enumerated, had been active in his mind for many years. It is natural to include the quantum theory among influences on him; my impression, however, is that this was to him a supporting illustration rather than a formative influence in the creation of his atomic pluralism.[6] As for the theory of relativity, Whitehead had already made his response to it.[7]

[6] Robert M. Palter, *Whitehead's Philosophy of Science* (Chicago, 1960) , pp. 214-218, explains the relation of Whitehead's idea about " non-uniform objects " (in the 1920 books) and " primates " (in SMW) to Bohr's theory of the atom, and notes the complete absence of allusions to the post-1924 developments in quantum theory (or to their authors) in Whitehead's works.

[7] It used to be argued in some quarters that Whitehead was led beyond

Probably the scientific influences whose force on Whitehead increased at this time are those which would naturally accompany the turning of his gaze upon the vastness of the universe. Such are the statistical theory of physical laws and the general theory of evolution. The latter, it must always be remembered, is for Whitehead—who was born in 1861, and once visited Darwin's house—a real and living force, not an item in intellectual history; and that is a great advantage which his thinking enjoys over that of the present generation.

My general conclusion on this subject is that we should accept Whitehead's statement in the Preface to *Process and Reality*, dated January, 1929, that he is endeavoring to " compress the material derived from years of meditation " (though we may have to allow that the meditation was intensified after 1918). Indeed, no other supposition is compatible with the fact that in but a few years—years of university work—he constructed so intricate and so vast a system of philosophy, and expounded it in several books.

---

the 1920 books by difficulties in reconciling his realistic position in them with the physical theory of relativity, but this line of argument has tended to disappear. I see no evidence in Whitehead's writings that he was aware of any such difficulties. In the Aristotelian Society papers of 1922, " The Philosophical Aspects of the Principle of Relativity" and " The Idealistic Interpretation of Einstein's Theory " he considered and rejected the difficulties of this sort which idealistic philosophers had presented to him. In the first paper—a very penetrating treatment of its topic—he concluded as follows about the philosophical importance of relativity: " The general character of its importance arises from the emphasis which it throws upon relatedness. It helps philosophy resolutely to turn its back upon the false lights of the Aristotelian logic " (IS p. 143; the second paper is also reprinted in IS, with a slight error in its title).

It has also been said that Whitehead set about constructing a philosophy of organism because of the influence of some biologists—J. S. Haldane and L. J. Henderson have been named—upon him. Evidence of this has not, I believe, been published. It would be wrong to assume that there must have been a special influence of that sort at that time. After all, a great deal of Whitehead's life had been spent in conversation with friends who were engaged in every branch of scientific activity; for example, there were Bateson and Sir Henry Head, on the biological side. Furthermore, the concept of organism in Whitehead's metaphysics is by no means cut altogether, or even for the most part, out of biological cloth (see Sect. III, below).

II

Whitehead recognized that many problems were raised by the 1920 books. For one thing, his definitions of spatial concepts needed reconsidering. Their defect was brought out by Theodore de Laguna in 1921: if the definitions were correct, men *could not* have known what they meant by "points" before the days of the Michelson-Morley experiment. That is contrary to common-sense meanings, and to Whitehead's own appeal to common-sense meanings in his arguments defending the concept of simultaneity against Einstein's criticism. (The new construction by which Whitehead in *Process and Reality* overcomes this defect was briefly noticed in our third chapter.[8] We may add that his carrying it through to a new definition of a straight line without making any reference to processes of measurement is the final issue of one of the lines of emphasis we picked up in expounding the *Universal Algebra*;[9] and that we should not be surprised when we find this thinker including the definitions of the most general geometrical properties of the world in a book on metaphysics.)

The other problems that were leading him to the speculative theories of *Science and the Modern World* (1925) appear in the brief Notes to the second edition of *Principles of Natural Knowledge*. Since these Notes are not intelligible to a person who has not freshly studied the book, the leading problems will bear enumeration here.

In the first place, full abandonment of the class theory necessitates a full reconsideration of the question: What, in empirical terms, is a physical object? It is, however, impossible to answer that question without introducing the concept of possibility in addition to that of actuality. Also, Whitehead had noted that his general distinction between an "object"— i. e., what *can* recur—and an "event" followed roughly the lines of the general division between possibility and actuality;

---

[8] At the end of Sect. IV. See notes 38 and 39 there for references to De Laguna.

[9] Chap. 6, Sect. IV, above.

he would like to work out that division. Another contrast, which he had already suggested to be associated with the event-object distinction, is that between continuity and atomism. What is the sense in which an event is one thing? We must particularly ask about the events we directly live through, which are perceptions of durations.

What is most striking in these Notes is that Whitehead uses for the first time the phrases, " social entity " and " realisation." " The main point [concerning ' fuller and more systematic treatment ' of the fundamental concepts of events and objects] hinges onto the ingression of objects into social entities, and onto the analysis of the process of the realisation of social entitics " (PNK Note I). He also writes of a " duration " as " the realisation of a social entity " (Note III). The difference between the words " relatedness " and " realisation " is precisely the difference between the standpoint of the 1920 books and that of *Science and the Modern World*. The former books had set forth the extensive relatedness displayed in every duration and in the passage of durations. Whitehead's mind is now probably following the simple and important thought that relatedness does not just happen, but is the skeleton of an active process of becoming which, in ways that he wishes to analyze, is both a complex of objects and an outcome of other becomings.[10]

The passage from " relatedness " to " realisation " can also be looked upon as indicating that Whitehead, having begun with *the percipient event as one entity*, is now asking what is its internal process of constitution.

These Notes suggest pretty clearly that Whitehead thinks of the metaphysical study toward which he is heading, as something which is to work out those " implications " of his earlier ideas which when he wrote the book " had not shaped themselves with sufficient emphasis in my mind " (Note I).

---

[10] This transition in thought seems also to be at the bottom of the more complex transition from " nature lifeless " to " nature alive," which is described in *Nature and Life* (1934), pp. 20 ff. (as reprinted in MT pp. 200 ff.) .

(I do not think we may read "implications" in a strictly limited sense. An intention "to embody the standpoint of [the 1920 books] in a more complete metaphysical study" strictly implies some movement beyond their standpoint.)

It seems to me that the idea of significance, above all others, was in need of further elaboration. This is an indispensable idea, but so far it had hardly been more than asserted and assigned a variety of tasks. What does "significance" come to, as a factor in the universe? If the converse of the doctrine is that "Relations are perceived in the making and because of the making" (PNK 3.7), what is the story of their making?

It is reasonable to suppose that when Whitehead wrote the 1920 books he had such metaphysical problems as this vaguely in the back of his mind. That was the impression I got from him in later conversations (1936). Although you can say only one thing at a time and must exclude the wider problems from your explicit consideration, he remarked, it is a desideratum for thoroughgoing work to have them in the back of your mind, vaguely.

III

Two series of Lowell Lectures gave him the opportunity to complete the kind of work that, on his own view, should precede a full-scale attempt at metaphysical construction. Such construction is really the boldest of imaginative generalizations. Consequently it "must have its origin in the generalization of particular factors discerned in particular topics of human interest; for example, in physics, or in physiology, or . . . In this way the prime requisite, that anyhow there shall be some important application, is secured" (PR I i ii). To start from an eclectic point of view is to assure a result befitting a dilettante. Whitehead already had hold of an origin. In *Science and the Modern World* one of the two strands in his main line of generalization—that coming from physics—is woven.

The critical portions of the early chapters of this book are essentially restatements of the previous examination of perceptual knowledge that was made for the sake of the foundations of physics. It was through the contrast between what in *Science and the Modern World* are called the " separative character " and the " prehensive character " of space (SMW p. 90) that he had in the first article of the *Principles of Natural Knowledge* sharply distinguished his assumptions from those of scientific materialism. Again, that no element in our perceptual knowledge has the characteristic of being " simply located " in space and time (this " simple location " being the defining characteristic of matter, and being " the very foundation of the seventeenth century scheme of nature " [SMW p. 81]), had been very clearly set forth—without the use of that phrase, but with the help of the same quotation from Berkeley that starts the discussion in *Science and the Modern World* [11]—in a very fundamental passage in the *Principles of Natural Knowledge* (3.5, 3.6). In the broad sense of " significance " which, as in " Uniformity and Contingency," includes the contingent relatedness of objects as well as the uniform relatedness of events, the assertion of significance is identical with the claim that " among the primary elements of nature as apprehended in our immediate experience, there is no element whatever which possesses this character of simple location " (SMW p. 81) .[12]

If this be granted, the " organic theory of nature " is readily

[11] P. 95. The quotation is from Sect. 10 of the Fourth Dialogue of Berkeley's *Alciphron*.

[12] In *The Revolt Against Dualism* (La Salle, Ill., 1930; Chap. V), A. O. Lovejoy found seven meanings of " simple location " in Whitehead's texts. I doubt that this would have been possible, had the critic remembered that Whitehead was concentrating on the contrast between the classical conception of matter and our actual observations of place. Also, it seems to me that Whitehead's remarks on the connection between the idea of simple location and the relational view of space might not have puzzled Lovejoy (*Revolt*, p. 160) if he had stuck to *Whitehead's* conception of the relational view, instead of going afield to find in a definition by C. D. Broad the usual—and, he seems to assume, most proper—statement of the relational view. Broad's definition is quite foreign to all Whitehead's discussions of that subject.

reached from the position of the 1920 books by thinking of their "percipient event" as a temporal process with an internal constitution, and making the following steps.[13]

1) The "unity of the perceptual field," which had been set down as an ultimate character of observations, is interpreted as "what it claims to be: the self-knowledge of our bodily event" (SMW p. 103).

2) The previously discriminated awareness, in the percipient event, of "significance" of all other events with respect to it as a focus, is converted into a process of awareness of aspects of all other events as "grasped into a unity," or "prehended," in the bodily event (p. 98). The unity is called an "organism," its constituents being concurrent (more accurately, as in *Process and Reality*, concrescent) prehensions. By "organism," Whitehead generally means a temporally bounded process which *organizes* a variety of given elements into a new fact.[14]

3) The occurrence of an organism is described as "something which is for its own sake," or the emergence of a particular *value* in the world. Whitehead argues, "These unities, which I call events, are the emergence into actuality of something. How are we to characterise the something which thus emerges? . . . no one word can be adequate. But conversely, nothing must be left out. . . . 'Value' is the word I use for the intrinsic reality of an event" (p. 131). This is extremely important.

4) On the principle that the bodily event is a natural event in nature, the generalization is made that every event in nature arises as a unity of concurrent prehensions (p. 103), and is an emergence of value.

5) This conception of natural events is applied to the problem of mechanism and freedom: since every event arises as a prehension of its environment, the characters of the events

[13] I do not say that Whitehead wrote *Science and the Modern World* by going through these steps.
[14] Sect. II of "Time," *Proceedings of the Sixth International Congress of Philosophy* (New York, 1927); reprinted in IS.

in the human body are not entirely determined by any absolute properties of the components of bodies in general (molecules), but are modified by the fact that the molecules are in the total organism of the body (the theory of " organic mechanism ") (pp. 108-112).

6) The persistence or endurance characteristic of matter is explained (pp. 152 ff.) as reiteration of the same pattern in a succession (the " nexus " of *Process and Reality*) of events that prehend each other.

7) It is explained how biological evolution, or the rise of complex organisms, is describable in terms of the maintenance and alteration of such nexūs. " Enduring things are . . . the outcome of a temporal process; . . . Only if you take *material* to be fundamental, this property of endurance is an arbitrary fact at the base of the order of nature; but if you take *organism* to be fundamental, this property is the result of evolution." [15] The concept later called " creativity " is introduced, as a " substantial activity " " underlying " the evolution of the organisms in which it is embodied; this is said to be required by the doctrine of evolution. (But the concept almost immediately becomes a universal category, not limited to processes of biological evolution.)

8) Whitehead had earlier said (CN p. 54) that the process of nature is more than a measurable extended continuum. He now says that the continuum omits the process by which an individual event comes into being. But that is what is happening. Temporal process, then, is a discrete succession of epochs, or arrests, each being the duration required for the emergence of a prehensive unity as a single fact (SMW p. 177). (This is the " epochal theory of time," which might better have been called the epochal or atomic theory of process.)

9) There is a general description of the quantum character

---

[15] SMW pp. 152, 154; cf. p. 152: " On the materialistic theory, there is material—such as matter or electricity—which endures. On the organic theory, the only endurances are structures of activity, and the structures are evolved."

of physical action as a fact to be expected if nature is conceived as a complex of organisms.

10) In each of the above steps, objects are implicated along with events, in accordance with their dual association as described in Whitehead's preceding books. In addition, the realm of objects is widened by being explicitly identified with the realm of possibility (pp. 222 ff.) . The emergence of new properties in events, which is required for (7) , is due to the prehension of objects other than those that characterize the events prehended.

This enumeration is not, of course, intended as a substitute for a logical analysis. The appeals to evidence are also omitted. (Their general character will appear in the final sections of this chapter and the opening section of the next.)

It may be useful to remark that Whitehead has not yet, at this point, got his labels fixed; so that he often uses " event," " prehension," and " organism " synonymously, and even says, " A ' prehension ' is a ' prehensive occasion ' " (SMW p. 101) . In *Process and Reality* a determinate terminology is introduced: " prehensions " are the threads of process, the vectors, between " actual occasions," which are concrescent unities analyzable into such threads.

In addition to the argument just summarized, Whitehead's writings contain another line, of comparable importance, which leads from physics to metaphysics. This second line is occasionally discussed in *Science and the Modern World* in connection with the main argument. It may be found clearly presented in its own unity in *Nature and Life* (1934) . It does not begin with Whitehead's own analysis of physical observation, but with the general character of physical theory in which mass is subordinated to energy, and " simple location " has evaporated, being replaced by vector relations and fields; Whitehead's generalization proceeds toward a panpsychistic type of metaphysics.

IV

We now come to the generalization from religious experience. It is the topic of the four Lowell Lectures which Whitehead gave in 1926 and published that year with the title, *Religion in the Making*. He published no extended discussion of religion before " Religion and Science," which appeared as a chapter of *Science and the Modern World* the year before. Our ignorance of what he earlier thought but did not publish is vast. Consequently, what we can say about religion in the development of his philosophy must be brief out of all proportion to its final importance.

We know from his Autobiographical Notes (LLP-W) that religion was an important element in his childhood and youth. Sir Edmund Whittaker wrote in his obituary notice of Whitehead: " His father, an Anglican of the Evangelical school, brought him up in an atmosphere of simple and even narrow piety. As an undergraduate, he talked openly and often to his friends about religion, and especially about his interest in Foreign Missions." [16] Bertrand Russell says, " As a young man, he was all but converted to Roman Catholicism by the influence of Cardinal Newman." [17] (The Whitehead we knew at Harvard held Newman as a thinker in high regard.) Lucien Price, reporting Whitehead's conversation of November 2, 1940, writes:

> He told of an episode early in their wedded life when they had read a great many books on theology. This study went on for years, eight of them, I think he said. When he had finished with the subject, for he *had* finished with it, he called in a Cambridge bookseller and asked what he would give for the lot.[18]

Whittaker records that Whitehead's early religious convictions

[16] *Obituary Notices of Fellows of the Royal Society*, VI (1948), p. 293.
[17] *Portraits from Memory*, p. 96.
[18] *Dialogues of Alfred North Whitehead* (Boston, 1954), Dialogue XIX.

" lost their hold on him [he mentions no year], and for a time he became an outspoken and even polemical agnostic." [19] Russell has confirmed this for me: " Throughout the time that I knew him well—that is to say, roughly, from 1898 to 1912—he was very definitely and emphatically agnostic." [20] According to Whittaker, " This phase again did not endure, and in mature life there was a reflux towards spiritual belief: *Process and Reality* is theistic . . ." We should add, that this element in *Process and Reality* is an original and profound philosophical theology.

Like the great majority of Whitehead readers, I find it impossible to read that theology and the discussions of religion in any of Whitehead's metaphysical books—beginning with the first, in 1925—except as written by a deeply religious man, though a man who retained a highly critical attitude toward church creeds and toward traditional separations of God from the world. When and how Whitehead ceased to be an agnostic is a question which we must leave to future biographers, if they wish to pursue it.

Because his concept of God is indispensable to the coherence of the realm of possibility with the realm of actuality, and because he endeavors to assimilate the formal characteristics of God to those of every other actual entity, it is sometimes supposed that Whitehead's God is a mere binder for the theoretical structure of the philosophy of organism, and lacks all religious character. The criticism is based either on a misunderstanding of what system is for Whitehead and why he seeks it, or on a limited range of religious feeling. For the extreme position taken by W. Mays throughout his *Philosophy of Whitehead* [21]—namely, that when Whitehead wrote about God he was only writing in obscure language about the logical structure of space-time—I have been unable to find in Whitehead's books any justification that goes beyond the sort of thing we noted on p. 110, above.

[19] *Loc. cit.*
[20] Letter of September 26, 1959.
[21] London and New York, 1959.

Though Whitehead's basic metaphysical concepts—creativity, prehension, eternal objects, actual occasions—had made their bow in the latter chapters of *Science and the Modern World*, the best introduction to their metaphysical relationships occurs in Chapter III, Section iii of *Religion in the Making*. That Section is preceded by a lucid statement of Whitehead's view of the relation between metaphysics and religion. Much of the remainder of the book is metaphysical exposition, and some of this, to my mind, is not lucid. Probably Whitehead was on his way to something further; at any rate, his expositions in later books often seem more comprehensible as well as more comprehensive.

To present a short description of the way in which the author of what I have called " the 1920 books " now handles religion, I cannot do better than quote Mason W. Gross: " Just as in his works on the philosophy of science Whitehead sought in experience the roots of the scientific concepts, so here he seeks the basis of religious concepts in religious experience and traces the growth of dogmatic theology from those roots " (N&G p. 469). It is a small book; it does not contain much history of theology, but the reflections on evil and on concepts of God, in addition to those on topics we discussed in Chapter 4, are priceless.

V

The most casual reader of *Science and the Modern World* will observe that no account of sense-perception alone can possibly provide an epistemology corresponding to the " organic theory of nature." That theory implies that our *general* response to nature, or prehension of our environment, includes a reception of causality: the " intrinsic reality " of one event is affected by the " extrinsic reality " of another. But this was not elaborated. The main outline of Whitehead's mature epistemology is laid down in another book (*Symbolism, Its*

Meaning and Effect [1927]) which precedes the publication of his metaphysics. Thereafter, he writes more about the Hume-Newton situation than about the Newtonian deposition. Two thoughts guide his criticism: that Hume's otherwise accurate description of sense impressions omitted the fact that they are perceived as significant of existent things; and that sense-perception is the superficial part of our experience, causal experience of existents being fundamental. In every succeeding book the strength and centrality of his conviction about the superficiality of sense-perception grows greater.

There is no need to hunt for a cause for the omission of the perception of causal efficacy from Whitehead's writings on the philosophy of natural science. Scientific observations are perceptions of sense-data. Whitehead comes to another kind of experience when he comes to consider other aspects of human activity. Even in the scientific field he had limited himself to the perceptual basis; he might, I imagine, have now proceeded by examination of the character of scientific laws.[22] His main course, perhaps more natural for an empiricist who is also trying to englobe physical science in a wider sphere, is a more general examination of experience—beginning with our feeling of the efficacy of the body in sense-perception.

An auxiliary course is more closely connected with Whitehead's earlier work: in a valuable paper of 1926 [23] he arrives at the causal character of physical prehension through an analysis of time. That paper includes Whitehead's first exposition of his new theory that the perception of sense-data is an act of "physical imagination, in a generalized sense of the word" [24]—an act that is useful because of a symbolic reference to causal actualities.

In *Symbolism*, Whitehead's theory of perception suffers from

[22] There were starting points for such an examination in his 1920 books, and in his paper of 1922 on "Uniformity and Contingency." Whitehead's final position on scientific laws appears in Chaps. VII and VIII of *Adventures of Ideas* (1933).
[23] "Time," *Proceedings of the Sixth International Congress of Philosophy*, pp. 59-64; reprinted in IS.
[24] *Ibid.*, Sect. v.

a confusion which seems to be due to his tendency to think
of the two elements of a dualism as on a par with each other.[25]
Thus he balances "the two pure modes of perception"
("causal efficacy" and "presentational immediacy"), and
discusses their "intersection." At the same time, he obviously
believes that perception of causal efficacy is by far the more
fundamental. In *Process and Reality* Whitehead will assign
an experience of "sensa" to even the lowest grades of
actual existents, after introducing a completely generalized
meaning of the term (we shall see the importance of this in
Chapter 14, Section IV). Readers must take care not to be
confused by his continued use of "sensum" and "sense-
perception" in many discussions (especially in *Adventures of
Ideas*) in their customary meanings, which presuppose an
organism with sense organs.

We should remember that Whitehead's thought in 1927 was
preceded by a stage in which—as I interpret it—causality was
not fully analyzed. A contemporary world of things was
assumed as a datum, and the characteristics of the sense-data
were related together by a primarily atemporal theory of their
multiple inherence in events. Their transmission and generation could not be fully treated in the absence of a theory of the
full functioning of events. There was a systematic relatedness
evident in nature which had to be got hold of somehow—
from some limited standpoint. One does not, at first trial,
find the conception that is adequate for all purposes. Whitehead got hold of "significance in a presented duration," and
expanded the notion and shifted its emphasis as he expanded
his field of inquiry. On passing from examination of perception to examination of experience, he adopted the view that
it is the *antecedent* environment that is the datum for an
occasion of experience.[26] Then there is no awareness of absolutely contemporary occasions: *they* constitute no datum for
the present. But after that we find, as we must expect, that
some of Whitehead's discussions of the contemporary world

---

[25] See p. 253, below.
[26] Why he adopted this will be discussed in Sect. VIII, below.

retain language which, as ordinarily used, is appropriate only if that world is considered as a datum.

It is of the essence of the philosophy of organism that its epistemological realism is based squarely on the rehabilitation of causality. If Hume is right about sense-data, then a realist must appeal to some other given, unless he is to abandon all idea of providing his " common world " with empirical credentials. In fact, this is no predicament, but an opportunity for the realist to build a much deeper realism than is possible on a phenomenalistic basis. For " experience," instead of being a " selection " of sense-data—a notion that is logically possible, but which has no evidence in its favor and requires a devious recasting (at best) of the physiological evidence—instead of this, experience becomes an individual reaction to things which exist for their own sakes and are felt as imposing their own weight and value on the experient. (A doctrine of " real " causality I take to be indispensable for a system of realistic pluralism. With causality accepted, one can proceed to work out a scheme in which, " though each event is necessary for the community of events, the weight of its contribution is determined by something intrinsic in itself " [SMW p. 147].)

One of the many important functions of the theory of symbolic reference in Whitehead's philosophy is to replace the principle of inferential constructions which we discussed earlier.[27] It was faulty psychology to try to explain our knowledge of common-sense objects entirely in terms of that principle (S 1 2). But on looking at this change from a broad point of view, we can see the similarity of approach as between Whitehead's prespeculative epistemology and the epistemology which he now develops to be the empirical anchorage of his metaphysics. Both were written out of an awareness of a fundamental contrast in experience—between elements of inescapable actuality, and the response of thought, creating elements that provide " accurate definition." The contrast is pushed to a deeper level in the second inquiry—that is all. The sense-perceptions which constituted the primordial pole

[27] Pp. 184-186, above.

THE PHILOSOPHY OF ORGANISM: V

in the first inquiry—rightly, in view of the limitation to the observational basis of natural science—have become the derivative pole now.

The intermediate period, in which common-sense objects have an independent but not clearly elucidated status with respect to sense-data, began with the adoption of "significance" and the event-object duality in the *Principles of Natural Knowledge*. Five years after its publication it appeared to Whitehead that he had been "wavering between the 'class-theory' of perceptual objects and the 'control-theory' of physical objects" (Note III to 2nd ed.). He added that he had been trying to get away from the class-theory, and no longer held it in any form. The word "control" first appeared in the Aristotelian Society address of November, 1922, "Uniformity and Contingency," as referring to control of the ingression of sense-objects into events by objects of other types. This notion of control was an expansion of the notion of significance.[28]

The theory of symbolic reference effects a considerable change, or rather expansion, of Whitehead's theory of space-time. The theory becomes more plausible (and also more complicated, so that it is difficult to understand its details from the imperfect exposition given in Part IV of *Process and Reality*). When nature is no longer conceived as only the terminus of sense-perception, but as a cumulative nexus of occurrences, it is hard to suppose that the spatio-temporal relatedness throughout the entire universe is uniform; in fact, it is impossible to do so while holding—as Whitehead does—that the spatio-temporal relations are the outcome of the natures of the occurrences, and with these natures shift from cosmic epoch to cosmic epoch. Thus the uniform geometry of the 1920 books does not characterize the universe

---

[28] See the discussion of the address in the preceding chapter; also Palter, *Whitehead's Philosophy of Science*, Chap. VII, Sects. 1, 6. An excellent detailed examination of Whitehead's successive treatments of perception was made by Prof. Paul F. Schmidt in his doctoral dissertation (Yale, 1952; unpublished). There are probably others.

itself. But that geometry was always assumed to be a public fact given in relation to a percipient standpoint, and such givenness is still held to occur; it becomes a natural event with its cause, context, and purpose. The act of "spatialization" (as it can accurately be called) is part of the process of responding to the qualitative and geometrical complexity of the world of things by transmuting it into a definitely colored and uniformly structured "projected" field which appears as given. This is an act which animals have learned to perform through long ages of the evolution of their sense-organs and nervous systems.

The theory of symbolic reference has, if I am not mistaken, a very great importance, entirely apart from the role it plays in Whitehead's speculative construction. But this is not the place to urge philosophers to work with it. My final comment on the theory must concern the belief of some philosophers, that it is its author's way of returning to the bifurcation of nature which he had previously condemned. To those who bifurcate nature, the connection between private sense-data and physical causes must finally be summed up in the word, "somehow" (sometimes dressed up as "animal faith" or "peculiar but well-known transcendent reference"); and only the sense-data are experienced. Whitehead admits, nay insists upon, the numerical and qualitative distinction between sense-data and things. But (1) he has offered a theory of the "somehow"; (2) this theory is based on an independently established doctrine that we experience causes. The defect I think I find in Whitehead's earlier description of nature has been mentioned above.[29] The supposition that he reaffirms the bifurcation he had previously condemned is often aided by passing in discussion from the 1920 books to *Symbolism*, in defiance of the difference between them in subject-matter and in the aim of the analysis.

[29] Chap. 8, end of Sect. IX.

VI

In the succession of Whitehead's books the generalizations from science and religion, and his epistemological statement, are followed by the full metaphysical scheme (*Process and Reality*). This statement will not be misleading if we remember that Whitehead had all his life been reflecting on (and probably generalizing about) other matters which are very important for his kind of metaphysics. Art and the history of European civilization should particularly be mentioned. His sustained treatment of them did not appear in print until *Adventures of Ideas* was published in 1933. But we are told in its Preface that some lectures given at Dartmouth College in 1926 "embodied a preliminary sketch" of its topic. This was but two years after he exchanged his obligations as a Dean and Professor of Applied Mathematics in the University of London for those of a Professor of Philosophy. Lucien Price reports that on June 19, 1945, Whitehead said: "My writings on philosophy were all after I came to this country; but the ideas had been germinating in me for the better part of a lifetime." [30]

In Chapters 1 and 2 we became acquainted with Whitehead's conception of the ideal of a metaphysical system. It is a foregone conclusion, as we can now see, that the form of his system will be semimathematical. An exposition closer than Whitehead's to the axiomatic method in mathematics may perhaps be made of this cosmology by someone in the future. The expression of metaphysical schemes in symbolic logic has not yet progressed very far. But it is important now to realize that the semimathematical method employed in *Process and Reality* is not a result of the *bare fact* that the author happened to have been a mathematician before he became a philosopher. The method is semimathematical because the

---

[30] *Dialogues of Alfred North Whitehead*, Dialogue XL. The impression I got from talking with Whitehead accords with this.

author is aiming at a single concept of the universe, in which
the various ideas form a natural circle from which none can
be excised without leaving a gap between principles concerning
the others—for each fundamental idea is metaphysical, i. e.,
expresses an ultimate factor relevant to everything that happens. Now the various ideas in a branch of mathematics form
such a natural circle. In fact mathematics, divested of its
limitation to quantity and number, is in Whitehead's view
nothing but the instrument for expressing such connectedness.
(Also, as in speculative philosophy, there are alternative circles,
some wider than others.)

I am not forgetting that one of the famous sentences in
Process and Reality is, "Philosophy has been misled by the
example of mathematics" (I i iii). What is referred to in
that dictum is the fact that the great historical branches of
mathematics have been able to start from premises which were
reasonably regarded as clear, distinct, and certain (and the
secondary fact that mathematicians have been able to use
ex absurdo arguments with a justified freedom, because in
practice there was little doubt as to which premise was at
fault). Philosophical discussion, Whitehead holds, is not
mathematical deduction, but an examination and generalization of experience. Neither the philosopher, nor the scientist,
should look *first* to mathematics—that is medievalism. But
when the universal factors of experience have been so far as
possible discerned, the effort to understand their operation
should proceed by conjecturing a scheme, in form analogous
to a set of interrelated assumptions, primitive ideas, and
definitions. The reason for this ideal is at bottom the same
as the reason for unitary theory in any science. *Whitehead*
could have recommended nothing else.

He places much emphasis upon the metaphysical desideratum which he calls "coherence." Its pursuit in a limited area
was evident in his philosophy of nature. Since critics of his
turn to metaphysics tend to forget this, I set down a few
passages from the 1920 books.

The false idea which we have to get rid of is that of nature as a mere aggregate of independent entities, each capable of isolation. According to this conception these entities, whose characters are capable of isolated definition, come together and by their accidental relations form the system of nature. . . . With this theory space might be without time, and time might be without space. [Compare Whitehead's reference to Descartes' philosophy as an example of " incoherence," in Section ii of the first chapter in *Process and Reality*.] . . . The explanation of nature which I urge as an alternative ideal to this accidental view of nature, is that nothing in nature could be what it is except as an ingredient in nature as it is. . . . An isolated event is not an event. . . . The isolation of an entity in thought, when we think of it as a bare ' it,' has no counterpart in any corresponding isolation in nature. Such isolation is merely part of the procedure of intellectual knowledge.—CN pp. 141 f.

The point of this doctrine [the doctrine of " significance "] on which I want to insist is that any factor, by virtue of its status as a limitation within totality, necessarily refers to factors of totality other than itself.—R p. 17.

And the key passage which we quoted in our last chapter:

. . . in the place of emphasising space and time in their capacity of disconnecting, we shall build up an account of their complex essences as derivative from the ultimate ways in which those things, ultimate in science, are interconnected.—PNK 1.5.

In *Process and Reality*, " the ideal of speculative philosophy that its fundamental notions shall not seem capable of abstraction from each other " is intended to be met by the cosmological principle that " the process, or concrescence, of any one actual entity involves the other actual entities among its components " (PR I i i, ii) .

Here a conviction which Whitehead probably acquired early in his association with Russell comes to play a role in the construction of his metaphysics: his conviction of the inadequacy of the subject-predicate logic. Whitehead thinks—I believe rightly—that the orthodox conception of " having an experience " has been shaped according to the subject-predicate mould: the experient is the subject, and is qualified by his sensations. In *The Principle of Relativity* Whitehead had said,

> If you once conceive fundamental fact as a multiplicity of subjects qualified by predicates, you must fail to give a coherent account of experience. The disjunction of subjects is the presupposition from which you start, and you can only account for conjunctive relations by some fallacious sleight of hand, such as Leibniz's metaphor of his monads engaged in mirroring. The alternative philosophic position must commence with denouncing the whole idea of ' subject qualified by predicate ' as a trap set for philosophers by the syntax of language.— R pp. 13 f.[31]

Thus Whitehead's philosophic endeavor is to state literally that coherence of ultimate factors which Leibniz could express only metaphorically.

In philosophy as it has come down to us, *dualisms* form, with multiple solipsisms, the two main types of incoherence. The source of multiple solipsisms is the dualism of subject and object, the private and the public. The *duality* of private subject and public object is a fundamental fact stamped on the face of experience. To achieve coherence, Whitehead begins with this principle: " The sole concrete facts, in terms of which actualities can be analysed, are prehensions [of objects by subjects]; and every prehension has its public side and its private side " (PR IV i v) . But, further, his basic conceptions are intended to be so inclusive in scope, and so interlocked, as to overcome all the classical dualisms of metaphysics: mind and matter, God and the world, permanence and transience, causality and teleology, atomism and continuity, sensation and emotion, internal and external relations, etc., as well as subject and object. Thus, e. g., " physical " inheritance from the environment and novel " mental " reaction to it, are

---

[31] See also: IS pp. 138 f., CN p. 150, AI VIII vii; on " experience," PR II vii i.

both, in principle, ascribed to *every* occasion, as respectively
its public basis and its private culmination. It makes no
difference that the "mentality" involved in inorganic occasions is slight in proportion as spontaneity is negligible. The
objections to this are not as good as the objections to calling
" zero " a number.

VII

There is a human temptation for idealists to believe that
in erecting his metaphysics Whitehead in fact turned his back
on "his previous realism." But, as may be seen from our
discussion in Section VIII of the preceding chapter, that
realism was relative to a limited purpose. The closure of
nature to the observing mind, interpreted as it was intended
to be interpreted, is not repudiated at any later point. In
Whitehead's metaphysics, it is true, sense-data are creations of
mentality; but this is *on Whitehead's definition* of mentality,
which is so far from the idealistic epistemologist's notion of
the conscious mentality of the observing human mind that
it might be called, *per contra*, biological. The creation is
really a transmutation (so evolved in man's history as to be
now automatic) of given elements which are physical. There
is compensation for idealists in the fact that Whitehead's
final account of the occurrence of sense-perception is equally
distant from the account given in G. E. Moore's " Refutation
of Idealism."

Idealists are right in seeing *a certain* kinship between Whitehead's pursuit of a coherent scheme and their pursuit of a
coherent system of experience; there is much difference in
the. *manner* of the pursuit.

The world, as Whitehead finally describes it, is in some
fundamental respects similar to the world idealism has traditionally pictured. His working hypothesis is that the structure
of every organism is analogous to that of an occasion of experience. (I do not see what other hypothesis would be compatible

with the aim at the coherence of all human experience and all nature.) The employment of the hypothesis consists in rounding out our immediate knowledge of our experiences by interpreting them in the light of what we know of other events in nature,[32] and conversely interpreting the other events in the light of the generic traits of the experiences we live through.[33] Thus Whitehead tries to make full utilization of natural science and of immediate experience.

A result is that he ascribes value, feeling, purpose to every actuality. This accords with the results of idealistic philosophies. But the setting of the metaphysical problem is realistic. What is "experience?" It is "the self-enjoyment of being one among many, and of being one arising out of the composition of many" (PR II vi i). Whitehead starts as the American realists did, with the notion of a "common world" in which we find ourselves, a world full of minds and of other things which also exist in their own right.

The important moral for idealism concerns the way in which teleology and value took their place in this philosophy. Whitehead's difference from others who arrive at idealism from the study of physics, lies in the fact that he did *not* look at the structure of the spatio-temporal continuum, or some other aspects of the physical scheme, and ask, "What role did mind play here?" or "How is all this understandable without teleology?" He first examined the logical and empirical defects in the orthodox scientific conception of nature ("scientific materialism"); then he proposed an amazingly detailed, comprehensive theory of nature—nature taken, as the scientist must take her, in and for herself; he next examined our immediate, naïve experience of nature and our practice of life (and appealed to the romantic poets to remind us "how strained and paradoxical is the view of nature which modern science imposes on our thoughts" [SMW p. 118]);

---

[32] For example, we know—and Whitehead takes it very seriously—that man is one of the animals.

[33] An example is the fourth step in the account I gave of the argument of *Science and the Modern World* (Sect. III, above).

then, and then only, guided by the rationalist ideal of one set of concepts in which human experience and physical nature are understood together, he framed such an account of the teleologic and nonteleologic factors involved in our experience as allows of their universal conjoint application in the understanding of existence. (Anybody can raise a cry about " the omissions of science.")

VIII

One very important originative factor in the development of Whitehead's philosophy has not yet been taken up in this Part. I shall introduce it by considering again the doctrine of the little book on *Symbolism*, which lies at the very heart of Whitehead's philosophy. When a student finishes the first two chapters of this book and turns to the third, where the meaning and effect of symbolism in human society are discussed, he is likely to stop because the epistemological analysis is over. If he does, he misses the true Whitehead altogether. Although the arguments of the first two chapters are not as a rule dependent on any other considerations for their validity, they are dependent on the third chapter for their full setting and import. The evidence from which the epistemology grows has a much wider base than inspection of given experience (about which disagreement is notorious) . Whitehead's central doctrine of causal inheritance seems to me to have sprung chiefly from his reflections on the characteristics of human society. The reflections are of the sort made, on a smaller scale, by Burke in his conception of " prejudice." Whitehead sees the actual, specific character of human individuals, and the specific character of a part of human society (say, New England) , and the specific character of a home, or of a tree, as the outcome of an inescapable inheritance transmitted from the past, and of sporadic or purposed deviations from that inheritance. Such a conclusion is obvious to an Englishman who dispassionately considers the institutions, the edifices, the customs about him. In an article on "The Education of an Englishman," [34] Whitehead describes this beautifully. But anyone can see the truth in his point of view, merely by observing the comparatively insignificant effect which the actually presented sense-data of the moment have in determining the diverse judgments, mental processes, and reactions of different men; the cumulative effect of personal and social history is what counts most.

Some critics, observing the humanistic setting of Whitehead's argument in *Symbolism,* condemned him for giving us generalities instead of the accurate logical analyses of his earlier books. They forgot that the subject matter was not the same. Eventually, Whitehead hoped, we may be able to use symbolic logic in the description of our experience generally, not merely of its spatio-temporal aspects. For the present, we must look for generic traits and formulate them as well as we can.

A cardinal point about his humanistic reflections on man is that the concept of evolution (not necessarily progress), biological, sociological, intellectual, constantly colored and reinforced them. Whitehead believed that when a philosopher talks, say about language and reality, he should not forget that the precise entities he is holding up "by the scruff of the neck" for examination did not long have their present character, and are not going to keep it for long; they are occurrences thrown up from a long, long past. The eternally fixed term ought to have gone out of philosophical discussion when the eternally fixed species went out of biology. The retention of the former gives a show of exactness; but "the exactness is a fake." [35]

When we discussed Whitehead's way of handling the scien-

---

[34] *Atlantic Monthly,* 138 (August, 1926), 192-198; reprinted in ESP and AESP.

[35] From Sect. xix of Whitehead's last lecture, "Immortality" (in LLP-W, ESP, and IS). For the connection with the presumption of the fixity of species, see his first paragraph in Sect. x.

tific concepts of space and time,[36] we became acquainted with
his view that exactness should be pursued but never assumed,
that humans ought to be aware of the roughness of their
knowledge, consider what assumptions they are making, and
advance by defining routes of approximation; and we noted
that he found this as true concerning social and political
matters as it is for points and instants. Here is a consistent
strain which runs through all of Whitehead's thought, bursts
into print with the doctrine of the rough world and the
smooth world in the essays of 1915 to 1917, and continues to
increase in force. An incidental fact, amusing if not significant, is that Whitehead's first serious publication, a paper in
mathematical physics dated 1888, bears the subtitle, "A
method of approximation." [37]

To recur to the doctrine of evolution. The bifurcation of
nature that Whitehead condemned in *The Concept of Nature*
became prominent as an effect of the transmission theories of
seventeenth-century physics on the common-sense conception
that matter is the passive support of qualities. But there is
also in modern philosophy a bifurcation of experience into
experience as given datum and experience as process of reaction to the environment. This bifurcation became acute for
cosmology with the emergence of evolutionary ideas and biological accounts of experience in the nineteenth century. It
is the foil of Whitehead's final delineation of experience. He
bridges it by designing an account of experience that applies
to the unborn child, the infant in the cradle, our hours of
sleep, as well as to "normal" sense-perception.

To understand Whitehead's central doctrine of causal inheritance, we should have in the backs of our minds Burke,
and evolution, and—we must not forget it—mathematics. The
logic of relations and series is an instrument with which the
dependence on each other of derivation-series of various com-

---

[36] Chap. 3, above—especially Sect. II and III.
[37] "On the Motion of Viscous Incompressible Fluids," *Quarterly Journal
of Pure and Applied Mathematics*, 23 (1888), 78-93.

plexity can be defined.[38] The definitions in *Process and Reality* of "society" in general, and of several types of societies, are examples (PR I iii ii; II iii, iv). The vector character of physics, and the absolute generality of the mathematical notion of a series, and the way in which the functioning of the human body is centered mainly toward the experience enjoyed by the brain: these are the reasons why the doctrine of inheritance, whose truth is discerned in human society, can be applied to all events in the universe. Physics and mathematics and physiology make possible a generalization from sociology.

As we know, in Whitehead's metaphysics the doctrine of inheritance from the past is always coupled with the idea of novel, individual reaction to that past. Every individual is new, and none merely repeats its past; it is animated by its own purpose. This idea too is suggested by the history of societies. But Whitehead's metaphysical generalization of the idea of new achievement is phrased in *aesthetic* terms— in terms like harmony and discord, rhythm, intensity, massive simplicity, narrowness and width, inhibition and contrast. He has been noticing these things all around him! As was said in our second chapter, his fundamental concept of order and the principles of his new teleology are, broadly speaking, aesthetic.

Of course there is no one line of generalization in this philosophy. Several lines, which have been meditated upon for years, mingle. In the succession of Whitehead's books we can easily see the line which comes from physics, and the line which comes from religion. But his philosophical theology is mainly expressed in aesthetic language, and he interprets physical wave-vibration as a simple union of repetition and contrast. It would be a mistake to think of Whitehead as writing his metaphysics primarily out of a scientific background, if "science" has its ordinary unsophisticated meaning, namely, the systematic study of the causes of various types

[38] Russell aptly said, "The old logic put thought in fetters, while the new logic gives it wings" (*Our Knowledge of the External World* [New York and London, 1914], p. 68).

of natural events. Whitehead was *aware* of all sorts of things; but the three most important sources of his metaphysical thought seem to me to be these: reflections on aesthetic unity; reflections on history and society; and the study of theory—the vision of the possibilities of mathematics in the widest sense, in which it is far more than the study of quantities.

The first two are inevitably put under the head of "Whitehead's humanistic background." That background included a very great deal. Whitehead noticed and thought about the conditions of achievement in art, and in science, and in education; and equally the conditions involved in the mere survival and destruction of societies. I suggest that thinking about the patterns discernible equally in—to take one example —the conditions of the growth of human individuals or societies, and the conditions of the growth of forests, is at the bottom of Whitehead's whole constructive effort. Ordinarily one does not join thoughts about such different things. Only a philosopher or a mathematician might be expected to do so. One would say that the philosopher was aiming at a synthesis, the mathematician making an abstraction. Both are " seeking the forms in the facts."

An essential part of Whitehead's greatness is his profound understanding of human life.[39] That he drew so much on this in building his philosophy, was probably inevitable. What might, by critics at least, be called the contribution that comes from his *amateur* side, had been a subject of meditation for decades; this appears plainly in every account he has ever given of his life's activities.[40]

Whitehead made no attempt to write as a research scholar in the humanistic field. Relying considerably on secondary sources, he repeated some old errors of historical fact. But

[39] Read the opening pages of Part V of *Process and Reality*!

[40] Lucien Price adds, " Whitehead's classical training stuck, it was cultivated by him for the rest of his days, and as the twentieth century went on and so many men of science were found to be lamentably lopsided, this benign balance in him between science and humanism became one of his unique distinctions. It was a common saying that ' Whitehead has both ' " (*Dialogues of Alfred North Whitehead*, Prologue) .

that does not affect his *philosophy*. Anyone who supposes that in criticizing him for such errors he criticizes Whitehead's thought, has a curious sense of importance. It would be more reasonable to wish that he had spent a little less time on social, political, and church history. When we remember that the system set forth in *Process and Reality* is an essay in cosmology, and reflect that its future may very well depend more on the scientists than on the philosophers, and also recall that on Whitehead's own grounds the system is a failure if science is not affected by it, we begin to wonder whether he might not to our advantage have done more to indicate possible uses of it in science. The discussion in *Process and Reality* of some of the general theories of some of the sciences, and of the divisions between sciences, is so short! New developments in psychology and the life sciences could have used some theoretical unification. Freud had taken the physics of Helmholtz's school for his model; according to Whitehead, that model was outdated. In psychoanalysis and elsewhere the concept of homeostasis was riding high when Whitehead came to America. If the mind is not a mechanism oriented toward a tensionless state, what Whiteheadian alternative was sufficiently worked out for scientists to use? —But I am probably being naïve; we have no assurance that these scientists would have used a more worked-out Whiteheadian framework any more than physicists used what he had produced for them. And doubtless this hypothetical Whitehead would have been not so complete and civilized a man as the real Whitehead was. Parts of *Adventures of Ideas*, too, would never have been written. Whitehead, of course, was not worried about his philosophy. Its real application may lie in a remote future.

IX

Having recognized Whitehead's historical bent, we are bound to balance our earlier notice of the importance of mathematical and physical ideas for his work by noting certain positive relations of the philosophy of organism to some of the great metaphysical depositions in Western thought. Among the ancients, Plato, Aristotle, and Epicurus are the only metaphysicians he discusses (unless we count Zeno the Eleatic). Although he loved Plato and did not love Aristotle, his own doctrine of forms is much more Aristotelian than Platonic. (It is also original, as Ivor Leclerc has shown by comparing Whitehead and Aristotle.[41]) Whitehead's relation to Epicurus is more negative than positive.

[41] "Form and Actuality," in *The Relevance of Whitehead*, ed. Ivor Leclerc (London and New York, 1961), pp. 169-189.

In his book, *Whitehead's Metaphysics: An Introductory Exposition* (London, 1958; reviewed by the present author in *Philosophy of Science*, 27 [October, 1960], 410-414), Leclerc expounds Whitehead's system as a modern endeavor to solve the classic metaphysical problem of the nature of being—more specifically, Aristotle's problem of describing that which has being in the primary or full sense of the term, to which all other being, such as the being of Platonic Forms, refers. (Whitehead wrote, "The final problem is to conceive a complete [παντελής] fact" [AI ix viii]). This way of interpreting Whitehead is very helpful, and is fairly justified by the fact that in *Process and Reality* and *Adventures of Ideas* he set forth his metaphysics in the context provided by the great thinkers of the European philosophical tradition. (He re-read them when he came to Harvard; his books pay little attention to philosophers of second rank in the historic stream, and he was probably not widely read in them.) It is a mistake to imagine that you cannot get a decent understanding of the philosophy of organism if you are ignorant of *Principia Mathematica*. But knowledge of Whitehead's first period does enlarge our understanding of his metaphysics.

In the recent strong renewal of interest in the philosophy of organism, interpretations which differ very widely on its relation to the early Whitehead have appeared. At one end of the spectrum we have a separation of Whitehead's work in England from his work in America, with the latter construed in Leclerc's manner. At the opposite end we have W. Mays's interpretation, which leans heavily on "Mathematical Concepts of the Material World," and scarcely permits its author to leave the English Cambridge. In his *Philosophy of Whitehead* Mays holds that ". . . the two key notions of Whitehead's later philosophy are the postulational method of modern logic with its emphasis on complex relational systems, and the field theory of modern physics with its emphasis on the historicity of physical systems" (London and New York, 1959; p. 20). "Looked at in this way," he explains, "Whitehead's account does not seem to be as outrageous nor as metaphysical as some philosophers have made it out to be, since what he seems to be doing is a sort of applied logic." On its positive side this type of interpretation also is helpful;

Before considering certain modern philosophers, I must con-
fess to sympathy with those critics who find Whitehead's piety
toward the great thinkers of the past excessive. It cannot be
salutary to tell the philosophers of the future that Plato
divined " seven notions " and that " All philosophical systems
are endeavours to express . . . [their] interweaving " (AI ix iv,
viii) .[42] Then there is the raising of John Locke to divinity. Of
course Locke is a very useful man to study—very: and that for
the reason Whitehead gives, his " admirable adequacy." Also,
this adequacy can be of use to a man engaged in Whitehead's
great investigation, cosmology. But the type of question raised
by Locke is so infinitely narrower! When, in the first paragraph of the preface to *Process and Reality*, Whitehead says,

> The writer who most fully anticipated the main positions of
> the philosophy of organism is John Locke in his *Essay*, especi-
> ally in its later books (Cf. Bk. IV, Ch. VI, Sec. 11),

one can be thankful that Whitehead's own work follows to
set the reader right. His statement that " the philosophy of
organism . . . does start with a generalization of Locke's account
of mental operations," and that " prehensions " in particular
" are a generalization from Descartes' mental ' cogitations,'
and from Locke's ' ideas ' " (PR I ii i) , is doubtless true in the

---

the negative side is another matter. The author of the memoir of 1906
is surely present in the pages of *Process and Reality*, but so is a serious
student of the metaphysical difficulties which beset Aristotle, Descartes,
Kant, and others; we may not treat his long discussions of his predecessors
as window-dressing. And it is not credible that when Whitehead framed
his own " description generalizations of experience " (as he called them)
after " his translation to Harvard "—Mays's give-away phrase—he used
his humanistic reflections of many years' growth merely to clothe his
real thought in verbal obscurities. In carrying out such an interpretation,
" experience " is necessarily replaced by " the perceptual field," and not
only Whitehead's new philosophical theology, but his new teleology, his
doctrine of causal experience, his appeal to practice, are reduced to
useless shadows.

[42] I. e., the interweaving of seven main factors of fact, divined and
crudely expressed by Plato. Whitehead appeals mainly to the *Timaeus*
and *Sophist*, but also to the *Statesman, Theaetetus, Laws* (Books V, X),
and *Symposium*.

double sense that there is a significant connection between his
concepts and theirs, and that he was reading and appreciating
these men when he began to expound his metaphysics; still
the statement is misleading if it is not supplemented by attention to the ideas, and the sources of the ideas, in his premetaphysical work.

The perhaps excessive space devoted to Locke and Descartes
in Whitehead's essay on cosmology is more than an effect of
his philosophical professorship. It is an effect of his strong
feeling for continuity in the history of ideas. It is, even more,
an effect of his belief that any new interpretation of human
experience has an obligation to test itself against previous
interpretations. This belief is one of the things that separates
Whitehead and Russell. If some support for a new thesis
cannot be found in a position proposed by any major philosopher in the long history of European thought, the thesis
is not credible to Whitehead. This method of partial confirmation is part of his appeal to a broader experiential base than
mere inspection of "the given" provides. (It was in the
course of explaining it that Whitehead made his celebrated
and usually misquoted statement," "The *safest general characterization* of the European philosophical *tradition* is that
it consists of a series of footnotes to Plato " [43] [PR II i i].)
When Whitehead says in his last book that, although process
is universal, "The essence of the universe is more than
process," he explains that "The alternative metaphysical
doctrine, of reality devoid of process, would never have held
the belief of great men, unless it expressed some fundamental
aspect of our experience " (MT v 8). A standing danger in
pursuing the ideal of *coherence* after Whitehead's manner
is, evidently, the acceptance of both poles of historically important antitheses as equally fundamental for metaphysics.

Some of Whitehead's appeals to Plato are weakened when

[43] My reason for italicizing certain words is that I have heard a scholar
of the highest reputation begin a paper by saying that according to
Whitehead the history of European philosophy is a series of footnotes
to Plato, and proceed to demonstrate that this is only half true.

the idea which he finds in a dialogue is considered more Whiteheadian than Platonic by specialists on Plato. Concerning Descartes and Locke, I may perhaps be allowed to opine that, since the future rests so much with the scientists, it was somewhat more important to emphasize what Whitehead remarked but can scarcely be said to have emphasized—the utilization of scientific and theoretical conceptions in the philosophy of organism, and the importance of the philosophy for such conceptions—than to make sure of gaining the authority of Descartes and Locke.

Some Whitehead scholars find that his completed system is closest to the metaphysics of Leibniz, which he never discussed in detail, and the metaphysics of Hegel, to which he made only passing references. I think this is true, but I should not go so far as to say that the philosophy of organism is in effect a revision and union of their positions.

Concerning Hegel, this delightful passage occurs in Whitehead's Autobiographical Notes:

> I have never been able to read Hegel: I initiated my attempt by studying some remarks of his on mathematics which struck me as complete nonsense. It was foolish of me, but I am not writing to explain my good sense.—LLP-W p. 7; ESP p. 7.

Earlier, Whitehead had said, " I remember when I was staying with Haldane at Cloan I read one page of Hegel. But it is true that I was influenced by Hegel " (ESP p. 117; IS p. 217). He explained that he had had many, many conversations with his close friend J. M. E. McTaggart and with Lord Haldane, and that he had read books about Hegel. Although my own first-hand acquaintance with Hegel is not much better than Whitehead's, I should like to set down three points which others have noticed and which I think should be borne in mind.

1) Max H. Fisch, upon surveying the classic period in American philosophy (which includes Whitehead) and remarking that, " Philosophically, the nineteenth century lived in the shadow of Hegel, . . . and the twentieth has scarcely emerged from it," wrote, " Whitehead's use of the term ' speculative philosophy ' and his general conception of it were in the Hegelian tradition." [44] Professor Fisch was well aware of the great differences between Whitehead and Hegel; I take it he was emphasizing the important fact that Whitehead shares with the Hegelian tradition the aim at a comprehensive interpretation of the experienceable world in process by a system of categories constructed for that purpose. The contrast between Hegelian construction and Kantian criticism comes to mind; more, though Whitehead in particular respects is a great deal closer sometimes to one and sometimes to another philosopher than to Hegel, he is in general more different from other nineteenth- and twentieth-century philosophers than from Hegel [45] (Samuel Alexander seems to me the outstanding exception) .

2) Concerning particular theses in the systems of Hegel and Whitehead, Professor Fisch makes this significant remark, which follows the quoted statement about speculative construction: " He [Whitehead] saw an analogy less obvious to others between the Hegelian development of an idea and the concrescence of an actual entity as the development of a subjective aim in his own philosophy."

3) The best short comparison of Whitehead's doctrines with Hegel's that I know was published by Gregory Vlastos in 1937.[46] In it Whitehead's pursuit of a coherence of contrasting conceptions, each requiring the other, is called dialectical (*Process and Reality* was preceded by what Vlastos refers to as the " dialectic of objects and events " in the 1920 books) ; but the contrast between this " heterogeneous " dia-

---

[44] *Classic American Philosophers* (New York, 1951) , pp. 17, 19.

[45] Prof. Fisch has referred me particularly to the long ninth and thirteenth paragraphs of the Preface to *Process and Reality*, which are indispensable keys for our understanding of Whitehead; and to pp. 16, 66 f., 152-154 of the second edition of Wallace's translation of Hegel's shorter *Logic* (Oxford, 1892) .

[46] " Organic Categories in Whitehead," *Journal of Philosophy* 34 (1937) , 253-262.

lectic, which is not based on contradiction, and Hegel's dialectic is made clear. I refer the present reader to Professor Vlastos' paper, though I am bound to say that if application of the term *dialectic* to Whitehead's philosophy were to become prevalent the misunderstandings would surely outweigh the benefits.

Whitehead's general comment on Hegel was made in a one-paragraph response to the reading of Professor Vlastos' paper: " He is a great thinker who claims respect. My criticism of his procedure is that when in his discussion he arrives at a contradiction, he construes it as a crisis in the universe. I am not so hopeful of our status in the nature of things. Hegel's philosophic attitude is that of a god " (ESP p. 131; IS p. 213). Whitehead's specific comments in *Process and Reality*, which supplement the one noticed by Professor Fisch, are only these: (1) " In the place of the Hegelian hierarchy of categories of thought, the philosophy of organism finds a hierarchy of categories of feeling " (II vii iv). (2) Whitehead finds an " analogy to philosophies of the Hegelian school " in his own theory of the transformation of actual occasions in the consequent nature of God. But his Preface, to which he refers the reader, mentions Bradley rather than Hegel. I suspect that even the analogy to Bradley was somewhat overestimated.

It remains to be said that in *Adventures of Ideas*—the only book of Whitehead's which is in large part devoted to discussion of institutions and the idea of civilization—Hegel gets no more than incidental mention. Whitehead's ideas on those subjects are his own wise response to history and the aesthetic element in experience. Only in his metaphysics—particularly in his doctrine of coherence—is a Hegelian influence notable. Had there never been a Hegel, I think Whitehead would still have been led to that by his instinctive acknowledgment that the truth is complex and that different thinkers have got hold of contrasting aspects of it.

It is neither Hegel nor Leibniz nor Descartes nor Locke, but Berkeley, who seems to me—judging from our examination of the foundations of Whitehead's philosophy of natural science—to have been the member of the European tradition in philosophy who was most relevant to Whitehead's own conceptions in their formative stage. I should not, however, ascribe to any philosopher an influence on him comparable to that of mathematical and physical conceptions. Even Plato, I think, primarily provided an illustration after the fact, though on a grand scale. Some of those who know Whitehead wonder if William Wordsworth did not influence him quite as much as any other man—and Shelley almost as much as Wordsworth.

X

In this Section we consider the possible importance of Whitehead's contemporary, Bergson, for his metaphysics. When Bertrand Russell reviewed *Science and the Modern World* he wrote: " What can we regard as really concrete? On this point, Dr. Whitehead is profoundly influenced by Bergson's belief in interpenetration, which he even carries further. . . . We are to understand that the world is a logical continuum, not validly analyzable into bits, and that, when it dreams of things to come, these things are already existing now in the dream." [47] This is evidently written from the point of view of logical atomism. Whitehead for his part was carrying out the idea he had expressed in " Uniformity and Contingency " of the significance of an event for earlier and later events. The only way of answering Hume that will yield a basis for induction is to find something in the immediate occasion which connects it with its past and future (SMW pp. 61 ff.). Possibly it was acquaintance with Bergson's thought which first led him so to think of the immediate occasion. Confirmation of this must be left to biographical research.

It is fatal to the understanding of Whitehead's constructive metaphysical effort to define it in Bergsonian terms. There

[47] *Nation and Athenaeum*, 39 (May 29, 1926) , 207. Russell adds, " The view that the world is a logical continuum had been made familiar by the Hegelians, before Bergson."

are many reasons for saying this besides the one given in the first section of the present chapter.

"It must be thoroughly understood," Whitehead wrote in his Preface to *Process and Reality*, "that the theme of these lectures is not a detached consideration of various traditional philosophical problems which acquire urgency in certain traditional systems of thought." But the topics to which Bergson devoted his successive works were just such problems, problems which acquired urgency for him in the Cartesian, Kantian and Spencerian systems—the nature of our consciousness of time and space, the reciprocal action of mind and body upon one another, the force behind evolution, the sources of morality and religion. When he goes about relating mind and body, Bergson ascribes to the events in the nervous system purely physical properties only—the power of receiving, preserving, and continuing movements; he comes close to swallowing Cartesian natural science whole. Whitehead's entire conception of the speculative reason and speculative metaphysics clearly stands beyond the orientation which Bergson advocated by writing (in 1922) : "To metaphysics, then, we assign a limited object, principally spirit, and a special method, mainly intuition"; and "Let us have done with great systems embracing all the possible, and sometimes even the impossible! Let us be content with the real, mind and matter." [48]

In sum, Whitehead comes to the metaphysics of experience as a Plato-loving theorist who wishes to construct an all-inclusive cosmological scheme; Bergson as a half-Cartesian intuitionist cleanly and systematically setting off his own meditation from other types and areas of thought.

The most significant passage on Bergson in Whitehead's metaphysical writings I take to be this:

> On the whole, the history of philosophy supports Bergson's charge that the human intellect 'spatializes the universe'; that is to say, that it tends to ignore the fluency, and to analyse

[48] "Introduction II" in *The Creative Mind*, trans. by Mabelle L. Andison (New York, 1946), pp. 42, 77; hereafter cited as "CM."

the world in terms of static categories. Indeed Bergson went further and conceived this tendency as an inherent necessity of the intellect. I do not believe this accusation; but I do hold that 'spatialization' is the shortest route to a clear-cut philosophy expressed in reasonably familiar language.—PR II x i.

As we saw earlier in this chapter, Whitehead also, in his theory of "presentational immediacy," generalizes the idea of spatialization far beyond its meaning in Bergson. Thus in place of the dualism of a living absolute (within which the philosopher and artist place themselves) and inert, perspectival relatives (the work of *homo faber*'s intellect) , he has a unitary cosmological theory of all existence as perspectival, perspectives being in diverse ways transformed into effective aesthetic simplicity by conceptual feeling, and their contents unconsciously displayed to the experient—spatialized—in its perceptive process. Note also how un-Bergsonian is Whitehead's treatment of teleology, and of the order and disorder of nature (Bergson repudiates the notion of disorder, and divides order into two kinds, vital and geometrical) .[49]
In his view of the general relation of conceptual language to philosophy, Whitehead contradicts Bergson by maintaining that the inadequacies of conceptual language are diminishable, though never eliminable. Their source lies beyond the tendency to spatialize process; it lies in the contrast between the pervasive traits of the infinite universe and that which is variable, special, and hence easily noticeable and namable by finite man; a further obstacle is the dominance of Aristotelian categories in the learned tradition. Here again Whitehead is the innovator, Bergson the conservative to whom logic is forever Aristotelian and the intellect forever excluded from metaphysical penetration. When Whitehead asks philosophy to mobilize and make manifest the basic experience which is lived, he is in accord with Bergson. "If you like to phrase it so," he grants in 1935, "philosophy is mystical. For mysti-

[49] *Creative Evolution*, trans. by Arthur Mitchell (New York, 1911) , pp. 220-236.

cism is direct insight into depths as yet unspoken" (MT Epilogue). But he continues as no Bergsonian can: ". . . the purpose of philosophy is to rationalize mysticism . . . by the introduction of novel verbal characterizations, rationally co-ordinated." Though "akin to poetry," philosophy "allies itself . . . to mathematic pattern." Metaphysics is decidedly not what Bergson said it was—"the science which claims to dispense with symbols." [50]

Whitehead's philosophy and Bergson's are both of them "process philosophies," but they are largely of opposed types. Throughout Whitehead's metaphysics the flux of things is taken as "*one* ultimate generalization around which we must weave our philosophical system"; [51] he shows the evidence for this necessity by referring not to Bergson but to the poetry of the Psalms, to Heraclitus, to the Anglo-Saxon story of the sparrow flitting through the banqueting hall of the Northumbrian king, to poetry in all stages of civilization (PR II x i). (His other "ultimate generalization" is the antithetical idea of permanence.) Whitehead expounds process in his elaborate theory of prehensions; Bergson, believing theory of no avail, uses poetic imagery to supplement his references to "melting" and "interpenetration." Both men hold that a true process is indivisible; but for Whitehead it always has the shape of an analyzable concrescence, whereas the issue of Bergson's meditation was an intuition of "pure, unadulterated inner continuity (duration), continuity whch was neither unity nor multiplicity, . . ." [52] For Whitehead, the continuity of the stream of experience is a surface feature prominent in consciousness, the underlying reality being a succession of "drops of experience"; for Bergson, continuity is the fundamental fact, and there are no drops in Whitehead's sense, but only static states artificially abstracted by our acts of attention or by psychological analysis. Whitehead applies his principles

[50] *An Introduction to Metaphysics*, trans. by T. E. Hulme (New York, 1912), p. 9.
[51] PR II x i; italics added.
[52] "Introduction I," CM p. 12.

of process to all existents, Bergson only to spiritual or at least living existents. Whitehead's concept of "creativity" cannot—A. E. Taylor [53] and other scholars to the contrary—be identical with Bergson's *élan vital*, for "creativity" does not admit of an inverse. Whitehead draws a distinction between becoming and change, Bergson does not.

Were these differences not present, we should still have to call Whitehead's and Bergson's opposed types of process philosophy, in virtue of the root fact that Whitehead always thinks of the creativeness of processes as their appetition for, and evocation of, timeless potentials, whereas in Bergson's eyes this mode of thought subjects change to the static. So in "The Possible and the Real," written in 1920,[54] Bergson denies that the possible is real. But *Process and Reality* sets as the central problem of Whitehead's metaphysical system the relation between process and reality which is more than process just because it harbors real possibility.

Quite possibly Bergson's homage to life impressed Whitehead; but we can hardly be surprised by his comment on the other's doctrine. "We all remember Bergson's doctrine of the *élan vital* and its relapse into matter. The double tendency of advance and relapse is here plainly stated. But we are not given any explanatory insight" (FR p. 23). While Bergson, as the historian Höffding well said, takes as his basis an absolute opposition between the organic and the inorganic, Whitehead works out their relative differences in novelty of appetition, in rhythm, and in structural integration. Another great divergence—concerning consciousness—joins this one. For the French dualist, but decidedly not for Whitehead, "the living is conscious by right," for life is "consciousness launched into matter." [55] (Bergson's conception of life is fundamentally monistic, Whitehead's pluralistic.) It is hard to imagine Whitehead seriously entertaining Bergson's conviction that

[53] *Dublin Review*, 181 (1927), 34 f.
[54] CM pp. 107-125.
[55] CM p. 108 (from Bergson's essay, "The Possible and the Real"); *Creative Evolution*, p. 181.

" the appearance of man or of some being of the same essence is the raison d'être of life on our planet." [56] And Whitehead rejects the comforting anthropocentric tradition (accepted by Bergson) which makes freedom co-extensive with consciousness.

Since Bergson is not much read today, I shall bring these comparisons to a close. Some day people will return to him. My concern has been to make it impossible then to look upon Whitehead as Bergson's mathematically trained *alter ego*. What is there in Bergson's thought that corresponds to the three conceptions—of actual entity, prehension, and nexus [57]— with which Whitehead tries to assure the concreteness of his own? How small a part of the Categoreal Scheme in *Process and Reality* parallels anything in Bergson's writings! [58]

The acknowledgment of indebtedness in the Preface to *Process and Reality* is often cited. After referring to " the English and American Realists," Whitehead wrote:

> I am also greatly indebted to Bergson, William James, and John Dewey. One of my preoccupations has been to rescue their type of thought from the charge of anti-intellectualism, which rightly or wrongly has been associated with it.

A survey of Whitehead's work suggests that the acknowledgments which occur in his various prefaces are somewhat overstated. I suggest that here Whitehead was paying a tribute to, and showing his sympathy with, the three men who had done most to encourage philosophers in the first quarter of

[56] " Introduction II," CM p. 69.
[57] See the first paragraph of Chap. 12, below.
[58] On the other side, see how un-Whiteheadian the main basis of Bergson's philosophy appears. A. O. Lovejoy summarized it as consisting of two Cartesian propositions, namely, the affirmation of a division between extended things and consciousness, and the proposition that consciousness is the more certainly known, and one Kantian proposition, to wit, that time is the essential characteristic of consciousness (" Some Antecedents of the Philosophy of Bergson," *Mind*, n. s., 22 [1913], 465 f.) . Although this summary seems not quite just to Bergson's originality of thought, it has a wide enough application to contrast strongly with its gross inapplicability to Whitehead.

THE PHILOSOPHY OF ORGANISM: XI

the twentieth century to think of the process of experience in terms other than those of pure cognition. His articulation of a rational metaphysics of living, emotional, purposive experience rescues their emphasis from the charge of anti-intellectualism. But we should remember that Whitehead's own attitude toward life and his own intellectual interests required him to adopt a wider-than-cognitive conception of experience.

XI

For the reasons detailed in the preceding Section, I think that in trying to understand Whitehead we are more likely to be misled than aided by bringing Bergson into the picture. The reverse is true in the case of James and Whitehead, for the difference between them immdiately strikes us, and we are more likely to underestimate the areas of contact. It is helpful to observe, for example, that when James wrote, " Perception changes pulsewise, but the pulses continue each other and melt their bounds," [59] he was not so much expressing a standpoint which he would develop until discreteness and continuity were conciliated in a new understanding, as a feeling for a state of affairs falsified by earlier theorists; that Whitehead makes the development by taking on a problem which James, prejudiced by the traditional empiricism in which he had been reared, rejected—the problem of how pulses of experience are formed; and that James's unmatched psychological observations provide the chief outside evidence to show that Whitehead's theory of prehensions is not a castle in the air.[60]

Whitehead's response to James's way of philosophizing is better called one of sympathy and of appreciation of " that adorable genius " (SMW p. 3) than a case of influence. In May, 1941, he said as much in conversation with the present

[59] *Some Problems of Philosophy* (New York, 1911) , pp. 87 f.
[60] This point is developed in Chap. 13, below.

author, adding that there was no question of James affecting
the direction of his thinking. Some writers assume that Whitehead's pluralism was partly an effect of James's arguments
that experience comes in drops. The similarity between their
pluralisms is important. But, remembering the force with
which Whitehead used to exclaim before his Harvard classes,
"Hang it all, there must be individual actual things!" and
the tenacity with which in a variety of ways he enforces this
conviction in all his philosophical writings,[61] I think it far
more likely that his pluralism expressed a conviction native
to the man. In 1939 he told me that he began with such a
general conviction, then found supporting examples. The
phrase, "drop of experience," used by Whitehead, is James's,
but what it names is the natural candidate for the unit of
existence in the eyes of a metaphysician who wants to develop
a new monadic theory of experience.[62]

I have known Whitehead, in a conversation about Bergson,[63]
to inject the remark that the contemporary from whom he
actually got most was Samuel Alexander: he and Alexander
"conceived the problem of metaphysics in the same way." In
particular, Alexander had the important idea that the unity
of the universe (Spinoza's emphasis) and the many individuals
(Leibniz') had somehow to be reconciled. Another common
element which I have heard him mention is the fact that
Alexander, almost alone among Whitehead's contemporaries,
did not, implicitly at least, assume that our experience is
basically an experience of sense-data. On the positive side,
Whitehead observed in *Process and Reality* (II i i) that his
basic term, "feeling," "has a close analogy to Alexander's
use of the term 'enjoyment.'" Another specific statement

[61] This is obvious in his metaphysical, educational, and historical
writings. Perhaps it appears also in his philosophy of physics: cf. PNK
17.4, CN pp. 5-15, and SMW pp. 98-102, 145, 185-189.
[62] From "William James's Pluralistic Metaphysics of Experience," *In
Commemoration of William James: 1842-1942* (New York, 1942), pp.
157-177, the reader may see how near, and how far, James at various
times came, in my judgment, to the pluralistic conceptions later elaborated
by Whitehead.
[63] In August, 1942.

concerns Whitehead's metaphysical concept of the primordial nature of God: " It is Alexander's *nisus* conceived as actual " (ESP p. 118; IS p. 219) . A sketch of Whitehead's world view in his last book (MT v 9) is written in terms of Alexander's title-phrase, " Space, Time, and Deity." In the Preface to his first metaphysical book, *Science and the Modern World*, Whitehead had said that he was " especially indebted to Alexander's great work," which he had found " very suggestive." (It had been published five years before.) Alexander, for his part, once observed that he thought Whitehead's cosmological scheme had superseded his own.

To this evidence several comparative observations could be added. For example, that according to both philosophies, activity and value exist throughout nature. Both philosophers work out an intimate union of static form and process. And Alexander's interpretation of perception, as consisting in a " compresence " of an object and a percipient who enjoys his " togetherness " with the object, is a rough adumbration of Whitehead's notion of " prehension ": thus Alexander offered an alternative to the idea of " simple location." The study of *Space, Time, and Deity* can sharpen our understanding of Whitehead by showing us the need of some of the concepts which he introduced into his more subtle system.

May we also conclude that Alexander exercised an indispensable influence on Whitehead's metaphysics? I doubt it, because these leading ideas of the philosophy of organism already had firm taproots in Whitehead himself. Besides, the pluralistic theory at which he aimed—as *Science and the Modern World* shows—is of a much thicker kind than Alexander's pluralism of point-instants. Alexander's metaphysics seems to have been elaborated in response to the early twentieth-century dispute between realism and idealism, which colors his whole work; Whitehead, paying much less attention to that dispute, aimed primarily at displacing scientific materialism. When we remember the memoir, " On Mathematical Concepts of the Material World," it seems better, in the absence of biographical investigations, to describe the relation between Alexander and Whitehead as more one of encouragement and sympathy than of indispensable influence.

What about Americans other than James, in the development of Whitehead's philosophy? Fascinating comparisons can be drawn between Peirce's and Whitehead's metaphysical doctrines; but in Whitehead's texts there is no evidence that before he wrote his philosophy of organism he was familiar with any of Peirce's work outside logic. The same is true of Royce, who is mentioned in a note in the " General Considerations " part of the memoir of 1906. I do not know when Whitehead first seriously studied Dewey. In his two-page contribution to the Dewey volume in " The Library of Living Philosophers " he both admires the man and subtly conveys his dissatisfaction with Dewey's limitation of philosophic thought to human problems.[64] Some students of Dewey think that his influence is manifest in the first appearance—in *Symbolism* (1927) —of Whitehead's doctrine of a direct experience of causality. Though it is possible that Dewey had something to do with this, I cannot believe that *Experience and Nature*, or any book of the nineteen-twenties, was half as influential on Whitehead as the deep-lying sources described in Section VIII of the present chapter. Dewey himself thought of Whitehead as a first-rate thinker whose scope and range were beyond his own—a man of such originality that his appreciation of a contemporary, though it could be a confirming or deflecting factor, can never be considered a primary one.

The significance of contemporary American philosophy for Whitehead's thought during his productive years here is difficult to estimate from his conversations, because he loved to savor, and to express his appreciation of, the many and varied intellectual adventures of his contemporaries; also he loved people, and his manners were supremely good. As a result, visitors often left his company with the feeling that their philo-

[64] *The Philosophy of John Dewey*, ed. P. A. Schilpp (Evanston and Chicago, 1939) ; Whitehead's contribution is reprinted in ESP. Cf. also his comparison of James and Dewey, as reported by Lucien Price, *Dialogues of Alfred North Whitehead*, Dialogue XLI; and our references in Chaps. 3 and 10 to Whitehead on Dewey.

sophical problems were what Professor Whitehead was most concerned with. That this concern continued in full force when he retired to his study to work at his own system, is a hazardous assumption; I suspect that it has largely contributed to the belief, held by some American philosophers, that one of the *main* objects of the author of *Process and Reality* was to come to terms with American analyses of experience.

On turning to the general circumstances which Harvard and America provided for Whitehead in his third period, it seems to me from Price's *Dialogues*. Hocking's article, and Whitehead's own statements (allowance being made for good manners), that the British detractors of his metaphysics are right in holding this country partly responsible, though I should not go so far as to join his American admirer, H. B. Van Wesep, in calling Whitehead "the latecoming but almost violent convert to America." [65] There is a certain congeniality between the outlook of Whitehead's American books and a great deal of what was best in American philosophy before him.[66]

We do well to keep a close watch on our readiness to discern influences from earlier philosophers in Whitehead's metaphysics. He was like one of his "actual occasions"—a prehension of manifold data, on which he imposed his own unique "subjective aim." [67] It is natural for us, upon looking into a new philosophy, to say forthwith, "I know where he got that idea!—and that one! and that one!" Natural, yes, but it is also likely to be nine-tenths projection. We have here, to use James's phrase, a disease of the philosophy-shop—or, rather, the typical fallacy of the well-read Ph. D. The gain, of course, is that we need not sweat for long over the idea if we read it as another version of one we know; or if,

[65] *Seven Sages: The Story of American Philosophy* (New York, 1960), p. xi.
[66] Cf. the General Introduction, by Max H. Fisch, in *Classic American Philosophers: Peirce, James Royce, Santayana, Dewey, Whitehead*, New York, 1951. In Van Wesep's *Story* Whitehead is preceded by chapters on Franklin, Emerson, James, Santayana, Dewey, and Peirce.
[67] I owe this *aperçu* to Prof. Raphael Demos.

when still puzzled, we assume that what puzzles us is only a new twist in the treatment of a familiar problem. Because philosophic ideas make up our frames of reference for understanding other ideas, the understanding of novelty is in this field peculiarly difficult, and the price of its exclusion ruinously high. First-rate philosophers, to be sure, *do* read books and *are* influenced by them, even when they misread them. But let us allow that they may see some things for themselves, and that the core of their thought must be grasped in its own terms, not those of earlier systems.

We can now understand more fully what was said about the philosophy of organism at the end of Section I in Chapter 2: It "can neither be subsumed under any movement of the twentieth century nor accurately represented as the joint influence of recent thinkers on its author." There is in Whitehead a touch of Bergson, a touch of James, a touch of Samuel Alexander, more of Wordsworth and Shelley, and a good deal of Plato (though not so much as Whitehead thought there was). His sympathies were wide; his work was his own.

Chapter 10

The Third Period of Whitehead's Work (Continued):

Adventures of Ideas and Later Writings

I

Adventures of Ideas was Whitehead's last long book. In the Preface, dated September, 1932, he groups it with *Science and the Modern World* and *Process and Reality*:

> The three books . . . are an endeavour to express a way of understanding the nature of things, and to point out how that way of understanding is illustrated by a survey of the mutations of human experience.

Adventures of Ideas is briefly described in our first chapter (p. 14), and drawn upon in all our discussions of the philosophy of organism; we need not say much about it now.

In placing this book in the sequence of Whitehead's writings, the first thought that comes to mind is that in devoting himself to the role of metaphysical ideas in the progress of European

civilization, Whitehead was following up his system of metaphysics with what to him was the natural commentary on it.
But that is too weak a statement. Part of what needs to be
added concerns human institutions, about which not enough
was said when we were discussing the humanistic background
of Whitehead's metaphysics. Their importance for the metaphysics is well shown in a paragraph from the slightly earlier
short book, *The Function of Reason*.[1] With it I quote the
preceding paragraph because I believe it fits Whitehead's 1920
books.

> The speculative Reason works in two ways so as to submit
> itself to the authority of facts without loss of its mission to
> transcend the existing analysis of facts. In one way it accepts
> the limitations of a special topic, such as a science or a practical
> methodology. It then seeks speculatively to enlarge and recast
> the categoreal ideas within the limits of that topic. This is
> speculative Reason in its closest alliance with the methodo-
> logical Reason.
>
> In the other way, it seeks to build a cosmology expressing
> the general nature of the world as disclosed in human interests.
> In order to keep such a cosmology in contact with reality
> account must be taken of the welter of established institutions
> constituting the structures of human society throughout the
> ages. It is only in this way that we can appeal to the wide-
> spread effective elements in the experience of mankind. What
> those institutions stood for in the experience of their con-
> temporaries, represents the massive facts of ultimate authority.—
> FR pp. 68 f.

Whitehead had already, in the Preface to *Science and the
Modern World*, said that " various human interests . . . suggest
cosmologies," and that one derived from science had acquired

---

[1] Lectures delivered at Princeton in March, 1929. From the Preface
to *Adventures of Ideas*, it appears probable that the portions of the
latter which were first written out—as more than a sketch—were written
for lectures delivered at Bryn Mawr College " during the session 1929-30."
   The two types of Reason to which the quoted passage refers were
indicated at the end of Chapter 1, above.

something too close to a monopoly. The appeal to institutions is an essential part of this broadening of the experiential base for speculative philosophy. They provide " broad, widespread testimony " about the stable experience of mankind (FR p. 62). The very discordance among human beliefs and purposes enables us to see that we all share such general notions as compulsion, purpose, alternatives of action, order and disorder. (FR p. 69; AI xv viii). From *Symbolism* (1927) on, Whitehead had also drawn on the *language* in which men interpret actions and social institutions. All this is made explicit, emphasized, and used in *Adventures of Ideas*.

Does not the position expressed by the emphatic last sentence of the quoted passage need qualification? Certainly it does, for anyone who takes the possibility of evolution seriously. This is most evident in the case of religious institutions. Whitehead had earlier referred to " the stage of satisfactory ritual and of satisfied belief without impulse towards higher things " as " the stage of religious evolution in which the masses of semi-civilized humanity have halted." His comment was: " Such religion satisfies the pragmatic test: It works, and thereby claims that it be awarded the prize for truth " (RM I iv). Whitehead, I take it, believes that impulse toward something new is a universal feature of human life, but that in any particular field it may become negligible for a shorter or longer time, and that " impulse towards higher things " *is* an essential part of civilized life.

In Whitehead's metaphysical work an appeal to *civilized* experience is added to his appeal to general experience:

> Whatever thread of presupposition characterizes social expression throughout the various epochs of rational society, must find its place in philosophic theory.—PR I i vi.

Another fact is important:

> Philosophy works slowly. Thoughts lie dormant for ages; and then, almost suddenly as it were, mankind finds that they have embodied themselves in institutions.—SMW Preface.

In all his metaphysical books Whitehead held that in flashes of insight men may grasp metaphysical notions beyond those which may be extracted from ordinary experience. A civilized society facilitates the formulation of such notions. And what is already presupposed in civilized experience must be satisfied by the metaphysics he constructs. This requirement becomes central in *Adventures of Ideas*. It is most emphatically stated on the last page of *Modes of Thought*: " Philosophy is akin to poetry, and both of them seek to express that ultimate good sense which we term civilization." [2]

II

Adventures of Ideas includes a general—not a professionally worked out—philosophy of history. The opening section of the first chapter makes a forceful succinct attack on the idea of " pure history." Whitehead's platform here will not surprise us; it was second nature to him.

> This notion of historians, of history devoid of aesthetic pre-judice, of history devoid of any reliance on metaphysical prin-ciples and cosmological generalizations, is a figment of the imagination. The belief in it can only occur to minds steeped in provinciality . . . minds unable to divine their own unspoken limitations.

Whitehead's own interpretation of the history of mankind revolves largely around the interplay of two factors: ideals which, like Christianity or democracy, are consciously enter-tained (general ideas which are successively clothed in par-ticular ways) , and senseless agencies, like the barbarian in-vasions of the Roman Empire. —But this view of Whitehead's is well known. For the same reason, I here pass over the abso-

---

[2] For further discussion of this idea, see Chap. 4, Sect. III, above; and Chap. 11, Sect. III, below.

lutely central concept of adventure, and the equally central concept of stability. They are of the essence of Whitehead's wisdom. And their prominence in *Adventures of Ideas* can come as no surprise to anyone familiar with his earlier educational and philosophic writings.

The chapter, " Beauty," opens with a general definition: " Beauty is the mutual adaptation of the several factors in an occasion of experience." The subsequent discussion, by elaborating this definition against the background of Whitehead's philosophy of organism, repays the debt which the metaphysics owed to its aesthetic sources. Of course it does more than that. To my mind, it gives fortunate expression to important truths about beauty, ideals, and good and evil.

Concerning the other developments in *Adventures of Ideas,* I shall do no more than mention a few of the most important ones.

The book's discussion of laws of nature rounds out Whitehead's position on causality, so that one sees how the " passing events " of the 1920 books had to get expanded into the " actual occasions " of the philosophy of organism, with their " objective immortality." [3] His technical theory of the relation of sense-perception to reality is further explained, and connected with the contrast between appearance and reality; [4] and his last word on the topic—the role of God—emerges.[5] The chapter on philosophic method is a superb discussion by an experienced and constructive philosopher; it includes an invaluable gloss on Part I of *Process and Reality* by providing an account of some sources of its terminology and a discussion of the relation of theory to evidence. The fine concise chapter, " Objects and Subjects," which was Whitehead's presidential

[3] Critics who think this expansion involves a great repudiation should observe that Whitehead had long before (1922) described the " passage of events " as one thing with their " significance " (R p. 68).

[4] Especially in XIV.

[5] XVI xi; XX ix-xi. Whitehead writes, ". . . we have to ask whether nature does not contain within itself a tendency to be in tune, an Eros urging towards perfection." He suggests the possibility of " a general drive " which would " constitute a factor in each occasion persuading an aim at such truth as is proper to the special appearance in question."

address to the Eastern Division of the American Philosophical
Association in 1931, will, I imagine, come to be considered the
locus classicus for Whitehead's conception of experience.
Those who object to Whitehead mainly because of his James-
like theory of personal unity will be pleased to find that in
Section 18 of this chapter he says that a problem remains; the
discussion of it which follows, however, proceeds along his
usual lines.

Adventures contains many enlightening ideas which cannot,
in the scope of the present volume, be given the attention they
deserve. For example, there are a dozen pages on art which
are priceless (xviii iii-vii; xix iv). But the line Whitehead
takes in his general discussion of civilization must be noticed.
That discussion has been too much neglected by philosophers
of the social sciences and by historians. Of course his concept
of civilization is normative rather than descriptive: " civilization is nothing other than the unremitting aim at the major
perfections of harmony " (xviii vi). Cautiously and more
explicitly, Whitehead writes:

> The notion of civilization is very baffling. We all know what
> it means. It suggests a certain ideal for life on this earth, and
> this ideal concerns both the individual human being and also
> societies of men. . . . We pronounce upon particular instances.
> We can say *this* is civilized, or *that* is savage. Yet somehow the
> general notion is elusive. . . .
>
> I put forward as a general definition of civilization, that a
> civilized society is exhibiting the five qualities of Truth, Beauty,
> Adventure, Art, Peace.—xix i.

Whitehead leaves mainly to others the relation of these
qualities to social structures; his effort is to depict their character as founded in the metaphysical nature of things, and
especially in relations between appearance and reality.[6] His
definitions of truth tacitly hark back to *Principia Mathe-*

[6] See Chap. 2, Sect. III, above.
[7] This was pointed out to me by Prof. Paul F. Schmidt.

matica.[7] Naturally nothing of the sort occurs in Whitehead's concluding chapter, "Peace." This—one of his finest achievements—speaks profoundly of many things (e. g., "The deepest definition of Youth is, Life as yet untouched by tragedy "), and presents his final response to tragedy.

As we noticed earlier in this section, *Science and the Modern World* made it plain that Whitehead would use aesthetic, ethical, and religious elements in his metaphysics. We should remember, further, that in his Tarner Lectures of November, 1919, Whitehead, calling attention to what he was *not* trying to do, had said, "The values of nature are perhaps the key to the metaphysical synthesis of existence " (CN p. 5). When he did attempt this synthesis, taking "nature" in the broadest possible sense—philosophic rather than scientific—values were the key. The mutual relevance of historic cosmologies and the values of civilized societies are emphasized and defended in *Adventures*:

> In each age of the world distinguished by high activity there will be found at its culmination, and among the agencies leading to that culmination, some profound cosmological outlook, implicitly accepted, impressing its own type upon the current springs of action.—II ii.[8]

III

The eight years between Whitehead's arrival in America and his completion of *Adventures of Ideas* were a marvelously productive period. Though his work in Harvard University was enough to satisfy the energies of an ordinary man, in that time he had constructed the most comprehensive cosmology in history and expounded it from a variety of points of view. I think that shortly thereafter he suffered a bit of

---

[8] Toynbee quoted this and said that it "surely hits the truth "; *A Study of History*, XII, "Reconsiderations " (Oxford, 1961), 279.

ill health; there was much more than a bit if it in his immediate family.[9] Besides *Adventures of Ideas*, only a few short
pieces were published in the remaining five years of active duty
at Harvard. The two lectures he gave at the University of
Chicago in 1933 were published the next year as *Nature and
Life*.[10] They are regularly drawn upon in books of philosophic
readings to introduce students in Whitehead's own words to his
novel world view. They also constitute an admirable preparation for the study of his system. The nature of Whitehead's final
contribution to mathematical logic, made in a 1934 paper,
"Indication, Classes, Numbers, Validation," we indicated in
Chapter 6, Section IX. Also in this period fall two published
addresses on education. The one called "Harvard: The
Future," [11] given during the tercentenary celebration of Harvard College, is superb.

In 1937 the response Whitehead made to papers on his philosophy at a symposium held the previous December was
published.[12] The other participants were John Dewey, A. P.
Ushenko, and Gregory Vlastos. The title, "Remarks," given
to Whitehead's response, is misleading; the paper is a connected discourse on the task which is set for human thought
by the interfusion of necessity and accident in our experience
of the universe. Dewey had asked Whitehead to choose between emphasis on a mathematical-formal interpretation of
his philosophic method and emphasis on a genetic-functional
interpretation; Whitehead of course declined to choose, and
said that the real problem for philosophers was the fusion
of these two ways of interpreting first principles. This leads
into a discussion of the vagueness of our understanding of the
connectedness of things, and that to a statement of the assumptions involved in using our best instrument for increasing

[9] See Lucien Price, *Dialogues of Alfred North Whitehead* (Boston,
1954), Dialogue I.
[10] Chicago, 1934; later included in MT.
[11] *Atlantic Monthly*, 158 (1936), 260-270; reprinted in ESP and AESP.
[12] *Philosophical Review*, 46 (1937), 178-186; reprinted in *Proceedings
and Addresses, American Philosophical Association*, Vol. 10; also in IS;
and in ESP pp. 122-131 as "Analysis of Meaning."

clarity—" the method of algebra." [13] There was a bit of a stir when Whitehead said, " We must end with my first love—Symbolic Logic," and predicted that " the symbolic examination of pattern with the use of real variables, will become the foundation of aesthetics," then conquer ethics and theology. But he placed these triumphs " in the distant future." [14]

IV

The Whitehead Bibliography in LLP-W lists the few other short pieces which Whitehead published in 1933-1937.[15] Then in 1938 there appeared what deserves to be one of the best-loved books, as *Science and the Modern World* is one of the most exciting books, that philosophy possesses. In *Modes of Thought* system is kept entirely in the background. The metaphysician sets aside his conceptual definitions, and writes " the first chapter in philosophical approach "—" a free examination of some ultimate notions, as they occur naturally in daily life " (MT ɪ 1). Whitehead leads off with the contrasting ideas of importance and matter-of-fact. They recur in various contexts again and again—along with such notions as expression, understanding, pattern, the infinite and the finite, clarity, form and

[13] This part of the " Remarks " was referred to in our discussion of the *Universal Algebra*: p. 142, above.

[14] *Philosophical Review*, 46 (1937), 186; ESP pp. 130 f.; IS p. 213. To Ushenko's criticism of the concept of " negative prehension " in the philosophy of organism, Whitehead replied that in some form or other that concept is required, because of the exclusiveness of every pattern of composition. On p. 255 we noticed Whitehead's brief response to Vlastos' paper, on Whitehead and Hegel, " Organic Categories in Whitehead."

[15] For the sake of completeness I should like to note here one item, of little philosophic importance, which escaped my notice when compiling that Bibliography. It is a Foreword on p. xvii of *The Farther Shore: An Anthology of World Opinion on the Immortality of the Soul*, ed. Nathaniel Edward Griffin and Lawrence Hunt (New York, 1934). Prof. Paul F. Schmidt brought it to my attention.

DEVELOPMENT OF WHITEHEAD'S PHILOSOPHY

process, potentiality, a perspective of the universe, abstraction, order and disorder, composition, deity. The reader gets a kind of distillation of Whitehead's Philosophy 3 and 3b lectures at Harvard, or rather, as he says in the Preface, " those features of my Harvard lectures which are incompletely presented in my published works." Whitehead was encouraged to do this by an invitation to give six public lectures at Wellesley College in 1937-38, the year after his retirement. *Modes of Thought* consists of these lectures, with the addition of the earlier *Nature and Life* and a short address of 1935, " The Aim of Philosophy."

Whitehead used to tell his students, in the thirties, that he could contemplate with pleasure a conflation of his philosophy with that of Samuel Alexander. That philosopher, he felt, had leaned a bit too much toward monism, whereas he himself in *Process and Reality* might have leaned a bit too much toward pluralism. How, if at all, he would revise the categoreal scheme of *Process and Reality* could not be discussed in a book like *Modes of Thought*. One sees a tendency, sometimes checked, to refer " importance " to the ultimate unity (the God of *Process and Reality*) , and the contrasting notion, " matter-of-fact," to finite individuals. But Whitehead is very far from going over to monism. " There is also equally fundamental in the Universe, a factor of multiplicity " (III 4) .

He is now especially concerned that philosophy should not be identified with the making of philosophic systems. Systematization is necessary, but it is *one* of " the two aspects of philosophy "; the other aspect, called " assemblage," is the free type of discussion to which he confines himself in the Wellesley Lectures. He associates systematization with science, and praises the intellectual life of William James as a " protest against the dismissal of experience in the interest of system " (I 1) .

One topic which recurs again and again is the contrast that was so emphatically set forth even on its first appearance, in *Symbolism*. " The doctrine dominating these lectures," Whitehead now writes in his Preface, is that factors in our experience are 'clear and distinct' in proportion to their variability, provided that they sustain themselves for that moderate period required for importance. The necessities are invariable, and for that reason remain in the background of thought, dimly and vaguely. Thus philosophic truth is to be sought in the presuppositions of language rather than in its express statements.

"Clear, conscious discrimination . . . is of the essence of our humanity," but "an accident of our existence" (vi 6).

Inseparable from this doctrine is Whitehead's renewed attack on the notion of independently existing entities. He explains that the derivation of modern thought from a brilliant past, and the very articulateness of our language, tempt us to conceive of a philosophic problem as that of figuring out interconnections between things each of which is clearly understood "apart from reference to anything else" (iv 1). I may add, that if this presupposition is attacked we attack the attacker by saying that he would permit philosophers to talk when they don't know precisely *what* they are talking about. I can hear Moore, Russell, and Broad—to mention but three—making just this retort. I do not know whether Whitehead had any of them in mind, for he never spends his energies attacking the views of individuals. Here he simply continues, "This presupposition is erroneous. Let us dismiss it, and assume that each entity, of whatever type, essentially involves its own connection with the universe of other things. This connection . . . can be termed the perspective of the universe for that entity" (iv 2). This notion of perspectives of the universe is explained, illustrated, and defended in one way or another throughout the fourth, fifth, and sixth lectures; he had, he says, discussed it, but not broadly enough, under the heading "Relational Essence" in Chapter x of *Science and the Modern World*. I should also say that he is now presenting in nontechnical terms various aspects of the metaphysics of "coherence."

V

Concerning mathematics, Whitehead had long since moved beyond his first conception of it, as having to do solely with "the inference of proposition from proposition," and had come to conceive of it as dealing with the connectedness between passing things insofar as the facts of connection are general, that is, form patterns. In the famous second chapter of *Science and the Modern World* the term, "occasion of experience," was introduced, and the abstract generality of mathematics (expressed by the use of "any") was basically referred to the indefinite variety of such occasions. The only limitation on this generality is the one which the relation of the thinker to his world imposes upon all general statements: if there is an occasion which enters into *no* relationship with his present occasion, he can say nothing about it beyond confessing his absolute ignorance of it. "The generality of mathematics is the most complete generality consistent with the community of occasions which constitutes our metaphysical situation" (SMW p. 37). Furthermore, the very notion of a set of postulates was metaphysically construed, as offering a key which unlocks every detail of a pattern of general conditions—conditions alike of the unity of a complex occasion, and of its status in the community of occasions. An endeavor to divine not what I called "a pattern," but *the* pattern, would be metaphysics, which thus appears as the widest mathematics. There were also, in those few pages on mathematics in *Science and the Modern World*, metaphysical statements about aesthetic relationships and the harmony of the logical reason. I suppose that Whitehead was there divining something, lucid consistent statement of which would have to come later. But to discover a consistent correlation between the terms he used in that chapter and the terms of the philosophy of organism is perhaps an impossible task even for Whitehead specialists. What we may be sure of is that in 1925 Whitehead thought of systematic metaphysics as the widest mathematics, and thought of mathematics in general as concerned with the actual world. He was infinitely far from thinking of mathematical formulas as strings of meaningless marks.

With the development of his metaphysics of process, the appropriate interpretation of ordinary mathematical propositions came out. The discussion of " one and one make two " in *Process and Reality* assumes the view which, as we noticed in our first chapter, is emphatically defended in *Modes of Thought*—that this is a statement about a process and its issue. We must be careful not to imagine here the slightest deviation from Whitehead's constant position that mathematics abstracts utterly from particular things and processes. It is just because mathematics endeavors to state truths which are absolutely universal, that an identification of it with metaphysics is possible. (I say, " an identification," because in another sense Whitehead of course identifies mathematics with logic.[16] Indeed, " one and one make two " was presented for discussion in *Process and Reality* as a *metaphysical* proposition. Upon defining " metaphysical proposition," [17] Whitehead remarked, " The propositions which seem to be most obviously metaphysical are the arithmetical theorems." He discussed " one and one make two " to show the justification both for believing that we entertain metaphysical propositions, and for reserving some scepticism. He concluded that this proposition is beyond a reasonable doubt true concerning our cosmic epoch, but is

---

[16] These relationships and others, e. g., to aesthetics and to natural knowledge, are concisely set forth in Robert Palter's excellent paper, " The Place of Mathematics in Whitehead's Philosophy," *Journal of Philosophy*, 58 (September 14, 1961), 565-576.

[17] " A metaphysical proposition—in the proper, general sense of the term ' metaphysical '—signifies a proposition which (i) has meaning for any actual occasion, as a subject entertaining it, and (ii) is ' general ', in the sense that its predicate potentially relates any and every set of actual occasions, providing the suitable number of logical subjects for the predicative pattern, and (iii) has a ' uniform ' truth-value, in the sense that, by reason of its form and scope, its truth-value is identical with the truth-value of each of the singular propositions to be obtained by restricting the application of the predicate to any one set of logical subjects. It is obvious that, if a metaphysical proposition be true, the third condition is unnecessary. For a general proposition can only be true if this condition be fulfilled " (PR II ix iv) .

not a metaphysical truth. (In place of the dictum that mathematical propositions are true in all possible worlds, Whitehead has the ultimate metaphysical ideal of truth for all cosmic epochs.) I should not call arithmetical truths cosmological, because it is only on occasion that Whitehead abides by the rule of giving " cosmology " a narrower meaning than " metaphysics."

From the doctrine of the essential connection of mathematical forms with the world there issues, in *Modes of Thought*, an arresting comparison of logical consistency with aesthetic consistency. Another consequence is Whitehead's belief that the logic of propositions, if based on inconsistency (H. M. Sheffer showed how the system of *Principia Mathematica* could be based on inconsistency as the sole undefined relation [18]) , reflects the fundamental fact of a pluralistic metaphysics of process; the existence of alternatives that are not conjointly realizable sets the problem for the becoming of every actual occasion.

The doctrine of the autonomy of form, and the worse doctrines of autonomy of propositional and linguistic forms, are pieces of bad metaphysics. They have—for one thing—the same defect as the absolute theory of space (which Whitehead had so long criticized) and the conception of natural laws as absolute: they forget that the relata always make a difference. But Whitehead fully recognizes that every science, as a science, progresses by making an abstraction, and considering the relata only in certain respects: thus spaciness is absent from geometry, process from arithmetic (MT III 2) .

In *Science and the Modern World* Whitehead presented philosophy as " the critic of abstractions." That was his first book on philosophy as such. In every one of his subsequent discussions of the nature of philosophy this theme recurs, usually with special attention to the relation between philos-

[18] *Transactions of the American Mathematical Society*, 14 (1913) , 481-488. Sheffer does not speak of the relation of inconsistency, but of an operation called " rejection " or " non-conjunction." See his review of the second edition of *Principia Mathematica*: *Isis,* 8 (1926) , 229.

ophy and science. It is in *Modes of Thought* that the topic of abstraction is most dwelt upon. " The final conclusion " of the Wellesley lectures was " the importance of a right adjustment of the process of abstraction " (VI 10) .

Philosophy is important because that adjustment is important. This is the very idea that is accounted worthless by the critics who suggest that when Whitehead turned to speculative philosophy a good mathematician attempted the impossible and became an enemy of scientific attitudes. Ernest Nagel's review of *Process and Reality*—reprinted in 1954— affords an illustration.

> . . . when Whitehead declares that by the " coherence " of ideas he understands that no entity be conceivable in " complete abstraction " from the system of the universe, one may retort that no relational way of thought can declare itself otherwise. But one must also add, that while there can be no " complete abstraction " in this sense, there undoubtedly is a " relative abstraction " so that one must not make the impossible demand that the nature of the whole universe be presupposed in whatever we may say.[19]

[19] *The Symposium*, 1 (1930) , 396; in Nagel, *Sovereign Reason* (Glencoe, Ill., 1954) , p. 157. I note:

1) The criticism begins by declaring agreement with Whitehead's ideal of coherence. How, then, are we supposed to offer the ideal more than lip-service?

2) The necessity of also making " relative abstractions " was unfortunately not emphasized as a general point in *Process and Reality*; and in *The Function of Reason* Whitehead in the heat of argument made statements which were either ambiguous or excessive—e. g., " Insofar as philosophers have failed, scientists do not know what they are talking about when they pursue their own methods " (p. 49) .

3) The passage in Nagel continues: " Whitehead's pursuit of truth as ' nothing else ' than how the composite natures of actualities receive representation in God's nature, is fortunately not his only occupation, otherwise the *Universal Algebra* and the *Principia* would never have been written." Probably that was not the meaning of " truth " for Whitehead in that earlier period; but neither was he describing *the pursuit of truth* in the passage Nagel refers to (PR I I v) ; he was stating a thesis about the mode of existence of the totality of truth. (I find the thesis

Some specific comments on this criticism of Nagel's are given in Note 19. I would add that I do not read Whitehead as making any demand about what we ought to presuppose when we talk. He seems in the main to be saying that our experiences arise in an interrelated universe which has a very general but not completely statable character throughout; that the individual consciously finds himself in a more special, variable setting, since consciousness is selective; that putting the general nature of the world into words is the business of man as philosopher; that for the scientist this general nature is context, not topic; and that we can have no assurance that in pursuing the topic we can indefinitely neglect the context. In *Adventures of Ideas* and *Modes of Thought* Whitehead repeatedly insists upon the necessity of making " relative abstractions." He holds that science and philosophy are engaged in a joint enterprise (AI IX) . Our knowledge is reached by stages; abstractions fall into clusters, of greater or less circumference. Whitehead's pursuit of both scientific and philosophic theory is the pursuit of the double necessity: " We have to analyse and to abstract, *and* to understand the natural status of our abstractions." [20] Thus the theory of Coördinate Division in Part IV of *Process and Reality* is to be read as the culmination of Whitehead's effort to provide a right place of relative independence for the abstractions of mathematical physics.

It must be distinctly understood that Whitehead never made general war on acts of abstraction; he always insisted that they are indispensable to the advance of thought, especially toward greater exactness. What he objected to was the assumption that only reckless or foolish men ever relinquish the relative exactness of scientific statements to think about the total universe of existence.

An even more frequent criticism of Whitehead's speculative philosophy is that it lacks verifiability in human experience.

---

dubious—or at best unclear—in terms of the philosophy of organism itself, and not subsequently emphasized; Professor Hartshorne, however, thinks it sound and necessary.)

[20] MT p. 173; italics added.

That, if true, would be serious indeed, for Whitehead had written, " The elucidation of immediate experience is the sole justification for any thought; and the starting point for thought is the analytic observation of components of this experience " (PR I ɪ ii). Let us look for a moment at the starting point before commenting on the matter of verifiability. I hope the reader will allow that experience suggests ideas for systematic development by philosophers. Problems arise, for many philosophers, when they realize that Whitehead thinks of general human experience as functioning in a way for which " suggests " is much too weak a word. His view is that experience *insists upon* the formulation of certain *kinds* of ideas by philosophers. It requires them to conceptualize, not anything they please, but the manyness of things, their interconnectedness, their becoming and perishing, the compulsion of events, the interweaving of necessity and accident, the purposive character of action, etc.

When a philosophic theory has been constructed, it is to be tested by " confrontation " with this insistent experience of ours. That is the point of Whitehead's repeated appeal to " the immediate deliverances of experience." Now, these appeals run all through Whitehead's work from 1915 on, and are defended with the utmost vigor by his teaching in *Modes of Thought* that " A correctly verbalized philosophy mobilizes this basic experience " (ɪɪɪ 3) . I suppose that many readers have found a contradiction between this and the conception of *speculative* philosophy in *Process and Reality*. But the act of appealing to immediate experience does not contradict the view that the philosopher's verbal characterizations can only be accomplished by systematic speculation and will never be wholly correct and complete. The two activities fit together.

If this be granted, the Whitehead reader may yet be shocked by the way Whitehead talks about *self-evidence* in *Modes of Thought*. Proof, he says, " is based upon abstraction." Philosophy, being a criticism of abstractions, cannot be proved. He concludes: " Philosophy is either self-evident, or it is not philosophy. The attempt of any philosophic discourse should be to produce self-evidence" (III 3). I do not think this is opposed to the description of metaphysics as speculative, presented in *Process and Reality*. Some of the shock will disappear if we first recognize that both are directed against the notion that a philosophy should consist of a chain of inferences. More of the shock goes when we read Whitehead's next sentence: "Of course it is impossible to achieve any such aim." In other words, self-evidence, in his sense, is always *partial and imperfect*. Understanding "always bears the character of a process of penetration," in which the area of self-evidence is enlarged (MT III 1). A detailed categoreal scheme, like the one offered in *Process and Reality*, must be sought; but it always keeps more of a hypothetical character than do such discussions as those in *Modes of Thought*. Mason W. Gross reports of Whitehead that "in his last years he expressed some doubts as to whether he had not sought a too precise elaboration" in Parts III and IV of the big book, which carry the technical elaboration farthest (N&G p. 565).

VI

Whitehead's last metaphysical writings are the lecture, "Mathematics and the Good," delivered at Harvard late in 1939, and his Ingersoll Lecture, "Immortality," of April, 1941. They were published in 1941.[21]

The first (initiated by a reference to Plato's famous lecture on the Good and placed in the context of the historical development of mathematics) is an additional expression of some of the ideas in *Modes of Thought*. The connection between mathematics and the good is the importance of pattern. (The idea of pattern is of course an old favorite of his.) "The essential characterization of mathematics is the study of pattern in abstraction from the particulars which are pat-

---

[21] In LLP-W; both are reprinted in ESP and IS.

terned" (xi). A longer quotation will bring out Whitehead's theme.

> The notion of the importance of pattern is as old as civilization. Every art is founded on the study of pattern. Also the cohesion of social systems depends on the maintenance of patterns of behaviour; and advances in civilization depend on the fortunate modification of such behaviour patterns. Thus the infusion of pattern into natural occurrences, and the stability of such patterns, and the modification of such patterns, is the necessary condition for the realization of the Good.
>
> Mathematics is the most powerful technique for the understanding of pattern, and for the analysis of the relationships of patterns. Here we reach the fundamental justification for the topic of Plato's lecture. Having regard to the immensity of its subject-matter mathematics, even modern mathematics, is a science in its babyhood. If civilization continues to advance, in the next two thousand years the overwhelming novelty in human thought will be the dominance of mathematical understanding—x.

This, D. H. Lawrence—had he been alive to read it—could have condemned from his own point of view without getting Whitehead all wrong.

Whitehead was not thinking of a monstrous extension of mechanics; to see his way of thinking of patterns, the chapters on "The Order of Nature" and "Organisms and Environment" in *Process and Reality* should be read along with "Mathematics and the Good." In the lecture itself he at once noted, "Pattern is only one factor in our realization of experience, . . ."; he went on to describe existence in terms of "the acquisition of pattern by feeling," and to emphasize the ultimate importance of finite individuality.

In the final paragraph of "Mathematics and the Good" Whitehead again mentions the general relation between philosophy and the process of abstraction. The creation of any finite individual, he says, involves abstraction from the infinite universe; and consciousness is a further abstraction, attending

to particular constituents of actual things. " This procedure
. . . is the basis of science. The task of philosophy is to reverse
this process and thus to exhibit the fusion of analysis with
actuality. It follows that Philosophy is not a science." Though
he did not say just this when he published the philosophy of
organism, it was implicit there. (The view of the relation of
the philosophic effort to consciousness was explicit in *Process
and Reality*.) I do not know whether it is now implied that
metaphysics, which in the 1920s he sometimes referred to as a
science, is not really one. The question is unimportant. Since
a metaphysical scheme attempts an analysis of the universe,
makes the widest possible abstraction, we may consider it the
analytic component in the larger activity of Philosophy.

I have been sketching Whitehead's final conception of philosophy in its relation to exact thought. The relation of
philosophy to life—from the point of view of this chapter, the
union of Whitehead's humanistic side with his aim at mathematical coherence—was beautifully stated in the final paragraph of *Modes of Thought*.

> Philosophy is akin to poetry, and both of them seek to express
> that ultimate good sense which we term civilization. In each
> case there is reference to form beyond the direct meanings of
> words. Poetry allies itself to metre, philosophy to mathematic
> pattern.

VII

The Ingersoll Lecture received some discussion in Chapter 4.
Two points which concern the development of Whitehead's
views need to be made here. The first point is that the concept
of a person, which was not given a metaphysically important
place in *Process and Reality*, now gets one: ". . . the World
of Change develops Enduring Personal Identity as its effective
aspect for the realization of value. Apart from some mode of
personality there is trivialization of value " (xiii). Does this

indicate an alteration in Whitehead's metaphysics? I doubt it. I do not think anything in *Process and Reality* precludes the addition of this to what was there said. Instead, I see Whitehead at these two times using two different routes for the analysis of existence.

The possibility of different routes is the second point I wish to make. Let us go back a bit. Whitehead's positive philosophy of natural science begins in Part II of his *Principles of Natural Knowledge* with Article 13, entitled, " The Diversification of Nature." Our diversification of nature, he there observes, " is performed in different ways, according to different procedures which yield different analyses of nature into component entities " (PNK 13.2; see also 3.8) . These entities are " radically different," as different as events, sense-objects, and scientific objects. One mode of analysis needs to be supplemented by another, and Whitehead does this. Moving beyond nature, let us note that he opens the metaphysical sections of *Religion in the Making* in the same way: " There are many ways of analyzing the universe, conceived as that which is comprehensive of all that there is "; and " different routes of analysis " require to be correlated (III iii) . Whitehead then sketches an initial analysis of the universe into " (1) the actual world, passing in time; and (2) those elements which go to its formation," to wit, creativity, the ideal forms, and God. After a few sentences about them, he writes: " A further elucidation of the status of these formative elements is only to be obtained by having recourse to another mode of analysis of the actual world." In it the temporal world is analyzed into a multiplicity of " epochal occasions "—called " actual occasions " in *Process and Reality*. That book presents the only general theory of existence which Whitehead fully elaborated. When we outlined it in Chapter 2 we noted that God is there introduced as a unique member of a pluralistic universe of actual entities. The categoreal scheme with which the theory begins does not mention him; its principles are supposed to hold for all actual entities, and to permit but not strictly require the addition of the concept of God. That concept,

290 DEVELOPMENT OF WHITEHEAD'S PHILOSOPHY

rather misleadingly, is called a "derivative notion." (The notions of a "society"—including that of a "personal society" [in brief, a person]—and of extension are also so designated.) However, this is mostly a matter of Whitehead's technical construction. As we suggested in our earlier chapter, the scheme cannot be systematically applied to temporal occasions without using the concept of God, which is thus necessary to the system, though not present in the opening categoreal scheme.

The subject of the Ingersoll Lecture is the relation of the World to God. Here the concept of God is not a derivative notion!

> The main thesis in this lecture is that we naturally simplify the complexity of the Universe by considering it in the guise of two abstractions—namely, the World of multiple Activities and the World of coördinated Value.—xiii.

What I suggest, then, is that we shall understand Whitehead's metaphysical thinking and his philosophy of organism better if we refrain from insisting that the layout in Part I, Chapters II and III of *Process* presents *the* definitive structure of his metaphysics. It is the only structure he elaborated, but it would be rash to suppose all his mature metaphysical thought followed just those lines. Not that he contradicted them; as between the elaborate portrayal of a pluralistic universe having God as one member, and these sketches of other analyses of the universe, I doubt that there is any incompatibility that is more than skin deep. They represent *different routes of analysis.* The addition of God as a first "derivative notion" to the categoreal scheme of *Process and Reality,* and the theory of the world's reaction on God, with which that book concludes, I incline to think of as effecting a correlation of two such routes, namely, the one stated in the categoreal scheme, and one like that which is used in "Immortality."

Another reason for believing it impossible to specify the exact logical structure of Whitehead's metaphysical position is, that in conversations he allowed and even suggested some

possible and desirable variations from the verbal formulation
that got into print in 1929. And the very idea of adequate
exact verbal formulations in metaphysics is contrary to the
entire spirit of his thought.

VIII

It is my impression that after 1941 Whitehead did not
attempt any further philosophical work. At any rate, a one-
page Preface to an article by William Morgan,[22] is, I believe,
his only published post-1941 piece of writing.

The reader who has had the courage to travel our road to
the end will see, I hope, that the only possible answer to the
question, "Mathematician or Philosopher?" is: "At all times,
both."[23] (This is a rough answer; there is no other kind.)
As an illustration of my meaning, consider Whitehead's battle
against the idea of an independently existing entity, which
his philosophy fought more than anything else. He began
as a mathematician; now a mathematical scheme is the complete denial—most emphatically so on Whitehead's philosophy
of mathematics—of entities which might exist independently
and merely happen to fall into relationships. As a mathematician, Whitehead was a bit unusual in that he worked so
much at bringing different schemes together, out of *their*
independence. Independent existence was exemplified in
physical thought primarily in the concepts of space and
material particle. Whitehead attacked each in turn. Then he
came to attack the Humian epistemology of perceptions which
carry no intrinsic reference to other perceptions.

[22] The article is cited on p. 88, above.
[23] I do not at all mean to doubt that Whitehead worked less and less
at mathematics, in the conventional sense, after World War I; in America
he probably did not study important new developments that would have
greatly interested him earlier. See Robert Palter, *Whitehead's Philosophy
of Science* (Chicago, 1960), pp. 214-218. An article on Whitehead's
mathematical ideas, by Prof. Palter, is expected.

To put before our minds the common character of the alternatives he created, the definition of Speculative Philosophy in *Process and Reality* is to my mind his own most useful statement.

> Speculative Philosophy is the endeavour to frame a coherent, logical, necessary system of general ideas in terms of which every element of our experience can be interpreted. By this notion of ' interpretation ' I mean that everything of which we are conscious, as enjoyed, perceived, willed, or thought, shall have the character of a particular instance of the general scheme.—I 1 i.[24]

In the 1920 books the experience concerned is limited to our perceptions of external nature and our thoughts of spatio-temporal relations. What Whitehead constructed for that field was a *framework*. This word (which people so often use loosely) really fits his objective c. 1920, and the objective of his speculative philosophy. It can also be used in connection with *Principia Mathematica*, the memoir of 1906, and the *Universal Algebra*. Mason Gross was quite right, I think, in calling the definition of speculative philosophy " the key to what Whitehead is trying to do in almost all his writings." [25]

There is thus something common to Whitehead's work that is called mathematical, and to the work that is called philosophical: his objectives and his ways of thinking in diverse areas have a common general character. There are also some identifiable interests which run through decades. An important one, which we traced back to 1905, is his interest in effecting an integral inclusion of geometry in the world of change.

Stronger ways of expressing the result of our survey, we had better avoid. It has not been shown here, and it is not credible

---

[24] Compare his conception of the goal of philosophy, uttered in 1919: " the attainment of some unifying concept which will set in assigned relationships within itself all that there is for knowledge, for feeling, and for emotion " (CN p. 2).

[25] Review of LLP-W in *Journal of Philosophy*, 40 (May 13, 1943), 273.

to me, that Whitehead's metaphysics is but an application of
mathematical principles which he worked with earlier. It has
not been shown that Whitehead's concept of a self-creative
organism, or any central thesis in his philosophy of organism,
is implied by anything in the work of his first period.[26] We did
see how natural was the expansion of the main ideas of the
later half of his second period into his metaphysical concepts
of prehensions, actual occasions, and the duality between occasions and eternal objects; but I have refrained from saying
that the relations here are relations of implication; if that is
said, the hypothetical character of the implications—their
dependence upon Whitehead's bringing to his metaphysics
other ideas from other sources—must be borne in mind.

Whitehead's first serious nonmathematical writings, so far
discovered, were the essays on education published in 1912
to 1917. They are now well known, and were not examined

[26] Prof. David Harrah offers a fresh perspective in his article, " The
Influence of Logic and Mathematics on Whitehead," *Journal of the
History of Ideas,* 20 (1959), 420-430. He argues that there are various
relations, which I should call relations of formal similarity, between the
central *content* of Whitehead's metaphysics and the *procedures* of a
creative mathematician. The metaphysical notion of many entities becoming one novel entity (Whitehead called it his " ultimate metaphysical
principle ") " derives from the mathematician's schemas of induction from
several species to an embracing genus and deduction from several premises
to one conclusion " (Harrah, p. 423). When stated so generally, and
accompanied by Harrah's allowance that the metaphysical notion derives
from other sources also, this type of interpretation is helpful. I do not
find his particular explanations—of the plurality of creative acts, the
functions assigned to God, the concepts of self-creation and objective
immortality, and so on—very convincing. Self-creation gets denatured.
And I get a better grasp of Whitehead's pluralism when I remember him
declaring to his Harvard students that a plurality of individuals in process
is an evident fact of experience (cf. his criticism of Spinoza in *Process
and Reality,* I i ii), than when I remember that a mathematician deduces
his conclusion from a plurality of premises. We might do well to
remember both. But the more compelling member will soon be put in
the shade if we use the terms with which Harrah characterizes Whitehead's
basic notions; he says they are " projections " of mathematical procedures
which were " sublimated." He believes he has caught " the basic ' root
metaphor ' in Whitehead's thinking " (p. 422). If we must fill that
position, aesthetic composition seems to me a better candidate.

here. It has been said that the views on education in these essays had as their basis the organic metaphysics which Whitehead worked out in detail after he came to Harvard. That is possible, and specific evidence which supports it may be unearthed; it is not to be inferred from the picture we have drawn. Because of the unexplained shift from agnosticism toward theism, which seems to have begun in Whitehead's second period (probably in the middle of it), we may not assume any earlier anticipations of that important side of his metaphysics; though I think that his pluralism, temporalism, moderate Platonism, and possibly his emphasis on value, were his quite early. If I have correctly interpreted his published works, they show that what he possessed even in the 1890s was a Whiteheadian method of thinking; and this is very important. The likely additional candidate is his view of human institutions and human life.

In sum: it cannot be assumed that Whitehead's conclusions at one time provide premises for later conclusions, without severe qualifications which destroy the simple notion of a " premise." There is a difference in the level of his discussions. The mistaken assumption rests on a naïve notion of the logic and the psychology involved in expanding investigations.

IX

Finally, let us glance at a few general conditions that made Whitehead's development possible. The nineteenth century was a peaceful century, and sheltered the pursuit of thought; Whitehead was fifty-three years old at the beginning of the First World War. As a youth, he went to Cambridge during one of her great ages. Fortunate occasions arose, at various times, for the exercise of his powers. But the division of his activity into distinct periods, each of high accomplishment, is equally the result of his extraordinary concentration. His first object was a great intellectual synthesis, universal algebra.

He went on to another,[27] and another, always one at a time—but in his conversations and reflections he was constantly touching on all the conditions involved in human existence. If it be also true that mathematics and metaphysics are naturally akin, then it is impossible to imagine a set of conditions more favorable to the creation of a philosophy. The man fitted the conditions perfectly. The philosophy of organism is the ultimate intellectual achievement of the nineteenth century.[28] The centuries to come will profit far more than we.

[27] Without, we remember, finishing his synthesis of algebras. He also left the program of *Principia* unfinished in order to move into a larger area. Philosophy was the chief beneficiary of these moves, which were quite natural ones for him to make. That no intellectual synthesis can be wholly adequate, became one of his mature convictions.

[28] Prof. Harrah, reading this statement in my "Development of Whitehead's Philosophy" (LLP-W), finds it "misleading" because "it suggests a finality and a datedness to this philosophy" and "a biological orientation" (David Harrah, *op. cit.*, p. 430). The context provided by the preceding paragraph and the final sentence of my essay (except for the addition of the footnote, they are unaltered here) should steer the reader away from any such suggestions. Prof. Harrah continues: "Instead, if we regard this philosophy as having a logical rootage and orientation [see Note 26] and reconsider its chief insights in the light of what we know since Gödel's discoveries concerning the ' openness ' of logical systems, we might come to regard the philosophy of Whitehead as belonging to the intellectual climate of the twentieth century." May not a system of metaphysics, created by a mathematician who matured under the remarkably favorable circumstances provided by the peaceful era that ended in 1914, also belong in certain respects to the intellectual climate of the twentieth century? Certainly it may; these are not mutually exclusive alternatives. I say, " in certain respects," because most of the intellectual activities of our time, including almost all the activities in mathematical logic, decision theory, etc., are unfortunately far removed from Whitehead's philosophical point of view (think of how much closer they are, say, to Carnap's, the very opposite of Whitehead's). Hence the hopeful prophecy audaciously expressed in my final sentence.

Whitehead, whose metaphysics was constructed before Gödel published his theorem in 1931, subsequently called it a " great truth," " the discovery embodied in a formal proof, that every finite set of premises must indicate notions which are excluded from its direct purview" (MT I 1—Whitehead's only reference in print to Gödel, I believe). The moral he drew for philosophy is that although we must have systems we must keep them open, and engage in philosophic "assemblage" to make sure we are not victimized by their inherent narrownesses. This advice is based upon his fundamental view of understanding as partial penetration into the infinite unanalyzed background of our conscious experience. That view, unfortunately, is far from common among students of Gödel's proof. But I must leave to others the question of possible implications of Gödel's discoveries for metaphysical method. (Harrah refers in a note to an article by John Myhill [*Review of Metaphysics*, 6 (1952), 165-198], which does not discuss Whitehead's method.)

In this book I have interpreted Whitehead's open-systems doctrine in the way in which he himself presented it, that is, as the inevitable doctrine for anyone who remembers the infinity of the universe and the finitude of man's powers of formulation—a doctrine which, if it is momentarily forgotten, we can be reminded of by the fate of the enormously successful Newtonian system of the world. Possibly the view of the British Hegelians, that no truth is wholly true, also had some positive effect on Whitehead. From his writings I conclude that he always in one way or another (see, e. g., CN p. 12 and PR III I ii) defended the reality of finite truths (which they questioned); that he always thought of partial truth in terms of the scope and limits of application of mathematical theories, not in terms of stages of a dialectic; and that he rejected the argument that truth's incompleteness shows that the finite entities which appear to be its logical subjects are not really its subjects nor wholly real. Still, we know too little about Whitehead's philosophical ideas during the years in which he was exposed to British Hegelianism to warrant us in ruling out the possibility of a positive connection. To my mind his own way of recommending his open-systems doctrine gives a sufficient explanation of its appeal to him.

PART III

EXPERIENCE AND METAPHYSICS

Chapter 11

An Approach to Metaphysics

I

In the last book that Whitehead wrote there is a passage which every April brings to my mind. He is saying that all human understanding is partial, but without permanent limits.

> For example, we know about the colour 'green' in some of its perspectives. But what green is capable of in other epochs of the universe, when other laws of nature are reigning, is beyond our present imaginations. And yet there is nothing intrinsically impossible in the notion that, as years pass, mankind may gain an imaginative insight into some alternative possibility of nature, and may therefore gain understanding of the possibilities of green in other imagined epochs.—MT iii 1.

In what other philosopher's writings could we expect to find what the professionals call a " sense-datum term " being used at once to call attention to the immediate value of sensory experience, to remind us of our ignorance, and to set forth the ideal of ever enlarging our conceptual horizons? My purpose in quoting the passage, however, is not to contrast various uses of sense-datum terms. It is to indicate one of the kinds of caution which a good metaphysician should have. What he hopes to be a quite general theory of existence may, for all he knows, be quite as special as three-dimensional Euclidean geometry. This caution is consequent upon a bold imagination concerning possibilities. The boldness makes trouble; there are obvious difficulties in the idea of a presumably infinite variety of cosmic epochs, and—for me—in the idea that green is an eternal object. I shall look at the second later. My present point is only that a metaphysics which does not boldly make a generous allowance for forms of existence "beyond our present imaginations," is in danger of a dogmatic provincialism.

Besides imagination, passion appears to be indispensable in metaphysical work. This should not surprise us; it is generally, if not quite universally, true in other fields of constructive endeavor that only those who entertain some ideas with emotional intensity have anything to say. All Whitehead's philosophical writings manifest this intensity. The Harvard students who came to the Whiteheads on Sunday evenings remember it too. What he talked about, he cared about; the care was so evident in his voice, that those who wanted a dialectical game coolly played, or who were too young to own (or too timid to show) philosophical convictions of their own, as well as those who were enjoying a flirtation with logical positivism, would say that he pontificated—which he did not.

Proper caution in metaphysics mainly has to do with temptations to stray from an objective in which one ought to be passionately interested. It depends on an active conscience, more than on detachment. Of course everyone who in reading metaphysics is doing more than going through the motions of reading, brings his metaphysical conscience to bear. When an idealist author uses the proposition that ideal knowledge defines reality, the realist reader cries "foul." The moralistic tone of the nominalist's "We do not believe in abstract entities" is unmistakable. Whitehead's repudiations were fervent.

The present author also has ideas about what should be

permitted in metaphysics and what should not. Of course
none of us has charge of the permissions in this field. But
one may clear the air by setting down what one would, and
what one would not, with good conscience permit one's self;
what does, and what does not, arouse one's skepticism when
it is read in others; and why. The whys I have in mind are
not comparisons with the one true metaphysics (a standard
not within human reach) ; they are comparisons with a definition of the metaphysical enterprise that is made explicit and
can be explicitly defended. This is what is to be done in the
present chapter. I shall be both using Whitehead's work, and
reacting against it.

II

To avoid getting bogged down at once in hopeless verbal
dispute, we must agree on an initial identification of metaphysics. The major tradition in Western " metaphysics " seeks
a general theory of existence.[1] The minor tradition aims at
a clear, coherent consciousness of our ways of thinking and
talking about the world. Such consciousness is obviously
desirable; and it appears to be sufficiently attainable to make
the pursuit worth while. Let us give it (though not necessarily
all forms of it) our blessing, and turn to metaphysics in Whitehead's sense, already suggested by the language of the first
paragraph of this chapter—as aiming at a general theory of
existence.

The most useful brief description of this business which I
know is given by Whitehead's phrase, " the effort after the
general characterization of the world around us." I am taking
this phrase, which appears in the second sentence of his 1933
Chicago lectures, " Nature and Life " (MT p. 173), out of
its immediate context—a discussion of our general concept of
Nature—but not out of the wider context which Whitehead

---

[1] It is wise to avoid the ambiguities inherent in " being."

before many pages explicitly provided, that is, the fusion of Nature with Life in a new conception of the evolving universe. For present purposes I take " the world " to mean the totality of all existence, including whatever gods exist. But as Whitehead's most frequent name for this totality is " the universe," and as it has the advantage of not automatically suggesting a contrast with God, I shall substitute it for " the world " in our defining phrase.

I am accustomed to using the several words in this definition as so many reminders of what I seek and what I would avoid in the pursuit of metaphysics. (They do not suggest all that needs to be said.)

I would first of all avoid the suggestion that metaphysics is an established body of principles about the universe—principles doubtless subject to refinement, and the set of them perhaps to some enlargement; but still, established, so that a student can take Metaphysics down from a bookshelf and learn it. If we begin our definition, " Metaphysics is . . .", we must immediately bring in a term like *effort* to forestall the natural expectation that we are defining something which is *there*, awaiting inspection. Naturally I do not mean that metaphysics is pure effort, without results and progress. —But all this has been set forth admirably by Whitehead in the opening chapter of *Process and Reality*.

The word *characterization* reminds us that the metaphysician's task is to describe something; as I like to say, existence in its most general features is the *formulandum* to which his formulations must be faithful. In talking about metaphysics, where the gap between the two is most formidable, " characterize " and " formulate " are better words than " describe," because they carry a positive suggestion of this gap. " Characterize " also implies that the primary aim is not to express or evoke experiences, whether private and special or widespread and sociocultural. Of course a metaphysics may have interest and value when it is read as an intellectual expression of cultural aspirations or forces; and some of the words used should be capable of arousing in the reader the feelings (about certain aspects of existence) which stirred the writer. But for all that, metaphysics is meant to be a kind of telling. Only as a metaphysics ignominiously fails to help us understand the experienceable world may we assign it, as Dewey once assigned philosophy in general, to the realm of cultural meaning (along with Shakespeare and Athenian civilization) rather than the realm of difficult, partial truth.[2] Such re-assessment must be separately made for each distinct metaphysical system, as a system. I have not seen any argument to show that all metaphysics is really something else, that did not either beg the question, or ask for too much.

General is a word of degree. The metaphysician is to get as high up the ladder of generality as he can. We have no trouble in recognizing relative heights; but much, if we try to define the ladder in a way which will not spoil the rest of our definition, e. g., by directing us from the universe around us to universes of discourse. The only direct clarification of that supreme generality which metaphysics seeks, I find in Whitehead's explanation (in terms of experience and its interpretation) of the *adequacy* of a metaphysical scheme. I shall come back to this shortly.

The universe, one should not need to say, is the biggest possible subject matter. One merit of insisting upon this term when defining metaphysics is that its use gives notice that no mere philosophy of man is to be advanced as a metaphysics. The history of modern philosophy shows, I think, that it is on this point much more than on the distinction of science from metaphysics that lapses must be guarded against. Also, we think of the universe as, relative to man, not only an ongoing, but an antecedent reality. Metaphysics, so far as it is successful, is a form of knowledge which resists Dewey's claim that the object known in knowledge is not an antecedent reality but is constituted by the consequences of directed operations, of changes instituted. It would be ridiculous to suppose that the operations of any metaphysician institute changes in the general characteristics of the universe.

[2] John Dewey, *Philosophy and Civilization* (New York, 1931), p. 5.

The universe to be characterized is *the* universe, the one and only actual universe—not a "possible world," and decidedly not "all possible worlds." The usual meaning of "possible" in connection with worlds (or universes [3]) is "consistently thinkable." Different applied meanings then arise, depending upon what one intends to be consistent with. Consistency with what is known marks out what ought to be called "epistemic possibility." For example, I know that there is now some money in my pocket, but I do not know how much. Suppose it is $11.30. Then a world which is just like the one I suppose actual, except that I have $11.35 in my pocket, is a possible world. Plainly, I can think of an indefinite number of worlds which are possible in this sense. But this plurality is already noticed and left behind in our statement of the metaphysical purpose as a *general* characterization of the universe. And that is the better way to describe the situation, because " possible " is too tricky a word in philosophical discussion to be used when it isn't needed. It *is* needed in the theory of human thought,[4] and in some types of metaphysics; but to say that metaphysical propositions, if true, are true of all possible worlds (where " possible " means " thinkable in terms which are self-consistent and consistent with our present empirical knowledge ") and " world " is meant in the inclusive sense stipulated above (not as denoting a sub-world such as the " created world " of Leibniz) , is an unnecessary, misleading, and grandiose way of saying that these propositions present the most general facts about the actual world.

Like Whitehead, I cannot understand actuality without making reference to possibilities. But even if one could understand them otherwise than as within the universe of actual entities, it would still be the case that the subject matter, for

[3] In discussing this point I revert from " universe " to " world," to be in accord with the customary phraseology.

[4] E. g., C. I. Lewis has shown this need in the theory of the meaning of terms and propositions: see Chap. III of *An Analysis of Knowledge and Valuation* (La Salle, Ill., 1946) (my illustration is a true-life form of his in Sect. 5) ; also my paper, " The Concept of the Individual," *Methodos*, 5 (1953) , especially 158 ff.

the sake of understanding which they were introduced, was the actual universe and not being in any other mode.

One reason why I have devoted a bit of space to a notion as indefensible as the notion that metaphysics has for subject matter not what is but what might be, is that it represents the bold romantic way, in contrast to divers cautious ways, in which philosophers try to find a distinctive work to do during this age of science. It was ardently presented as the path of glory by the late William Pepperell Montague, who pleaded with philosophers to give the earth to the scientists and devote themselves to exploring the ocean of possibilities.[5] By imagination and vision philosophy should propose possibilities, and let science dispose of them. An emphatic subsistentialist metaphysics underlay this simple notion of the division of labor between science and philosophy. The necessity of imagination in metaphysics is undeniable. But is it addressed to anything but the actual world? It is truer to say that a first-rate metaphysician loves the world (and so is motivated to construct a vision of it), than that he becomes a metaphysician by casting off from it.

"... the universe *around us*." The last two words remind us of a fact on which the very possibility of the metaphysical effort depends, namely, that the universe is the metaphysician's environment, indefinitely extended. His subject is not out beyond the bounds of space and time; it is all around him— under his nose, in his dreams, in his memories. What is commonly called " experience " is his foothold in his environment, his point of departure for imaginative thought. It is his datum, what he must interpret; and the testing ground to which he must return. It is careless to say that metaphysical systems are so many " interpretations of the world." " Interpret," carefully used, takes as object something which is a datum and so may be inspected and consulted. The world to be characterized is no such datum; only conscious experience can play that role. In short, we interpret our conscious experi-

[5] Prologue in his *Great Visions of Philosophy* (La Salle, Ill., 1950).

ence by characterizing the universe or some part of it; and conversely. Whitehead's repeated statements, that the actual world is the datum for philosophy, and is what we experience though we are conscious of much less, will mislead unless we remember that only what can emerge in consciousness (e. g., the conscious sense of a vague totality, and the corresponding, consciously noticeable characteristics of everyday language), can be suggestive for thought or be empirical evidence for or against what we think.

" The universe around us " is meant in the sense in which it would normally be understood—as including ourselves. The exclusive sense in which someone might take it is not merely not intended; it is implicitly condemned as a falsification of the relation of experience to nature. There is a continuity here which, though it must not foolishly be supposed to preclude differences, has got to be remembered. Whitehead liked to remind philosophers (and Dewey emphatically agreed with him) that " the living organ of experience is the living body as a whole," and that though experience " seems to be more particularly related to the activities of the brain,"

> We cannot determine with what molecules the brain begins and the rest of the body ends. Further, we cannot tell with what molecules the body ends and the external world begins.[6] The truth is that the brain is continuous with the body, and the body is continuous with the rest of the natural world.— AI xv vi.

As we know, Whitehead argued that all experience-events exhibit a common " texture," causal and purposive, which we can discover if we permit our attention to be drawn from the special details of experiences. It is to be used to suggest cosmological categories; and our knowledge of our environment is to be used to inform us of what we might otherwise miss concerning immediate experience. The maxim, that ex-

[6] He often said just this, usually in the form of a challenging question, in his lectures at Harvard.

periences are natural events, is thus a two-edged instrument. This position is a convincing one.

In additional respects given experience is for Whitehead alive with suggestions which quietly start an empirical philosopher's interpretations of it in just one direction. I do not find all these suggestions binding. Still, given experience is for metaphysical purposes much more than the epistemological absolute which a pure theorist of perceptual knowledge, e. g., C. I. Lewis, demands. (The adjective which Whitehead usually attaches to "experience" is not "given," but "concrete." Experience for him is not a flat display; it has depths and meanings which may be caught intuitively by poets and others. There is a good deal of truth in such a conception of experience; but the dangers which it presents to the ordinary thinker are obvious.)

Our interpretations of experience naturally vary with our purposes. In that way many equally true characterizations of existing things can arise. When the purposes are identical, this latitude disappears. Even if all metaphysicians pursue the same purpose, their imaginative powers are so limited by the varying special characteristics of their first-hand experience, their intellectual period, etc., that we must expect great differences between metaphysical systems. In attending to the purpose of metaphysics we are concentrating upon the source of those other large differences, which are theoretically, though not practically or perhaps always desirably, eliminable.

III

The metaphysical objective, then, is a general characterization of the universe, capable of making every type of experience intelligible; a scheme of ideas such that (in Whitehead's words) "everything of which we are conscious, as enjoyed, perceived, willed, or thought, shall have the character of a particular instance of the general scheme" (PR I ɪɪ i) —when that scheme is applied under the circumstances (planetary, human, etc.) of the experiences we have, or believe others to have had. The test of metaphysical truth is the "general success" of the system in such applications.

The desired *scheme* of ideas is not revealed to us by any rational, or mystical, power of intuition. There is nothing for it but to try to frame one, and see if it will interpret diverse areas of experience better than earlier systems did. The first positive act of the cautious metaphysician is to grant permission to speculate—not at random, but under conditions of which Whitehead has given the classic statement (in the opening chapter of *Process and Reality* [7]).

The permission to speculate is also a permission to go in thought "behind the scenes" (as a hostile critic would say) — to explain what is perceived by something conceived. This sounds very bad to many modern ears, but is not. Our everyday thought interprets conscious experience by characterizing some part of the universe; for example, we interpret a sound when we conceive what produced it, and how. The phenomenalist language, which some philosophers try to insist upon, generally gives way to causal language when they try by illustrations to convince us that their doctrine can be applied. An intelligible conception of the sources of experience must of course maintain analogies with what is experienced; for example, no *event* can be explained by reference to an ultimate being which in its own nature does not involve temporality.[8]

It is not so much in relation to sense perception as in relation to the emotional and practical demands of human beings that the approach to metaphysics calls for an attitude of restraint. William James wrote in his first notable prag-

---

[7] Discussions of various aspects of this in the present volume are indexed under "Speculative Philosophy." See also Dr. Ivor Leclerc's excellent summary of Whitehead's position in Sect. 6 of his book, *Whitehead's Metaphysics: An Introductory Exposition* (London and New York, 1958).

[8] The difficulties and requirements of empiricism in metaphysics are briefly discussed in the following chapter.

matistic essay, " The Sentiment of Rationality ": " Man needs a rule for his will, and will invent one if one be not given him." [9] It is the business of a complete philosophy to give him a rule—but not the business of metaphysics. James of course argued the contrary. Each and all of the " great periods of revival, of expansion of the human mind," he wrote, ". . . have said to the human being, ' The inmost nature of the reality is congenial to *powers* which you possess.' " [10] James's statement is very likely true; but the question of what general characterization of the universe makes it most congenial to man is pertinent only to our understanding of man.

There are other ways in which illegitimate requirements of this sort have been imposed upon the metaphysical effort. John Dewey wrote a classic description of one, and himself eagerly embraced another. Men, as he often said, seek stability in a precarious environment; and philosophers have depicted " reality " as

> what existence would be if our reasonably justified preferences were so completely established in nature as to exhaust and define its entire being and thereby render search and struggle unnecessary. . . . Then the problem of metaphysics alters: instead of being a detection and description of the generic traits of existence, it becomes an endeavor to adjust or reconcile to each other two separate realms of being.[11]

Namely, the realms of actual experience, and of the " reality " depicted. Dewey never hid his own nonmetaphysical motive for being interested in what, quite misleadingly, he called " the generic traits of existence." His discussions of them are entirely concerned with those features of man's situation in nature which are both irreducible matter of fact, and always important for the experimental art of controlling human

---

[9] *The Will to Believe and Other Essays in Popular Philosophy* (New York, 1937; first published in 1896) , p. 86.
[10] *Ibid.*, p. 86; italics in text.
[11] *Experience and Nature* (2nd ed.; Chicago, 1929) , p. 54.

affairs. In the end, fortunately, Dewey stopped calling the detection and description of such traits "metaphysics." [12]

In Whitehead's metaphysics there are two worlds—a world of finite existents and a divine being—but both are equally real, and everything he says about them is shaped by the requirement that they be in essential communion with each other. Also, Whitehead never tried to conceive "reality" in such a way as to render human search, struggle, and experiment unnecessary. But there is a disturbing element in the exposition of the theistic side of his metaphysical system. In some passages he seems to be suggesting that the satisfaction of our deepest emotional cravings is an added merit in a metaphysics. In Chapter 4 we briefly examined Whitehead's way of dealing with the religious craving, and saw that his language conveys at the same time the idea of religious knowledge by intuition. We commented:

> This mutual involvement of craving and insight inevitably makes the value of religious evidence for metaphysics problematic for those who have had no personal experience of insight. The occurrence of just such experience demands explanation, but does not determine the soundest mode of explanation. We know too little about ourselves to eliminate the possibility that no religious experience, frequent or infrequent, reveals anything about the universe.

On the other hand, we said, if a thinker produces a metaphysics which, among other things, justifies an insistent religious craving, this result does not discredit the metaphysics. "The zest of self-forgetful transcendence belonging to Civilization at its height" (AI xx xi) must sooner or later be explained, in one way or another, and it is an achievement to offer an explanation which coheres as perfectly with metaphysics drawn from ordinary experience as Whitehead's explanation does. The conclusion drawn in Chapter 4 was that

---

[12] "Experience and Existence: A Comment," *Philosophy and Phenomenological Research*, 9 (June, 1949), 712.

" the marvelous coherence of Whitehead's completed metaphysics constitutes the strongest argument for the theistic element in it—provided this general characterization of the universe has any considerable success as an interpretation of mundane experience "—as I think it does.

It would be unrealistic to suppose that any human being can produce a substantial work of metaphysics which is motivated simply and solely by desire to frame a general characterization of the universe around us, capable of making every type of experience intelligible. Being an emotional animal and a civilized animal, he is bound to desire one kind of characterization more than another. This additional motive shows, whether you consider Spinoza, or Bergson, or Russell—or any philosopher. But the coherence and the empirical verification of the system are the only grounds for accepting it. The satisfaction of a mere craving—any craving—cannot be an added *metaphysical* merit of a general theory of existence. We are justified, then, in giving special scrutiny to those elements in a philosophy which make the universe support what the metaphysician, or mankind at large, cherishes; and we are always saddled with this task. There is also a danger that, leaning over backward, a metaphysician might fall over backward, as Nietzsche might be said to have done.

Whitehead nowhere, so far as I can remember, says that the universe is " just," or demands that it be just; he was too wise and too loving to take that line. But Lecture Six of *Modes of Thought* is entitled " Civilized Universe," and begins, " In this lecture we seek the evidence for that conception of the universe which is the justification for the ideals characterizing the civilized phases of human society." I shudder to think of what metaphysics could become if this sentence and title-phrase were to be widely adopted as guides in man's approach to metaphysics. Whitehead kept his discussion, for the most part, genuinely metaphysical, by founding it upon discernible features of the general texture of our experience—

beginning with the vague, omnipresent sense of maintenance
or discard, and the differentiation of this value-experience
into the feeling of the ego, the others, and the totality. This
level of experience, Whitehead rightly insisted, is much more
fundamental than the clear discrimination of sense-data. A
refusal to use it would be a case of misplaced caution.

The cautious metaphysician may be strongly tempted to
secure himself in advance against all kinds of wishful thinking,
by laying down the broad rule that *no* value-concept is to be
introduced in philosophy beyond the boundaries of the philosophy of man, or of sentient beings generally. He will appeal
to common sense: is it not silly to try to think up a value-
concept with general ontological application? Now this is
quite a different question from that of the cosmic significance
of religious experience and human ideals. It concerns intrinsic
value; but not in the forms which are most familiar in moral
philosophy, like pleasurable experience—nor does it concern
value as any object of any interest. The question is whether
we are so surely right when we habitually characterize most
of the population of the universe as sheer matter of fact
devoid of intrinsic value.[13] Probably we are simply being
unimaginative, and substituting a parochially human point
of view for a metaphysical one. The world view which sits
easiest with our desires is just the one which *restricts* the
occurrence of intrinsic value to ourselves, the higher animals,
creatures like us and them who may exist on planets of other
suns, and God if he exists. Of course, it *would* be absurd to
ascribe any kind of intrinsic value to an object like a type-
writer. The great challenge for " pan-valuism "—if I may introduce an awkward label—is to devise a conception of what
the individuals of the universe are if all possess some definable
for-itself character. Whitehead devised such a conception,
which to my mind definitely supersedes the panpsychisms of
the history of metaphysics. In general: the question whether
value in some form is an ontological attribute, is one which in
the approach to metaphysics should be looked upon as an

---

[13] This is what Whitehead called " vacuous actuality."

open question. As there is no empirical evidence against the possibility of pan-valuism, we are not debarred from favoring a hypothesis of this type when indirect reasons for favoring it appear—the superior coherence of a metaphysical system of which it is a part, for instance.

By way of contrast, consider a type of metaphysics which, because of the unwarranted transfer to metaphysics of a necessity in the theory of perceptual knowledge, has sometimes been said to be the only possible one. I mean the respectable view that the things, not ourselves, which make up the world (or including ourselves, in James's world of strands of " pure experience ") are just those sensa which are given in sense-perception, plus unsensed sensa; or are aggregates of these. This view is rendered improbable by a mass of physiological and psychological evidence to the effect that sense perception is a transforming, partly creative, agency. That thinkers should strain at intrinsic value as an ultimate feature of actualities while swallowing a phenomenalistic *ontology,* is one of the curiosities in the history of tough-mindedness among philosophers.

What is the general significance of essential features of human practice for metaphysics? Whitehead said, " Metaphysics is nothing but the description of the generalities which apply to all the details of practice " (PR I ɪ v). The word to underline here is *generalities.* Then we may give this Whiteheadian illustration of the principle: a metaphysics that does not in a generalized form embody our practice of expecting a future which will continue some characteristics of the present and deviate from others, does not describe the world we live in. It is obvious, however, that the burden of explaining our practices (more generally, of interpreting our experience) never falls on metaphysics alone. It falls on a complex conjunct, consisting of the general theory of existence, plus the philosophy of man, plus the biological and cultural sciences of man. If some invariable feature of human practice contradicts, or stands in no relation to, this conjunct, some member of the conjunct is defective. It is not always easy to say which one this is.

314 EXPERIENCE AND METAPHYSICS

IV

Let us turn to alleged necessities of language and of thought, in their relation to the metaphysical effort.

Do necessities of speech have metaphysical significance? Plainly, the universe is under no obligation to be such that *homo sapiens* can talk about it. He *can* talk about it—for the same reason that he can talk about poltergeists: he possesses a conceiving brain, vocal chords, and culture. Any universe in which these can arise is one that can be babbled about. The real problem is how it is possible for some of these babblings to approximate truth.

We should look with the utmost suspicion on every dilemma of the form, " Either you accept this metaphysical position, or you deny the possibility of meaningful speech "—or as people used to say, " of significant discourse." The necessities posed may reflect nothing more than the limitations of the author's vocabulary or the characteristics of the language in which he writes. Hence the potential value of new ways of talking metaphysics. Not that we can ever hope to possess a perfect metaphysical language; but we may hope to continue the progress which has occurred. It is an achievement to show that some things cannot be said in English without paradox, but it is mere intellectual conservatism to anathematize all efforts to talk in new ways. As Whitehead somewhere says, our language was formed for the market place, not for metaphysical purposes. His reminders of the inadequacies of language have been misunderstood as complaints and condemnations, and said to be " completely nongenuine " [14] because he saw the redesigning of language as an endless task. What other view of the relation of language *to metaphysics* would be sensible?

In Whitehead's view, this endless task serves another process of endless approximation, that of constructing an adequate

[14] Alice Ambrose, " The Problem of Linguistic Inadequacy," in *Philosophical Analysis*, ed. Max Black (Ithaca, N. Y., 1950), pp. 15-37, esp. pp. 15-20.

network of metaphysical concepts. The nature of things out-runs human thought, and thought may outrun speech. When some metaphysical thesis is presented to us as a logical necessity and we find no logical mistake, we should remember that the author is not the universe but a human thinker. The necessity flows from his initial concepts, his meanings. So we search our stock of concepts for better beginnings. And we may never assume that this stock is perfect.

In contrast to particular alleged necessities of thought, which are always in reality hypothetical, stands the broad requirement of consistency. But it is a genuine necessity for metaphysics only because of our daily evidence that the world is not literally " a fiction . . . made up of contradiction." I have never heard anyone report that for a moment he saw something as both red all over and not red all over. If the universe were in large part made up of contradiction, consistency would be a demerit in a metaphysical system, though it might still be a convenience to an occasional reader.

A second broad necessity for metaphysics is coherence, in Whitehead's sense: the general features of existence are to be so formulated that the full understanding of any one, as formulated, will take you to the others. Otherwise your system falls into unrelated parts (as Descartes's did). So far, this is only coherence as an ideal of the understanding. To be more than that, the coherences which the system exhibits must be findable in experience, and pervasive enough to warrant generalization to metaphysical status. This is generally the case with Whitehead's metaphysics. The immediate experience which is myself now, includes a feeling of its own derivation from other actualities, which collectively compose its environment; and also includes appetition for unrealized potentialities. This single sentence must suffice here as a sample of Whitehead's empirical warrant for developing his theory of the coherence of the universe, as that of a process in which actual entities come into being by prehending other actual entities and eternal objects.

That the universe, or being, is intelligible, is often said to

be an indispensable and undeniable premise of metaphysics.
But Whitehead has shown how the matter can and should be
conceived:

> That we fail to find in experience any elements intrinsically
> incapable of exhibition as examples of general theory, is the
> hope of rationalism. This hope is not a metaphysical premise.
> It is the faith which forms the motive for the pursuit of all
> sciences alike, including metaphysics.
>
> In so far as metaphysics enables us to apprehend the ration-
> ality of things, the claim is justified. It is always open to us,
> having regard to the imperfections of all metaphysical systems,
> to lose hope at the exact point where we find ourselves. The
> preservation of such faith must depend on an ultimate moral
> intuition into the nature of intellectual action—that it should
> embody the adventure of hope.—PR II i ii.

I wish next, and finally, to note and briefly consider necessities for definiteness and distinctness. The human animal
cannot think clearly without defining the object of his thought.
This introduces a danger for metaphysics. Actualities are
bigger than human concepts; the moment a metaphysician
forgets this he ascribes to existence some limitation of his
thought, and makes the universe foot the bill for his own
clarity. It is not too much to suggest that whatever he clearly
and distinctly conceives to be the case cannot be the case in
the universe—unless his thought has been as obedient to the
coherences intimated in experience, as to Bishop Butler's
"Everything is what it is, and not another thing." That
dictum is a dangerous rule for metaphysical discussion because
it is too easily used to sanction the erection of fences which
may not exist in reality or in given experience but only
between our concepts. The obvious example of such dicta-
torial thinking is the out of hand rejection of Bergson's
metaphysics on the ground that it is sheer confusion of concepts
to imagine that any kind of "interpenetration" can occur in
the temporal world. I do not suggest and do not believe that
his metaphysics should be accepted; I am saying only that con-

ceptual thought has no business forbidding one existent from embodying something of or from another. Furthermore, it is not a genuine necessity of thought to do this. James showed the preposterousness of it in his protest against the attempt of some monistic idealists to rule out pluralism with the argument that when you say there are many individuals in the universe you are logically bound to say that no connections exist between them. But in *A Pluralistic Universe* James professed to find no positive alternative other than one drawn largely along Bergsonian lines.[15] The man who, by doing it full-scale, showed that perfectly definite ontological concepts of intrinsic connection between individuals can be framed was Whitehead.

He has often been charged with abandoning the intellectual ideals of clarity and definiteness in his metaphysics of process. If our civilization is allowed to continue, the historians of philosophy two hundred years from now are likely to find this reckless charge amusingly misplaced. It is a bit like saying that the designers of the first submarines did not believe in travel by water. A thoroughgoing conceptualization of process —done with an insistence on the absolute self-identity of concepts rather than by making each turn into its opposite—is odd evidence of disloyalty to the intellect.

It would be more sensible to inquire whether his approach to metaphysical construction was not in one sense too intellectualistic. I am thinking of his category of eternal objects, which roughly corresponds to the historic category of universals. The use of universals is of course no vice of the intellect but a necessity of thought. I pass by the old question of whether they must also be considered a category for metaphysics, in order to discuss briefly the larger form which that sort of question takes concerning Whitehead's eternal objects, (William A. Christian has included in his recent book, *An Interpretation of Whitehead's Metaphysics*,[16] a needed reminder of the ways in which Whitehead dissented from the traditional view at the base of the old disputes—the view that

---

[15] See William James, *A Pluralistic Universe*, Lects. II, VI, VII.
[16] New Haven, 1959; Chapter 13.

the main use of universals is to classify individuals into genera and species.)

Things have characters. Some philosophers will not budge from the thesis that the characters of particular things are particulars rather than universals. That seems an untenable extreme view. Whitehead went all the way in the opposite direction. In his metaphysics the actual world is a process composed of individual processes; but he insists that none of these, nor any group of them, nor any element in any one of them, nor *anything* in the world, could be a definite entity *unless* it exemplified a form of definiteness which bears in itself no temporal limitation whatsoever. To Whitehead this is obvious, and probably always appeared obvious.[17] It is not quite obvious to me. Granted that an existent has a character, and that at least component characters of this character can be exemplified elsewhere, I am not convinced that in conceiving them as eternal objects we are being faithful to their mode of existence in the universe. We may be converting a normal step—possibly a necessity—of conceptual thought into a necessity for metaphysics. We must remember that Whitehead's eternal objects are " ideal entities," and " in themselves not actual," but " such that they are exemplified in everything that is actual, according to some proportion of relevance " (RM III iii). We must not think of them as things which *do* something in the world; Whitehead's position is the sound one that eternal objects are abstract entities, and only actual entities act. Nevertheless his language, in all the books in which he writes about eternal objects, is half the time suggesting either too much or too little: that they *are* agents, or that they " express " the definiteness of actualities. Plainly, Whitehead's doctrine that eternal forms of definiteness are exemplified in actualities is *his* way of expressing the definiteness of actualities. He often claims that without such forms no rational *description* of actual things is possible. If this were true, it would of course not prove that forms of definiteness

---

[17] See Part II of his premetaphysical book, PNK, and Note II to the second edition; also Chapter 6, Section VII, above.

are eternal in the universe, but only that if they are not, we must either write metaphysics as if they were or not write metaphysics. But I doubt that Whitehead's assertion is altogether true.

If every form of definiteness is eternal, it must be because each always has some relevance to whatever is happening, no matter how far that happening, or the whole universe in that stage of its history, may be from realizing this form. That which is relevant to a process but not certain to be realized in it must be called a potential for it. Now the metaphysician has not only to note that there are actual things and that they have characters; his formulations must describe the general way in which, in arising, they get their characters. This means using some notion of potentiality. Those who refuse to do this are abstracting from ongoing time—looking at the universe (either in their approach to metaphysics or at some point in their construction) as if it were a completed whole, spread out before them. They can then announce that it consists of the totality of actual things and nothing else; that is "what there is." But the universe we face is not like that. It has a tomorrow. Thus we need the notion that today contains potentialities (one or many) for tomorrow. The notion will take different forms, depending upon whether we think that new existence arises by efficient causation or by final causation or by both. In no case may we eliminate the notion of potentiality when we undertake to write the metaphysics of an ongoing universe.[18]

However, I do not think we need carry to this task the full sweep of the notion, as Whitehead did. He introduced his forms of definiteness as "pure potentials," each to all eternity a potential for every process. It is the maintenance of this eternal potentiality which first required a concept of God in Whitehead's system. Whatever we may conclude about

[18] Two suggestive discussions are: Grace A. de Laguna, "Existence and Potentiality," *Philosophical Review*, 60 (1951), 155-176; Charles Hartshorne, "On Some Criticisms of Whitehead's Philosophy," *ibid.*, 44 (1935), esp. 335 ff.

this conception of the universe, we are bound to admit its magnificence. Of course his boundless realm of possibility staggers the imagination. I can't quite believe in it; but I don't find it an unintelligible notion. One alternative, which I do not think has been mentioned by any of Whitehead's unconvinced admirers, is that we may just possibly be able to construct a metaphysical theory of potentiality which does not assume eternal objects, by exploiting (with alterations) another of his categories of existence: " propositions." These are *limited*, " impure " potentials, " matters of fact in potential determination." They are not timeless logical entities, but natural entities which come into being in the history of the universe.[19] Perhaps we can think of such propositions as embodying all the effective potentiality that there is. Some of them may be for practical purposes almost eternal,[20] but none completely so. The notion of a form of definiteness would appear in such a metaphysics as that of a predicate abstracted from a proposition; and the eternalization of such a form (a quality, relation, or pattern) would be a further abstraction which is performed by human thought and discussed in the philosophy of man, not in metaphysics.[21] There

[19] Whitehead is explicit on this: see, in I II ii of *Process and Reality*, the third Category of Explanation; also the fifteenth, and the sixth Category of Existence. A reference to p. 42, above, may be helpful. For Whitehead's general discussion of these entities one might turn first to AI xvi iii, then to PR II ix i and III iv i, ii. When Whitehead reminds us that " every idea once was new, and for that reason was then vague, ill-defined, with glorious possibilities or with hideous consequences " (ESP p. 203) —which is " the great secret of history "—his examples are the propositions suggested by the words, " that two and two make four," " that Caesar should be murdered," " that Caesar had been murdered." Note also: " The unconscious entertainment of propositions [by an actual occasion] is a stage in the transition from the Reality of the initial phase of experience to the Appearance of the final phase " (AI xvi iii) .

[20] " One and one make two," as discussed by Whitehead in PR II ix iv, is an example.

[21] The distinction between these fields will be touched upon again in Chap. 14, Sect. V. In Whitehead's system, propositions of course presuppose eternal objects. " A proposition is the abstract possibility of some specified nexus of actualities realizing some eternal object, which may

are surely problems here, e. g., the problem of the status to be given to mathematical propositions, and to what we are pleased to call the "metaphysical propositions" which we entertain in our stabs at characterizing the universe. We shan't know how difficult these problems are until someone works with this approach.[22]

Whitehead was always warning against turning inabilities

either be simple, or may be a complex pattern of simpler objects" (AI *loc. cit.*). The proposition is "a manner of germaneness" of the eternal object(s) to the actualities. This is the clean way to introduce the Proposition, as a type of entity, into metaphysics. The line I suggest would be more complicated, but possibly more faithful to the way the creative advance of the world proceeds. "Proposition" would be undefined, and Whitehead's definition, just quoted, would first appear not in metaphysics but in the theory of human thought, subsequent to the introduction there of atemporal, or pseudo-eternal, objects.

Any revision of *Whitehead's* metaphysics in which the category of eternal objects was eliminated would affect everything in his system. No such scheme can be much more than half Whiteheadian.

[22] Eternal objects are eliminated in a different way by Dr. Lucio Chiaraviglio, who substitutes special sets of becoming entities. One of the most interesting things yet done with the philosophy of organism is his formalization—and reformulation—of part of it. This particularly concerns Part IV, "The Theory of Extension," of *Process and Reality*. In "Strains" (*Journal of Philosophy* 58, September 14, 1961, 528-534), Dr. Chiaraviglio sketches a formalized theory of feelings and of extension in terms of set theory. He has kindly shown me two other papers. In his "Extension and Abstraction" (to be published in that collection of essays in honor of Charles Hartshorne mentioned in Chap. 1, n. 13, above), the construction is more detailed, and his reformulation of Whitehead's theory of the transmission of feelings is developed. In a later paper on "Eternal Objects" he uses a variant of the same approach to highlight the elimination of these entities.

The general metaphysical idea I have been emphasizing, potentiality, is omitted, and I suppose must be omitted, in Dr. Chiaraviglio's theory. So are other essential ideas of the philosophy of organism, such as subjective aim and subjective immediacy. I am uncertain about "organism" itself, and about the fate of the category of existence which Whitehead named "contrasts." (Contrasts are not relations, but modes of synthesis of entities in a prehension, and a multiple contrast is not an aggregate of dual contrasts.) It is to be hoped that Dr. Chiaraviglio will further expound and develop his theory of actuality. I have grave doubts about set theory as a language for metaphysics, but in any case his papers should be valuable to logicians interested in important new uses of set theory.

of our imagination into limitations of the universe. Metaphysics has also to remember that in some ways our thought tends to go beyond what is effective in the process of the universe.

V

It is mainly because of its tendency to slight the difference between metaphysics and the philosophy of man that I do not like to use an approach to metaphysics which can quote Whitehead's authority but differs from the approach sketched in this chapter. It conceives of philosophy as Henry Sidgwick did, in a remark which Whitehead quoted with approval: "It is the primary aim of philosophy to unify completely, bring into clear coherence, all departments of rational thought, . . ." [23] A statement of this sort does not tell us what to look for in the various fields, or how to put what we find to metaphysical use. It is really only a beginning for a definition. Whitehead's way of completing it is suggested by his statement that it is one of the functions of philosophy " to harmonise, refashion, and justify divergent intuitions as to the nature of things " (SMW Preface). This brings the ordinary thinker up against the question, What intuitions are genuine? Suppose we substitute a weaker notion, e. g., that of the *point of view* which is characteristic of a field, e. g., of jurisprudence, or ethics, or physics. Unfortunately it is not true that all recognized " departments of rational thought " are co-ordinate in their possible metaphysical significance. Those which deal with human peculiarities must be somewhat discounted, and the notion of the universe brought in. Whitehead remarked that " The various human interests which suggest cosmologies, and also are influenced by them, are science, aesthetics, ethics, religion " (SMW Preface). If ethics be replaced by sociology,

[23] From *Henry Sidgwick: A Memoir*, Appendix I (London and New York, 1906) ; quoted in SMW p. 197; see also SMW pp. 26, 122.

this is a fair list of the areas which Whitehead himself drew upon. Other thinkers with wide sympathies will prefer a different list. Under the modern departmentalization of knowledge, the whole "integration of diverse fields" approach to metaphysics is in constant danger of encouraging a mere reconciliation of the different human standpoints embodied in the current division of intellectual labor. Its value for philosophy lies chiefly in the reminder that philosophy is to be a constant and constructive critic of abstractions; its value for metaphysics, in the insistence that the physicists' perspective of the universe around us must be confronted with other perspectives.

If you ask a scholar to define the metaphysical effort, he will take you first to Aristotle: "There is a science which investigates being as being and the attributes which belong to this in virtue of its own nature." He may elucidate this as meaning inquiry into the nature of that which has "being" or "existence" in the primary and full sense of the term, to which all other being, such as (for Aristotle) the being of Platonic forms, refers. A conception of this sort is to be found also in Whitehead's *Adventures of Ideas*: "It [philosophy] seeks those generalities which characterize the complete reality of fact, and apart from which any fact must sink into an abstraction." [24] Aristotle's definition of metaphysics is not easy to understand. And probably the statement from Whitehead, which looks somewhat clearer to me, means little to readers who know nothing else in Whitehead. Most descriptions of the metaphysical enterprise, naturally enough, refer to something historical, like Aristotle's difference from Plato, or to something other than existence (as Aristotle's description [25] referred to the different ways in which we *say* that things have being), or to our sense of contrast between "concrete existence" and "abstract existence," or to the contrasting words, "appearance" and "reality" (whereby we are nudged into

[24] AI ix iii. See Chap. 9, n. 41, above, and Leclerc, *Whitehead's Metaphysics*, esp. pp. 17-34.
[25] *Metaphysica*, Book Gamma, 1-2.

an epistemological approach to metaphysics). All these definitions, carefully used, are helpful. In this chapter I have tried
to define metaphysics in a way which requires no such auxiliaries, and is understandable by anyone who has a living general
wonder about existence. (You may call it the naïve approach
to the subject; I have tried to show that fidelity to it requires
more than naïveté.) It embodies, I hope, the spirit in which
Whitehead wrote of philosophy in the opening sentences of
" Nature and Life ":

> Philosophy is the product of wonder. The effort after the
> general characterization of the world around us is the romance
> of human thought.—MT p. 173.

and on his last page:

> Philosophy begins in wonder. And, at the end, when philo-
> sophic thought has done its best, the wonder remains. There
> have been added, however, some grasp of the immensity of
> things, some purification of emotion by understanding.—MT
> p. 232.

Chapter 12

Empirical Method in Metaphysics

I

The common reaction against Whitehead's metaphysics is a protest that it is intolerably abstract. What *is* all this talk about actual entities and prehensions and nexūs? Yet Whitehead wrote (PR I II i) that in framing these three notions he was trying to base philosophical thought upon what is most concrete! Surely—the reaction runs—the concrete things are the identifiable bodies around us, and all our knowledge is knowledge of the behaviors of identifiable bodies of one sort or another, got by observing them and framing theories about them. A philosophy of actual entities, prehensions, and nexūs can only be written by someone who deems himself to have a way of knowing that is superior to the way of science.

A similar reaction, on a smaller scale, could have been made —and was made—to the concept of nature in Whitehead's 1920 books. He elaborated a theory of events, and a theory of various types of objects. But surely the concrete things in nature are neither events as such nor objects as such, but enduring objects whose behavior we can observe! Whitehead

was aware of this view, and criticized it several times.¹
Evidently we have a head-on collision of opinions about what
it is that men concretely experience.

Enough has been said in earlier chapters about this collision
in the theory of natural science. What is harder to be fully
aware of is the sense in which Whitehead's metaphysical
thought can be concrete when he adopts the same procedure
there. It really is the same. When explaining it in *Process
and Reality* he referred in a footnote to the second chapter
of *The Principle of Relativity*.² There we find such passages
as: ". . . the Tower of London is a particular aspect of the
universe in its relation to the banks of the Thames. Thus an
entity is an abstraction from the concrete, which in its fullest
sense means totality " (R p. 17). The position he took in
his metaphysical books is shortly put in the statement, "We
experience more than we can analyse," and the explanation,
" For we experience the universe, and we analyse in our consciousness a minute selection of its details " (MT v 3). This
doctrine will be familiar from our discussion of Whitehead
on abstraction, in Chapter 10. I want to add now, emphatically, that if the doctrine is fully accepted, the terms of any
metaphysical scheme constructed in accordance with it will of
necessity be intangibles to common sense; and the identifiable
bodies of common sense and science will appear as constructs.
The ultimates must be intangibles, because whatever is marked
out for us by our hands or eyes, and whatever we are conscious
of as an individual object in the external world, is an individual only in the special way in which objects of its kind are
individuals and/or taken as individuals relative to our particular purposes and our perceptive organs. We must then
permit *thought* rather than sense, thought not limited to particular purposes, to frame the shapes of the metaphysically
ultimate entities. Not that anything proposed by thought will

¹ A good example, not well enough known, is his criticism (R pp. 53 f.)
of the view " that our notions of space merely arise from our endeavours
to express the relations of these bodies to each other."
² He could also have referred to CN I.

serve; as we know, Whitehead holds that nothing we can propose will be wholly satisfactory. And he is aware of the risks we run in unleashing pure thought. " The speculative methods of metaphysics are dangerous, easily perverted " (AI xx xi). But, " in spite of much association with arbitrary fancifulness and atavistic mysticism, types of Platonic philosophy retain their abiding appeal; they seek the forms in the facts " (PR I ii i). The general form of actuality which Whitehead speculatively defined in that totality of fact, the universe, is the one he named " actual entity."

Well! (it will be said) —If Whitehead wants to call concrete things abstracta and call his intangibles the really concrete things, at least we know that this is not an empiricist approach to metaphysics. Ah, but if we pass that judgment, we must also say that only a crazy empiricism begins with " we experience the universe." And that is not self-evident to Whitehead. He considered the classic doctrine that we experience impressions and ideas a pretty unempirical one. Among empiricisms, Whitehead had most in common with James's; we shall explore this in our next chapter.

Among other empiricisms not of the classic type but held by English-speaking philosophers in the twentieth century, one stands in a particularly enlightening contrast to Whitehead's. The naturalistic empiricism, inspired by Aristotle, that was nourished by F. J. E. Woodbridge at Columbia was meant to be a doctrine for metaphysics. The " empirical metaphysics " which thus arose was not confined to the behaviors of identifiable bodies; its analysis of experience was organized around the subject matters of the various sciences and of types of human activity. In a Symposium, " The Nature of Metaphysics: Its Function, Criteria, and Method," held at a meeting of the American Philosophical Association (Eastern Division) in 1946, one of the three speakers, W. E. Hocking, defended a view which, very roughly speaking, continues the tradition of Plato, Hegel, and Royce; the two others, J. H. Randall, Jr., and Sterling P. Lamprecht, very largely coincided in recommending the position, stemming from Woodbridge, which I have just mentioned. Professors Randall and Lamprecht have continued the advocacy and practice of this kind of metaphysical analysis, and the former reprinted his contribution to the Symposium of 1946 a dozen years later, in his book, *Nature and Historical Experience*.[3] To me, the papers of 1946 [4] opened up the whole question of "empirical method in metaphysics." In a paper so entitled, read to the same philosophical association at the end of that year as part of a program on Empirical Method, I tried to state the general empiricist ideal and to show how speculation is necessarily involved in its application to metaphysics. I believe the paper brings out as well as I can the reasons why an empiricist should take a Whiteheadian approach to that field rather than approaches which at first sight look more concrete. The remainder of this chapter consists of that paper, with practically no alterations. As I have not tried to remove the polemical edge, it should be noticed that in the passages which criticize "empirical metaphysics" I am criticizing a type of metaphysics, not the complex positions taken by either Professor Lamprecht or Professor Randall; nor could I take account of their later published specimens of metaphysical analysis without disproportionately enlarging this part of my book.

II

We smile when we read that once many German philosophers fell into the habit of asking themselves, "Was ist deutsch?" Perhaps we should smile a little at ourselves as we ponder the question, "What is empirical method?" We are, I think, quite sure that empiricism is a great common bond uniting us, that no nonempirical blood runs through our philosophic veins; [5] and we wish to heighten our conscious-

---

[3] New York, 1958.
[4] Originally published in *Journal of Philosophy*, 43 (1946).
[5] This was a bit of an overstatement in 1946, and "empiricism" is no

ness of this characteristic, to discuss its implications, and so help ourselves keep true in practice to what we all are in essence. Perhaps we *should* assume that a genuine empiricism will be off the line of our mental habits, and that nowadays we violate it even when we think we are being most empirical.

This would be but a smug proposal to use words perversely, were the attitude I shall recommend not needed to fulfill a basic ideal of empiricism which we all recognize—the ideal that thought should progressively satisfy experience. " Satisfy " may be too vague a word to satisfy you, but I shall not go into its meaning now. I shall discuss what precedes the verifying process. We often unwittingly hamstring this basic empirical ideal in advance of verification.

To become aware of this, we must first remember that we use ideas, as C. I. Lewis once aptly said, to play a perpetual " animal, vegetable, or mineral? " game with given experience. Now I am reminded that the last time I played this parlor game with my wife, she was thinking of the letters engraved on a silver cup, and in answer to my first question, " Animal, vegetable, or mineral? " she replied, " It's a sort of absence of mineral." Had she been less generous, she might have made no answer, and charged me with a question that was a sheer loss. As the thing she was thinking of was just itself, and not necessarily either animal, vegetable, or mineral, so, empiricism holds, experience is just itself, and is not necessarily isomorphic with any category in our mental stockroom. To assume the contrary is partially to nullify the submission of thought to experience.[6] It is to commit what Whitehead called " The

---

longer the word of widespread praise which it was then. Nevertheless, I think it is by their appeals to experience (including linguistic experience) that most English-speaking philosophers make their difference from Whitehead known.

[6] Some degree of isomorphism is, of course, presupposed by the possibility of using categories to put questions to experience. But if any set of philosophical categories which man has formulated were predetermined to be completely isomorphic with experience as it is had, empirical testing would be confined to subordinate matters of detail; it would be eliminated from philosophy. And surely the truth is that the repeated empirical testing of ideas concerning details is at the same time a long-range testing

Fallacy of the Perfect Dictionary," which consists in "the belief, the very natural belief, that mankind has consciously entertained all the fundamental ideas which are applicable to its experience," together with the assumption " that human language, in single words or in phrases, explicitly expresses these ideas " (MT p. 235). As I have not time to discuss language, I shall concentrate on the aforementioned " very natural belief," to which the assumption about language is merely a natural supplement.

History shows us that the displacement of old ideas, whether scientific or philosophical, by new ones which achieve a wider and more precise coverage of experience, is a real possibility. This is so obvious in the history of science that it is hard for a scientist to persist unchallenged in the Fallacy of the Perfect Dictionary. But we generally get away with its use as a staple of metaphysical argument. I illustrate by a passage on pluralism, drawn from Hastings' *Encyclopaedia of Religion and Ethics:*—" If the monads are absolutely separate, it is not obvious how a cosmos can arise; while, if they are inter-related, there is no intelligible sense in which they can be ultimate." [7] Here the phrase, " there is no intelligible sense," should warn us that a conventionally accepted, " intelligible " notion of relatedness is being dogmatically applied to prevent metaphysicians from trying out novel conceptions of individuality. The fallacy is hardest of all to detect when the instrument of its application is not consistency with " intelligible " categories, but fidelity to " the empirical." [8] Yet the history of thought warns us that new ideas which eventually prove most advan-

---

by experience of the general success of those philosophic ideas which, functioning as the framework of our testing apparatus, enjoy in each particular test a relative independence of that particular experience.

[7] W. D. Niven, " Good and Evil," Vol. VI, p. 323 (edition of 1914). There is no later edition. It can plausibly be said, however, that this way of thinking is now practised anew in much " Oxford philosophy."

[8] I do not wish to suggest a hard and fast distinction between two ways of committing the Fallacy of the Perfect Dictionary. The empiricist sinner, just as much as the rationalist, is proud of pinning philosophy down to " intelligible " categories, universally recognizable and untranscendable.

tageous often, perhaps usually, look queer from an empirical
point of view when they are first introduced. Therefore we
must carefully examine every restriction which anyone, in the
name of empiricism, may propose to place on ideas in advance
of the tests of future experience.

III

By way of illustration, let us examine the restrictions implicit in a current view of what constitutes proper empirical
procedure for metaphysicians. The procedure recommended
is an analytic survey of the various universes of discourse presented by the sciences and by human activities, so as to identify
the properties which their subject matters in common present.
This will be an analysis of " existence as existence," and our
conclusion will be a statement of " the generic traits of existence." Though we generalize as we pass from one universe
of discourse to all, we avoid the notion of synthesis, because
we believe that we shall lose our empirical purity if we start
to talk about " the Whole." When, by our comparative
method, we have identified and carefully stated such traits as
causality and contingency, structure and process, individuality,
or continuity, we have the good sense to accept them, instead
of trying to " explain " them. We respect the meanings of
ideas in ordinary experience, giving each a chance to be considered the generic meaning, and choosing fairly between them.
We become great admirers of Aristotle, and recommend as
models those books of his *Metaphysics* in which he did this
with such masterly impartiality.

In asking what more may be desired, I do not wish to attack
what Messrs. Lamprecht and Randall said at the Symposium
on Metaphysics in February, 1946. My concern is not with
the complex position taken by any individual, but with what
is distinctive of this " empirical metaphysics," and what we
shall neglect if we choose to pursue it rather than a speculative
metaphysics of experience such as Whitehead's.

Knowledge of the generic traits of existence is rightly much
to be desired. My questions concern the method recommended. "Analysis" in the sciences is an application of
theoretical concepts to something observable. It is easy for
the metaphysician to say that he will analyze, but dare he
assume that he has the tools for it in his pocket? That would
be the Fallacy of the Perfect Dictionary at its worst. How,
then, shall he get those tools? How analyze?

It will be obvious, to begin with, that a sheer *survey* of
diverse universes of discourse will discover no idea which is
the same in all of them; we may find the same term employed,
but in different senses. Thus no idea, as it appears in our
survey, expresses a generic trait of existence; some wider form
of it may. The problem is to state that wider form, and is
not to be thought of as just the separation of the more general
from the less general in our stock of concepts. "Empirical
metaphysics" rises to the problem by suggesting a "clarification" of these concepts. I take this to be a process of extrusion
and abstraction, by which the hard generic core in any given
concept is separated from the indefinite shell of extra meanings
which it has in use.

An illustration will let us see how far this gets us. Individuality and continuity, we suspect, are generic traits of existence.
We say that a man, a beetle, an experience, an atom, a quality,
an element in a mathematical manifold, a universal, a work
of art, an act, all have individuality; but in different senses.
Clarify, refine each of these senses as much as we please, will
the common result of our labors be anything more than the
truism that everything mentionable is *ipso facto* individual?
That hardly helps us to conceive the individuality which is
a generic trait of existence, or to conceive its generic relation
to continuity, which is in the same leaky boat. Shall our
generic continuity be that of the mathematicians, which they
have fortunately already clarified for us? or the continuity
exhibited in the growth of organisms? or of minds? Shall it
be the continuity of which Bergson spoke? or that of James,
when he said, "Perception changes pulsewise, but the pulses

continue each other and melt their bounds "? [9] Mathematical, biological, and perceptual continuity are not only vastly different: they are not even commensurable at this level of inquiry. We must tackle the status of mathematical forms, and of life, and of perception, in the world. Their status is part of our problem from the start.

Further illustration would be tedious. It is a recognized principle that thought and observation grow but meagerly in the absence of a working hypothesis which embraces the field to be investigated. What reason is there to think that the observing, formulating, and interrelating of the generic traits of existence is any exception to this rule? [10]

Of course the advocate of " empirical metaphysics " does not take this lying down. He protests that he approves of hypotheses—he merely wants them to be derived from the facts. He strives for interrelatedness, but he will not buy it by supposing that existence forms a single system, a Whole; he sensibly studies existences *distributively*,[11] and if the result be modest, it is empirically sound. But here he may be a little ahead of the game. Possibly his demand that existences be studied distributively signifies merely a preference for pluralism over monism—a preference I share. But if it implies that their unity is simply that of members of a *class*, this is empirically a most unwarranted assumption. The physical uni-

[9] *Some Problems of Philosophy* (New York, 1911), pp. 87 f.
[10] It may be objected that I have dealt with " analysis " in but one of its meanings. Another, commonly used when our situation is that of relative ignorance, signifies selective emphasis on some observed trait which, it is hoped, contains a clue to understanding. But as Dewey— from whose *How We Think* ([rev. ed.; Boston, 1933], pp. 127, 157, 197) I take this statement of the second meaning—tells us, the clue is developed by conjecturing the existence of systematic interconnections in the situation. In a highly general problem, this means that, starting from some selected aspect, we construct a general working hypothesis. It does not mean just " clarification," of the sort whose self-sufficiency I am questioning.
[11] This way of putting the matter was employed by both Prof. Lamprecht (*Journal of Philosophy*, 43 [1946], 397) and Prof. Randall (*ibid.*, p. 406). I think it was unfortunate. Prof. Lamprecht tells me he does not embrace the natural connotation which I proceed to criticize, and I do not suppose Prof. Randall would accept it either.

verse has more unity than that, in the eyes of a physicist; an
organism-environment " transaction," in the eyes of a Deweyite;
the many data of a single experience, to its experiencer. A
purely classial unity is *quite* hard to discover empirically;
it appears to be an artifact of thought. The outcry about the
Whole drowns out the distinction between togetherness which
is more than classial [12] and togetherness in a Cosmic Being.
A purely distributive study would cripple the production of
metaphysical ideas adequate to experience, by declaring that
only one favored type of relational concept—the classial—is
worth testing.

As the next item to be considered—the plausible demand
that hypotheses be derived from the facts—is not peculiar to
" empirical metaphysics," I now take my leave of that doctrine,
with the thought that it will never reach the generic traits
of existence so long as it is faithful (as Aristotle was not) to
a method which locks us inside a partitioned mental stockroom. " Seeing in context " is required not only where Professor Randall recommended it [13]—in the metaphysical study
of a specific subject matter—but (in the form of a general
metaphysical hypothesis) in our search for the generic traits
of existence.

IV

Turning to the " derivation " of metaphysical hypotheses
from the facts of experience, we repeat that if the facts meant
are those presented by the various departments of knowledge,
the traits they offer us are too narrow. And we fool ourselves
if we imagine that, upon adding to these what are called " the
data of common experience," we shall have everything we
need. The experience of the woman who lists her occupation
as " housewife " is not as partial as that of a mathematician

---

[12] The formulation of this in twentieth-century metaphysical thought is
well illustrated by Whitehead's concept of a nexus and Samuel Alexander's
concept of compresence.
[13] *Op. cit.*, pp. 410 f.

or a bacteriologist. But it is still partial, in that, from moment to moment, she is consciously preoccupied with the accidents of existence, whereas metaphysics seeks the factors that are always with us. Common experience certainly has an essential place in the construction of metaphysical hypotheses; but we, like the natural scientist, can literally *derive* generic ideas from it only by reconceiving it—which is not what our empiricists usually have in mind. But unless they have it in mind, they commit the Fallacy of the Perfect Dictionary.

Our empiricists, I think, want metaphysics to use only the sort of method that Francis Bacon proposed for science. But as Galileo reconceived the material world, the truly empirical metaphysician has to reconceive the nature of experience—not just survey what it plainly displays. Unfortunately, and in spite of the lessons to be found in modern philosophy, the belief persists that " experience " should always mean something given, not also something to be conceived. I think this dative view is a half-truth masquerading as the whole, and I should like to dispose of it; but the problem is very complex, and I do not flatter myself that I can dispose of that view now. It will be enough to suggest two of the difficulties in its way.

One is, that the dative view of experience is not open to anyone who holds, as most empiricists today hold (and they are right) , that every experience is a natural event. For every natural event has its natural constitution, only a small part of which is dative, if the event be an occasion of experience. Do we take " dative " to mean " given in at least some conscious experience " (especially such as have occurred in laboratories) , we still have not reached the integral natural constitution of an experience. That is something which we conceive rather than observe. And in the natural sciences, what a theory offers for verification is in effect an explanation of dative experience as an outcome of experience broadly conceived, so as to include its genetic constitution. In practice many " dative " empiricists unhesitatingly import into their philosophies the novel notions about the constitution of human experience which have recently been developed in the biological sciences. The original insistence that experience must only be employed datively may deservedly be named " single-track empiricism."

A second defect of the dative view is this: does it not demand that the philosopher give up all distinction between experience and conscious experience, between what is undergone and what is given? But extension of the notion of experience beyond the conscious has proved too valuable to be given up. And our only way of getting at the extended area is by some speculative conception. In fact, every philosopher employs some conception of what occasions of experience generically are. These conceptions should be made explicit.

It may be objected that I would elevate experiences into actual entities, whereas " experience " has usually been employed adjectivally, to signify a context which things acquire. Experience is at least that. But surely if we accept the view than an experience is a natural event, we must also hold that there is such a natural entity as " an experience "—an integrative process possessing its essential constitution.

V

Turning now to a closing consideration of what empirical procedure might be in metaphysics, I should like to ask: If the metaphysician wants to formulate the interrelatedness of generic traits of existence, should he not, like the scientist with his atoms and genes, conceive his existents, not just talk discursively about trait after trait? The tameness and sterility of most current empiricist literature springs largely from its merely adjectival mode of thought—something not remedied by piling adjectives on top of each other.

It may be thought that generic traits are the metaphysician's only possible topic, because his actual entities are presented by everyday life and adequately defined by the various departments of knowledge. Now it is all very well to say that metaphysics deals only with those tables and animals and actions which everybody perceives; and doubtless this facilitates exposition in the seminar room. But if you grant that "individuality" (for example) applies to these things in different senses, how do you escape determining what it applies to in a basic sense, of which the applications to tables, animals, and actions are special forms reflecting the composite nature and special place of those things in the world? Granted, those things are as real as anything. But we show little respect for their reality if we assume that their mode of existence is completely given to ordinary, mildly interested, human sense-perception. As Whitehead would say, humility before subject-matter demands our utmost efforts of imaginative thought.

As for the different departments of knowledge, each conceives existences in its own way, and none attempts to state the full nature of that existent which is empirically of critical importance: the occasion of experience. No, the metaphysician can not take over anybody else's conception of the existences of this universe. He must sweat that out himself.

He may do it by conceiving of some type of beings or being which is related to our occasions of experience as their source; or, concentrating, to begin with, on those occasions themselves, he may conceive other existences as composed of elements analogous to them (he will then be applying to the universe " descriptive generalizations of experience "—a procedure practiced by Whitehead, and praised by Dewey [14]) . Each way has its dangers—as what thinking that is of consequence does not? If we choose the second, we must always remember that all occasions of human experience have in common some traits, such as dependence on a nervous system, which are surely not present in all existences. Then, as the chemist had to generalize beyond fire and flame to achieve a theory of combustion, so we have to conceive human perception in a generalized form (such as " prehension," for example) from which are omitted

[14] John Dewey, "Whitehead's Philosophy," *Philosophical Review*, 46 (1937), 170. This procedure is also illustrated—though, I think, in an unnecessarily limited manner—by W. T. Stace's phenomenalist metaphysics.

EXPERIENCE AND METAPHYSICS

all characteristics which there is positive reason to believe are only human or animal. I state this requirement in terms of positive reasons; it would be a great mistake to insist upon the rigid exclusion of traits which "there is no reason to believe" characterize inorganic existence. This customary phrase, "there is no reason" (with the implication that there could be none) expresses a determination to keep one's mind closed, and one's beliefs sensible at all costs; in human intercourse it is the mark of an unimaginative man. Metaphysicians must go on the principle that the human experience-event is in some sense on the same level as all events; but they cannot escape having to use imagination and judgment in applying the principle.

The other way of conceiving existence is illustrated by most concepts of God, by the One, the Idea of the Good, and the Epicurean atoms in their void. The generic traits become the constitution of a necessary being or beings, and the common characteristic of human experiences is but that of a theatre wherein special traits appear as variable effects of the allegedly generic. To state this procedure is to become suspicious of it. Yet it is regularly employed by common sense, and—as the modern theories of the gene and the atom illustrate —in the natural sciences. There, the frequency of the various effects can be analyzed in detail, and the method of difference employed in experimentation. As philosophers do not enjoy these advantages, it is dangerous for them to theorize about sources. But of course they will continue to do so. Many of the scientifically-minded do so today, especially in limited fields where the risks are less: an instance is the type of ethics which conjectures a hypothetical structure of needs, inherent in the animal organism, as the sole source of human conduct.

In metaphysics, the method which thinks of existences as analogous to occasions of experience deserves an empiricist's preference. The mansion it builds is closer to home, yet as large as we can wish: for we can only get at the generic traits of existence, and their interrelatedness, as they come together in our experiences; and any trait or relatedness of traits which does not exist in the experience-event is, in virtue of that fact, not generic. Furthermore, as experience is essentially a process, this metaphysical method will never picture being as "an everlasting fixture." [15]

In reality the two modes of thought cannot be kept apart. We all know what happens when a metaphysician conceives the sources of our experiences as having but faint analogy with them. On the other hand, an experience which was not, if only vaguely, *of* sources, would be a solipsist's experience. Thus in conceiving the typical togetherness of items in an experience, the metaphysician is introducing sources—but in their experiential context.[16]

I hope that nothing in this chapter will be construed as encouragement to clothe experience in fancy dresses of the sort the post-Kantian German idealists designed. The position taken bases itself rather on the conviction that an experience is a natural event whose nature is only partly bared by scientific investigation. The work recommended is, roughly speaking, a development into a systematic conceptual scheme of the experiential naturalism which Dewey discursively suggested in *Experience and Nature*. It would contrast with "methodological naturalism" (as I call his antimetaphysical exaltation of scientific method). My idea of empirical metaphysics is closest to Whitehead's; but it could be developed in a more naturalistic, less Platonic, way.

What we have to cast off is the habit of supposing that empirical conceptions in philosophy are those which anybody can recognize—merely by chasing speculation out of his head and opening his eyes. Democratic, this notion may sound; but it can nourish neither science nor philosophy. What we require, in advance of the testing of our ideas, is the contrasting notion of arduous *flights toward* the empirical, seeking to penetrate to the essence of experience and more adequately to express it. We enjoy that essence, but nature has not laid it open in our laps.

[15] Plato, *Sophist*, 249a (Jowett's trans.).
[16] See Whitehead's strong argument against accepting any other meaning of "togetherness," except as derived from this type: PR II ix ii.

Chapter 13

William James and Whitehead's Doctrine of Prehensions

I

We indicated earlier that the evidence to which Whitehead appeals on behalf of his philosophy has a much broader base than inspection of given experience; disagreement over that, we said, is notorious among philosophers.[1] Still, what a philosopher believes is present for awareness in any occasion of human experience, is extremely important; and there are not really as many beliefs about this as there are philosophers. Whitehead's conceptualization of given experience is often thought peculiar. We may become more at home with it if we consider how it is supported by the empiricism of William James. Pluralism is the subject of the most obvious kinship between their philosophies; we shall have it in mind, but this chapter is devoted to their empiricism. We shall come to the central common doctrine in Section II. We have first to note some matters of agreement in their orientations.

[1] P. 245, above, and Chap. 10, Sect. 1. See also p. iii.

The proper general method of philosophy, both men believe, is that of the "working hypothesis." [2] James's attitude toward Whitehead's technique of construction would have been one of distaste touched with awe; but Whitehead's "rationalism" is nothing like that which James fought. Anyhow, the crucial point concerns the experiential materials used to suggest and to test the working hypothesis. And here James and Whitehead are in remarkable agreement. The sole purpose of the hypothesis, they say, is to elucidate immediate experience. Let it then be tested by every kind and type of experience that can be found. That wonderful purple passage in one of the last chapters of *Process and Reality*,[3] beginning, "The chief danger to philosophy is narrowness in the selection of evidence," and ending with, ". . . the fairies dance, and Christ is nailed to the cross," is not in James's style, but he would have placed a heavy check-mark opposite it in the margin. In the conclusion of *A Pluralistic Universe*, James insisted only on "one point of method,"—that "the basis of discussion" in metaphysical questions needs to be "broadened and thickened up." [4] James was at least as emphatic as Whitehead that what is in the clear focus of consciousness can tell nothing like the whole story in the appeal to experience. Whitehead sometimes uses James's name, "the fringe," for the rest; and at other times, preferring the imagery of physical science, he calls this "the penumbra,"—a word occasionally to be found in James. James also, as Ralph Barton Perry observed, preceded Whitehead in suggesting that "feelings" was "the best term to employ" for the components of immediate experience.[5]

---

[2] James, *A Pluralistic Universe* (New York, 1909), pp. 292, 328; hereafter "PU." Whitehead, AI xv i, iii, xv; PR Preface and I i.
[3] V i i.
[4] P. 330.
[5] R. B. Perry, *In the Spirit of William James* (New Haven, 1938), p. 82.

II

The fulcrum of Whitehead's philosophy is his doctrine of the transmission of feelings. If he can convince you that you actually feel your experience of a moment ago growing into your present experience and compelling some conformation to it, then it is likely that you will give his philosophy sympathetic study. If his argument fails to take hold at this point, he is in the position of a book agent who has neglected to put one foot inside your doorway. Now William James for twenty-five years propounded a similar doctrine with great vigor. In his *Principles of Psychology* he described the moment of experience as inheriting and appropriating the contents of prior experiences. In the unfinished book *Some Problems of Philosophy* he suggested that the true account of causation was that " a whole subsequent field grow[s] continuously out of a whole antecedent field because it seems to yield new being of the nature called for, while the feeling of causality-at-work flavors the entire concrete sequence [of experiences] as salt flavors the water in which it is dissolved." [6]

The similarity between James and Whitehead on this point runs through connected accounts too long to be quoted. If we pick up Whitehead's address, " Objects and Subjects " (AI xi), which contains what is probably the classical exposition of his experientialism, we shall be startled by its likeness to James's classical description of the " Stream of Thought." [7] The words are different, for Whitehead wanted terms that could be used for describing Nature, as well as our mental life; and he uses " sense-perception " in a narrower meaning than does James. But the two sets of words tell the same story, and the same conclusion—that we are directly acquainted with the efficacy of our own immediate past—is drawn. And this is enforced by the same main illustration—a speaker

[6] P. 218.
[7] *The Principles of Psychology* (New York, 1890), I, Chap. IX. The likeness is most striking in Sect. 12-14 of Whitehead's address.

uttering a phrase.[8] *Whitehead's "non-sensuous perception" is what James later called "the plain conjunctive experience";* [9] it has no one name in the *Psychology*, but is described under a number of headings such as "feelings of relation" and "feelings of tendency."

That excellent name, "*radical* empiricism," was applied by James to almost all of his ideas and attitudes not labeled "pragmatism." But if we consult his definition of the doctrine, and then his statements on the meaning of the adjective, we shall find that radical empiricism concerns the relational element in our experience, and that it is primarily directed upon the immediate temporal relation, or "felt transition," which is displayed in "the plain conjunctive experience."[10] The evidence for felt transitions is mainly in the *Psychology*. Radical empiricism as a program aims to develop those transitions into the tie rods of a pluralistic universe.[11] Generalization is needed, since very few of the transitions we know about are consciously felt in ordinary human experience. Now James had a confident faith in the felt-transition hypothesis, and he discussed the epistemological problems of his time in the light of his faith, but he did little to develop his working hypothesis along general lines. That—in the context of our discussion here—is the role of Whitehead's theory of "prehensions."

Setting aside prehensions of eternal objects,[12] a prehension is a specific transition from any antecedent occasion in the pluralistic universe to the present occasion of experience.[13] The simplest case of prehension, and the easiest one to observe in human experience, occurs when the earlier occasion is the

[8] *Psychology*, I, 249-264 and 278-283.

[9] *Essays in Radical Empiricism* (New York, 1912), p. 51; hereafter "ERE."

[10] *The Meaning of Truth* (New York, 1909), pp. xii f., also ERE pp. xii, 42-51; PU p. 326.

[11] See, for example, the conclusion of the second Introduction which James wrote in 1903 for a projected book on "The Many and the One." (The Introduction is printed in R. B. Perry's *Thought and Character of William James* [Boston, 1935], II, 378-380.)

[12] We return to them in the concluding section of this chapter.

[13] See, for example, PR II i i, vi; III i i.

immediately antecedent experience in the history of what we call " the same self." The contours of the general theory are drawn on the basis, first, of our direct acquaintance with this simplest case,[14] then of our more complex acquaintance with the external world, and then of our indirect knowledge.[15] In the simplest case a prehension is nothing else than James's felt transition from one " passing thought," or " drop " of experience, to the next. " Prehension " may be looked upon as concentrating in one concept the " generalized conclusion " of radical empiricism: " The parts of experience hold together from next to next *by relations that are themselves parts of experience.*" [16] If one asks just what James meant by " parts of experience," it can be shown (though I have not the space to do so here) that the correct expansion of his declaration is, in all probability, " The drops of experience hold together from next to next by transitions that are felt as components contributing to the drops of experience."

We have here a temporalistic doctrine of immanence. I have stated it very briefly. In the development of the theme it will be wise, in view of the suspicion with which all doctrines of immanence are regarded, to center attention on the immanence effected by prehensions, and the alternatives to it.

III

It is clear, to begin with, that James felt experience plainly testified to an immanence of the past in the present. The " appropriation " emphasized in his *Psychology* can not there be safely interpreted with entire literalness, as producing literal immanence.[17] But he finally declared it to be such, and

---

[14] Whitehead made this explicit in AI xv i.

[15] " Objects and Subjects " exhibits the construction in brief.

[16] James, *The Meaning of Truth*, pp. xii f., or ERE p. xii. (My italics.)

[17] Notice how James presented the idea through a layer of similes put in inverted commas: appropriation is the inheritance of a " title," or it is " this trick which the nascent thought has of immediately taking up the

his declaration was the natural outcome of a long trend in his thought.[18] Again, in "A World of Pure Experience"— possibly the most important, if not the most startling, philosophical essay of his maturity—James assailed the "over-subtle intellects" who have said that "'Sameness must be a stark numerical identity; it can't run on from next to next.'" On the contrary, he asserted, the primary meaning of sameness is to be found in "the plain conjunctive experience."[19] And *A Pluralistic Universe* is filled with striking observations which are summed up in the conclusion that "the simplest bits of immediate experience are their own others. . . . There is no datum so small as not to show this mystery, if mystery it be."[20]

James's idea of a "drop" of experience did not advance far enough beyond metaphor to allow a precise discussion of the nature of the immanence of the drops. But the issue at this stage is a simple one. In terms of conjunctive transition: if the transition produce no immanence, how can it be successful? The past occasion can be experienced only by becoming *itself* present in the experience that is now. *It* must be *appropriated*. This may, if you like, be called the truism that that which is to be experienced must be brought within the experient occasion. What is not a truism is the identification— by the most gifted introspective observer and reporter in all modern philosophy—of felt transitions as the observable elements by which an experience is found to be concrete of what was outside it; thus the truism is saved from being a mere predicament. There is no mystery, because what was outside

---

expiring thought and 'adopting' it" (*Psychology*, I, 339). Every student of the *Psychology* knows, too, that it is in strictness impossible to say what is asserted in it without making reservations and explanations.

[18] The trend is described in my paper, "William James's Pluralistic Metaphysics of Experience," pp. 157-177 of *In Commemoration of William James: 1842-1942* (New York, 1942). In James, see PU, Chap. V and VII; and the selections from James's notebooks of 1905-1908, printed as Appendix X in Perry's *Thought and Character*, II (esp. 760-765). This trend is also manifested in the development of James's tychism: see Perry, *op. cit.*, II, 411-412, 663-664.

[19] ERE pp. 50, 70.

[20] PU p. 282.

came inside. There is no solipsism of the present moment, because what is inside is felt as having come from outside. If it be said that this makes everything too easy, I reply that it is too hard to make the transition found by introspection mean anything else.

We are hard-boiled, let us say. Are we prepared to dismiss James's psychological findings as errors of observation? To deny that " the *feeling* of the thunder is also a feeling of the silence as just gone "? [21] That when a man is angry over a period of a minute, the feeling of anger as enjoyed by him a quarter of a second ago is, as Whitehead puts it, present in his experience *now* as datum felt? (AI xi 14).

Perhaps the way out that really is too easy is the one we are likely to take if we do not dismiss James's introspective results, but are unwilling to admit that they have the metaphysical significance claimed for them. All that happens, we may say, is that an earlier occasion is succeeded by a later occasion, and that some overlapping is observed in the qualities they display. We shall not hold that we know the meaning of the earlier-later relation in virtue of an intuition of the passage of Time-in-itself; nothing like that is needed, we shall say, because the earlier-later relation for short spans of time is directly given in experience. But an empiricist will reply that what is given is always specific, so that we can not say, without falling back on an intuition of Time, that the earlier-later relation we are acquainted with is a general dyadic form. What is given is the lateness of *this* now to *that* earlier. The problem thrown in our laps is how *this* lateness *can* be given if *that* earlier occasion be not conveyed into this present. If we reply that the earlier is *remembered* whereas the present is perceived, we bring in a new word but nothing more, for we have still to distinguish remembrance from invention and recollection, and to explain the remembrance of *that* earlier

[21] *Psychology*, I, 241 (italics in text). Of course I do not claim infallibility for James's psychological report. It seems to me true. I adopt it in this chapter on the ground that it is about as plain and evident a basis for discussion as one can expect a description of " the given " to be.

occasion. If we appeal to the akoluthic character of brain-processes we forsake the principle that the meaning of the earlier-later relation is directly given in experience.

It has been necessary to repeat an argument often presented by Whitehead and others; since few philosophers are likely to dismiss James's report of introspection, we had to be sure that this other way of escape, which is a very natural way, was blocked. The argument also blocks a plausible proposal to avoid Whitehead's immanence-producing prehensions by " taking relations seriously," that is, by allowing historic process to consist simply of things (drops of experience, in the present application) related by a " relation," which relates without requiring the help of prehensions in this world or of the idealist's Absolute in the next. For this proposal evidently rephrases the objection I have just considered. The empiricist answer that was given applies, unless we affirm the relation to be an (abstract) universal—in which case it is enough to point out that two experiences and a universal are not two connected experiences. The connectedness of two drops of experience may be said to exemplify an abstract universal, but it is not itself a universal; it is a real particular fact in the history of a particular person.[22]

The proposal just mentioned represents a line of thought which was characteristic of much of the new realism. That school, or the major part of it, tended to suppose that no general account of how relatedness happens is needed. Its attitude was rather like the classical empiricist attitude toward sense-data. Relations, it said in effect, arise in the world originally from unknown causes; as logicians we must assume them to be primitive material; and of themselves they can never cause trouble, because " the business of a relation is to relate," just as it is the business of a sense-datum to be sensed. I do not dispute the right of the logician to assume relations. But the value of an appeal to the proper business of a philosophic category evidently depends on how clearly every man

[22] This answer is taken from Whitehead's argument in AI xv xi.

in his experience can see the business actually being done by the philosopher's category. Most of us would not think Hume's destructive analysis of the idea of necessary connection was sufficiently answered by asserting that the business of a necessary connection is to necessarily-connect. We would continue to ask for the original of the idea. Let us also ask for the original of the really troublesome type of relation—temporal relation. If, as I believe, what we find is a feeling bearing the characteristics of what James called a felt transition and Whitehead calls a prehension, then a temporalist, for one, surely, ought to conclude that *prehension* is a better ultimate than *relation*. The concept of prehension describes how temporal "relation" *happens*.

I bear no animus against the general concept of relation. My concern is that all attempts to dismiss Whitehead's prehensions should be confronted by James's radical empiricism, according to which the relatedness of the stream of human experience is achieved by *transitions* that are *felt* in the drops of experience. We may reject James's doctrine, but in that case there is at least a gain in the definition of the standpoint from which we pass judgment on Whitehead.

We must, however, be careful not to suppose that James and Whitehead assert, or need to assert, that the *entire* past occasion becomes immanent in the present. Each occasion consists of feelings, and it is necessary only to say that in so far as the past is a cause, feeling passes from the old to the new occasion. It is necessary that we should not think that we have finished with the situation and are free to talk of "correlations," once we have remarked that of course every occasion includes reverberations of the past. There remains the question, What is the status of a reverberation? We should either admit that something which was external to the present occasion has become internal to it, or we should claim an intuition of the passage of Time-in-itself.

IV

We have to consider next the possibility that we may suppose these prehensions, however desirable, to be procurable only at a prohibitive price. The price is direct apprehension of the past, which may be held to be impossible because it obliterates the distinction between present and past. But let us make sure that we are not being frightened by a bogeyman. There is nothing we know better than the difference and the connection between present and past. We are acquainted with the emergence of a new particular, and with the change in the status of its predecessor, which suffers loss. Thus a double description of the passage of time is required. Almost all of *Process and Reality*, Whitehead said, can be read as an attempt to analyze *perishing* on the same level as Aristotle analyzed *becoming* (ESP p. 117; IS p. 218).

Now the distinction between present and past would be obliterated only if "direct apprehension of the past" meant the holding, in the present moment, of the past with that creative, growing quality of immediacy which *it* had when *it* was present. But perishing has intervened. The past has had its chance at becoming; it transfers the opportunity to the next runner. The past is now there to be apprehended, but not to grow and change. The present is creatively active but is not apprehended. It is only if we deny this distinction—which naturally falls into those old niches, "object" and "subject" —that direct apprehension of the past becomes a contradiction in terms. It is only when—as James often did—we talk loosely of the past as "living" in a present with which it "coalesces," that we provide our opponents with reason for saying that the direct apprehension of the past is a ridiculous notion.

It must not be supposed that we are committed to a line which excludes the possibility of errors in judgment or perception. "Direct apprehension"—"rock of error": these twain have been inseparably linked in modern criticism. But the apprehension of the past here discussed is not a direct knowledge of *propositions about* the past; it is not cognition in that sense of the word, and the fact is marked in Whitehead's discussion by the regular use of "prehension" instead of "apprehension." All that "prehension" means is the broad and, as it seems to me, unavoidable fact that the past is built into the make-up of the present.[23] "Prehension" is that fact, formulated for an assumed plurality of occasions. My point now is, that while we must agree with the common saying (which everyone in his actual life accepts) that the dead hand of the past is laid upon the living present, we are not by that admission required to say that the present can not imagine the shape of the hand as somewhat different from what it is in fact. In order to allow for the possibility of error, consistent with the immanence of the past in the present, we need only recognize that a limited activity of transmutation and "representation" comes into play as we pass from blind physical experience, which makes no anticipation and no mistakes, to conscious perception of "objects" and thence to the formulation of judgments and theories. The possibility of this activity is part of an essential freedom which, according to both James and Whitehead, belongs to every occasion of experience.[24] Under the name of the Theory of Symbolic Reference, Whitehead offered a fairly full account of this transmuting activity and of its relations to the dumb immanence of the past in the present. The theory—we met it in earlier chapters [25]—seems to me a remarkably successful auxiliary to the theory of prehensions, bringing illumination to a great many of those confusedly lighted corners where epistemology and metaphysics meet.

There have been, and probably always will be, some philosophers to claim that whoever says that the past is in *some*

[23] "Prehension" actually stands for more than this in Whitehead's system; but it does so only in virtue of the type of prehension he called "conceptual," which we have temporarily excluded from the discussion.

The use of active verbs like "prehend" and "appropriate" is justified by the self-creative role which the present, in human experience at least, plays in determining the final result of the building-up process.

[24] Thus, Whitehead's description of freedom at the close of Sect. 12 in "Objects and Subjects" expresses James's thought as well as his own.

[25] Chap. 2, Sect. III; Chap. 9, Sect. V.

respect a constituent of the present, contradicts himself; to
claim that if something is past—whether by a year or only by
a hundredth of a second—it is altogether past, and *only* a representation of it can be present. " Everything is what it is and
not another thing " is their motto. From the truth that any
entity which is an individual is when it is and where it is,
they conclude that no such entity, nor any constituent of it
which is particular, can in any respect or degree be also at
another time or place. It can't, because they have erected a
conceptual fence to prevent just that. As a proposition about
the world, this is the doctrine of simple location. It would
be true of unextended instants and points—if Time and Space
were absolutes, composed of them. How the doctrine permits
any experiencer to know that he lives in a world of other
things, has never been explained. More specifically, the introspective evidence presented by James, and also by Whitehead,
is dead against the pure representation theory. We note also
that the theory belongs to the class of theories which are
rejected by radical empiricism; for the principle of that doctrine is that the drops of experience *themselves* hold together
from next to next.

V

We can accept the prehensional theory of immanence without supposing that the neorealists were entirely wrong in the
famous battle over " external relations " which they fought
with the idealists. If what they were fighting for was the
doctrine that " everything in the world has a real environment,
that is, a relation to something which is genuinely other than
itself, and which it is compelled to meet and take account of
without any sort of antecedent complicity," [26] this doctrine is
not denied, but on the contrary is asserted. It is the doctrine
of external relations that James fought for, and it is of the

[26] R. B. Perry, *op. cit.*, II, 586; see also James, PU, p. 321.

essence of pluralism in metaphysics. If, however, we consider the center of the dispute to have been the thesis that relations do not necessarily alter their terms, then it is to be observed that the controversy went wrong because it was discussed in terms of *terms*,—as abstract a way as is possible.

The important point about James's position on this problem is that he did not call for the elimination of immanence, but for a pluralistic conception of it:

> Here, then, you have the plain alternative, and the full mystery of the difference between pluralism and monism, . . . It packs up into a nutshell:—Is the manyness in oneness that indubitably characterizes the world we inhabit, a property only of the absolute whole of things, . . . or can the finite elements have their own aboriginal forms of manyness in oneness, . . . ? [27]

Philosophers would hardly have been human had they not tended to throw out all effective manyness in oneness in their efforts to make sure we were saved from the block-universe. The historical result is to be contrasted with that at which James was aiming. If the external relationists retained the term " immanence," they used it to signify the entrance of a thing, unchanged, into membership in a new group of things. The analogy to their theory, in a discussion confined to the stream of experience, is the analytic psychology James had fought—the psychology which supposed that a thought of " the pack of cards is on the table " is composed of thoughts of " the," " pack," " of," and so on, all these being now together in a new contingent grouping. I admit that the endeavor to think of complex things as ordered classes of simpler elements has a perennial attractiveness and is a sound approach to certain problems. It can be observed as at some time an ingredient in both James's thought and Whitehead's. James's theory of pure experience leaned in this direction, and Whitehead's earliest philosophical essays aimed to explore the possibilities of the class-method in the philosophy of science. In

[27] PU pp. 326-327.

both instances the line of thought was caught up and pushed by an entire school, while the philosopher began to think in another way.[28]

When we consider all of James's work, we must say that he was aiming no more at the thin " immanence " of a unit in a collection than at the thick immanence of the part in the cosmic Whole which swallows it up. Neither view considers time, or, I should say, historic process, with James's emphasis. He realized that the sting of the block-universe lay in its elimination [29] of time, and in his radical empiricism he indicated a temporalist approach to the problem of relations. We are to fix our gaze on what Whitehead was to call " the rush of immediate transition " (PR II iv x) ; and instead of the logical possibilities concerning terms or semipermanent things [30] with respect to membership in classes, we are to consider the " co-conscious transition " [31] as it occurs between two drops of experience. We may then conceive of the earlier occasion, which is what it is, becoming related to the later, by *itself* (the neorealists were surely right in insisting on that

[28] Whitehead, Preface and last three chapters of AE; PNK 2nd ed., Note III; James, PU; Perry, *op. cit.*, Appendix X (selections from James's notebooks). On Whitehead, see Chap. 8, Sect. II, IV, VII, above; on James, pp. 165-177 of the paper cited in n. 18 of this chapter.

[29] Read " transcendence," if you prefer.

[30] In Russell's *Principles of Mathematics*, every term is eternal. In using the phrase, " semipermanent things," I have R. B. Perry's discussions in mind, e. g., his discussion of a perceiver's relation to a tulip, to the planet Mars, etc. in his *Present Philosophical Tendencies* (London, New York, and Toronto, 1912). However, Perry summed up his position by saying (Chap. XIII, Sect. 6) , " The realist, in short, must resist every impulse to provide a home for the elements of experience, even in ' experience ' itself. . . . the realist must be satisfied to say that in the last analysis the elements of experience are not anywhere; they simply are what they are." " Elements " (conveniently vague word!) that are not anywhere cannot be temporally anywhere; this is absolute Platonism. For Whitehead, on the contrary, " the elements of experience " are of specific types; all elements that are not eternal objects are necessarily somewhere, and so are the drops of experience themselves; even eternal objects are somewhere (in God's primordial nature, and throughout the temporal world in various gradations of realization) .

[31] Another name for " felt transition," ERE pp. 47-48.

word) passing into the later experience, which thereby comes to be. Each occasion, in its becoming, is a part of nothing else; but in perishing it becomes part of other occasions (and this may be taken to provide the fundamental meaning of " part " in a temporalistic pluralism). Pluralism and immanence are reconciled in this form of temporalism; and our acknowledgment of that central feature of the world as experienced which the leader of the neorealists, Perry, called " the indepndence of the immanent," [32] begins to shape a cosmology of events instead of affirming a logical possibility for " terms."

VI

As the immanence believed in by James, and worked out by Whitehead, supports rather than undermines pluralism, so also it really helps the cause of realism. What more solid empirical basis is likely to be found for realism than the premise that a feeling of derivation from external occasions is found in the present occasion of experience? As Whitehead says, " There can only be evidence of a world of actual entities, if the immediate actual entity discloses them as essential to its own composition." [33] I do not see on what other assumption we can develop a realistic philosophy. For it seems to me that the realist's problem (after he has exposed the uncompelling character of the arguments for idealism) is just this: the construction of a metaphysics which shall be realistic and yet in accord with that subjectivist or experiential bias of modern philosophy, which is accepted as in some sense true by almost all who are not neoscholastics or behaviorists. Realism is the requirement that the experient occasion be conceived as one among many others, with no privileged status except that it happens to be now experiencing. The subjectivist bias requires that we be able to say this solely on the basis of a full

[32] *Op. cit.*, Chap. XIII, Sect. 4.
[33] PR II vi i; see also Sect. 9 of " Objects and Subjects."

description of the experient. How can we, if the experient be not made up of feelings of others?

In another meaning, realism is a theory which guarantees the possibility of perceiving objects as they are in themselves, without the modification which they must suffer if they become immanent in an experience conceived as a process. The desire for this guarantee has been one of the traditional motives of realism. But a temporalist, for one, must give it up.

VII

There remains to be noticed but one more supposedly objectionable characteristic of the immanence required by the doctrine of prehensions. The immediate occasion is both an agent responsible for the specific immanence that arises, and the product of that process. That an occasion of experience should be *both* these things, both feeler and emergent feeling—in Whitehead's terminology, both a " subject " and a " superject " —seemed to W. M. Urban (and doubtless to many other philosophers) utterly unintelligible.[34] I do not think it is; but if it is, so is James's doctrine of the "passing thought" which is the thinker in his *Psychology*. James described the passing thought as an " integral pulse " of thought or feeling [35] which grows out of prior pulses but is also the active agent, and the only agent, which thinks or feels them together. There is no antecedent subject which relates together. (Radical empiricism prohibits that.) Some of the most vivid appeals to experience and the most persuasive analogies in James's treatise are devoted to making this description seem natural.[36] But it will seem paradoxical so long as the moment of experience be spoken of only as the *subject* of its thoughts or feelings. White-

[34] Urban, "Elements of Unintelligibility in Whitehead," *Journal of Philosophy*, 35 (November 10, 1938) , 626.
[35] As James explained (I, 185-186) , he uses " thought " and " feeling " synonymously, and in wider senses than are usual.
[36] *Ibid.*, I, 336-342.

head's introduction of the term, "superject," to be coupled
with "subject," is therefore a considerable advance on the
theoretic side.

   Urban did think that James's account of the moment of
experience is intrinsically as unintelligible as Whitehead's.[37]
The main point in criticism, however, was that Whitehead
is forced—"constantly tricked . . . by the truth "—to speak of
the occasion as the subject of its feelings (a way of talking
which this critic understood) as well as their superject (an
expression which he found fantastic). The criticism was misplaced, for the duality in Whitehead's language is deliberate.
And the duality is rightly introduced, since an experiential,
temporalistic pluralism must assign to the drop of experience
functions which other types of metaphysics can distribute
among other entities. The true critical question is whether
the duality which Whitehead's language is intended to bring
out is really to be found in each drop of experience.[38]

   [37] Urban, in LLP-W p. 317.
   [38] Urban's reply (LLP-W p. 318) to this sentence when it appeared
(*Journal of Philosophy*, 38 [February 27, 1941], 125) in the article on
which the present chapter is based, was: ". . . Even if we experience felt
transitions within, such feelings or intuitions must be communicated;
. . ." And: "An 'experiential temporalistic pluralism' does, indeed,
assign to the drop of experience functions which other types of metaphysics can distribute among other entities; but it ought not to do so. . . .
In order to express itself intelligibly Whitehead's philosophy must use
the categories of the traditional categorial scheme." If we ask the question,
"'Intelligibly' to whom?," the only possible answer anyone can truthfully
give is, "To me and to all others who think entirely in terms of the
one and only traditional categorial scheme." Whitehead had already given
a concise answer to this position: We have used it earlier in this book,
and now quote it in full: "There is an insistent presupposition continually sterilizing philosophic thought. It is the belief, the very natural
belief, that mankind has consciously entertained all the fundamental ideas
which are applicable to its experience. Further it is held that human
language, in single words or in phrases, explicitly expresses these ideas.
I will term this presupposition, The Fallacy of the Perfect Dictionary"
(MT Epilogue).
   One of Urban's chief criticisms of Whitehead's metaphysics was that
in its use of familiar terms they were "redesigned . . . out of all *recognition*" (LLP-W p. 319; Urban's italics). A great many philosophers
reacted in this way to *Process and Reality*. They must read Whitehead's
answer; it is in AI xv ix-xiii.

Another text which should help smooth the way toward understanding this aspect of Whitehead's philosophy of experience is James's defense of radical empiricism's attempt to " understand forwards " against the objections of B. H. Bode; it is the ninth of the *Essays in Radical Empiricism*. At the least, these texts from James may lessen the feeling that Whiteheadian points of view are unique in their perversity.

VIII

Everything that has been said in this chapter can be evaded, and very simply, by denying that " transitions " are felt. Their function of relating the moments of experience together may be reserved for thought or for language, or condemned as an illusion. If we persevere in those courses after reading James's psychology and radical empiricism, it is probably useless to take *Process and Reality* in hand. If, however, we accept James's account of our experience of transition, we may no longer dismiss " prehension " as an obscurantist notion. We may object to those respects in which Whitehead's exploitation of the notion extends beyond James's, but we must at least put into " prehension " as much of sense as there is in James's descriptions. And we might hope for much, in philosophy, from a combination of vivid description and theoretic adequacy.

IX

Finally, what is to be said about the prehensions which we have so far set aside in this chapter—prehensions of eternal objects? " Any entity whose conceptual recognition does not involve a necessary reference to any definite actual entities of the temporal world is called an ' eternal object ' " (PR II I iii). In occasions of human experience there is no scarcity of entities which satisfy this description. (But I do not think we know how they got there.) Whitehead's theory of eternal objects gives them two main roles, which are then combined in a variety of ways. In one main role they are ideal forms, not yet realized in the temporal world. It is by positive prehension of them that a new occasion has a new character; this is the theory of "appetition." This side of the doctrine of eternal objects was briefly criticized in Section IV of our eleventh chapter. There is another main role for eternal objects because prehensions of them are essentially involved in an actual occasion's reception of the world of antecedent occasions; this is Whitehead's theory of the "objectification" of the antecedent universe, and it directly concerns us here. In recent studies—especially by Professors Leclerc and Christian—interpretations of his theory of objectification which vary on this point have appeared.

Is there anything in William James which can help us to understand Whitehead better on the role of eternal objects in objectification, or to see the boundless realm of unrealized forms in a more convincing light? Alas, there is nothing that I know of. The rejection of Aristotelian essences in his *Psychology* is clear enough, but scarcely *supports* Whitehead. His later discussions of the objects of conceptual recognition I find confusing; they seem to me to be written by a man whose natural position is very like Bergson's, but whose intellectual sympathy for the young men around him—probably Perry in particular—leads him at times to profess something like their logical realism. However that may be, I see nothing in James that helps us with Whitehead's theory of eternal objects.

The present volume is not the place to enter upon the details of Leclerc's and Christian's interpretations of the theory of objectification.[39] We are concerned only with the possibility

---

[39] Ivor Leclerc, "Form and Actuality," pp. 169-189 in *The Relevance of Whitehead*, ed. Leclerc (London and New York, 1961); Leclerc, *Whitehead's Metaphysics* (London and New York, 1958), esp. Chap. VII, VIII, XII, XIII; William A. Christian, *An Interpretation of Whitehead's Metaphysics* (New Haven, 1959), esp. Chaps. 6-9, 11. Other interpretations have been suggested by reviewers of these books.

that recognition of the functioning of eternal objects in objectification may undermine the doctrine of the literal immanence
of antecedent actual occasions in new occasions. It is easy to
drift into a substitution of the former for the latter. When
Whitehead uses the words "re-enaction" and "repetition,"
universals naturally come to mind. Are they not precisely the
sort of things that can be repeated? So we read Whitehead
on immanence as saying merely that previously realized eternal
objects are being realized again. He does mean to say that;
but it is not all he means to say. And saying that is not saying
very much; for, if you grant that the character of a thing is
an eternal object, a prehension of the thing which did not
once more realize that eternal object would be either negative
prehension, or prehension of a characterless thing. In fact,
the evidence is overwhelming that Whitehead's view was the
common-sense one: what is given us by the antecedent world
from which our experience arises is not a set of characters, but
a nexus of things with their characters. There are his repeated
statements to the effect that we experience particular existents;
there is his laying down the principle that the feeling of an
already realized universal *purely* as a universal is *derived from*
a feeling of the existent which realized it [40] (his whole lengthy
account of the later stages of concrescence is written in accordance with this principle) ; there is his remark that his metaphysics is mainly devoted to making clear the idea of one
actual entity being present in another (PR II I v) ; there is his
continual criticism of the disastrous idea that the data of
experience consist wholly of qualities, figures, and other universals, from which the subject must *infer* a world of actual
things.

I suggest that we read the first half of Whitehead's much
discussed sentence, " The organic philosophy does not hold
that the ' particular existents ' are prehended apart from universals; on the contrary, it holds that they are prehended by
the mediation of universals " (PR II VI iv) , as a rejection
of the impossible notion of prehending a characterless datum.

---

[40] Categoreal Obligation iv, in PR I II iii.

How to read the second half so that it does not conflict with the evidence just noted? I should interpret it as a particular instance of a general assumption which Whitehead always made, in every field he dealt with—that synthesis, or any kind of connection between diverse things, implies that they share a common character. I should not read the sentence as implying that the repeated realization of universals is an adequate categorial expression, for Whitehead's philosophy, of the immanence of the past in the present. If that were so, we should have to go outside the philosophy to express the fact that process, as he somewhere says, is the accumulation of the universe, and not a stage play about it.[41] Whitehead's categorial expression of this fact was, that every new occasion incorporates in itself every occasion in its past, by feeling some of the feelings (the positive prehensions) which came into being as constituents of the past occasion, and forever bear its mark (PR III ii i).[42]

It must be admitted that many philosophers laid down *Process and Reality* unconvinced that the author had said clearly how one actual entity can be present in another. Whitehead himself, I think, put his finger on the most frequent cause of their trouble: ". . . the truism that we can only *conceive* in terms of universals has been stretched to mean that we can only *feel* in terms of universals. This is untrue." [43]

[41] The second paragraph of ix in PR III i may be read as an illustration.
[42] Cf. Chap. 2, Sect. II, above.
[43] PR III i ix; italics in text. For a clear fuller statement, see IS pp. 241 f.

PART IV

CONCLUSION

Chapter 14

Learning from Whitehead

I

The title of our final chapter is to be understood in the broad sense, in which one may learn from a thinker's oversights as well as from his contributions. But nothing that remotely approaches a comprehensive evaluation of Whitehead's philosophy will be attempted in this short space. And a real attempt to *assess* some part of it requires detailed studies which have not been made in this book. The most that I can do is to offer a few suggestions.

These are not suggested as answers to the question that is usually set for symposia on Whitehead, namely, What is valid in this philosophy? With Whitehead one must be especially careful to ask the right questions. Strictly speaking, only a philosopher's arguments are valid or invalid. One of the many ways in which Whitehead was unusual is that so much of his work consists of analytical description and speculative construction, so little of argument. If we construe "argument" broadly enough to avoid this objection, it becomes necessary that we first make sure we agree on the criteria of validity. Then, alas, the discussion may never get around to Whitehead.

Rather than assume that I have the reader's agreement on
criteria of *validity*, I drop that strong word altogether.

Similar prior questions could be asked if " true " or " valuable " were substituted for " valid." But " valuable " has the
advantage of not advertising the possession of precise criteria
which are in fact lacking, and so, of not inviting us to paint
a picture in black and white alone. Let me, then, notice and
briefly discuss a few of the distinctive general aspects of Whitehead's philosophy which seem to me most valuable. These
are things which it is good, I think, for anyone who philoso-
phizes to bear in mind. I shall also suggest a criticism of
Whitehead. The discussion will be carried on in the light of a
standard of value that is appropriate to his philosophy, not
impossibly precise, and accepted by many philosophers as well
as by Whitehead himself. His view was that philosophy is not
argument but " the search for premises " (MT vi 1) , and that
the value of whatever premises may be offered lies in their
power to elucidate human experience. (This statement tacitly
includes his requirement that the set of premises be not merely
self-consistent but coherent, since otherwise the connections
between diverse aspects of experience will not receive elucidation.) The use of this general standard, too, at once runs into
trouble; but the trouble is itself instructive. I shall be satisfied
if the reader, when he lays down this book, has received an
idea of what one requires for an evaluation of Whitehead.

II

In the reception of this philosophy, nothing is more striking
than the uncompromising differences of opinion about its
elucidatory power. Some thinkers (both theists and atheists)
insist that his conceptions of God and the temporal world are
irrelevant to the understanding of religious experience; other
theists and atheists say that they get a profound understanding
from those conceptions. So it goes with every topic in White-

head's philosophy. I do not see that these sharp disagreements will ever diminish unless one condition, so simple as to be almost utopian, is fulfilled more often: the condition that we come to his work with an open mind. It is all too obvious that no scheme of ideas will elucidate your experience unless you give it a chance. Unfortunately, one man may not consider his experience elucidated unless it heightens his sense of what has been called the " terrible chasm between us and all sub-human things." [1] Another has embraced precisely the opposite position; perhaps he is, in addition, wedded to methodological naturalism, and so can approve only those methods of thought which have been so successful in the natural sciences. A third will admit enlightenment only by a dialectic of spirit, a fourth only by a materialist dialectic. And so on. It is not merely that we would-be evaluators of Whitehead cannot fairly assess him without contradicting our antecedent preferences; we are often under strong psychological compulsions, whenever a philosophical discussion begins, to fight for *this* cause or to defend *that* technique or instrument—say, ordinary language—against all comers. Until we have stilled our agitations and enlarged our minds, we are ill qualified to serve on this jury.

—On this jury, above all. I think that any experienced reader of philosophy who does not come to Whitehead as someone else's man, can perceive in his writings an unusual degree of philosophic candor. The always bland dispassionateness of George Santayana only makes us look more eagerly for concealed causes, and ask just what makes him tick. Not so with Whitehead. It would indeed be inaccurate to suggest that he was not a man, subject to some human weakness. But the watchful reader seldom feels that Whitehead has let himself be induced to favor a conclusion which is not suggested by some important evidence. In his remarkable candor, Whitehead excels among philosophers.

Accordingly, the first question I would discuss concerning the value of his philosophy is this: What, specifically, can we

[1] John Wild, *The Challenge of Existentialism* (Bloomington, Ind., 1955), p. 77.

learn from him about the working attitude of an unprejudiced philosophic mind? I begin with something which we might learn about the use of reason in philosophy.

As we know, Whitehead was a Platonist—but with that circumspection which, though it is not, ought to be a matter of course by this time, twenty-three centuries after Aristotle. Whitehead the metaphysician held that "there is an essence to the universe which forbids relationships beyond itself, as a violation of its rationality" (PR I 1 i), and he sought that essence with unexampled boldness and care, by offering original formulations—the best his powerful mind could devise— of those forms and interconnections of forms which may be found in observable facts of existence. He stated well and frequently the moral for philosophical *discussion* which fits the example of his work. For instance, at the end of *Adventures of Ideas* he wrote that fundamental notions are not to be justified by argument; their discussion "is merely for the purpose of disclosing their coherence, their compatibility, and the specializations which can be derived from their conjunction" (xx x). Logical arguments "are merely subsidiary helps for the conscious realization of metaphysical intuitions." He added that St. Ambrose's saying, *Non in dialectica complacuit Deo salvum facere populum suum*, "should be the motto of every metaphysician" (AI xx xi). Some others have agreed: Cardinal Newman put it on the title page of his *Grammar of Assent*. But Whitehead's next sentence is strictly Whiteheadian: "He [the metaphysician] is seeking, amid the dim recesses of his ape-like consciousness and beyond the reach of dictionary language, for the premises implicit in all reasoning." [2]

I am taking space to praise Whitehead on this issue because, much as we admire him and wish we had his contructive

---

[2] Cf. his definition of mathematics in the *Britannica* article of 1910: "the science concerned with the logical deduction of consequences from the general premises of all reasoning." (The article was described in Chapter 6, Section IX, above, and Whitehead's final view of the relation between mathematics and metaphysics in Chapter 10, pp. 280 f.)

abilities, almost no one is really willing to *let the dialectic go.*
Professional philosophers feel that a request to do so is almost
a blow in the face. Of course Whitehead himself prepared
a hearing for his new ideas by arguing against older positions
and for his own approach to metaphysics; and he did this
very effectively. What is almost absent from his work but
customary in philosophy is the use of dialectic to validate
positive conclusions.[3] An obvious example of it is Royce's
claim to have conducted his reader ineluctably, by mere " dry
logic," to the reality of the Larger Self. More recently, we
remember Russell's argument that though the anti-Platonist
should eliminate all other universals, one, *similarity*, must
remain. It is hard to imagine Whitehead's offering such a
defense of Platonism. It would have been more like him to
say that Platonism rests on a slender basis indeed if this is
its final defense. Whitehead in fact called " proof," in the
strict sense of that term, " a feeble second-rate procedure "
(MT III 3). This goes contrary to all our usual evaluations.
I wonder whose mind, besides his own (and perhaps William
James's), Whitehead was thinking of in his next sentence:
" When the word ' proof ' has been uttered, the next notion to
enter the mind is ' half-heartedness.' " It should indeed be
obvious that when a metaphysician seeks the general forms, or
categories, by conceptual analysis and reasoning, all he can be
sure of demonstrating is the impingement of one conceptual
pattern upon another. He may thus spell out the terms in
which he and his friends habitually interpret experience, and
triumph over adversaries who have set foot on the same road
without thinking much about where it leads. For intellectual
self-clarification—a good thing, surely—proof is a crucial, not
a second-rate, procedure. But Whitehead was never content
to think of such clarification as a sufficient purpose for any
philosophy. Even *analysis*, as he used the word, is not of

---

[3] I make no objection to the careful use of what has been called
" empirical dialectic "—argument which furthers the search for more
adequate premises than we possess by giving a defective premise all the
rope it needs to hang itself. Socrates was adept at this.

concepts but of processes and things, and their entry into experience. It is from this explorer's standpoint that he called logical proof a second-rate procedure: in what an argument can say about the nature of things, its force is borrowed from that persistent experience upon which its own premises depend for evidence of truth. This must be granted. Yet among Whitehead's teachings, " Let the dialectic go " (as I have somewhat dramatically put it) is the one that is almost universally passed over. This seems to me a pity; for although many philosophers have downgraded logical argument, his positive ideal of speculative philosophy makes him unique among them. The desirability of serving this ideal *as well as we can* is not destroyed by the rarity of Whitehead's breadth of observation and powers of conceptual formulation. Our service of it *is* hindered by fondness for argument.

I turn now to what we can learn from Whitehead about philosophy's appeal to experience. His main point was that the chief appeal should not be to those factors in experience of which we enjoy clear consciousness, for these are the variable, and hence the metaphysically superficial, ones; we are to look instead for factors which are always present, and so not usually in the focus of attention; for example, the derivation of our experience from its antecedent environment, and our exercise of purpose. Whitehead contrasted this orientation with that of Hume and his philosophical descendants; today its chief contrast is probably with Oxford philosophy. Concern with showing the specific use and point of making typical statements in ordinary language has its value in the analysis of meaning; in metaphysics and in moral philosophy (broadly understood) Whitehead's advice is to look for that which ordinary speech sees no point in saying, because it so pervades our experience that it is taken for granted. This Whiteheadian thesis is now familiar. One fact about his expression of it, however, has not been sufficiently noticed. It is especially important for those whose inspiration is not ordinary language but the writings of the existentialists. When Whitehead directs us toward " the rush of immediate transition " or to other

LEARNING FROM WHITEHEAD: II

pervasive features of experience, he does it in a straightforward way which uses the words " pervasive," " immediate," " concrete " and " abstract " in senses which are either obvious or explained by him. It is not by weaving into his statements such advertiser's adjectives as " genuine " and " authentic " that he seeks to persuade us; [4] nor does he ever supercharge the words " being " and " existence." I am referring to a temptation which besets our excitable age, even as the temptation to turn discussion into edification sometimes beset idealists in the late nineteenth century. I am saying that we can learn from Whitehead to make our appeals to experience dispassionate, and *let the epithets go.* This does not mean that the ideal philosopher will be a passionless creature; certainly Whitehead was not. What I mean is that if we become zealots in our appeal to experience, the appeal is spoiled.

Any philosopher who follows Whitehead in the use of reason and in the appeal to experience will always be on guard against what, in his last course of lectures at Harvard (February to May, 1937), he called the trap of the clear-headed man— the assumption that questions for which there is no room in a precise " logical syntax of language " are meaningless. Mankind, he said, is always hunting for a formula that will enable it to avoid questions. The opposite danger, the trap of the mystic and the muddle-headed man, is the notion that whatever can be articulated must be unimportant. One does not became a philosopher, however, simply by avoiding these extremes; he must be ready to learn from everybody—from these men, and from the plain man, the emotional man, the religious man, the near-lunatic man (Whitehead in a Harvard lecture mentioned William Blake), and so on. His mind will not seek to find repose solely in any one of these attitudes. Every attitude, said Whitehead, reveals something to consciousness, and conceals something from consciousness. These are

---

[4] I am not criticizing the introduction of " authentic " by a systematic thinker to express a strictly defined meaning. In the speech of existentialism's American admirers, unfortunately, the word is almost inevitably a selling word.

not the words of a phenomenologist *qua* phenomenologist; they are simply the words of a wise metaphysician who desired a broad basis for understanding the universe. The ability to work from such a basis without falling into eclecticism is the final test of greatness in philosophy.

If we wonder how this is possible for any man, part of the answer is given by a positive rule which doubtless came naturally to the author of *A Treatise On Universal Algebra*, and which he considered "more important even than Occam's doctrine of parsimony—if it be not another aspect of the same": "In framing a philosophic scheme, each metaphysical notion should be given the widest extension of which it seems capable. It is only in this way that the true adjustment of ideas can be explored" (AI xv xvii). Would that there were more interest today in this kind of exploration!

III

The term "elucidate," used as a name for what philosophers systematically attempt for human experience, covers a wide variety of pursuits. At one extreme, the logical positivist offers a precise spelling out of current scientific concepts, procedures, and theories which, applied to phenomena, enable the prediction of definite observations. At the opposite extreme, systematic elucidation to Whitehead means a speculative formulation of the way in which process and form, final and efficient causation, becoming and perishing, individuality and continuity, and all other generic contrasting features of our experience are inseparably together in the process by which finite immediacies of experience arise from the infinite universe. This is a truly titanic mode of elucidation. Many large questions are involved in understanding and evaluating it. One, for example, is whether Whitehead was right in believing that all ultimate reasons are in terms of aim at value.

Linked with that question is another, posed by Whitehead's

concept of organism. It is surprising how small a portion of the published discussion of the philosophy of organism has been directed upon the idea from which Whitehead drew the name. In *Process and Reality* he left his readers in no doubt about its meaning. Probably many of them were taken aback by his complete temporalization of the notion of holistic pattern. His unit process of becoming, an "actual entity," is a self-guided integration of given data: "the actual entity, in a state of process during which it is not fully definite, determines its own ultimate definiteness" (PR III III v). This notion is difficult, if not unintelligible, for common sense. When we think of anything as half formed (like the drop of water at the faucet) or half grown, we customarily think of its state as perfectly definite. Probably this merely manifests our uncritical pictorial habit of supposing that there is a definite distribution of matter at every state—even every instant—of a process. In Whitehead's philosophy of organism a different kind of definiteness obtains: definite alternative potentialities (eternal obects and not yet realized propositions) are there. Explanation is also given for the initiation of the actual occasion's progressive resolution of indeterminations, by reference to the primordial nature of God. Now I think we should agree with Whitehead that every metaphysics in some form or other attributes self-causation to whatever it takes to be ultimate actuality. What in this respect is good in Whitehead's metaphysics is his explicitness. "Self-realization is the ultimate fact of facts. An actuality is self-realizing, and whatever is self-realizing is an actuality" (PR III I iv). What is radical is his fidelity to this requirement, in assigning self-causation to the becoming of every puff of existence. We have seen his reasons for doing that. To recall one reason: he thereby avoids a dualism of self-determining men and wholly unfree lower forms of existence. Finally, what is interesting is the question whether a comparably broad and rationally articulated conception of self-determining organisms which does not rely upon an eternal divine reservoir of potentiality can be constructed. This seems to me extremely difficult to do without

compromising the principle of temporalism—the principle that
"if process be fundamental to actuality, then each ultimate
individual fact must be describable as process" (MT v 3).[5]

It should be noted that although an answer to the question
of the soundness of the concept of a self-creating organic process is likely to be presupposed when philosophers assess
Whitehead's metaphysics, his work is at the same time an
important piece of evidence bearing on the determination of
the right answer to that particular question. A similar situation obtains for most—possibly for all—of the larger questions
involved in understanding and evaluating Whitehead.

IV

Whitehead's system, almost alone among cosmologies, has
a richness which is not many orders of magnitude removed
from that of the world. If we ask what the substance of his
universe is, there are many answers to be given, and we must
bring them all in. That is one of the great difficulties preliminary to evaluating this metaphysics. For example, after
mentioning the three most obvious answers—creativity, structured immediacies of process (his "actual entities"), and
feeling—it is absolutely essential to remember that Whitehead
also understands the universe, so far at it is not a chaos, to
be composed of societies of actual entities, and societies within
societies. Although "society," for excellent reasons, is introduced as a "derivative notion" in *Process and Reality*, it
alone enables the reader to compare Whitehead's world with
that of everyday things. The addition of other brief descriptive statements would bring us closer to a just answer to our
question. I wish particularly to show that there is a respect
in which Whitehead's world is made up of what in *Process*

---

[5] The proposal made at the end of Sect. IV of Chap. 11, above, may
be useful as a first step toward an alternative construction which does not
compromise the principle of temporalism.

and Reality he describes as *sensa*, for I doubt that their role in the philosophy of organism is often enough appreciated. The probable reasons are that Whitehead put more emphasis on our direct experience of the causal efficacy of our sense organs and of other actualities than on experience of sensa; and that he sometimes used " sensa " itself as a name for the variable tactile, visual, etc., data of the conscious sense perceptions which occur only because the human animal, on the planet Earth, has just those sense organs.

But we remember Whitehead's famous protest in *Science and the Modern World* against stripping nature of qualities. " The poets are entirely mistaken. They should address their lyrics to themselves, and should turn them into odes of self-congratulation on the excellency of the human mind " (p. 77) . In the same book our mathematician-philosopher, giving his first systematic account of eternal objects (Chapter x) , marked a grade the members of which are of " zero complexity," each being in itself (in its " individual essence ") " simple," not analyzable into a relationship of others. Such an eternal object must be a wholly qualitative entity. *It* is what he terms a sensum in *Process and Reality.* Apart from some emotional qualities which may have the requisite character but which educated observers seldom consider directly perceivable (AI xvi v) , sensa can be exhibited to our minds only as simple qualities of sensation, e. g., green of a definite shade. But Whitehead put to use the notion, suggested by reflection on unsophisticated experience, that the primitive core of every such quality is an indefinable definiteness of emotion. Until continuing research on sensory processes should give conclusive evidence against it—something which may not be easy to determine—we may not dismiss his thesis that the eye receives the green light as an emotional quality which then is intensified, supplemented, raised to consciousness, and projected upon the green leaf seen. Unless something like this is the case, I do not see how the poets' attitude toward nature can be other than mistaken (so long as they take the leaf and the light as natural things rather than divine symbols) .

I very much doubt that any philosopher *knows* whether
Whitehead's bold alternative to the bifurcation of nature is
true. But I would call attention to the unrestricted scope
which he gave to his idea that sensa are simple emotional
forms transmitted from occasion to occasion. "The simplest
grade of actual occasions," he wrote, "must be conceived as
experiencing a few sensa, with the minimum of patterned
contrast" (PR II iv iii). These are "the actual occasions in
so-called 'empty space'" (PR II viii iv). Whitehead also
suggested that sensa (and the vibrations associated with them)
which are characteristic of our "cosmic epoch" may—like the
fundamental particles of our physics and the three dimensions
of our geometry—not be characteristic of other epochs. However, a striking remark in *Modes of Thought* implies that in
his universe some sensa are by no means provincial. "We
know about the colour 'green' in some of its perspectives.
But what green is capable of in other epochs of the universe,
when other laws of nature are reigning, is beyond our present
imagination." [6] He added that "there is nothing intrinsically
impossible" in the notion that men may eventually gain
some understanding of these other possibilities of green; that
is (to put it in a way which accords more strictly with the
roles of eternal objects and actual occasions in his metaphysics),
we may become able to imagine something of the contexts
in which green can be realized by actual occasions in other
cosmic epochs, and something of the new syntheses of value
which may thus arise. Whether such imaginative understanding be possible or not, it is plain that any type of entity about
which the remark I have quoted may be made is, in the world
view of the man who makes it, part of the very alphabet of
being.

So far I have not used the term "value" in connection with
sensa as Whitehead conceived them. Without doubt, it must
be used. Eternal objects are possibilities, and their essential
role is to define possibilities of value. But the mathematical

[6] III 1. This passage was quoted at the beginning of Chap. 11, above,
where another significance of it was noticed.

Platonic forms do not do this directly; rather, they define conditions of value. The eternal objects which can be realized by actual occasions as subjective forms of feeling, or elements of their subjective forms, directly comprise all the values for existence. Sensa constitute the simplest category of these elements. The others are constrasts, contrasts of contrasts, and yet higher contrasts of sensa.

William James once suggested (and only suggested) a naïve metaphysics of "pure experience," according to which the primordial reality consists of "sensible natures" which get synthesized in various ways. As we know from Chapter 13, he also entertained an idea (of doubtful compatibility with this one) that the drop or moment of experience is the unit of existence. Whatever may be wrong with Whitehead's theory of actual entities and his theory of sensa, at least they work out systematically a way of conceiving process as at once qualitative, structured, and individualized. Far removed from all phenomenalisms, Whitehead's metaphysics does more than any of them for the reality of qualities.

V

One reaction to the philosophy of organism, sometimes expressed (and, I suspect, more often felt), is that the world can't be as complicated as all that. This strikes me as quite unphilosophical. Metaphysics, at least, is alive only when metaphysicians systematically dream of more things than are known to exist in heaven and earth. It is rather when we come to certain topics in the philosophy of man, such as the theory of human knowledge, that we may say with some truth that Whitehead went too far, and as a result did not adequately elucidate these matters. I confine myself first to the theory of empirical knowledge.

In the first three decades of this century epistemological realists insisted (among other things) that empirical knowl-

edge is basically "knowledge by acquaintance," whereas the
pragmatists (except for William James) insisted that there is
no such thing. The dispute was bound to be futile, for the
real concerns of the two parties were far from identical. The
pragmatist, looking out his window, wished to know whether
the green expanse which he perceived was a meadow or a lake,
and whether he would find it where it appeared to be. The
general principles of correct (warranted) classification and of
the confirmation of implicit expectations then make up the
theory of empirical knowledge. C. I. Lewis concentrated on it,
and was content simply to *acknowledge* that diverse perceptions occurring under the same conditions were due to diverse
dispositional properties of external objects. But the realist
was a metaphysician from the start—a man who was wondering
whether what he saw as green grass was in itself really green,
or at least greenish. Both questions are meaningful; but attack
on the second, if it is not to be naïve, must begin by admitting
the skepticism implied by our knowledge of the transformations which our own sensory processes effect upon their initial
data, and it can overcome this skepticism only by going beyond
the principles definitive of verifiable identification of such
things as meadows. Whitehead appealed finally to the immanence of God in the world (AI xvi x, xi; xx ix).

But first he made an essential contribution to the debate by
exhibiting the basis of our acknowledgment that the perceived
greenness has a source: we experience this derivation of the
sense-datum, by "perception in the mode of causal efficacy."
Unfortunately there is one point, crucial for epistemology, to
which he did not, I think, give due weight. Let it be granted
not only that we experience the general fact of derivation, but
also that at the subconscious levels of experience there are
causal "feelings" of all actual occasions on the route of transmission from the external object to the percipient occasion in
the brain. This is important for the general theory of the
causal constitution of temporal existents. It is irrelevant to
epistemology. Only what is indubitably given to *conscious*
experience can be particular evidence of perceptual truth or

error. Hence Whitehead's explanation of error as a mistaken symbolic transference from perception of presented sense-data to perception in the mode of causal efficacy is epistemologically useless. As he himself wrote,

> In the case of perceived organisms external to the human body, the spatial discrimination involved in the human perception of their pure causal efficacy is so feeble, that practically there is no check on this symbolic transference, apart from the indirect check of pragmatic consequences,—in other words, either survival-value, or self-satisfaction, logical and aesthetic.—S p. 80.

Long before we come to survival-value, the correctness of a sense-perception is testable in a way on which the pragmatists dwelt—testable by those further sense perceptions which occur when we act upon the perceptual judgment. Causal experience merely assures us that, whether our perceptions are right or wrong, they come from existent sources. What the effective distinction of perceptual truth from perceptual error requires is expectation which moves from one perception in the mode of presentational immediacy to others. (The empirical character of the object perceived is filled out—as the pragmatists seldom noticed—by the imaginable content of nonfutural hypothetical sense perceptions: by what the perceiver, or someone like him, supposes he would observe from other places or would have observed at other times.)

I think that Whitehead also handled the conceptual element in perceptual knowledge on the wrong plane—metaphysical rather than epistemological. It is curious that a thinker who enriched philosophy with so many new concepts should have said so little about the nature of concepts: they are " merely the analytic functioning of universals " (PR II i vi). Doubtless they are merely that—from Whitehead's *metaphysical* point of view. In human knowledge, however, they play a role which he did not fully appreciate. Notice of it would have fitted easily onto his profound observations about the role of theories, had he not assumed, with the neorealists, that human minds cannot apply a common conceptual pattern to their environ-

ment unless they enjoy sense-data in common (SMW p. 126).
Grant, with Whitehead, that these data are not confined to
the moment of perception but are recurrable eternal objects,
and also that they are continuous with rather than separated
from qualities which are enjoyed by the perceiver's sense
organs and which may be ingredient in events beyond his
body. It is still possible that, when an object is placed before
several observers, the exact quality which each perceives is
confined to him and *his* body. That this does not make knowledge of the object impossible, can only be due to the way in
which men frame, use, and express their concepts. I think
that the true, and epistemologically sufficient, account of the
matter was well stated by Lewis in 1929:

> As between different minds, the assumption that a concept
> which is common is correlated with sensory contents which are
> qualitatively identical, is to an extent verifiably false, is im-
> plausible to a further extent, and in the nature of the case can
> never be verified as holding even when it may reasonably be
> presumed. Nevertheless, community of meaning is secured if
> each discover, within his own experience, that complex of
> content which this common concept will fit.[7]

One moral which I draw here is that, though the conception
of distinct individuals which Whitehead provided in his theory
of actual occasions and societies of occasions may be sufficient
and admirable for metaphysics (as I rather think it is), when
we come to epistemology (and many other topics in the philosophy of man) it is essential to take the individual person
as the primary unit in terms of which problems should be
discussed.

A system of metaphysics should try to describe the universe
in a way which permits all human activities to be exhibited
as various highly specialized instances of the operation of
generic metaphysical factors. It is the responsibility not of
metaphysics but of a general theory of man to show the distinc-

-----
[7] *Mind and the World-Order* (New York, 1929), pp. 115 f.

tive features of diverse groups of such instances—e. g., of moral conduct, historical inquiry, political organization, and civilized life. In *Adventures of Ideas, Modes of Thought,* and the undeservedly neglected last chapter of *Symbolism,* Whitehead illuminated many of these topics as no one else could. In doing so he was consciously applying his metaphysics—not bestowing ontological titles (as many philosophers now do) upon those special features of human existence which are important to us. If the preceding discussion of his view of perceptual knowledge is correct, however, it shows that he did not always take certain specifically human factors into account. I also suggest that although eternal objects, or universals, may be metaphysical factors, concepts are human factors, whose special nature the theory of human thought must determine. And although Whitehead's introduction into metaphysics of propositions as a category of existence, consisting of " impure potentials " functioning as lures for feeling (generally unconscious) in the processes of the world, was an original contribution of great importance, the proposition as a union of concepts—a union which must be consciously entertainable— is another and much more special thing, and must still be treated as a topic in the theory of human thought. That theory must assume responsibility for clarifying the criteria by which the propositions thought by men may be accounted true or false, probable or improbable, accurate or inaccurate, etc. These propositions are human proposals; they are not *appearances* which have or lack a certain relation to reality. Whitehead's profound discussion of the " truth-relation " of appearance to reality (AI xvi) has only an indirect relevance to them.

In view of the magnitude of Whitehead's work it would be out of place to dwell on his tendency to ontologize these concerns of the human mind. He wanted his philosophy to be used. My critical suggestion is that in its future use a nice discrimination between the theory of being and the theory of man will sometimes need to be supplied.

VI

If the reader will turn back to Section VII of Chapter 1, he will see some of the things which we can learn from Whitehead in framing our social and political philosophies. There is nothing on earth that is more urgently needed than wisdom in that task. Whitehead had it in the highest degree that I have seen. This statement is not to be justified here; Part I, " Sociological," and Chapter xix, " Adventure," in *Adventures of Ideas* must be studied. You will not find there analyses of the theory of natural law, utilitarianism, historicism, or the organic theory of the state. The stock alternatives have often been examined and revised. In Whitehead we have a broader view of society, and a way of thinking about ideals which makes them absolutely fundamental and is yet perfectly sane.

He wrote: " Life can only be understood as an aim at that perfection which the conditions of its environment allow. But the aim is always beyond the attained fact " (AI v v). In this sense the civilization of the Roman Empire in the West was not alive. The Empire itself " was a purely defensive institution, in its sociological functionings and in its external behaviour." That is one pattern which must not be repeated in our time.

Whitehead declared totalitarianism " hateful ": " If the man be wholly subordinated to the common life, he is dwarfed. His complete nature lies idle, and withers " (ESP p. 65; AESP p. 125). But he never supposed that courage and love of freedom, backed by technical progress, are enough. " In the region of large political affairs, the test of success is twofold— namely, survival power and compromise. . . . Some English statesmen of vigorous decisiveness . . . try to decide and impose. They are the failures in modern English history, much beloved by vivid intellectuals " (ESP p. 72; AESP pp. 132 f.). This does not apply to Englishmen only! Whitehead added, " Political solutions devoid of compromise are failures from the ideal of statesmanship." Surveying our postwar world, he did not hesitate to recommend "sympathetic compromise" (ESP p. 53 n.) . Choice among ideals (bad ones are as numerous as good ones) , coordination and compromise, provision of more opportunity for individuals, courage, reverence for the human soul, care that the foundations of civilized society be not destroyed: all are essential. A Bertrand Russell and a Sidney Hook, alive at 100 A. D., might have agreed on the necessity of abolishing slavery in the Empire; not so Whitehead (see AI II vi) . His imaginativeness was as many-sided as it was keen, and it was perfectly united with a firm common sense.

Dewey liked to quote Whitehead's statement, " Mankind is that factor *in* Nature which exhibits in its most intense form the plasticity of nature." [8] In general, the relation of Whitehead's social philosophy to his metaphysics conforms well to the ideal stated in the preceding section. Mankind's social experience, familiar to him from his lifelong historical reading, receives a signal, though of course partial, elucidation from the metaphysics, mediated by his fine sense of historical importance and of what constitutes civilization.[9]

The world-process is not merely the motion, consolidation, and dispersal of matter and energy, sometimes accompanied by pain and pleasure; nor is it the enactment of the opera called Dialectical Materialism. What then is it? Whitehead's Platonic-organismic cosmology is a grand alternative to these. To be sure, not all social philosophers assume that some kind of materialism is the only possible view of nature and of man. An experienced planner of American foreign policy has just worked out a political philosophy in terms of a dualistic metaphysics of existential things and the perfection of Platonic

[8] AI v v; italics in text.

[9] " Elucidation " does *not* mean that the course of history can be deduced from the metaphysics. Another common imputation is that any use of a metaphysical idea or a judgment of importance is a claim to possess some " privileged information " or " special knowledge." Opponents of philosophy substitute this tic for a quiet look at their own general assumptions.

forms.[10] But Professor Halle's Platonism is naïve and tame in comparison with Whitehead's.

We Whitehead readers cannot hope to acquire everything— beginning with his creative mathematician's feeling for general patterns—that is in his philosophy. But we can be encouraged to widen our sensitivity to human values and the values of nature,[11] whether or not we share his religious sense of "the coordination and eternity of realized value." We can become wiser in our understanding of the history of the race and our attitudes toward its problems. And we can recover "the old doctrine that breadth of thought reacting with intensity of sensitive experience stands out as an ultimate claim of existence" (PR I i vi).

Philosophy is intellectual, and practical: "an endeavor to obtain a self-consistent understanding of things observed" (MT p. 208), and "an attempt to clarify those fundamental beliefs which finally determine the emphasis of attention that lies at the base of character." [12] In philosophy, the feeling of clarity that comes from mental subtraction is a cheat. By his example even more than by his teaching, Whitehead continually impels his reader toward wider and subtler observation, and toward greater imaginativeness in thought. This impulsion is the best of all the good things which his philosophy gives to the world.

[10] Louis J. Halle, *Men and Nations* (Princeton, 1962).

[11] Anyone who with Lewis Mumford is appalled by the morals of extermination and is attracted by that writer's good campaign for "the renewal of life" but desires a more dispassionate wisdom and a more articulated metaphysics will find them in Whitehead.

[12] AI vi vi. The context is a condsideration of the ways in which populations may react to the crises they encounter.

Index

Entries for each of Whitehead's writings which receive more than passing mention are included, but quotations per se are not indexed. Within entries, the abbreviations listed on pp. xv-xvi are used; and Whitehead is shortened to W.

A

A priori principles, 185
Abstraction, 42, 50, 241, 278, 320, 332
  method of extensive. *See* Extensive abstraction and natural science, 23, 50
  philosophy as critic of, 2, 181, 282-84, 285, 287f, 323
Abstractness of W's philosophy, 325-27
Action, 271
  at a distance, 167, 200
Actual entities, 42, 108, 202, 255, 262, 264, 304, 310, 318, 325, 327, 354, 359, 372, 375
  general account, 36f, 46, 315, 336, 371
  See also Actual occasion(s); Experience, drop(s) of
Actual occasion(s), 37, 85, 100, 202, 233, 256, 273, 289, 293, 320n, 374, 376, 378
  genetic analysis, 48-54
  morphological analysis, 48, 54f
  time span of, 55f
  unity of an, 50. *See also* Individuality; Synthesis
Actual world of an actual entity, 45, 48
Actualities, 232, 304, 315, 316, 318, 327, 371
  but one kind of, 37
Adequacy of a metaphysical scheme, 87, 303, 307f
Adjective, cognizance by, 204
Adventure, 6, 273, 274. *See also* Novelty
Adventures of Ideas, 14, 91, 94, 95, 98, 239, 250, 256, 269-75, 366, 379, 380

Aesthetic:
  achievement, 20, 50
  composition, 249, 293
  concepts in W's metaphysics, 248
  order, 101n, 111
  values, 52, 103
Aesthetics, 46, 111, 277, 322
Affective tone and sense perception, 51
Agar, W. E., 23, 88&n
Aggregation, Principle of, 190
Agnosticism, W's, 232, 294
Aims of Education, 15, 126, 180n
Aim, subjective. *See* Subjective aim
Alexander, Samuel, 255, 268, 278, 334n
  influence on W, 221, 264-66
Algebra, 131, 175
  enlargement of, 133
  of logic, 130, 136&n, 137n, 143
  method of, 277
  spatial interpretations of, 133, 139
  species of, 135
  universal, 133, 135, 151, 294
Ambrose, St., 366
Ambrose, Alice, 314n
America, W's philosophy and, 251-52n, 239, 266f
Analysis, 332, 333n, 367
  different routes of, 289, 290
  of perceptual basis of scientific concepts, 188
"Anatomy of Some Scientific Ideas, The," 185, 188
Animal faith, 238
Antecedent reality, 49, 303
Anthropocentrism, 261f